Child Sacrifice in Ancient Israel

Explorations in Ancient Near Eastern Civilizations

Series Editors

Grant Frame
University of Pennsylvania

Brent A. Strawn
Emory University

Niek Veldhuis
University of California, Berkeley

1. *Of Courtiers and Kings: The Biblical Daniel Narratives and Ancient Story-Collections*, by Tawny L. Holm
2. *The Sacrificial Economy: Assessors, Contractors, and Thieves in the Management of Sacrificial Sheep at the Eanna Temple of Uruk (ca. 625–520* B.C.*)*, by Michael Kozuh
3. *Children in the Ancient Near Eastern Household*, by Kristine Henriksen Garroway
4. *Fishers of Fish and Fishers of Men: Fishing Imagery in the Hebrew Bible and in the Ancient Near East*, by Tyler R. Yoder
5. *Child Sacrifice in Ancient Israel*, by Heath D. Dewrell
6. *The Dragon, the Mountain, and the Nations: An Old Testament Myth, Its Origins, and Its Afterlives*, by Robert D. Miller II

Child Sacrifice in Ancient Israel

Heath D. Dewrell

Winona Lake, Indiana
Eisenbrauns
2017

www.eisenbrauns.com

Library of Congress Cataloging-in-Publication Data

Names: Dewrell, Heath D., author.
Title: Child sacrifice in ancient Israel / Heath D. Dewrell.
Description: Winona Lake, Indiana : Eisenbrauns, [2017] | Series: Explorations in ancient Near Eastern civilizations | Includes bibliographical references and indexes.
Identifiers: LCCN 2017008375 (print) | LCCN 2017010022 (ebook) | ISBN 9781575064949 (hardback : alk. paper) | ISBN 9781575064956 (ePDF) ISBN 9781646024186 (paper)
Subjects: LCSH: Child sacrifice in the Bible. | Child sacrifice—Judaism. | Children—Palestine—History—To 1500. | Bible. Old Testament—Criticism, interpretation, etc. | Palestine—History—To 70 A.D.
Classification: LCC BS680.C45 .D47 2017 (print) | LCC BS680.C45 (ebook) | DDC 203/.420933—dc23
LC record available at https://lccn.loc.gov/2017008375

The paper used in this publication meets the minimum requirements of the American National Standard for Information Sciences—Permanence of Paper for Printed Library Materials, ANSI Z39.48–1984.♾™

GPSR Authorized Representative: Logos Europe, 9 rue Nicolas Poussin, 17000 La Rochelle, France, contact@logoseurope.eu.

for Kimberly

Contents

Acknowledgments

My work on child sacrifice has a history dating back at least a decade, with portions of the present work having their origins in papers for various courses during my graduate work at the Johns Hopkins University and especially in my doctoral dissertation on the same topic. Since defending the dissertation, I have reworked, rewritten, and expanded it in many regards, which has had the effect of augmenting the number of individuals to whom its completion is indebted.

My fascination with the ancient Israelites and their literature owes much to my mother and father, who instilled in me a love for the Bible from childhood. I earned my first allowance in exchange for memorizing Bible verses, which set me on the path toward earning my living through working with Scripture at an early age. My undergraduate professors introduced me to the academic study of the Bible. Of special note in this regard are Donald R. Vance, who taught me Hebrew, Jeffrey S. Lamp, who served as my adviser, as well as James B. Shelton and Edward W. Watson. Thanks are also due to John J. Collins, who served as my academic adviser and frequent professor at Yale Divinity School, and Robert R. Wilson, in whose Israelite Religion class I encountered the topic of Israelite child sacrifice for the first time. I also owe much to the faculty in the Near Eastern Studies department at the Johns Hopkins University with whom I took courses during my graduate studies, including Raymond Westbrook, Paul Delnero, Glenn M. Schwartz, Betsy M. Bryan, Richard Jasnow, and P. Kyle McCarter Jr., who also served as second reader on my dissertation. I further thank Jacob Lauinger, Pier M. Larson, and Steven R. David, who served on my dissertation committee and made numerous helpful comments and suggestions.

Of all my teachers, Theodore J. Lewis stands apart as meriting special thanks. As both my residence adviser during my doctoral work and as my dissertation adviser, he consistently demanded excellence from his students, albeit always tempering his criticism with encouragement and guidance. When he returned an exam or paper, I could be sure that it would be slathered in red ink; no nit went unpicked under his careful eye. I could also be sure, however, that I would find on the last page a detailed description of the merits of my work, how it could be improved, and a personal message of encouragement. That he managed to devote so much time and energy to each of his students on every assignment—from a thirty-page paper to a Ugaritic final exam—is a testament to his devotion to the task of raising up the next generation of scholars. I am grateful to have had him as a mentor, and I hope that I've done him proud here.

To my friends and colleagues: I survived coursework in general and comprehensive exams in particular with the aid of my fellow sufferer Heather Dana Davis Parker—epigrapher extraordinaire, connoisseur of fine bourbons, and hostess of the most glorious Halloween celebrations that a Hampden rowhouse ever saw. I thank Christopher D. Brinker and Adam S. Maskevich, who know that the best conversations involve stratigraphy, cuneiform, and a pint of ale. I also thank my classmates Erin E. Fleming, Michael Simone, Laura Wright, Andrew R. Davis, Isabel Cranz, and Jaime L. Waters for their collegiality and friendship. Special thanks are also due to Matthew Neujahr and T. M. Lemos, on whom I have come to depend for scholarly feedback on my work, as well as for the occasional distraction from it. Jeremy Pope has saved me from embarrassing myself in matters Egyptological on more than one occasion, and Alexandra Kleinerman taught me first-year Akkadian with all the patience and kindness that one would expect from a Sumerologist. Of all my classmates, however, I owe the most to my good friend Andrew Knapp. I especially thank Andrew (as should the reader) for volunteering to read through a previous draft of the book. His remarkably acute eye and sundry suggestions for improvement have greatly contributed to its quality. Special thanks in this regard are also due to my editor, Jim Eisenbraun. In addition to the enormous amount of work that he poured into the present volume, the contributions that he and Eisenbrauns have made to the study of the ancient Near East in general, in the form of consistently producing high-quality and affordable resources, are incalculable. I am quite proud that my first monograph bears a little ibex on the spine.

I have presented portions of my research on child sacrifice in various venues, including at the Columbia Seminar for the Study of the Hebrew Bible, where Mark S. Smith provided a helpful and gracious response; at the Old Testament Research Colloquium at Princeton Theological Seminary, with F. W. "Chip" Dobbs-Allsopp and Hannah S. An responding; and at a session of the Children in the Biblical World section at the Annual Meeting of the Society of Biblical Literature. I received constructive feedback at each of these venues. I thank my former and current colleagues at Princeton Theological Seminary, especially my Old Testament colleagues—Choon-Leong Seow, F. W. "Chip" Dobbs-Allsopp, Jacqueline E. Lapsley, Mark S. Smith, Dennis T. Olson, Brian Rainey, and Elizabeth Bloch-Smith—for their help and encouragement in both my research and my teaching. I also thank the staffs at the Milton S. Eisenhower Library at the Johns Hopkins University, the Knott Library at St. Mary's Seminary and University, and the Princeton Theological Seminary Library for providing the resources necessary for my research. Special thanks are due to Kate Skrebutenas, who went above and beyond the call of a research librarian on more than one occasion. Her ability to track down rare volumes by obscure presses from faraway places was of great help; much of the second chapter in particular was completed with her assistance.

Finally, and most of all, I thank my wife Kimberly and our son Stephen for their love and encouragement. Over the last decade and a half, the support that Kimberly has offered has been extraordinary. She has followed me from Tulsa to New Haven to Baltimore to Princeton as I have pursued my studies, uprooting her own life and career at each step along the way. I cannot begin to enumerate the sacrifices that she has made on my behalf, and this book is just as much a product of her effort as it is of mine. It is with much love that I dedicate it to her.

Abbreviations

3R	Rawlinson, H. C., and G. Smith. *A Selection from the Miscellaneous Inscriptions of Assyria*. Volume 3 of *The Cuneiform Inscriptions of Western Asia*. London: R. E. Bowler, 1870.
AASOR	Annual of the American Schools of Oriental Research
AB	The Anchor Bible
ABD	Freedman, D. N., ed. *The Anchor Bible Dictionary*. 6 vols. New York: Doubleday, 1992.
ABS	Archaeology and Biblical Studies
AfO	*Archiv für Orientforschung*
AHw	Soden, W. von. *Akkadisches Handwörterbuch: unter Benutzung des lexikalischen Nachlasses von Bruno Meissner (1868–1947)*. 3 vols. Wiesbaden: Harrassowitz, 1959–1981.
AIPHOS	*Annuaire de l'Institut de philologie et d'histoire orientales et slaves*
AJA	*American Journal of Archaeology*
AnBib	Analecta Biblica
ANEM	Ancient Near East Monographs
AOAT	Alter Orient und Altes Testament
AR	*Archiv für Religionswissenschaft*
ARES	Archivi reali di Ebla, Studi
ARMT	Archives royales de Mari, transcrite et traduite
ASOR	American Schools of Oriental Research
ATA	Alttestamentliche Abhandlungen
ATD	Das Alte Testament Deutsch
AThANT	Abhandlungen zur Theologie des Alten und Neuen Testaments
AYB	The Anchor Yale Bible
BA	*Biblical Archaeologist*
BAR	*Biblical Archaeology Review*
BBVO	Berliner Beiträge zum Vorderen Orient
BDB	Brown, F., S. R. Driver, and C. A. Briggs. *A Hebrew and English Lexicon of the Old Testament*. Oxford: Clarendon, 1907.
BETL	Bibliotheca Ephemeridum Theologicarum Lovaniensium
BFCT	Beiträge zur Förderung christlicher Theologie
Bib	*Biblica*
BibInt	*Biblical Interpretation*
BJS	Brown Judaic Studies
BN	*Biblische Notizen*
Brockelmann	Brockelmann, C. *Lexicon Syriacum*. Edinburgh: T. & T. Clark, 1895.
BVSAWLPHK	Berichte über die Verhandlungen der Sächsischen Akademie der Wissenschaften zu Leipzig: Philologisch-historische Klasse
BZABR	Beihefte zur Zeitschrift für altorientalische und biblische Rechtsgeschichte

BZAW	Beihefte zur Zeitschrift für die alttestamentliche Wissenschaft
CAD	Gelb, I., et al., eds. *The Assyrian Dictionary of the Oriental Institute of the University of Chicago*. 21 vols. Chicago: The Oriental Institute, 1956–2010.
CahRB	Cahiers de la Revue biblique
CBC	Cambridge Bible Commentary
CBQ	*Catholic Biblical Quarterly*
CBQMS	Catholic Biblical Quarterly Monograph Series
CBSC	The Cambridge Bible for Schools and Colleges
CC	Continental Commentaries
CHANE	Culture and History of the Ancient Near East
CIS	*Corpus inscriptionum semiticarum*
COS	Hallo, W. W., and K. L. Younger Jr., eds. *The Context of Scripture*. 3 vols. Leiden: Brill, 1997–2002.
CRAI	*Comptes rendus de l'Académie des inscriptions et belles lettres*
DCH	Clines, D. J. A., ed. *The Dictionary of Classical Hebrew*. 9 vols. Sheffield: Sheffield Academic, 1993–2016.
DDD[2]	Toorn, K. van der, B. Becking, and P. W. van der Horst, eds. *Dictionary of Deities and Demons in the Bible*. 2nd ed. Leiden: Brill, 1999.
DNWSI	Hoftijzer, J., and K. Jongeling. *Dictionary of the North-West Semitic Inscriptions*. 2 vols. Leiden: Brill, 1995.
EANEC	Explorations in Ancient Near Eastern Civilizations
EBR	*The Encyclopedia of the Bible and Its Reception*. Edited by H.-J. Klauck et al. Berlin: de Gruyter, 2009–.
EH	Berthier, A., and R. Charlier. *Le sanctuaire punique d'el-Hofra à Constantine*. 2 vols. Paris: Arts et métiers graphiques, 1955.
EHAT	Exegetisches Handbuch zum Alten Testament
ES	Emerging Scholars
FAT	Forschungen zum Alten Testament
FAT 2	Forschungen zum Alten Testament 2. Reihe
FFC	FF (Folklore Fellows) Communications
FGrH	Jacoby, F. *Die Fragmente der griechischen Historiker*. Berlin: Weidmann, 1923–.
FRLANT	Forschungen zur Religion und Literatur des Alten und Neuen Testaments
HAG	Handbücher der alten Geschichte
HALOT	Koehler, L., W. Baumgartner, and J. J. Stamm. *The Hebrew and Aramaic Lexicon of the Old Testament*. Translated and edited under the supervision of M. E. J. Richardson. 4 vols. Leiden: Brill, 1994–99.
HAR	*Hebrew Annual Review*
HAT	Handbuch zum Alten Testament
HBM	Hebrew Bible Monographs
HBS	Herders biblische Studien
HKAT	Handkommentar zum Alten Testament
HNPI	Jongeling, K. *Handbook of Neo-Punic Inscriptions*. Tübingen: Mohr Siebeck, 2008.
HSAT	Die Heilige Schrift des Alten Testaments
HSM	Harvard Semitic Monographs

HSS	Harvard Semitic Series/Studies
HSS 10	Meek, T. J. *Old Akkadian, Sumerian, and Cappadocian Texts from Nuzi*. Vol. 3 of *Excavations at Nuzi*. HSS 10. Cambridge: Harvard University Press, 1935.
HThKAT	Herders Theologischer Kommentar zum Alten Testament
ICC	International Critical Commentary
JA	*Journal asiatique*
JAJ	*Journal of Ancient Judaism*
JANES	*Journal of the Ancient Near Eastern Society of Columbia University*
JAOS	*Journal of the American Oriental Society*
JBL	*Journal of Biblical Literature*
JNES	*Journal of Near Eastern Studies*
JNSL	*Journal of Northwest Semitic Languages*
JPOS	*Journal of the Palestine Oriental Society*
JPSTC	The JPS Torah Commentary
JSJSup	Supplements to the Journal for the Study of Judaism
JSOTSup	Journal for the Study of the Old Testament Supplement Series
JSSEA	*Journal of the Society for the Study of Egyptian Antiquities*
KAI	Donner, H., and W. Röllig. *Kanaanäische und aramäische Inschriften*. 2nd ed. 3 vols. Wiesbaden: Harrassowitz, 1966–69.
KAI[5]	Donner, H. and W. Röllig. *Kanaanäische und aramäische Inschriften*. Vol. 1. 5th ed. Wiesbaden: Harrassowitz, 2002.
KAT	Kommentar zum Alten Testament
KAV	Schroeder, O. *Keilschrifttexte aus Assur verschiedenen Inhalts*. WVDOG 35. Leipzig: J. C. Hinrichs, 1920.
KeHAT	Kurzgefasstes exegetisches Handbuch zum Alten Testament
KHC	Kurzer Hand-Commentar zum Alten Testament
KTU[3]	Dietrich, M., O. Loretz, and J. Sanmartín. *Die keilalphabetischen Texte aus Ugarit, Ras Ibn Hani und anderen Orten/The Cuneiform Alphabetic Texts from Ugarit, Ras Ibn Hani and Other Places*. 3rd ed. Münster: Ugarit-Verlag, 2013.
LHBOTS	Library of Hebrew Bible/Old Testament Studies
MAD	Materials for the Assyrian Dictionary
NCBC	New Century Bible Commentary
NIBCOT	New International Biblical Commentary on the Old Testament
OBC	Orientalia Biblica et Christiana
OBO	Orbis Biblicus et Orientalis
OIC	Oriental Institute Communications
OLZ	*Orientalistische Literaturzeitung*
OTL	Old Testament Library
OTS	Old Testament Studies
Payne-Smith	Payne-Smith, J., ed. *A Compendious Syriac Dictionary, Founded upon the Thesaurus Syriacus of R. Payne Smith*. Oxford: Clarendon, 1903.
PEFQS	*Palestine Exploration Fund Quarterly Statement*
PEQ	*Palestinian Exploration Quarterly*
RB	*Revue biblique*
RBL	*Review of Biblical Literature*

RBS	Resources for Biblical Study
REJ	*Revue des études juives*
RES	*Répertoire d'épigraphie sémitique*
RGRW	Religions in the Graeco-Roman World
RHR	*Revue de l'histoire des religions*
RIDA	*Revue internationale des droits de l'antiquité*
RS	Ras Shamra
RSF	*Rivista di studi fenici*
RSOu	Ras Shamra–Ougarit
SAA	State Archives of Assyria
SBAB	Stuttgarter biblische Aufsatzbände
SBLDS	Society of Biblical Literature Dissertation Series
SBLMS	Society of Biblical Literature Monograph Series
SBT	Studies in Biblical Theology
SBTS	Sources for Biblical and Theological Study
SCS	Septuagint and Cognate Studies
SEL	*Studi epigrafici e linguistici sul Vicino Oriente antico*
SHANE	Studies in the History of the Ancient Near East
SHCANE	Studies in the History and Culture of the Ancient Near East
SHR	Studies in the History of Religions (supplements to *Numen*)
SJOT	*Scandinavian Journal of the Old Testament*
Sokoloff	Sokoloff, M. *A Syriac Lexicon: A Translation from the Latin: Correction, Expansion, and Update of C. Brockelmann's Lexicon Syriacum*. 2nd corrected printing. Winona Lake, IN: Eisenbrauns, 2012.
TDOT	Botterweck, G. J., H. Ringgren, and H.-J. Fabry, eds. *Theological Dictionary of the Old Testament*. Translated by J. T. Willis, G. W. Bromiley, and D. E. Green. 15 vols. Grand Rapids, MI: Eerdmans, 1974–.
TLZ	*Theologische Literaturzeitung*
TuL	Ebeling, E. *Tod und Leben nach den Vorstellungen der Babylonier*. Berlin: Walter de Gruyter, 1931.
UF	*Ugarit-Forschungen*
Ug. V	Nougayrol, J., E. Laroche, C. Virolleaud, and C. F. A. Schaeffer. *Ugaritica V: nouveaux textes accadiens, hourrites et ugaritiques des archives et bibliothèques privées d'Ugarit*. Mission de Ras Shamra 16. Paris: Imprimerie nationale, 1968.
VT	*Vetus Testamentum*
VTSup	Supplements to Vetus Testamentum
VWGT	Veröffentlichungen der Wissenschaftlichen Gesellschaft für Theologie
Waltke-O'Connor	Waltke, B. K., and M. O'Connor. *An Introduction to Biblical Hebrew Syntax*. Winona Lake, IN: Eisenbrauns, 1990.
WAW	Writings from the Ancient World
WBC	Word Biblical Commentary
WMANT	Wissenschaftliche Monographien zum Alten und Neuen Testament
WVDOG	Wissenschaftliche Veröffentlichungen der deutschen Orient-Gesellschaft
ZABR	*Zeitschrift für altorientalische und biblische Rechtsgeschichte*
ZAW	*Zeitschrift für die Alttestamentliche Wissenschaft*
ZDPV	*Zeitschrift des deutschen Palästina-Vereins*

Introduction

The act of sacrificing one's own child is to most audiences among the most horrifying religious practices imaginable. While many religious acts described in the Hebrew Bible are discomforting to say the least, few can compete with child sacrifice. Animal sacrifice and blood manipulation may seem strange and exotic to modern Western audiences, and slaughtering conquered enemies as offerings to the gods conjures up uncomfortable images of genocide and holy war, but the sacrifice of innocent children—and specifically one's own children—evokes a level of horror that easily overshadows them both. Nonetheless, there is ample evidence that child sacrifice occurred in ancient Israel. This is an uncomfortable fact for modern Jewish and Christian faith communities who trace their own religious heritage back to Iron Age Israel. It is unsurprising then that an enormous body of scholarly work has been devoted to exploring the topic of ancient Israelite child sacrifice, and, as the examination below will reveal, debates concerning Israelite child sacrifice have raged for over a century now, with little in the way of a consensus on many important issues.

Scholarly discussion up to this point, however, has primarily focused on the question of whether children were actually sacrificed in ancient Israel or not. Among those who believe that child sacrifice did indeed occur to some degree or another (the vast majority of contemporary scholars), secondary questions have centered on whether Yahweh himself was understood as the recipient of such offerings or if Israelite child sacrifice instead represents an example of foreign syncretism and apostasy in the form of the Israelites offering up their children to foreign gods. These debates typically turn on how to interpret specific biblical passages, and in some cases even the meanings of individual terms. The present work will of necessity address such questions and weigh in on these longstanding debates. In this regard, though, it will cover well-worn territory and address issues that have been debated for the last century.

While there of course may be some value in providing an up-to-date overview of scholarly debates surrounding Israelite child sacrifice—especially in gathering together an abundance of potentially relevant epigraphic, iconographic, and archaeological material all in one place—one might justifiably ask whether the world really needs yet another study of Israelite child sacrifice. The present work, however, will attempt to move beyond simply addressing questions concerning whether Israelite children were ever sacrificed and, if so, to whom. It will additionally attempt to untangle the apparent variety of child sacrifice rituals attested in the Hebrew Bible. That is, the biblical evidence actually indicates that more than one sort of child sacrifice occurred in ancient Israel. While these various rites did share in common that children served as the victim in each, conflating various forms of child sacrifice and treating them all as essentially the same or as only variations on a theme obscures the diversity of belief and practice that gave rise to several distinct, and often in practice incompatible, forms of Israelite child sacrifice.

In addition, just as there are a variety of forms of child sacrifice attested in the Hebrew Bible, the biblical writers who condemned such rites employed a variety of rhetorical strategies for combatting them. For instance, some deny that Yahweh ever desired that children be offered to him at all, while others claim that Yahweh did in fact have a claim to some children, especially firstborn children. Various biblical writers nonetheless found creative, and often conflicting, ways of avoiding the conclusion that children actually ought to be killed and offered to Yahweh. The present examination, especially in its final chapter, will attempt to untangle the various rhetorical threads represented in the Hebrew Bible surrounding Israelite child sacrifice and to discern why certain biblical writers adopted the particular rhetorical strategies that they did.

Thus in what follows, I hope not only to demonstrate the historical reality of Israelite child sacrifice, but also to trace the individual histories of several different rites that involved the sacrifice of Israelite children. While gaps in our evidence will require speculation on some points and uncertain silence on others, there does appear to be enough evidence to suggest that at least three different sorts of Israelite child sacrifice likely existed. Further, I also hope to show that the various biblical writers who inhabited and participated in their own particular streams of Israelite Yahwism (e.g., Deuteronomism, the Holiness School, etc.) adopted divergent, and sometimes even directly contradictory rhetorical strategies in opposing various forms of child sacrifice. Further, in some cases one can even trace the development of a particular argument as it was taken up from earlier texts and reframed in later ones. In this way, the history of biblical rhetoric surrounding Israelite child sacrifice will be just as much a topic of examination here as the historical reality of the practice. Before moving on to such questions concerning the rhetoric surrounding child sacrifice, however, it is probably best to begin by examining the evidence for the historical existence of such rites. Here we will begin with one of the best attested forms of Israelite child sacrifice—the so-called "Molek" sacrifices.

Chapter 1

Children Sacrificed as Part of a "Molek" Rite

The best-known example of Israelite child sacrifice probably is the practice associated with the Hebrew term מֹלֶךְ, traditionally understood as the proper name of a god or demon, usually rendered "Moloch" (following the Septuagint and Vulgate) or "Molek/Molech" (following the Tiberian tradition and the Authorized Version). According to the traditional understanding, this terrible Moloch/Molek being delighted in the sacrifice of human children delivered to him by reprobate Israelites during the monarchic period. Probably most influential for modern conceptions of this alleged demon or deity is Milton's description of the character in *Paradise Lost*. When Satan and Beelzebub rouse the hosts of hell, the first listed among them is "Moloch," whom Milton describes as follows:

> First *Moloch*, horrid King besmear'd with blood
> Of human sacrifice, and parents tears,
> Though for the noyse of Drums and Timbrels loud
> Their childrens cries unheard, that past through fire
> To his grim Idol. Him the *Ammonite*
> Worshipt in *Rabba* and her watry Plain,
> In *Argob* and in *Basan*, to the stream
> Of utmost *Arnon*. Nor content with such
> Audacious neighbourhood, the wisest heart
> Of *Solomon* he led by fraud to build
> His Temple right against the Temple of God
> On that opprobrious Hill, and made his Grove
> The pleasant Vally of *Hinnom*, *Tophet* thence
> And black *Gehenna* call'd, the Type of Hell.[1]

1. Milton, *Paradise Lost*, Book I, 392–405.

Later in the epic, the figure's character develops when Satan invites proposals for how the fallen angels should proceed following their expulsion from heaven. Moloch opens the discussion by calling for open war between the forces of hell and heaven and advocates bringing all the terrors of hell into heaven itself:

> [L]et us rather choose
> Arm'd with Hell flames and fury all at once
> O're Heav'ns high Towrs to force resistless way,
> Turning our Tortures into horrid Arms
> Against the Torturer; when to meet the noise
> Of his Almighty Engin he shall hear
> Infernal Thunder, and for Lightning see
> Black fire and horror shot with equal rage
> Among his Angels; and his Throne it self
> Mixt with *Tartarean* Sulphur, and strange fire,
> His own invented Torments.[2]

Although Moloch's suggestion is ultimately rejected in favor of Beelzebub's plan instead to gain vengeance against heaven by corrupting humanity, the character of Moloch, that "horrid King besmear'd with blood of human sacrifice," is here again established as an entirely malevolent being who desires nothing other than death and destruction.

This picture of Moloch has lived on in popular imagination. Tennyson's "The Dawn" characterizes the barbarism of past generations (in contrast to the barbarism of the present) with the stirring image of "Screams of a babe in the red-hot palms of a Moloch of Tyre."[3] Likewise, in his "Howl, Part II," when Ginsberg sought to identify all of the evils oppressing his generation—capitalism, poverty, pollution, war—he found no better term for the sum of it all than "Moloch," a word that appears as a refrain some thirty-nine times in the short jeremiad.[4] Thus, ancient "Moloch" has come to serve as a personification of cruelty, destruction, and barbarism, which should probably come as no surprise given its apparent historical connection with the gruesome practice of child sacrifice.

2. *Paradise Lost*, Book II, 60–70.
3. A. Tennyson, *The Death of Œnone, and Other Poems* (New York: Macmillan, 1892), 81.
4. A. Ginsberg, *Howl and Other Poems* (The Pocket Poets Series 4; New York: City Lights Books, 1956), 21–22.

It is worth observing that Milton's depiction of "Moloch," as colorful and compelling as it may be, is significantly more developed than the picture presented by the Hebrew Bible itself. Indeed, the Bible contains relatively little information about this so-called מֹלֶךְ. The term appears in two places in Leviticus (18:21 and 20:1–5), once in Kings (2 Kgs 23:10), and once in Jeremiah (32:35).[5] In each case, one's offspring, either referred to as one's "seed" (זרע; so Leviticus) or one's "son(s) and daughter(s)" (בן/בנים and בת/בנות; so Kings and Jeremiah), are sacrificed as part of the ritual. Specifically, the parent either "causes to pass over" (√עבר Hiphil) or "gives" (√נתן) the child לַמֹּלֶךְ, literally, "to the *mōlek*." There are also a handful of other passages that mention parents "causing to pass over" (√עבר, Hiphil) their children, without explicitly specifying that they were passed over למלך (Deut 18:10; 2 Kgs 16:3; 17:17; 21:6 [//2 Chr 33:6]; Ezek 16:21; 20:31; 23:37). Some of these passages also indicate that the victims were passed over "in fire" (באש; Deut 18:10; 2 Kgs 16:3; 17:17; 21:6 [//2 Chr 33:6]; 23:10; Ezek 20:31). Likewise, once, where Kings has "cause to pass over," the Chronicles parallel has the more explicit "burn" (√בער Piel; 2 Chr 28:3//2 Kgs 16:3). Finally, 2 Kgs 23:10 indicates that these offerings were made in a place called a תֹּפֶת[6] in the Valley of Ben-Hinnom, a location also mentioned in conjunction with child sacrifice several times in the book of Jeremiah (7:31–32; 19:1–14; 32:35). Only here, in 2 Kgs 23:10, which describes Josiah's defilement of this "tophet," is all of this information about the rite gathered together in a single place:

> וטמא את התפת אשר בגי בני הנם[7] לבלתי להעביר איש את בנו את בתו באש למלך
>
> And he defiled the *tophet* which is in the Ben-Hinnom Valley, so that a man would not cause his son or daughter to pass over in fire *lmlk*.

---

5. The MT of 1 Kgs 11:7, which alleges that Solomon built a shrine "for Molek the abomination of the Ammonites" (למלך שקץ בני עמון) is a rather obvious corruption of "for Milcom" (למלכם), the national deity of Ammon (see elsewhere in the same chapter, 1 Kgs 11:5, 33; as well as 2 Kgs 23:13). OG τῷ βασιλεῖ αὐτῶν, representing a Hebrew *Vorlage* למלכם, further supports this conclusion, despite its having (mis)understood the term as a common noun with a 3mp possessive suffix, rather than as a divine name.

6. There has as of yet still been no convincing etymology offered for this term. For a thorough and convenient overview of previous suggestions, see M. J. Mulder, "תֹּפֶת *tōpet*," *TDOT* 15 (2006): 753–65.

7. So K; Q בן הנם.

If one then takes the sum total of the biblical evidence, one might suggest that the למלך rite involved sacrificing one's child via burning in a cultic location called a *tophet*, which was located in the Ben-Hinnom Valley, just south of Jerusalem (see Josh 15:8; 18:16).

A major difficulty in attempting to say anything more about the nature of the rite is the meaning of the phrase למלך itself. The traditional way of understanding the phrase is "to (the) Molek," taking "Molek" as the name or title of some sort of supernatural being who was the intended recipient of these sacrifices. This is how the phrase has been interpreted at least as early as the Hellenistic period. The various Old Greek translators differ somewhat in how they render the phrase: in 2 Kgs 23:10, the translator simply transliterates τῷ Μολοχ "to the Moloch"; the translator of Lev 18:21 and 20:2–4 opts for ἄρχοντι "to a ruler,"[8] apparently taking מלך as a Qal active participle from √מלך; and the OG translator of Jeremiah opts for τῷ βασιλεῖ "to the king" (39:35; MT 32:35). Thus, in all cases, it is clear that the OG translators understood the phrase למלך as referring to the sacrifice's recipient, probably a deity, either with the name "Moloch" or with the title "ruler/king." From this early understanding it is not difficult to trace the thread that runs to Milton's terrible archdemon.

This understanding of the phrase is not the only possibility, however. Modern historical-critical scholarship has challenged the traditional understanding, and many now argue that the term has been misunderstood and deny that a "Molech/Moloch/Molek"[9] deity was ever venerated in ancient Israel. On the other hand, others continue to argue in favor of the traditional interpretation and maintain that identifying "Molek" as some sort of deity or demon remains the most convincing explanation. Still others argue that Molek is in fact a deity but that this deity is none other than Yahweh himself. The debate among scholars holding these various positions has been especially energetic over the last century; nonetheless, nothing resembling a consensus on the matter has resulted. Although an exhaustive history of scholarship on the topic is beyond the scope of the present study,[10] the

8. On εἰς τοὺς ἄρχοντας for MT אחרי המלך in Lev 20:5, see below.

9. The Anglicization of the name of this alleged deity varies by author. In what follows, I default to "Molek" unless quoting the work of another scholar.

10. Scholarship on the topic over the last century has been vast. While the following outline is intended to present the work of the most important and representative voices in the conversation, not every study on the topic has been included here. For a more thorough history of scholarship, see my dissertation, "Child Sacrifice in Ancient Israel and Its Opponents," (Ph.D. diss.; The Johns Hopkins University, 2012), 3–73.

discussion below will attempt to present both the historical and the current range of scholarly opinion, especially focusing on arguments made in more recent decades.

Those Who Deny the Existence of a God "Molek"

Nearly a century ago, Otto Eissfeldt, in his *Molk als Opferbegriff im Punischen und Hebräischen und das Ende des Gottes Moloch*,[11] made the striking claim there never was any "Molek" deity. Instead, he argued that the Hebrew phrase למלך actually meant "as a *mōlek*-sacrifice" and that the term referred to the victim of the sacrifice, not to its recipient. The impetus for this suggestion was archaeological evidence that had recently come to light from the Punic colonies of the central Mediterranean.

Historians since ancient times had assumed that Punic colonists practiced child sacrifice, primarily due to accusations leveled by classical authors as early as the fifth century BCE and as late as the fifth century CE.[12] Probably the most colorful description of these rites is found in the writings of first-century-BCE historian Diodorus Siculus. In his description of the siege of Carthage by Agathocles of Syracuse ca. 310 BCE, he alleges that, among other religious reforms, the Carthaginians reinstituted the ancient but neglected practice of sacrificing the children of elites to Kronos:

> ᾐτιῶντο δὲ καὶ τὸν Κρόνον αὐτοῖς ἐναντιοῦσθαι, καθ᾽ ὅσον ἐν τοῖς ἔμπροσθεν χρόνοις θύοντες τούτῳ τῷ θεῷ τῶν υἱῶν τοὺς κρατίστους ὕστερον ὠνούμενοι λάθρᾳ παῖδας καὶ θρέψαντες ἔπεμπον ἐπὶ τὴν θυσίαν· καὶ ζητήσεως γενομένης εὑρέθησάν τινες τῶν καθιερουργημένων ὑποβολιμαῖοι γεγονόντες. τούτων δὲ λαβόντες ἔννοιαν καὶ τοὺς πολεμίους πρὸς τοῖς τείχεσιν ὁρῶντες στρατοπεδεύοντας ἐδεισιδαιμόνουν ὡς καταλελυκότες τὰς πατρίους τῶν θεῶν τιμάς. διορθώσασθαι δὲ τὰς ἀγνοίας σπεύδοντες διακοσίους μὲν τῶν ἐπιφανεστάτων παίδων προκρίναντες ἔθυσαν δημοσίᾳ· ἄλλοι δ᾽ ἐν διαβολαῖς ὄντες ἑκουσίως ἑαυτοὺς ἔδοσαν, οὐκ ἐλάττους ὄντες τριακοσίων. ἦν δὲ παρ᾽ αὐτοῖς

11. O. Eissfeldt, *Molk as Opferbegriff im Punischen und Hebräischen und das Ende des Gottes Moloch* (Beiträge zur Religionsgeschichte des Altertums 3; Halle: Niemeyer, 1935).

12. For a convenient collection of classical allegations of Punic child sacrifice, see P. G. Mosca, "Child Sacrifice in Canaanite and Israelite Religion: A Study in *Mulk* and מלך" (Ph.D. diss.; Harvard University, 1975), 2–23, or J. Day, *Molech: A God of Human Sacrifice in the Old Testament* (University of Cambridge Oriental Publications 41; Cambridge: Cambridge University Press, 1989), 86–91.

> ἀνδριὰς Κρόνου χαλκοῦς, ἐκτετακὼς τὰς χεῖρας ὑπτίας ἐγκεκλιμένας ἐπὶ τὴν γῆν, ὥστε τὸν ἐπιτεθέντα τῶν παίδων ἀποκυλίεσθαι καὶ πίπτειν ἔις τι χάσμα πλῆρες πυρός.[13]
>
> They were claiming that Kronos was opposing them inasmuch as, while they had sacrificed the best of their sons in former times, later secretly buying and raising children, they sent them for the sacrifice instead. An inquiry being made, some of those who were sacrificed were found to have been covertly substituted. Having considered these things and seeing their enemies encamped before their walls, they were superstitiously afraid, as they had neglected the ancestral honors of the gods. Eager to correct their mistakes, selecting two hundred of the most distinguished children, they sacrificed them publicly; and others who were under accusation willingly gave themselves—no fewer than three hundred. There was among them a bronze statue of Kronos, having outstretched hands, palms up and sloping toward the ground, so that one of the children placed there would roll down and fall into a pit full of fire.

This description jibes well with what Philo of Byblos says about the ancient Phoenicians, as preserved in Eusebius's *Praeparatio evangelica*:

> Ἔθος ἦν τοῖς παλαιοῖς ἐν ταῖς μεγάλαις συμφοραῖς τῶν κινδύνων ἀντι τῆς πάντων φθορᾶς τὸ ἠγαπημένον τῶν τέκνων τοὺς κρατοῦωτας ἢ πολεως ἢ ἔθνους εἰς σφαγὴν ἐπιδιδόναι, λύτρον τοῖς τιμωροῖς δαίμοσιν· κατεσφάττοντο δὲ οἱ διδόμενοι μυστικῶς. Κρόνος τοίνυν, ὃν οἱ Φοίνικες Ἦλ προσαγορεύουσιν, βασιλεύων τῆς χώρας καὶ ὕστερον μετὰ τὴν τοῦ βίου τελευτὴν ἐπὶ τὸν τοῦ Κρόνου ἀστέρα καθιερωθείς, ἐξ ἐπιχωρίας νύμφης Ἀνωβρὲτ λεγομένης υἱὸν ἔχων μονογενῆ τελευτὴν (ὃν διὰ τοῦτο Ἰεοὺδ ἐκάλουν, τοῦ μονογενοῦς ὅυτως ἔτι καὶ νῦν καλουμένου παρὰ τοῖς Φοίνιξι) κινδύνων ἐκ πολέμου μεγίστων κατειληφότων τὴν χώραν βασιλικῷ κοσμήσας σχήματι τὸν υἱὸν βωμόν τε κατασκευασάμενος κατέθυσεν.[14]
>
> There was a custom among the ancients in great and dangerous circumstances—rather than the destruction of everything—for the

13. *Bibliotheca historica* 20.14.4–6. All translations are my own unless otherwise noted.

14. *Praep. ev.* 1.10.44=4.16.11. The Greek text here follows H. W. Attridge and R. A. Oden Jr., *Philo of Byblos, The Phoenician History: Introduction, Critical Text, Translation, Notes* (CBQMS 9; Washington, DC: Catholic Biblical Association of America, 1981), 60–62.

> rulers of a city or a people to hand over the most beloved of their children for slaughter, as a ransom to the avenging gods, and those handed over were slaughtered secretly.[15] Now Kronos, whom the Phoenicians call "El" and who was ruler of the land and later after his death consecrated as the star of Kronos, had an only son by a local bride named Anobret (whom they therefore called "Ieoud," and likewise still today among the Phoenicians an only son is so called). The greatest dangers of war having seized the land, he dressed the son in kingly dress and, constructing an altar, sacrificed him.

While there are differences between Philo's account and that of Diodorus—for example, whether the sacrifice took place secretly or publicly and how many children were offered—both agree that the occasions for such sacrifices were times of distress. It is also interesting that Kronos is associated with each, although Diodorus presents Kronos as the recipient of the offering and Philo presents him as having originally instituted the practice when he was a human ruler, prior to his death and deification. These accusations are hardly unique to these two authors though, and classical literature is replete with references to Phoenician and Carthaginian child sacrifice,[16] albeit typically in less detail than the examples presented above.

In modern times, popular audiences have encountered similar descriptions of the ancient practice of Carthaginian child sacrifice through the lens of Flaubert's *Salammbô*, where the rite, as is typical for the novel, is depicted in exotic and Orientalist fashion. First, there is the description of the statue of "Moloch," which had seven compartments through which sacrifices could be delivered into its fiery belly. In Flaubert's depiction, human children were conveyed to one of these compartments via the statue's arms, which were in turn operated by a series of chains. "Pontiffs of Moloch" officiated over the ceremony, offering child after child at an increasingly frenzied pace:

> Moloch's brazen arms moved more rapidly; they no longer paused. Each time a child was placed upon them, the priests of Moloch extended their hands over the victim to charge upon it the sins of the people, vociferating:
>
> "These are not men, but oxen!" and the multitude around repeated, "Oxen! Oxen!" The Devotees screamed out, "Lord! Eat!" and the priests of Prosperine, conforming in terror to Carthage's need, mumbled their Eleu-

15. Alternatively, "according to a secret ritual"; see Attridge and Oden, *Philo of Byblos*, 63.
16. Again, the reader is directed to Mosca, "Child Sacrifice," 2–23, or Day, *Molech*, 86–91 for a comprehensive collection of relevant classical sources.

> sian formula: "Pour forth fain! conceive!" No sooner were the victims placed on the verge of the aperture than they vanished, like a drop of water on a red-hot plate, and whiffs of white smoke curled up through the scarlet glow.
>
> Yet the appetite of the God was not appeased: he still wanted more. In order to supply him, the children were piled on his hands, and were retained there by a great chain.
>
> In the beginning, Devotees tried to count them, in order to note if the total number corresponded to the days of the solar year; but now so many were piled on that it was impossible to distinguish them during the dizzy movements of those horrible arms. All this lasted a long time, until nightfall. Then the interior divisions gave a most sombre glare. For the first time, the burning flesh was visible. Some people even fancied that they recognised hair, limbs, and entire bodies.[17]

Thus, long before Eissfeldt's time it was widely assumed that the Carthaginians had sacrificed their children, and these sacrifices had already been conflated with biblical "Molek" in the popular imagination in the work of Flaubert. There was as yet, however, no corroborating evidence from Carthage itself to support the claims of the classical writers.

Beginning in 1921, however, excavations at Carthage, led first by F. Icard, then by L. Poinsott and R. Lantier, and finally by F. Kelsey, unearthed the remains of both animals and human children in what appeared to be a sacred precinct. This was quickly taken as archaeological corroboration for the claims of Classical authors concerning the practice of human sacrifice among the Carthaginians.[18] In addition, excavations at N'Gaous, Algeria led by J. and P. Alquier revealed three stelae inscribed in Latin, which were published along with two other similar stelae from the same region.[19] Stelae I and III, the best preserved of the five, read as follows:

---

17. G. Flaubert, *Salammbô* (trans. M. F. Sheldon; London: Saxon, 1886), 355–56.

18. L. Poinssot and R. Lantier, "Un sanctuaire de Tanit à Carthage," *RHR* 87 (1923): 32–68; F. W. Kelsey, *Excavations at Carthage, 1925: A Preliminary Report* (New York: Macmillan, 1926); D. B. Harden, "Punic Urns from the Precinct of Tanit at Carthage," *AJA* 31 (1927): 297–310; idem, "The Pottery from the Precinct of Tanit at Salammbo, Carthage," *Iraq* 4 (1937): 59–89. For a convenient summary of the excavations of Carthage in the 1920s, see L. E. Stager, "Carthage: A View from the Tophet," in *Phönizier im Westen: die Beiträge des Internationalen Symposiums über "Die Phönizische Expansion im Westlichen Mittelmeerraum" in Köln vom 24. bis 27. April, 1979* (ed. H. G. Niemeyer; Mainz am Rhein: Zabern, 1982), 156–57. It should be noted that the interpretation of this archaeological evidence is now disputed, on which see the discussion in chapter 2 below, pp. 44–50.

19. A. Alquier and J. Alquier, "Stèles votives à Saturne découvertes près de N'Gaous (Algérie)," *CRAI* (1931): 21–26.

Ngaous I:[20]
[Q]*uod bonum faus* | [*tu*]*m feliciter fac* | [*tu*]*m sit*
domino sanc | [*t*]*o Saturno*
sacrum | [*m*]*ag*(*num*) *nocturnum mor* | [*c*]*homor*
ex voto Aqui | [*li*]*us Victor et Aelia Ruffina* | [*co*]*niux eius*
pro impetrato fil(*io*)
v(*otum*) | *l*(*ibentes*) *s*(*olverunt*) *a*(*gnum*) *v*(*i*)*k*(*arium*)

That it may made good, favorable, and happy
to the holy lord Saturn,
a great nocturnal offering—a *morchomor*,
because of a vow of Aquilius Victor and Aelia Ruffina his wife
for procuring a son,
a gift they willingly offer—a lamb as a substitute.

Ngaous III:[21]
Q(*uod*) *b*(*onum*) *et faustum f*(*actum*) *s*(*it*)
d(*omino*) *s*(*ancto*) *S*(*aturno*)
s(*acrum*) *m*(*agnum*) | *nocturnum*
anima pr[*o*] *anima sanguine pro sanguine* | *vita pro vita*
pro Con[*ces*] | *se salute*⟨*m*⟩
ex viso et voto
[*sa*] | *crum reddiderunt molc*[*ho*]*mor*
Felix et Diodora libentes | *animo*
agnum pro vika(*rio*)

That it may be made good and favorable
to the holy lord Saturn,
a great nocturnal offering,
soul for soul, blood for blood, life for life,
for the health of Concessa

20. The restoration and translation here primarily follows that of A. and J. Alquier, taking into account the later corrections by R. Charlier, "La nouvelle série de stèles puniques de Constantine et la question des sacrifices dits '*molchomor*,' en relation avec l'expression '*bsrm btm*,'" *Karthago* 4 (1953): 8. It should be noted that in the original reading, followed by Eissfeldt, *pro impetrato fil. v. l. s. a. vk.* was read *pro imperato eius audito*, "in obedience to his request," making it much less obvious that a substitutionary ritual is at issue. This text, along with other similar inscriptions are helpfully collected in Mosca, "Child Sacrifice," 55–97.

21. This restoration and translation follows that of A. and J. Alquier, as corrected by J. Carcopino, "Survivances par substitution des sacrifices d'enfants dans l'Afrique romaine," *RHR* 106 (1932): 597–98.

because of a vision and a vow
Felix and Diodora, willing in soul,
have given an offering, a *molchomor*,
a sheep for a substitute.

In a brief remark appended to the Alquiers' edition,[22] J. Chabot made a connection between the *morchomor/molchomor* of these Latin inscriptions and the term *mlkʾmr* attested in two then extant Punic inscriptions, which read as follows:

CIS 1 307:
lrbt ltnt pn bʿl
wlʾdn lbʿl ḥmn
ʾš ndr ʾršt bt
bdʿštrt mlk
[ʾ]*mr*

To the Lady, to Tanit, Face of Baʿl,
and to the Lord, to Baʿl Hammon
which ʾArisut daughter
of Bod-ʿAstart vowed, a *mlk*-
ʾmr.

JA 11:10, 49–50:
[. . . . . *nd*]
r bdʿšrt bn
mlkytn mlk ʾ
mr kšmʿ qlʾ brkʾ

[. . . . . vow-]
-ed did Bod-ʿAstart son of
Milk-Yaton, a *mlk-ʾ*
mr. For he heard his voice; he blessed him.

Taking the Latin and Punic evidence together, Chabot suggested that *mlkʾmr*, as well as the various Latin transliterations of it (*molchomor*, *morchomor*, etc.), means the "promise" (cognate to Syriac *mlk*[23]) "of a lamb" (*ʾimmōr*; see

22. J.-B. Chabot, "Note complémentaire," *CRAI* 75 (1931): 26–27.
23. Sokoloff, 771; Payne-Smith, 277; Brockelmann, 188.

Hebrew אמר).[24] Thus, according to Chabot's reading, a *mlkʾmr* is "the offering of a lamb" in fulfillment of a vow.

Building on Chabot's work, J. Carcopino noted that the offerer's identity typically differs from that of the individual being blessed. In Carcopino's reconstruction of the ritual, the offerers should be understood as a child's parent or parents. The recipients of the benedictions, on the other hand, were children to whom Saturn had a rightful claim but for whom a sheep had been offered and accepted in their place. Carcopino posited that this substitutionary ritual indicates that by the time of the composition of these inscriptions the old Punic practice of human sacrifice had been replaced by a more humane custom of offering vicarious animal sacrifices instead, likely under Roman pressure/influence. He also noted that the very names of those who had been spared—Concessa, Donatus, Saturninus, etc.—all imply gratitude to Saturn for accepting a substitute offering in the Latinized cult of Saturn/Baʿl Hammon.[25]

It was in the wake of this work that Eissfeldt addressed another problematic term that appears in several Punic inscriptions—*mlkʾdm*.[26] Two notable attestations are found in *RES* 339 and 334:

RES 339 (= Costa 93):
lʾdn lbʿl ḥmn mlk
ʾdm ndr ʾš ndr bʿlpdʾ
bn mgn šmʾ qlʾ
brkʾ

To the Lord, to Baʿl Hammon, a *mlk*
ʾdm, the vow which Baʿl-Padoʾ
son of Magon vowed. He heard his voice;
he blessed him.

RES 334 (= Costa 8):
lʾdn lbʿl ḥmn wlrbt ltnt pʿn bʿl
ndr ʾš ndr ḥmlkt bn bʿštrt
bn nbl mlk ʾdm bšʿrm btm
kšmʿ qlʾ brkyʾ

24. Chabot, "Note complémentaire," 26–27.
25. J. Carcopino, "Survivances par substitution des sacrifices," 592–99.
26. For a convenient collection of inscriptions containing this term, see Mosca, "Child Sacrifice," 61–63.

To the lord, to Baʿl Hammon, and to the Lady to Tanit, the Face of Baʿl,
an oath which Hamilkat son of Bo-ʿAstart,
son of Nabal vowed, a *mlk ʾdm bšʿrm btm.*[27]
For he heard his voice; he blessed him.

While previous scholars had been somewhat perplexed by the meaning of this *mlkʾdm*,[28] Eissfeldt made the connection between the enigmatic phrase and

27. As of yet, there is no satisfactory explanation for the meaning of *bšʿrm btm*. The first term appears variously as *bšr/bšʾr/bšʿr/bšrm/bšʾrm/bšʿrm/bšʾry/bšryʾ* with or without the second term, variously written as *btm/bntm/bnty/btn*. Mosca has collected the attestations and presented previous scholarly suggestions concerning the meaning of the terms ("Child Sacrifice," 85–97). Suggestions include understanding *šʿrm btm* as a place name (so *CIS* 1 294; P. Berger, "Les inscriptions de Constantine au Musée du Louvre," *Actes du 11e Congrès international des Orientalistes, 4e Section* [Paris: Imprimerie nationale, 1898], 287–88; M. Lidzbarski, *Ephemeris für semitische Epigraphik* [vol. 1; Giessen: Ricker'sche (Töpelmann), 1902], 42; and J.-B. Chabot, "Punica XVIII: Stèles puniques de Constantine," *JA* 11:10 [1917]: 66); as a term describing the state of the offerer (so *CIS* 1 3822; J.-B. Chabot, "Mélanges épigraphiques et archéologiques," *Le Muséon* 37 [1924]: 164; R. de Vaux, review of O. Eissfeldt, *Molk als Opferbegriff*, *RB* 45 [1924]: 279); as "das Fleisch im Vollkommenheit" (Eissfeldt, *Molk als Opferbegriff*, 20); or taking *btm* as "at his own expense" (G. Levi Della Vida, "Iscrizioni neopuniche di Tripolitania," *Rendiconti delle sedute dell'Accademia Nazionale dei Lincei: Classe di Scienze morali, storiche e filologiche* 8 [1949]: 399–406). More recent suggestions include "en échange d'un enfant (littéralement: d'une 'chair')" (J. G. Février, "Molchomor," *RHR* 143 [1953]: 10–15; idem, "Essai de reconstitution du sacrifice *molek*," *JA* 248 [1960]: 172); "sein eigenes Kind in vollkommener Zustand" (J. Hoftijzer, "Eine Notiz zum punischen Kinderopfer," *VT* 8 [1958]: 290–92); "his own child, totally" (R. de Vaux, *Studies in Old Testament Sacrifice* [Cardiff: University of Wales Press, 1964]: 78); and "(whose) body (is) intact" (W. F. Albright, *Yahweh and the Gods of Canaan: A Historical Analysis of Two Contrasting Faiths* [Jordan Lectures on Comparitive Religion 7; London: Athlone, 1968], 236, n. 79).

Mosca reviews these options, rightly finds all of them problematic, and tentatively suggests *bšr* as *b-šr*, understanding *šr* as a byform to *ṣr* "distress," and hence "in distress." Thus, in Mosca's view the phrase describes the difficult circumstances under which the offerer's vow was made. Alternatively, he posits that *bšr* might instead be a contraction of *b-yšr* "in uprightness" and *b(n)tm* may be cognate to Hebrew *b-tm* "in uprightness, in purity," in which case *bšr btm* would describe the righteous state of the offerers. Mosca admits, however, that even his own suggestions are not entirely satisfactory (Mosca, "Child Sacrifice," 92–97). Alternatively, F. M. Cross suggests that *bšr* means "of his flesh"—that is, that the child is kin to the offerer ("A Phoenician Inscription from Idalion: Some Old and New Inscriptions Relating to Child Sacrifice," in *Leaves from an Epigrapher's Notebook: Collected Papers in Hebrew and West Semitic Palaeography and Epigraphy* [HSS 51; Winona Lake, IN: Eisenbrauns, 2003], 235–36). Fortunately, for the purposes of this study, the precise meaning of the terms is of relatively little consequence.

28. For some earlier suggestions, see P. Berger, "Les inscriptions de Constantine au Musée du Louvre," 291; M. Lidzbarski, *Ephemeris* 1, 42; idem, "Neue Götter," *Nachrichten von der königlichen Gesellschaft der Wissenschaften zu Göttingen, Phil.-hist. Klasse* (1916): 90–91; and *RES* 334.

mlkʾmr. If *mlkʾmr* means "the sacrifice of a sheep," he posited, then *mlkʾdm* would naturally mean "the sacrifice of a human" (*ʾdm*). Given the numerous claims in Classical sources that child sacrifice occurred in the Punic colonies, this reading should occasion no surprise. These Punic inscriptions would simply represent native corroboration for the Classical accusations. Once this step was taken, Eissfeldt's next conclusion was an ingenious but fairly simple one: these Punic *mlk* sacrifices and the biblical למלך sacrifice, both of which involved the sacrifice of children, are actually one and the same! A key piece of evidence for this claim is Eissfeldt's reading of a Neo-Punic inscription from Constantine, first published by Lidzbarski as Neopun. 30:

> *lʿdn lbʿl hqd* | *š bym nʿm lmlk*[29]
>
> To the holy Lord Baʿl, in a fortunate day, for a *mlk*.

As with the biblical "Molek" sacrifices, where a child is said to be offered למלך, here in a Neo-Punic inscription Eissfeldt found not only the same term but even identical syntax, *lmlk*, used in connection with a ritual that involved the sacrifice of a human child. Eissfeldt thus concluded that when the Hebrew Bible mentions a sacrifice offered למלך, one should understand it to mean "as a *mōlek* offering," just as in the case of the Punic inscriptions, rather than as it had traditionally been understood, "to (a god) Molek." In Eissfeldt's view, any attempt to identify a "Molek" deity venerated in ancient Israel is misguided from the outset. Eissfeldt further surmised that Israel's own god, Yahweh, would have been the obvious recipient of such sacrifices. On the basis of texts like the Aqedah (Gen 22), the story of Jephthah's vow (Judg 11), the testimony of the prophet Micah (6:7), and the use of tophet imagery by the prophet Isaiah (30:33), Eissfeldt argued that child sacrifice was in fact a very old part of Israelite Yahwistic religion and only fell into disfavor with the rise of Deuteronomism.[30]

---

29. Lidzbarski had read *lʾdn lbʿl hqd* | *š-yʾn ʿhlmlk* (*Handbuch der nordsemitischen Epigraphik nebst ausgewählten Inschriften* [Weimar: Felber, 1898], 438). Chabot's reexamination, however, resulted in *lʾdn lbʿl hqd* | *š bym nʿm mlk*, "To the holy Lord Baʿal in the day of fortune, Malik" ("Punica, XVIII. Stèles puniques de Constantine," *JA* 11:10 [1917]: 72–73). Eissfeldt's reading (with the addition of the *l-* before *mlk*; *Molk als Opferbegriff*, 30) has been confirmed by Février, "Glanes néopuniques," *JA* 255 (1967): 63. It should be noted that Eissfeldt's translation of this inscription is not undisputed, even among those who follow his views in other regards. K. Jongeling, who elsewhere understands *mlk* as "a certain type of sacrifice," believes that *lmlk* here should be read as "for Malik," who, in Jongeling's view, is the individual who dedicated the inscription (*HNPI*, 211–12, 396).

30. Eissfeldt, *Molk als Opferbegriff*, 31–71.

Many scholars writing in Eissfeldt's wake were convinced to one degree or another by his radical new proposal,[31] but the most thorough and able defense of Eissfeldt's thesis to date has been P. Mosca's 1975 Harvard dissertation,[32] which not only champions Eissfeldt's general ideas concerning the למלך ritual but has also done more to build on Eissfeldt's conclusions than any other work since. One of the most valuable features of Mosca's work is that he gathered together in one place all of the relevant texts, both Classical and epigraphic, regarding Punic child sacrifice. In his first chapter, Mosca presents thirty-three references to the practice in Greek and Latin sources, dating from the fifth century BCE to the fifth century CE. Mosca observes that the combined testimony of the Classical material suggests that child sacrifice was a rite that took place in the Punic colonies. According to these sources, a child of noble birth was offered to Kronos/Saturn = Baʿal-Hammon/El, either as part of an annual ritual, in response to a great favor, or during a time of crisis.

Next, Mosca examines the Latin and Punic epigraphic material that had served as the primary evidence for Eissfeldt's thesis in the first place. After a brief discussion of archaeological evidence for the sacred precincts in which children were sacrificed at Carthage (see chapter 2 below for an overview of this and related evidence), Mosca presents more than sixty inscriptions from the Punic central Mediterranean, classified according to the type of offering mentioned in the text: *mlkʾmr* or *mlkʾdm*, as well as another problematic term, *mlkbʿl*. Mosca follows Eissfeldt in interpreting *mlkʾmr* as "the *mulk*-sacrifice of a lamb." He argues, however, that *mlkʾdm* should be translated "the *mulk*-sacrifice of a commoner," while *mlkbʿl* refers to "the *mulk*-sacrifice of a 'baal' (i.e., the scion of a wealthy mercantile or estate-owning family)." Both of

31. Among Eissfeldt's most fervent early defenders was R. Dussaud, who wrote two reviews of Eissfeldt's monograph: review of O. Eissfeldt, *Molk als Opferbegriff*, *Syria* 16 (1935): 407–9; and review of O. Eissfeldt, *Molk als Opferbegriff*, *AfO* 11 (1936): 167–68. In each, he defended Eissfeldt against detractors such as R. de Vaux (review of O. Eissfeldt, *Molk als Opferbegriff*, *RB* 45 [1936]: 278–82). Among the most prolific authors on the topic during this period was J. G. Février, who wrote five different articles on Punic and/or Hebrew *mlk* between 1953 and 1964 ("Molchomor," *RHR* 143 [1953]: 8–18; "Le vocabulaire sacrificiel punique," *JA* 243 [1955]: 49–63; "Essai de reconstitution du sacrifice Molek," *JA* 248 [1960]: 167–87; "Le rite de substitution dans les textes de N'Gaous," *JA* 250 (1962): 1–10; "Les rites sacrificiels chez les Hébreux et à Carthage," *REJ* 123 [1964]: 7–18). Although he consistently agreed with Eissfeldt that *mlk* should be understood as a sacrificial term, not as a divine epithet, Février often disagreed with Eissfeldt on the implications of this conclusion, sometimes even rejecting the idea that human sacrifice was involved at all. Further, he consistently disputed the claim that the practice was native to Israel rather than being a late import from Phoenicia.

32. Mosca, "Child Sacrifice."

these, he claims, involved child sacrifice, the difference apparently being the social status of the victim('s family).[33] Mosca concludes that the epigraphic evidence generally confirms the picture presented by the Classical sources and argues that Punic inscriptions themselves indicate that child sacrifice was indeed practiced in the colonies. He does note, however, that the epigraphic material appears to imply that the sacrifices had more to do with personal vows than with annual rites or national emergencies, despite what the Classical sources often indicate.[34]

Turning to the biblical testimony, Mosca argues that למלך rites must be distinguished from firstborn sacrifices (Exod 22:28 [Eng. 22:29]; on which, see chapter 3 below). In his view, Israelite firstborn offerings always involved redemption, while the למלך sacrifice involved child sacrifice. Based on his careful examination of the biblical evidence, Mosca concludes that Israelite child sacrifice was closely connected with the Phoenician/Punic rite bearing the same name, was extant in both Israel and Judah from at least as early as the eighth century BCE (possibly even as early as the tenth), was repudiated as idolatrous during the Josianic reform, and was reinterpreted as being the non-Yahwistic cult of a pagan deity "Molek" in the centuries after its abolition. Thus, while Eissfeldt provided the seminal insight that connected Israelite למלך with Punic *mlk*, it was Mosca who did the work of gathering all of the relevant evidence necessary to support the thesis and expand upon it.

In addition to Mosca, a number of more recent studies have followed Eissfeldt's thesis, despite some disagreement in the details. H.-P. Müller and K. A. D. Smelik,[35] for example, follow Eissfeldt rather closely in most important regards. On the other hand, S. Ackerman largely follows both Eissfeldt and Mosca, but she disagrees with Mosca that the Israelite למלך ritual and the offering of firstborn children should be seen as fundamentally different rites. Instead she argues that למלך offerings originally only involved firstborn children but that over time more and more children came to be viewed as eligible for sacrifice.[36] P. D. Miller also agrees that the rite is related to the

33. Mosca, "Child Sacrifice," 77.

34. Mosca, "Child Sacrifice,"102–3.

35. H.-P. Müller, "מֹלֶךְ *molæk*," *TDOT* 8, 375–88, and "Hebraisch מֹלֶךְ und punisch *ml(ʾ)k(t)*" in *Michael: Historical, Epigraphical and Biblical Studies in Honor of Prof. Michael Heltzer* (ed. Y. Avishur and R. Deutsch; Tel Aviv: Archaeological Center Publications, 1999), 243–53; K. A. D. Smelik, "Moloch, Molekh, or Molk-Sacrifice? A Reassessment of the Evidence Concerning the Hebrew Term Molekh," *SJOT* 9 (1995): 133–42.

36. S. Ackerman, *Under Every Green Tree: Popular Religion in Sixth-Century Judah* (HSM 46; Atlanta: Scholars Press, 1992), 117–43.

Punic *mlk* sacrifices but argues, contra Eissfeldt and Mosca, that it was imported to Judah at a late date rather than being a relatively old element of the Yahwistic cult.[37] On the other hand, F. Stavrakopoulou follows Eissfeldt's argument that למלך refers to a ritual rather than to a deity but argues, contra Miller, that the למלך sacrifices should not be naively accepted as borrowed and "foreign," as the biblical authors present the case. On the contrary, in her view, למלך sacrifices were native to Israel, a "royal specialization of the fertility rite of the firstborn sacrifice, in which a royal pregnancy was promised as a gift to *Yhwh*, the patron-deity of the Judahite royal family, and sacrificed in fire shortly after the birth as a means of encouraging the divine perpetuation of the royal dynasty."[38] Stavrakopoulou argues that biblical writers intentionally distorted the historical reality of Yahwistic child sacrifice in order to absolve Yahweh of any involvement in such rituals, despite their ancient roots in the Yahwistic cult.[39]

Thus, even among those who agree with Eissfeldt in viewing מלך as an *Opferbegriff* rather than as the name or title of a deity, his defenders often disagree on whether the rite was native or imported, for how long it existed in Judah, the purpose of these sacrifices, and so on. These issues will be treated in due course below (see especially chapter 4), but for now it is important to note that the full diversity of scholarly opinion goes much further than simply the variations on Eissfeldt's thesis outlined above. Indeed, from the time that Eissfeldt's monograph first appeared until the present there have been those who have rejected his central thesis entirely and who have sought to resurrect the traditional view that למלך means "to Molek," a foreign deity who was worshiped via the sacrifice of Israelite children.

---

37. P. D. Miller, *The Religion of Ancient Israel* (Louisville: Westminster John Knox, 2000), 59.

38. F. Stavrakopoulou, *King Manasseh and Child Sacrifice: Biblical Distortions of Historical Realities* (BZAW 338; Berlin: de Gruyter, 2004), 134.

39. Other studies that have followed Eissfeldt on the meaning of Hebrew למלך include E. Noort, "Child Sacrifice in Ancient Israel: The *Status Quaestionis*," in *The Strange World of Human Sacrifice* (ed. J. N. Bremmer; Studies in the History of Anthropology of Religion 1; Leuven: Peeters, 2007), 103–25; B. H. Reynolds, "Molek: Dead or Alive? The Meaning and Derivation of *mlk* and למלך," in *Human Sacrifice in the Jewish and Christian Tradition* (ed. K. Finsterbusch, A. Lange, and K. F. D. Römheld; SHR 112; Leiden: Brill, 2007), 133–50; and M. Bauks, "Kinderopfer als Weihe- oder Gabeopfer: Anmerkungen zum *mlk*-Opfer," in *Israeliten und Phönizier: Ihre Beziehungen im Spiegel der Archäologie und der Literatur des Alten Testaments und seiner Umwelt* (ed. M. Witte and J. F. Diehl; OBO 235; Fribourg: Academic Press, 2008), 233–51.

Scholars Who Continue to Argue That "Molek" Was a Deity

Among Eissfeldt's earliest critics was M. Buber,[40] who argued that Eissfeldt was wrong to understand מלך as a sacrificial term, even in the Punic inscriptions. According to Buber, Punic *mlkʾmr* is not "the *mlk* offering of a sheep" but "the Malk has spoken." Likewise, *mlkʾdm* is not "the *mlk* offering of a human" but merely a variant of *mlkʾdn* "the Malk is Lord." Further, in an argument that would prove crucial for nearly all later opponents of Eissfeldt's thesis, Buber pointed to Lev 20:5, which forbids "whoring after the *mōlek*" (לזנות אחרי המלך). Elsewhere in the Hebrew Bible, only gods, demons, and idols are "whored after" (see Exod 34:15–16; Lev 17:7; Judg 8:27; etc.), but in no other case is a type of sacrifice "whored after." Thus whatever the term might have meant at Carthage or elsewhere, the authors of the Hebrew Bible seem to have assumed that it referred to some sort of supernatural being. Notably, though, Buber did not suggest that this is an instance of Israelite polytheism or that one should attempt to identify a "Molek" deity to whom children were sacrificed. Instead, in Buber's view, "Molek" refers to "*Melekh JHWH*," a popular, syncretistic mutation of the Yahwistic cult centered in the Hinnom Valley.[41] Thus, while Buber's view of the philological evidence stands in stark contrast to Eissfeldt's, their ideas concerning the relationship of the למלך sacrifices to the Yahwistic cult are actually not all that different. Both Eissfeldt and Buber view the sacrifices as Yahwistic or at least as perceived as such by those offering the sacrifices, despite their disagreement on whether the sacrifices were broadly conceived of as a legitimate aspect of the Yahwistic cult prior to the rise of Deuteronomism.

For his part, R. de Vaux took issue with Eissfeldt's reading of both the Punic material and the biblical evidence.[42] Although he agreed with Eissfeldt contra Buber that *mlk* referred to a type of sacrifice in the Punic inscriptions, he finds it more likely, contra Eissfeldt, that *mlkʾdm* should be understood as "a sacrifice *by* a human" rather than "the sacrifice *of* a human." Furthermore, he argued that there is ample evidence for Canaanite deities with "*mlk*" titles (e.g., *mlk-qrt* → *mlqrt* = "Melqart"), and there is thus no need to turn to a Punic *mlk* sacrifice to explain the biblical term rather than following the traditional interpretation and concluding that Israelite children were likely

40. M. Buber, *Königtum Gottes* (2nd ed.; Berlin: Schocken, 1936), 211–25.
41. Buber, *Königtum Gottes*, 217.
42. R. de Vaux, review of O. Eissfeldt, *Molk als Opferbegriff*, *RB* 45 (1936): 278–82.

sacrificed to one of these foreign *mlk* deities. In his later work, however, de Vaux softened his opposition to Eissfeldt's thesis. He came to acknowledge that Punic *mlkʾdm*, analogous to *mlkʾmr* "sacrifice of a sheep," probably does in fact refer to "the sacrifice of a human" and that it was indeed likely cognate to the Israelite למלך rite. De Vaux continued to insist, however, that "the practice was introduced late in the history of Israel and from the outside and it was condemned by all the spokesmen of Yahwism—the Deuteronomist, the prophets, and the Priestly editors. It never formed part of the Israelite ritual for sacrifices."[43] Further, de Vaux argued that, despite the evidence for a Punic *mlk* ritual, the existence of a "Malik" god both in Assyria and at Ugarit makes it likely that the Israelites (mis)understood the sacrifice that they borrowed as being offered "to Malik," not "as a *mlk*-sacrifice." In this regard, he leans heavily on Buber's observations concerning the syntax of Lev 20:5, which de Vaux agreed precludes interpreting biblical *mlk* as a type of sacrifice rather than as a divine name or epithet.[44]

W. F. Albright's views on the topic shifted rather dramatically over the course of his career. He was initially convinced by Eissfeldt, describing his argument as "an important thesis, convincingly established, viz., that there never was a Canaanite god Moloch at all, but that the Canaanite-Hebrew common noun *molk* refers to a kind of votive offering." He even went so far as to claim that Eissfeldt's work "settles one of the obscurest problems in the history of the religion of Israel."[45] In his later *Archaeology and the Religion of Israel*, however, although he continued to agree with Eissfeldt's conclusions concerning the Punic *mlk* offerings, he suggested that "the original conception [of the Israelite sacrifices] was more complex than he was able to guess at the time."[46] Pointing to the Amorite deity "Muluk," Albright posited that Ahaz, who was known for other cultic innovations, borrowed both the deity and the practice of child sacrifice from Syria. Although Albright would not rule out the possibility that children were sacrificed in Israel prior to the Deuteronomistic reform (but if they were, it could have only occurred under

43. De Vaux, *Ancient Israel: Its Life and Institutions* (trans. J. McHugh; New York: McGraw Hill, 1961), 445.

44. De Vaux, *Les sacrifices de l'Ancien Testament* (CahRB 1; Paris: Galbalda, 1964), 67–81. On similar grounds, A. Bea, "Kinderopfer für Moloch oder für Jahwe?" *Bib* 18 (1937): 95–107, and E. Dhorme, review of O. Eissfeldt, *Molk als Opferbegriff*, *RHR* 113 (1936): 276–78, argued that, whatever *mlk* might have meant outside Israel, מלך in the Hebrew Bible must be understood as the name or epithet of a deity.

45. W. F. Albright, review of O. Eissfeldt, *Molk als Opferbegriff*, *JPOS* 15 (1935): 344.

46. W. F. Albright, *Archaeology and the Religion of Israel* (Baltimore: The Johns Hopkins University Press, 1942), 162.

foreign Canaanite influence, in his view), he had come to reject entirely Eissfeldt's contention that the practice was ever accepted as part of the Yahwistic cult or that children were ever sacrificed to Yahweh himself.[47] In his still later *Yahweh and the Gods of Canaan*,[48] however, Albright once again modified his views, moving back closer to Eissfeldt's understanding of the relationship between the Punic and Israelite *mlk* rituals, going so far as to state: "There are probably few competent scholars who now believe that a god Moloch is intended in any biblical passage referring to human sacrifice."[49] He continued to maintain, however, that all of the למלך sacrifices ultimately derived etymologically from a *mlk* deity and that they were introduced into Jerusalem relatively late in Judah's history, during the reign of Ahaz. Thus, while Albright's disagreements with Eissfeldt were not always as sharp of those of de Vaux, at least in some points during his career he did disagree with Eissfeldt's specific conclusions and differed with him significantly regarding whether or not the למלך offerings were "native" to Yahwism.[50]

Among those who continue to argue for the existence of a biblical Molek deity, no one has done so in as thoroughgoing a manner as G. C. Heider. In his *The Cult of Molek: A Reassessment*,[51] Heider offers what appears to be definitive evidence for the existence of a pan-Near Eastern "Malik" deity, of which biblical Molek was only one manifestation. His impressive and extensive survey of ancient Near Eastern material includes Eblaite and Amorite proper names, Ugaritic literature, Akkadian god-lists, and other Near Eastern textual evidence. He offers an overwhelming number of attestations, especially from Ebla, of a deity named "Malik," who is sometimes equated with or linked to the Mesopotamian underworld deity Nergal. After collecting all of this data, his examination leads him to conclude: "[T]he Syro-Palestinian Malik was a significant underworld figure, especially in the popular cult,

47. A. R. W. Green essentially follows Albright's thesis in his own survey of the "Molek" material in *The Role of Human Sacrifice in the Ancient Near East* (ASOR Dissertation Series 1; Missoula, MT: Scholar's Press, 1975), 179–87.

48. Albright, *Yahweh and the Gods of Canaan*, 236–44.

49. Albright, *Yahweh and the Gods of Canaan*, 236.

50. Other scholars of this period who favored understanding *mlk* as a divine name or epithet include J. Gray, "The Desert God ʿAṯtr in the Literature and Religion of Canaan," *JNES* 8 (1949): 72–83; idem, *The Legacy of Canaan: The Ras Shamra Texts and Their Relevance to the Old Testament* (Leiden: Brill, 1957), 125–27; W. Kornfeld, "Der Moloch: eine Untersuchung zur Theorie O. Eissfeldts," *WZKM* 51 (1951): 287–313; and K. Dronkert, *De Molochdienst in het Oude Testament (with a Summary in English)* (Leiden: Luctor et Emergo, 1953).

51. G. C. Heider, *The Cult of Molek: A Reassessment* (JSOTSup 43; Sheffield: JSOT Press, 1985).

whose character bore dimensions both of fertility and of death."[52] The Punic evidence for a type of sacrifice denoted by the term *mlk*, on the other hand, he views as a "unicum" and argues that any connection between it and the Israelite למלך sacrifice remains "conjectural."[53] His specific conclusions will be examined in more detail below, but it is important to note here the impact that Heider's work has had. Not only did Heider also author the entry on "Molech" in the influential *Anchor Bible Dictionary*,[54] but in his well-known and widely read *The Death and Resurrection of the Beloved Son*, J. D. Levenson surveys the various suggestions concerning the meaning of למלך and ultimately echoes Heider's assessment: "The best conclusion is that biblical Molech was a chthonic deity honored through the sacrifice of little boys and girls."[55]

Bolstering this new majority view, J. Day, writing shortly after Heider, presents a similar thesis in his *Molech: A God of Human Sacrifice in the Old Testament*. In his opinion, there are three major problems with viewing למלך as a sacrificial term. The first of these is Buber's observation that nowhere outside of Lev 20:5 does one "whore after" (לזנות אחרי) a type of sacrifice; thus, the term should more naturally be understood as referring to a deity rather than to a type of sacrifice.[56] Second, Day acknowledges that, syntactically speaking, √עבר (Hiphil)/נתן/שרף can be followed by ל + a sacrificial term as Eissfeldt had suggested, but he counters that examples of this syntactical construction almost always also contain ל + the divine recipient *alongside* ל + the sacrificial term. On the contrary, ל + a sacrificial term almost never occurs alone. Day does, however, acknowledge one exception to this general rule in 1 Chr 21:23, where one finds נתתי הבקר לעלות "I give the cattle for burnt offerings." Finally, Day points out that following Eissfeldt's thesis requires assuming that the earliest translators of the Hebrew Bible, none of whom understand מלך as a type of sacrifice, all misunderstood the nature of the term מלך, a prospect that he finds unlikely.[57] Having argued that children were indeed sacrificed to a מלך deity, Day turns his attention to determining what kind of deity this "Molech" might have been. Here he points to the repeated biblical claims that the cult derives from the Canaanites whom the Israelites

52. Heider, *The Cult of Molek*, 163.

53. Ibid., 188.

54. G. C. Heider, "Molech," *ABD*, 895–98.

55. J. D. Levenson, *The Death and Resurrection of the Beloved Son: The Transformation of Child Sacrifice in Judaism and Christianity* (New Haven: Yale University Press, 1995), 19.

56. Day, *Molech*, 11.

57. Ibid., 10–13.

drove out of the land (Lev 18:3, 21, 24–25, 27; 20:2–5, 23; Deut 12:31, 18:9–10; 2 Kgs 16:3; 21:2, 11; Isa 57:5, 7, 9; Jer 19:5; Ezek 16:2–3, 20–21, 36; Ps 106:37–38). In his attempt to identify this Canaanite (= Jebusite[58]) deity, he presents a solution almost identical to that of Heider: Molech = Ugaritic *mlk* = Akkadian Malik, all three of which correspond to an underworld deity such as Nergal.[59] Finally, after surveying the relevant biblical texts, Day concludes that Molech and Yahweh were never identified but that at least some participants in the cult of Molech probably considered themselves to be good Yahwists and saw no contradiction in their venerating both deities simultaneously.[60]

More recently, T. Römer has also rejected the idea that מלך refers to a ritual rather than a deity, primarily on the basis of Lev 20:5, which "s'oppose à la comprehension de *molek* comme désignant d'un type d'offrande."[61] Contrary to Day and Heider, however, he also rejects the view that מלך is the title of a foreign non-Yahwistic deity. Instead, echoing the thesis of Buber, Römer argues that מלך was originally *melek*, a title for Yahweh. Pointing to Mesha's sacrifice (2 Kgs 3:26–27), he argues that these sacrifices were offered during especially dire circumstances. In further support of this conclusion, Römer notes that the two Judahite kings who are said to have sacrificed their children, Ahaz (2 Kgs 16:3) and Manasseh (2 Kgs 21:6), both faced military crises, the Syro-Ephraimite war and Assyrian occupation, respectively.[62]

Thus, although the scholars surveyed in this overview differ on precisely who "Molek" was, they do have in common that they all find Eissfeldt's basic thesis—that is, that biblical מלך is a sacrificial term, not a divine name or epithet—to be untenable. In this regard, there are two primary pieces of evidence typically brought to bear against Eissfeldt's thesis: extrabiblical attestations of a "Malik" deity and the phrase "whore after the Molek" (לזנות

58. Ibid., 55.

59. Ibid., 46–52.

60. Ibid., 65–71; for a more recent but in its particulars essentially unchanged presentation of Day's views, see his *Yahweh and the Gods and Godesses of Canaan* (JSOTSup 265; Sheffield: Sheffield Academic, 2000), 209–16.

61. T. Römer, "Le sacrifice humain en Juda et Israël au premier millénaire avant notre ère," *Archiv für Religionsgeschichte* 1 (1999): 23.

62. Ibid., 24. In his own work on the topic, J. Tatlock takes a similar position: *mlk* is an epithet for a deity, but that deity is none other than Yahweh (J. Tatlock, "How in Ancient Times They Sacrificed People: Human Immolation in the Eastern Mediterranean Basin with Special Emphasis on Ancient Israel and the Near East" [Ph.D. diss., The University of Michigan, 2006], esp. 210–20).

אחרי המלך) in Lev 20:5. As will become clear below, however, neither of these objections can withstand careful scrutiny.[63]

"Molek" Disappears Once Again

As observed above, scholars who have sought to resurrect a Molek deity who was venerated in ancient Israel have done so primarily based on two pieces of evidence: the syntax of Lev 20:5 and comparative Near Eastern evidence for the existence of a chthonic "Malik" deity. The most thorough attempt to support the latter idea was made by Heider. In his survey of ancient Near Eastern texts, Heider gathered an impressive body of evidence for the existence of an underworld deity named Malik. A closer examination of this evidence, however, reveals that many of his claims are more problematic than they first appear. First, it is true that "Malik" does in fact appear in Ur III, Babylonian, and Ugaritic god-lists and that sometimes he is equated with Nergal (see RS 20.121[= Ug. V 119]:81; *KAV* 63.2:37; *KAV*

63. One final theory concerning the למלך rite worth noting is the suggestion that it never involved child sacrifice at all. This thesis was most extensively defended by M. Weinfeld, "The Worship of Molech and the Queen of Heaven and Its Background," *UF* 4 (1972): 133–54. After dispensing with the biblical evidence as either ambiguous or "tendentious poetical fancy" ("The Worship of Molech," 141), he points to Neo-Assyrian temple contracts that stipulate that children of an offending party will be "burned" if the agreement is violated. According to Weinfeld, the child is typically described as being "burned" to Adad-Milki. Weinfeld then argues that, since Mesopotamian sacrifice rarely involved slaughter of any kind, much less *human* sacrifice, the "burning" here must refer to some sort of dedicatory rite, not a sacrifice, and that the biblical למלך rite is cognate to it, both lexically and ritually. In his view, "The children born of cultic prostitution associated with Molech were presumably delivered to the idolatrous priests, even as the offspring of a regular marriage may have been handed over to Molech" ("The Worship of Molech," 144). This theory was challenged in a rebuttal by M. Smith, "A Note on Burning Babies," *JAOS* 95 (1975): 477–79, who argued that both the biblical and Neo-Assyrian material refer to actual child sacrifice, not to a dedicatory ritual. Weinfeld then wrote a rejoinder to Smith, primarily reiterating the points of his previous article ("Burning Babies in Ancient Israel: A Rejoinder to Morton Smith's Article in *JAOS* 95 (1975), pp. 477–479," *UF* 10 [1978]: 411–13).

Although the argument could have ended at an impasse over the interpretation of the evidence, S. A. Kaufman demonstrated that all alleged occurrences of "Adad-Milki"—cuneiform ^{d}X.XX = ^{d}U.MAN = ^{d}Adad-Milki, in Weinfeld's view—should actually be read ^{d}XXX = ^{d}Sîn. Especially damning for Weinfeld's case is that in one instance ^{d}XXX is followed by the gloss SIG, phonetically read *si*(ʾ), the Aramaic name for Sîn (Kaufman, "The Enigmatic Adad-Milki," *JNES* 37 [1978]: 101–9). Thus, the alleged Neo-Assyrian parallels in reality refer to the Mesopotamian god Sîn, not to a deity named Adad-Milki, which severs any philological connection to Hebrew מלך and thus eliminates the key piece of evidence for Weinfeld's thesis.

42.1:32; and 3R 66, 2:9). Additionally, Ugaritic *mlk ʿθtrth/mlk bʿθtrt* (KTU³ 1.100/KTU³ 1.107) does appear to be evidence for a *mlk* deity, perhaps with chthonic characteristics,[64] although it is unclear that this is a deity named "Malik" rather than "Milku."[65] Also, "Malik" does appear as a theophoric element marked by the divine determinative in a handful of Old Akkadian personal names,[66] and the presence of the divine determinative may indicate that it is to be understood as a divine name rather than merely serving as a title or epithet, meaning something like "adviser" (or, less likely in an East Semitic context, "ruler").[67] Thus, despite my argument below, Heider is correct that there does appear to have been a "Malik" deity in various places at various times in the ancient Near Eastern. But I contend that much of the additional evidence that Heider presents is less straightforward and that this deity is far less widely attested than he claims.

For instance, Heider leans especially heavily on the ubiquity of Syrian, especially Eblaite, personal names with "Malik" in the theophoric position. It is true that "Malik" is indeed a very common theophoric element in Eblaite personal names,[68] but it is not at all clear that this theophoric element is the name of a deity, rather than an epithet or title. Either "ruler" (West Semitic) or "adviser" (East Semitic) would be an appropriate divine epithet for any number of deities.[69] Anticipating this counterargument, Heider points to the

---

64. But see B. Schmidt, who doubts that one can ascribe a chthonic character to *mlk* on the basis of available evidence (*Israel's Beneficent Dead: Ancestor Cult and Necromancy in Ancient Israelite Religion and Tradition* [FAT 11; Tübingen: Mohr Siebeck, 1994], 93–97).

65. So, for instance, D. Pardee, *Ritual and Cult at Ugarit* (WAW 10; Society of Biblical Literature: Atlanta, 2002), 177 and 281.

66. These include *I-gu-ᵈma-lik* (= *Ikûn-ᵈMalik*, "Malik is firm"), *Ìr-am-ᵈma-lik* (= *Irām-ᵈMalik*, "Malik loves"), *Ìr-e-ᵈma-lik* (= *Irē-ᵈMalik*, "Malik shepherded"), *ᵈMa-lik-zi-in-su* (= *ᵈMalik-ṣīnšu*, "Malik is his help"), PÙ.ŠA-*ᵈma-lik* (= *Puzur-ᵈMalik*, "Shelter of Malik"), *Šum-ᵈma-lik* (= *Šum-ᵈMalik*, "Name of Malik"), *U-ṣi-ᵈma-lik* (= *Uṣi-ᵈMalik*, "Malik went forth"). See Heider, *The Cult of Molek: A Reassessment*, 150; and earlier: J. J. M. Roberts, *The Earliest Semitic Pantheon: A Study of the Semitic Deities Attested in Mesopotamia before Ur III* (Baltimore: The Johns Hopkins University Press, 1972), 42–43; and I. J. Gelb, *Glossary of Old Akkadian* (MAD 3; Chicago: University of Chicago Press, 1957), 176–77.

67. But even this is not necessarily the case, as these examples could merely be evidence of "divinized epithets." So S. M. Olyan and M. S. Smith, review of G. C. Heider, *The Cult of Molek*, *RB* 94 (1987): 273.

68. See F. Pomponio and P. Xella, *Les dieux d'Ebla: Étude analytique des divinités éblaïtes à l'époque des archives royales du IIIe millénaire* (AOAT 245; Münster: Ugarit-Verlag, 1997), 458–65, for a list of attested "Malik" names.

69. J. J. M. Roberts had already suggested the god Dagan as a likely candidate (*The Earliest Semitic Pantheon*, 43).

few cases at Ebla where "Malik" appears to be preceded by the divine determinative (the DINGIR sign). Although divine epithets are not usually preceded by the divine determinative, divine names typically are. Thus, if Heider were able to produce onomastic evidence from Syria with "Malik" in a theophoric position also preceded by a divine determinative, then he would have a much stronger basis for arguing that Malik was a deity in his own right in Syria.

Unfortunately for Heider's case, however, despite the large number of Eblaite Malik names, he is able to produce only a small handful that mark the theophoric element with the divine determinative, and even the few cases he does produce are dubious.[70] For example, Heider reads one name *Dar-^{d}ma-lik*. But the AN/DINGIR sign should be read *am_6* rather than DINGIR here: *Dar-am_6-ma-lik* (= *Tarām-Malik*, "You loved, O Ruler/Counselor"; or perhaps "The Ruler [fem.] loved").[71] Heider's reading *Dar-^{d}ma-lik*, on the other hand, would be gibberish. Likewise, although *Ìr-^{d}ma-lik* could theoretically be understood as (*W*)*arad-^{d}Malik* ("Servant of Malik"), it more likely should be read *Ìr-am_6-ma-lik* (= *Irām-Malik*, "The Ruler has loved").[72] Once these two examples are eliminated, no other proper names containing "Malik" marked by the divine determinative from Ebla remain. Similarly, Heider's single example of *Malik* marked with the divine determinative in a proper name from Nuzi is *Gu-^{d}ma-lik*, but this is almost certainly a misreading. Although it is possible that GU is used here as a Sumerogram for *qû*(*m*), "flax, thread, string, filament, capillary, net, web,"[73] and thus Heider's reading could at least theoretically result in a name "The flax/thread/net of Malik," this would be an odd Semitic personal name, especially since there are no other "GU-names" attested at Nuzi. If this example is examined more closely, however, even the presence of "GU" itself is far from certain: only the last bit of the alleged sign is preserved, in a broken context.[74] Depending on how the sign should

70. For a convenient collection of the onomastic data that he brings to bear on the issue, see Appendix A in Heider, *The Cult of Molek*, 409–19.

71. So also M. Krebernik, *Die Personennamen der Ebla-Texte: Eine Zwischenbilanz* (BBVO 7; Berlin: Reimer, 1988), 81; J. M. Pagan, *A Morphological and Lexical Study of Personal Names in the Ebla Texts* (ARES 3; Rome: Missione Archeologica Italiana in Siria, 1998), 10, 300; and Pomponio and Xella, *Les dieux d'Ebla*, 459.

72. So Krebernik, *Die Personennamen der Ebla-Texte*, 225; Pagan, *A Morphological and Lexical Study of Personal Names in the Ebla Texts*, 8, 337; and Pomponio and Xella, *Les dieux d'Ebla*, 462.

73. See *CAD* Q 285–88.

74. For the hand-copy of the tablet, see HSS 10 86:7. In the other alleged attestation of the name, HSS 10 159.v.3, the alleged "GU" is absent entirely; the tablet is broken where it would appear.

be read, it is possible that the following sign should be taken as having a syllabic value rather than serving as the DINGIR determinative. Further, even if this were an example of a personal name containing ^{d}*Malik*, it would be the only example of such a name at Nuzi, despite the fact that there are several attested "Malik" names in clearer contexts, none of which mark the term with the divine determinative (e.g., *Mālik-nāṣir*, "The Ruler is guarding"; *Ilu-mālik*, "The God is ruling"; ^{d}*Sîn-mālik*, "Sin is ruling"; *Šarru-mālik*, "The King is ruling").[75] Thus the weight of the evidence suggests that "malik" elements in Nuzi personal names, like those at Ebla, should be understood as meaning either "adviser" or "ruler," not as a divine name "Malik."

Heider also conflates "Malik" with the *mālikū* at Mari, which is problematic. Variously translated "conseillers(?),"[76] "les esprits infernaux(?),"[77] "departed men of distinction,"[78] "Totengeister oder Unterweltsgötter,"[79] and "a nether-world god or demon,"[80] the *mālikū* are believed to have had a chthonic character due to their association with the *kispum*.[81] The *kispum* rites involved funerary offerings,[82] and since these offerings appear in lists that also include offerings given *ana mālikī*, it is natural to assume that the latter were also associated with death and the underworld. It is a matter of debate whether these *mālikū* figures are to be understood as "counselors" (assuming an East Semitic etymology[83]) or as "kings/rulers" (from a West Semitic root[84]). Somewhat splitting the difference, Schmidt argues that the *mālikū* are in fact rulers but not on the same level as the *šarrānū* (East Semitic "kings"), alongside whom the *mālikū* are frequently listed and who consistently receive larger offerings

75. See I. Gelb, P. Purves, and A. MacRae, *Nuzi Personal Names* (Chicago: University of Chicago Press, 1943), esp. 308.

76. ARMT 9 89:12.

77. ARMT 12 30:10.

78. D. J. Wiseman, review of M. L. Burke, *Textes administratifs de la salle 111 du palais*, *JSS* 10 (1965): 125.

79. J. Aro, review of M. Birot, *Textes administratifs de la salle 5*, *OLZ* 56 (1961): 604.

80. *CAD* M/1 168.

81. For a list of the relevant texts, see A. Tsukimoto, *Untersuchungen zur Totenpflege* (kispum) *im alten Mesopotamien* (AOAT 216; Kevelaer: Butzon und Bercker/Neukirchen-Vluyn: Neukirchener Verlag, 1985), 65 nn. 254–55.

82. See *AHw*, 487 and *CAD* K 425–27.

83. So J. Bottéro, *Textes économiques et administratifs* (ARMT 7; Paris: Imprimerie nationale 1957), 190.

84. So D. Charpin and J.-M. Durand, "Fils de Sim'al: les origines tribales des rois de Mari," *RA* 80 (1986): 169.

than the *mālikū*.[85] Schmidt suggests, "The *malikū* at Mari might represent rulers of vassal kingdoms under Mari's hegemony. . . . In other words, these former rulers of local city-states have become the deceased recipients of offerings alongside the former kings of Mari, the *šarrānu*."[86] Whether Schmidt is correct about their precise identification, one suspects he is on the right track in attempting to see the *mālikū* and the *šarrānū* as different more in degree than in kind; both are probably deceased rulers to whom offerings were given.

Based on three attestations (one of which is restored) that read the singular *ana mālikim* instead of the typical plural *ana malikī*,[87] Heider suggests that in at least a few cases these offerings were given "to [the god] Malik" rather than "to the deceased king(s)." He further posits, "While these cases could be scribal errors, it is tempting to see in them exceptional instances where the offerings were made to a single being, just as there is a single instance where the *kispum* was offered to one king, Yaḫdun-Lim (ARM 3.40)."[88] In his own important work on the texts, Tsukimoto had already noted instances in which a singular form appears, but he wrote them off as either scribal errors or singulars used as collectives.[89] In any case, there is very little reason to assume that these *mālikū* and the epithet "Malik" that serves as a theophoric element in some Syrian personal names were in any way connected. Thus, contra Heider, there is little to no evidence that there existed at Mari any deity called "Malik."[90]

85. See, for example, ARMT 9 89.

86. B. Schmidt, *Israel's Benficent Dead*, 32–33.

87. ARMT 9 121.v:43; ARMT 9 123:12 (restored); and ARMT 12 85:10.

88. Heider, *The Cult of Molek*, 111.

89. Tsukimoto, *Untersuchungen zur Totenpflege*, 66–67.

90. Especially problematic for connecting a "Malik" deity with the city of Mari is Heider's use of *TuL* 2, which contains a god-list with the entry ^{d}*ma-lik* // LUGAL *ša má-rí* ^{ki} "Malik // the king of Mari." Heider concludes on the basis of this entry, "Malik's importance in Mari is strongly indicated, if not proved, by a later, Standard Babylonian list of underworld deities and their addresses, which calls '^{d}*Malik*' '*šarru ša má-rí* ^{ki}'" (*The Cult of Molek*, 111). As W. von Soden pointed out long ago, however, *TuL* 2 is a parody text, the purpose of which appears to be to poke fun at all branches of scribal learning (review of E. Ebeling, *Tod und Leben nach den Vorstellungen der Babylonier*, *OLZ* 37 [1934]: 415). Especially relevant for present purposes is B. R. Foster's observation that the list of deities and their cities "in their present form do not correspond" ("Humor and Cuneiform Literature," *JANES* 6 [1974]: 75). That is, the entire point of the text is to link deities with cities with which they were *not* associated, probably for humorous effect, and thus one cannot take its claim that Malik was the "king of Mari" as evidence that this was in fact the case. Indeed, for the humor to work, Malik obviously would have to have been *not* associated with Mari. (I owe this observation to Jacob Lauinger, who brought the relevant literature on this text to my attention.)

Finally, and most importantly, as K. Koch rightly observes,[91] the biggest problem with Heider's thesis is that he is unable to demonstrate that any Near Eastern *mlk* deity was ever the recipient of child sacrifice. Even if one were able to demonstrate that there was a pan-Near Eastern chthonic Malik deity, there is no reason to assume that a deity's chthonic nature would have necessarily made it a natural recipient of child sacrifice. Indeed, Koch argues that *astral* deities may actually be more obvious recipients, since the smoke from burning children would have ascended to the heavens.[92] Heider's attempt to connect child sacrifice to underworld beings is mere speculation without any supporting evidence. Thus, whatever one makes of Heider's hypothetical chthonic "Malik," there is no reason to assume that a deity of this kind ever received child sacrifices or that it was in any way connected to the למלך child sacrifice rites in Jerusalem. The Punic *mlk* offerings on the other hand, which like the Israelite למלך sacrifices *did* involve the sacrifice of children, remain an obvious parallel. In sum, one of the key reasons for rejecting Eissfeldt's thesis—that is, the apparent ubiquity of Near Eastern "Malik" deities—is far less substantial than it first appears; the alleged deity is much less well attested than has been suggested, and in no case is such a deity ever connected to child sacrifice.

This still leaves, however, the other major reason typically offered for rejecting Eissfeldt's hypothesis: Buber's observation concerning Lev 20:5, where the phrase "to whore after the Molek" (לזנות אחרי המלך) appears. As outlined above, Buber observed that in other biblical instances of the phrase "to whore after," the thing "whored after" is either a god, a spirit, or an idol (Exod 34:15–16; Lev 17:7; 20:6; Deut 31:16; Judg 2:17; 8:27, 33; Ezek 6:9; 1 Chr 5:25). Given these parallels, Lev 20:5 appears most naturally to indicate that biblical "Molek" should also be understood as a god, a spirit, or an idol, regardless of what the term meant at Carthage or elsewhere. If one examines the textual history of Lev 20:5 itself, though, one finds that the evidence is less clear-cut than it first seems to be.

Appearing at the conclusion of a relatively lengthy prohibition against offering one's children למלך, the Masoretic Text of Lev 20:5 reads:

> ושמתי אני את פני באיש ההוא ובמשפחתו והכרתי אתו ואת כל הזנים אחריו
> לזנות אחרי המלך מקרב עמם

91. K. Koch, "Molek astral," in *Mythos im Alten Testament und seiner Umwelt: Festschrift für Hans-Peter Müller zum 65. Geburtstag* (ed. A. Lange, H. Lichtenberger, and D. Römheld; BZAW 278; Berlin: de Gruyter, 1999), 33.

92. Koch, "Molek astral," 44–45.

And I myself will set my face against that man and against his family.
I will cut him off and all who whore after him, **by whoring after the Molek,** from the midst of their people.

Buber and others are correct to note that the most natural reading here is to understand "Molek" as an idol or deity rather than as the name of a sacrifice, although one must also admit that it is at least possible that a type of sacrifice could in fact be "whored after" and that this is simply the only instance in the Hebrew Bible.[93] Significantly, however, in precisely this spot an important but largely overlooked textual variant exists—one that may actually preserve a superior reading.[94] Specifically, where MT reads לזנות אחרי המלך "to whore after the Molek," LXX has ὥστε ἐκπορνεύειν αὐτοὺς εἰς τοὺς ἄρχοντας "their whoring away into the rulers." The variant cannot be dismissed out of hand as simply a loose rendering, because LXX Leviticus generally presents a quite wooden translation,[95] and although this translation philosophy often leads to a less than aesthetically pleasant translation, it does have the benefit of enabling the modern textual critic to reconstruct LXX's Hebrew *Vorlage* with relative confidence.

For this reason, establishing the probable *Vorlage* of ὥστε ἐκπορνεύειν αὐτοὺς is fairly straightforward; ὥστε + infinitive (+ accusative pronoun) is a standard way for LXX Leviticus to render Hebrew ל + infinitive (+ pronominal suffix).[96] Thus, one would expect ὥστε ἐκπορνεύειν αὐτοὺς to represent a Hebrew *Vorlage* לזנתם "for their whoring," rather than MT לזנות "to whore." This is not the only discrepancy. Even more significant is LXX εἰς τοὺς ἄρχοντας, which corresponds to MT אחרי המלך. First, LXX preserves a plural form rather than a singular one as in MT, and there is no obvious

93. So Mosca, who observes the wide variety of things whored after in the Hebrew Bible—"goat-demons (Lev. 17:1), 'that man' (Lev. 20:5), ghosts and spirits (Lev. 20:6), and 'your own heart' and 'your own eyes' (Num. 15:39), in addition to המלך (Lev. 20:5)." Mosca argues that there is no reason to believe that *only* supernatural beings could be "whored after" and thus concludes that this verse can only be used to argue against the idea that מלך was a sacrificial term "from probability" but "not from necessity" ("Child Sacrifice," 156–57). Nonetheless, it does remain the case that Lev 20:5 (or at least the MT version of it; see further below) does appear to tilt the "probability" of the argument against Eissfeldt's thesis.

94. For a previous presentation of the argument presented here, see H. D. Dewrell, "'Whoring after the *mōlek*' in Leviticus 20,5. A Text-Critical Examination," *ZAW* 127 (2016): 628–35.

95. J. W. Wevers characterizes it as an "isolate type of translation" more than a "contextual one"—that is, it tends to translate word for word rather than phrase for phrase (Wevers, *Notes on the Greek Text of Leviticus* [SCS 44; Atlanta: Scholars Press, 1997], ix).

96. So Lev 5:22; 7:30; 8:34; 14:21; 15:32; 16:10; 20:6; 22:33; 23:37; 26:15, 44.

reason for an LXX translator to have rendered the singular המלך with a plural form.[97] Even more surprising, though, is the anomalous correspondence of MT אחרי to LXX εἰς. The normal way for the LXX of Leviticus (and the Old Greek translations of the Hebrew Bible in general) to render אחרי/אחר is with either μετά[98] (sometimes followed by τοῦτο/ταῦτα) or ὀπίσω.[99] Considering the matter from the other direction, when the LXX reads εἰς in Leviticus (and the OG in general), it typically translates Hebrew ל,[100] אל,[101] or ב,[102] with a few exceptions.[103] In no case other than Lev 20:5 does εἰς correspond to אחרי/אחר. Furthermore, when we broaden the scope of investigation to the Hebrew Bible in general, every other MT attestation of √זנה followed by אחרי has an OG correspondence in the form of (ἐκ)πορνεύω +

97. The suggestion that the plural in the LXX "may be due to the fact that the translator read the plural המלכם into his Hebrew text, erroneously attracting the *mem* of the following word and reading it twice" (J. Lust, "Molek and ΑΡΧΩΝ," in *Phoenicia and the Bible* [ed. E. Lipiński; Studia Phoenicia 11; Leuven: Peeters, 1991], 200) is speculative and not especially convincing, especially if one considers the possibility that it may well be that MT's reading is secondary rather than LXX. Wevers is likewise puzzled by the verse, asking: "Did the translator think of the plural in terms of each individual having his own idolatrous ἄρχων?" and noting: "The C″ *n s* text has the singular τον αρχοντα, which is what one would expect" (*Notes on the Greek Text of Leviticus*, 317). Like Lust, Wevers does not appear to entertain the possibility that the LXX reading may be superior and that the MT is secondary.

98. So Lev 13:7, 35, 55, 56; 14:8, 19, 36, 43(3×), 48; 15:28; 16:1, 26, 28; 25:15, 46, 48; 27:18.

99. So Lev 17:7; 20:6. Two exceptions are Lev 22:7, where the LXX has τότε for MT adverbial אחר, and Lev 26:33, which reads καὶ ἐξαναλώσει ὑμᾶς ἐπιπορευομένη ἡ μάχαιρα "and coming upon you, the sword will consume" for MT והריקתי אחריכם חרב "I will unsheathe a sword after you." This second instance probably indicates a true textual variant. In any case and most significant for present purposes, in neither of these two instances does MT אחרי/אחר correspond to LXX εἰς as in Lev 20:5.

100. So Lev 1:10; 2:12; 3:17; 4:31; 5:7, 18, 25 (LXX 6:6); 6:11 (LXX 6:18); 7:24 (LXX 7:14), 36 (LXX 7:26); 8:21; 9:2, 3, 4; 10:9; 12:6; 13:17, 59; 14:21 (2×), 23; 15:13; 16:3, 5, 10 (2×), 26; 17:6, 7; 18:23; 21:4, 17; 22:3, 18, 21, 23, 27, 29; 23:12, 14, 19, 21, 31, 41; 24:2, 3, 7 (2×); 25:7, 19, 21, 23, 27, 28, 30, 45, 46; 26:5, 20.

101. So Lev 1:16; 4:12, 16; 6:4, 23 (LXX 6:30); 9:23, 10:9, 18; 11:33(?); 12:4; 14:5, 8, 34, 40, 41, 45, 46, 50, 53 (פני אל); 16:2 (2×), 3, 22, 23 (2×), 26, 28; 19:23; 23:10; 25:2, 10 (2×), 13, 41 (2×); 26:25

102. So Lev 3:17; 4:6; 9:9; 11:32; 13:25; 14:6, 32, 51; 23:37; 24:12; 26:25 (2×, once for בתוך), 33, 36.

103. Cases in which LXX εἰς lacks a corresponding word in the MT (frequently in construct chains) include: Lev 3:17; 5:7; 6:13 (LXX 6:20); 8:18; 12:8; 13:20; 14:10, 21, 22, 31; 15:15, 30; 16:21, 22; 22:22; 27:18. Other correspondences include: עד (Lev 7:15 [LXX 7:5], 22:30, 25:52), אשר (Lev 11:33[?], 11:34, 18:3, 20:22), על פני (Lev 14:7), and עצם (Lev 23:14). Finally, the two occurrences of εἰς in LXX Lev 17:4 appear in a clause not attested in the MT.

ὀπίσω/ὄπισθεν.[104] Significantly, one of these instances appears in Lev 20:6, immediately following our verse. Thus, if the LXX translator of 20:5 did have לזנות אחרי before him, he chose to translate the phrase differently from one verse to the next. In sum, the correspondence of MT לזנות אחרי המלך to LXX ὥστε ἐκπορνεύειν αὐτοὺς εἰς τοὺς ἄρχοντας is odd.[105] It should thus come as no surprise that the recensions of Aquila, Symmachus, and Theodotion all exhibit discomfort with LXX and correct to ὀπίσω τοῦ μολοχ, which unlike LXX does correspond nicely to the Hebrew of the Masoretic tradition.

If the possibility of a true textual variant is entertained, then the LXX εἰς τοὺς ἄρχοντας should reflect a Hebrew *Vorlage* of either למלכים, במלכים, or אל מלכים. Unfortunately, there is no clear text-critical criterion for deciding among these three possibilities. Since the phrase זנה ל appears nowhere else in the Hebrew Bible, this option can tentatively be excluded from consideration. The phrase זנה אל does appear three times (Num 25:1; Ezek 16:26, 28). In all of these cases, however, the objects of the whoring are foreigners—the daughters of Moab (Num 25:1), the Egyptians (Ezek 16:26), or the Assyrians (Ezek 16:28)—and the phrase consistently refers to having illicit sexual relations with these foreigners. This meaning is unlikely in Lev 20:5, since there is no reason to believe that the term מלך ever refers to foreign *persons*; whatever מלך is, it is somehow associated with sacrifice, and there is no reason to believe that a person could have sexual relations with a מלך. Thus, a *Vorlage* אל מלכים is also unlikely. The combination זנה ב is also attested elsewhere in the Hebrew Bible: in Ezek 16:17; 23:3, 19; and Ps 106:39. The two attestations in Ezek 23 are irrelevant since the object of the preposition is the land of Egypt: "to whore *in* Egypt." Whatever מלך may be, it is certainly not a place, so these two attestations can be set aside. In Ezek 16:17, the objects "whored ב" are "male images" (צלמי זכר) and seem to be the instruments employed for "whoring," perhaps idols. This parallel would fit if מלך is the name of a cultic object of some sort, but this seems unlikely based on what we can discern about מלך from elsewhere. In Ps 106:39, however, one finds ויזנו במעללהם "and they whored in their deeds." Here the ב marks the *actions* that constitute the whoring. This final attestation accords well with

104. Exod 34:15, 16 (2×); Lev 17:7; 20:6; Num 15:39; Deut 31:16; Judg 2:17; 8:27, 33; Ezek 6:9; 20:30; 23:30; Hos 1:2; 1 Chr 5:25.

105. Lust's suggestion that the LXX translator intentionally chose to (mis-)translate אחרי with εἰς in order to contrast with the preposition ἐκ ("Molek and ΑΡΧΩΝ," 199) is theoretically possible, but it once again assumes from the outset that the MT reading is original and the LXX is interpretive, rather than taking seriously the possibility that the LXX preserves a genuine textual variant and a better reading.

the suggestion that מלך is a type of sacrifice, since "to whore *by means of* their deeds" and "to whore *by means of* מלך-offerings" would be conceptually parallel. Perhaps most significant of all is the fact that the "deeds" mentioned in Ps 106:36–39 are specifically child sacrifices:

They served their idols;	ועבדו את עצביהם
they were a snare to them.	ויהיו להם למוקש
They sacrificed their sons;	ויזבחו את בניהם
and their daughters to *šēdîm*.	ואת בנותיהם לשדים
They poured out innocent blood,	וישפכו דם נקי
the blood of their sons and daughters,	דם בניהם ובנותיהם
which they sacrificed to the idols of Canaan.	אשר זבחו לעצבי כנען
The land was polluted with blood.	ותחנף הארץ בדמים
They were defiled in their actions;	ויטמאו במעשיהם
They whored in their deeds.	ויזנו במעלליהם
	(Ps 106:36–39)

Although the text is influenced by late polemic regarding *šēdîm* (on which see chapter 5 below), what is important for the discussion here is that זנה ב clearly means "to whore by doing X," and the "X" that is done is child sacrifice. In light of this, LXX Lev 20:5 εἰς τοὺς ἄρχοντας most plausibly represents a Hebrew *Vorlage* of במלכים, and one may reconstruct the *Vorlage* of the LXX of Lev 20:5 as:

> ושמתי אני את פני באיש ההוא ובמשפחתו והכרתי אתו ואת כל הזנים אחריו
> לזנותם במלכים מקרב עמם
>
> And I myself will set my face against that man and against his family. I will cut him off and all who whore after him, **for their whoring by means of *mlk*-offerings**, from the midst of their people.

Furthermore, it appears that the LXX probably preserves the original reading. Although there is no obvious reason for a scribe to miscopy לזנותם במלכים (LXX *Vorlage*) instead of לזנות אחרי המלך (MT), there are several reasons why the opposite might occur. As noted above, the phrase "to whore after" is fairly common. Indeed, it appears in the very next verse (20:6), which forbids turning to "ghosts" and "spirits" (אבות and ידענים) and "whoring after them" (לזנות אחריהם). Furthermore, in 20:5 itself, immediately prior to our phrase, the phrase הזנים אחריו "those who whore after him" occurs, referring to those who follow the example of a man who gives his seed למלך. Thus, the relatively uncommon phrase ב + זנה was sandwiched between two instances of the much more common biblical idiom אחרי + זנה; it would thus not be surprising that a scribe miscopied the more common phrase in place of the less common one. In addition, the fact that מלך eventually came to be understood as the name of a deity, "to whore after Molek" would have made perfect sense to a later copyist, while "to whore in מלכים" would probably have been confusing. For all these reasons, not only does the LXX present a reading that comports well with Eissfeldt's hypothesis, but there is good reason to suspect that it preserves the superior reading. Of course, textual criticism always deals in probabilities, and the arguments presented above may not be entirely presuasive in all their details to all readers. Nevertheless, at the very least, the fact that the verse presents so many textual difficulties precisely in its most crucial section makes it difficult to argue that this verse demands that מלך must be understood as the name of a deity.

In sum, neither of the two major pieces of evidence proffered by those who wish to argue that biblical מלך was in fact a deity stands up to careful scrutiny. Although there is some evidence for a Near Eastern "Malik" deity, this evidence is not nearly as widespread as has been claimed, and in any case, there is no evidence whatsoever that this deity was ever associated with child sacrifice. Second, the single verse that appears to preclude understanding מלך as a sacrificial term, Lev 20:5, is textually problematic at the very least and, depending how one assesses the text-critical evidence, may in fact actually weigh in favor of understanding מלך as a type of sacrifice. Finally, the connection between biblical מלך and Punic *mlk* still has much to commend it: the one thing that we can say with certainty about biblical מלך is that it involved the sacrifice of children, just like the Punic rite with the same name.

Although various biblical references to offering children למלך will be treated in later chapters, it is worth noting here that, in some cases, the very condemnation of such rites itself reveals that Yahweh, not "Molek," was understood as the recipient of the offerings. For example, Deut 12:30–31 forbids the Israelites to worship Yahweh in the same manner that the Canaanites worship their gods. Although the Canaanites "even burn their sons and daughters for their gods," the Israelites are warned "you shall not do likewise *for Yahweh your God*" (לא תעשה כן ליהוה אלהיך). The fact that the command is directed against sacrificing children to Yahweh, not "to Molek," indicates that those who were offering their children למלך understood the rites as Yahwistic. Likewise, Lev 18:21 forbids offering a child למלך and thus "profaning the name of your God; I am Yahweh." Once again, the assumption is that these offerings were in some way associated with Yahweh, although obviously not legitimately so in the eyes of the Leviticus scribe. That is, while it is rather obvious how one could conceive of making illicit sacrifices to Yahweh as "profaning his name," it is less clear how making such offerings to a foreign "Molek" deity would do so. Even while rejecting the idea that Yahweh ever desired to receive למלך offerings, the biblical rhetoric implies that those who were making such offerings believed that they were worshiping Yahweh.

For all these reasons, despite the scholarly resurrection of a foreign "Molek" deity to whom children were sacrificed, Eissfeldt's thesis remains the most convincing explanation of the biblical phrase למלך. The purpose, function, and history of the rite will be explored below in chapter 4, but for now it will suffice to conclude that מלך probably was an *Opferbegriff*, as Eissfeldt suggested long ago, and that biblical למלך offerings involved the sacrifice of children to Yahweh, at least when offered in Jerusalem. As the following chapters will argue, this is not the only Israelite rite involving child sacrifice attested in the Hebrew Bible. Before turning to other forms of child sacrifice, however, I will first survey archaeological, iconographic, and epigraphic evidence in order to determine how much extra-biblical evidence for child sacrifice the material record provides.

CHAPTER 2

Archaeological, Iconographic, and Epigraphic Evidence for Child Sacrifice in the Levant and Central Mediterranean

The previous chapter was confined primarily to textual evidence, a characteristic that it shares with most recent discussions of Israelite child sacrifice. Most work on biblical למלך sacrifices and, to a lesser degree Israelite child sacrifice in general, has focused on textual, especially biblical, evidence, paying only secondary attention, if any at all, to nontextual archaeological evidence. On the one hand, this is understandable: if our concern is with the meaning and function of a sacrifice specifically referred to by the term מלך, then textual evidence will probably provide our most useful body of data, since non-textual artifacts by definition do not typically convey information concerning specific words and their meanings—at least not obviously and directly. On the other hand, if our interest is in the broader question of whether children were sacrificed and how prevalent this practice was, then we cannot afford to ignore the archaeological record. How can we be certain that the biblical evidence does in fact refer to actual child sacrifice, rather than merely representing polemical rhetoric against a sacrifice that was never practiced?[1] Further, even if we believe that our texts do refer to child sacrifice and that their claims are in fact trustworthy, how can we determine the extent of the practice geographically and temporally? In this regard, the archaeological record has the potential to provide valuable corroborating evidence. Unfortunately, however, as will become clear below, although previous studies have

1. While few today would dispute the idea that at least some Israelite children were in fact sacrificed as part of a למלך ritual, this has not always been the case. For instance, M. Weinfeld proposed that children were merely dedicated as part of the rite, not sacrificed (see p. 25 n. 63 above).

often claimed to have found evidence for child sacrifice in the archaeological record at a variety of locations, only a handful of these claims stand up to careful scrutiny. In addition to nontextual data, the survey below will also examine inscriptions that have been brought to bear on the question of child sacrifice in the Levant and central Mediterranean. But we shall see, although several of these inscriptions appear promising at first, in the end very few provide solid evidence for child sacrifice either.

Megiddo, Gezer, and Taanach

During the first decades of the twentieth century, three separate excavations unearthed what came to be viewed as definitive evidence for child sacrifice in Bronze Age Canaan. At Middle Bronze Megiddo, G. Schumacher reported finding burials of infants in jars in the foundations of walls in the "Nordburg" of "der dritten Schicht,"[2] two layers below "die fünfte Schicht" in which the famous Shema seal was found.[3] Around the same time, at Middle to Late Bronze Gezer, R. Macalister found several infants in jars in the vicinity of a structure that he dubbed the "High Place," and he interpreted these burials as evidence for Canaanite child sacrifice.[4] Finally, at Middle Bronze Taanach, E. Sellin found a collection of jars containing the bones of infants within a relatively compact area. Partially under the influence of Macalister's finds, Sellin entertained the possibility that these discoveries also might represent the remains of child sacrifices, although he failed to unearth any apparent "High Place" structure in the vicinity of the jars similar to the structure at Gezer.[5] In the wake of these finds, Megiddo, Gezer, and Taanach became the trio of sites that were cited as providing definitive archaeological evidence for child sacrifice in pre-Israelite Canaan.[6]

But this evidence has turned out not to be as definitive as it first appeared. One of the difficulties for identifying child sacrifice in the archaeological record is demonstrating that infant remains present evidence of intentional sacrificial killing, rather than simply being the burials of infants who died of other causes. Without a clear textual marker, such as a stele recording "Here

2. G. Schumacher, *Tell el-Mutesellim* (vol. 1; Leipzig: Haupt, 1908), 45 and 54–55.

3. Schumacher, *Tell el-Mutesellim*, 99–100.

4. R. Macalister, *The Excavation of Gezer* (vol. 2; London: John Murray, 1912), 402–6.

5. E. Sellin, *Tell Taʿannek* (Denkschriften der Kaiserlichen Akademie der Wissenschaften in Wien, Philosophisch-Historische Klasse, Band 50:4; Vienna: Kaiserliche Akademie der Wissenschaften, 1904), 32–37.

6. See, for example, G. A. Barton, *Archaeology and the Bible* (Philadelphia: American Sunday-School Union, 1916), 128–29.

person X sacrificed child Y," archaeologists must resort to circumstantial evidence to distinguish child sacrifices from ordinary burials. Human interments can be distinguished without textual markers, of course; but a sound methodology for doing so must be established. G. M. Schwartz, for instance, has suggested the following criteria:

> The case of a person killed as an offering to the gods might be hypothesized if a complete or near-complete skeleton is deposited in a context understood as religious, especially if there is evidence for a violent death or binding of the limbs. . . . The larger the number of such individuals in a given location the more vigorous a case for sacrifice could be made. It will be necessary to distinguish the primary deposition of the bones, which might imply sacrifice, from a secondary deposition that is less likely to be interpretable as sacrificial. . . . Human sacrifice would also be a plausible interpretation if skeletal evidence of persons who died violent deaths is found in association with architectural types otherwise associated with sacrifice[.][7]

As this list of criteria rightly suggests, identifying human remains as evidence of human sacrifice is always a matter of plausibility and probability. One can almost never definitively prove or disprove that a given collection of human remains are the result of human sacrifice. If, however, a large number of human remains are found together in a sacred precinct, especially if the persons are all of a similar age and/or gender,[8] the likelihood that this is evidence of human sacrifice increases.

Originally, the evidence from Gezer appeared to fulfill several of these requirements. Large numbers of infants were found similarly interred in a sacred precinct, Macalister's "High Place." This evidence became problematic, however, when the connection between the burials and the "High Place" disappeared upon further investigation. In his re-excavation of the area, W. G. Dever discovered that the infant burials (MB IIA) actually pre-date the construction of the "High Place" (MB IIC); the burials could not have been interred at the installation, which did not exist at the time of the infant burials.[9] Without a cultic installation as the burial site for the infants, the more mundane explanation, that the area served as a simple infant cemetery,

7. G. M. Schwartz, "Archaeology and Sacrifice," in *Sacred Killing: The Archaeology of Sacrifice in the Ancient Near East* (ed. A. M. Porter and G. M. Schwartz; Winona Lake, IN: Eisenbrauns, 2012), 12–13.

8. Schwartz, "Archaeology and Sacrifice," 13, Table 2.

9. W. G. Dever, "The Gezer Fortifications and the 'High Place': An Illustration of Stratigraphic Methods and Problems," *PEQ* 105 (1973): 68–70.

became the more likely one. Furthermore, since the evidence at Gezer was the linchpin for arguing that the infant burials at Megiddo and Taanach also were infant sacrifices, eliminating the Gezer evidence meant that there was nothing to suggest that the burials at the other two sites should be understood as anything other than mundane infant burials. Thus disappeared any archaeological evidence for child sacrifice in Bronze Age Cisjordan Canaan.

The Amman Airport Temple and Umm el-Marra

Not far outside Israel's borders, however, there are two sites that may preserve evidence of human sacrifice. The first comes from excavations carried out at the Amman Airport in Jordan. These excavations, led first by J. B. Hennessy and then by L. G. Herr, unearthed a structure dating to the thirteenth century BCE and dubbed the "Amman Airport Temple."[10] The most interesting aspect of the structure is the large amount of burned human remains that it contains, concentrated in its cella.[11] The presence of burned human remains in what appears to be a cultic structure naturally suggested to Hennessy that the temple might have been a site at which human sacrifices were offered.[12] Herr disagrees, however, noting that all but one of more than a thousand bones belong to adults. He instead argues that the remains are evidence of post-mortem cremation, not human sacrifice. Herr also points out that cremation is rarely attested among Semitic peoples during this period and suggests that the remains may be evidence that Hittite inhabitants lived at the site.[13] Thus, although the temple and its burned human remains are tantalizing evidence, there is no consensus that they necessarily are evidence of human sacrifice. Even if the remains are the result of human sacrifice, they would be of limited use for our purposes, since the Israelite rites involved parents sacrificing their own children. The sacrifice of human adults, while certainly interesting in its own right, is not a close enough parallel to serve as a helpful point of comparison with child sacrifice as described in the He-

10. J. B. Hennessy, "Excavation of a Late Bronze Age Temple at Amman," *PEQ* 98 (1966): 155–62; idem, "Thirteenth Century B.C. Temple of Human Sacrifice at Amman," in *Phoenicia and Its Neighbors* (Studia Phoenicia 3; Leuven: Peeters, 1985), 85–104; L. G. Herr, *The Amman Airport Excavations, 1976* (AASOR 48; Philadelphia: American Schools of Oriental Research, 1981); idem, "The Amman Airport Structure and the Geopolitics of Ancient Transjordan," *BA* 46 (1983): 223–29.

11. Hennessy, "Thirteenth Century B.C. Temple of Human Sacrifice," 94–95.

12. Ibid., 104.

13. Herr, "The Amman Airport Structure," 223–29.

brew Bible. Thus, although the evidence from the Amman Airport structure is somewhat more promising than that from Megiddo, Gezer, and Taanach, it does little to confirm or deny the possibility of child sacrifice in Iron Age Israel.

A bit farther afield, there is stronger evidence for child sacrifice at Early Bronze Umm el-Marra, Syria. Led by G. M. Schwartz and H. H. Curvers, excavations there turned up an elite mortuary complex.[14] Among the burials were human infant remains in installations apparently constructed for the purpose of equid burials. In her examination of the equid skeletons, J. A. Weber demonstrates that these animals were probably hybrids of onagers and donkeys, referred to as "kunga" in ancient sources. Although such elaborate burials might seem odd for beasts of burden, kunga were associated with royalty and divinity, which makes their special funerary treatment comprehensible.[15] In some cases, what appear to be offerings—including puppies, a spouted vessel, and human infants—were deposited after the burial of the kunga. Since these deposits could be interpreted as funerary gifts, the presence of infants among the items deposited led Schwartz tentatively to suggest that they may represent child sacrifices,[16] a suggestion that seems plausible, given the archaeological context.

Although the Umm el-Marra equid installations may provide a helpful rebuttal to any claim that child sacrifice was simply unknown or unimaginable in the ancient Near East, it is only of limited use for our discussion here. First, the offerings took place at least a millennium and a half prior to the alleged Israelite child sacrifices. Second, even assuming that these remains do represent infant sacrifices, they were apparently associated with some sort of

14. G. M. Schwartz et al., "A Third-Millennium B.C. Elite Mortuary Complex at Umm el-Marra, Syria: 2002 and 2004 Excavations," *AJA* 110 (2006): 603–41; Schwartz, "Archaeology and Sacrifice," 22–23. Elsewhere, however, Schwartz acknowledges that the children interred there may have died of natural causes rather than being sacrificed; see Schwartz, "Era of the Living Dead: Funerary Praxis and Symbol in Third Millennium BC Syria,"in *(Re-)Constructing Funerary Rituals in the Ancient Near East* (ed. P. Pfälzner et al.; Wiesbaden: Harrassowitz, 2012), 71; idem, "Memory and its Demolition: Ancestors, Animals and Sacrifice at Umm el-Marra, Syria," *Cambridge Archaeological Journal* 23 (2013): 499.

15. J. A. Weber, "Elite Equids: Redefining Equid Burials of the Mid- to Late 3rd Millennium BC from Umm el-Marra, Syria," in *Archaeozoology of the Near East* (ed. E. Vila et al.; Lyon: Maison de l'Orient et de la Méditerranée, 2006), 8.499–519.

16. Schwartz et al., "A Third-Millennium Elite Mortuary Complex," 632; Schwartz, "Status, Ideology, and Memory in Third-Millennium Syria: 'Royal' Tombs at Umm el-Marra," in *Performing Death: Social Analyses of Funerary Traditions in the Ancient Near East and Mediterranean* (ed. N. Laneri; Oriental Institute Seminars 3; Chicago: The Oriental Institute, 2007), 52.

equid funerary cult. There are no known parallels for this sort of cult in Iron Age Israel, and there is certainly no reason to think that the למלך offerings in particular were tied to equid burials. It is therefore unlikely that there is any connection between the apparent child sacrifices at Umm el-Marra and the למלך rite. Ultimately, the only real similarity between the two sacrifices is that both involved child sacrifice. Thus, despite the fascinating nature of the evidence, the Umm el-Marra excavations shed little light on Israelite child sacrifice.

Alleged Depictions of Canaanite Child Sacrifice in Egyptian Art

Although archaeological remains from Syria-Palestine have thus far provided little relevant material to help understand the biblical למלך rite, some have found evidence for Canaanite child sacrifice in the Egyptian iconographic record. Specifically, wall reliefs from Karnak and Beit el-Wali dating to the late 14th–early 13th centuries BCE depict the Egyptian pharaoh (either Ramesses II or Merneptah) besieging Canaanite cities. In some of these reliefs, the beleaguered inhabitants appear at the top of their city walls with hands upraised. Frequently, one of the individuals is holding a brazier, with or without flames rising from it. In addition, in a few of these reliefs, one or more children are being dangled from the walls of the city in proximity to the figure with the brazier.[17] Whether these reliefs are relevant for the present discussion hangs on the significance of the dangled children. Are they being offered as hostages to the Egyptians, or are they Canaanite child sacrifices offered to the gods out of desperation in the face of an overwhelming assault?

Rejecting the idea that these dangled children are hostages offered to the pharaoh, P. Derchain observes that they would have made rather poor hostages after having fallen some ten meters from the top of a city wall.[18] He instead argues that the children are being offered as sacrifices during a desperate siege. He points to three major pieces of evidence in support of this interpretation. First, the second-century CE Greek work *De Dea Syria*, attributed to Lucian of Samosata, describes a ritual practiced in the north Syrian city of Hieropolis. The rite involved dropping children, as well as animals,

17. For an overview of this corpus of wall reliefs, see A. J. Spalinger, "A Canaanite Ritual Found in Egyptian Reliefs," *JSSEA* 8 (1978): 47–60.

18. P. Derchain, "Les plus anciens témoignages de sacrifices d'enfants chez les sémites occidentaux," *VT* 20 (1970): 351–55.

from walls. Specifically, the children were first bundled in sacks and officially declared to be "not children but cattle" before being dropped alive from the city gates.[19] To this testimony, Derchain adds Philo of Byblos's claim that in ancient times the Phoenicians would sacrifice their sons during times of particular distress.[20] Finally, he points to the account of Mesha's sacrifice of his firstborn son during Israel's war with Moab, as recorded in 2 Kgs 3. In view of all this, Derchain argues that there may have existed a ritual in which children were ritually dropped from city walls as sacrifices during particularly dire circumstances such as sieges and that this rite is what the Egyptian reliefs depict.

A few years later, building on Derchain's work, A. Spalinger made a similar argument concerning these reliefs.[21] Spalinger is especially interested in demonstrating that the children were being offered to Canaanite deities, not to the Egyptian pharaoh. He stresses the fact that the scenes depicting the children dangling from walls typically also include several individuals with their hands raised toward the heavens and an individual holding a brazier. In addition, in no case does the brazier or dangling child appear in a scene in which a city has already fallen. These scenes consistently portray the city as still undefeated, although clearly hard pressed by the Egyptians; it would not yet be the appropriate time in the battle for the city's inhabitants to be handing over their children as hostages. Spalinger's key piece of evidence, however, is a caption contained in one of the reliefs preserved in the temple at Beit el-Wali, depicting Ramesses II. It reads: "Said by the vile prince in extolling the Lord of the Two Lands, '(I) believe that there is no other like Baʿal, (and) the Ruler is his true son forever'" (*ḏd n wr ẖsj m sʿꜣ nb tꜣ.wy ỉb.ḫr=(ỉ) nn wn kjj mj Bʿr pꜣ ḥqꜣ sꜣ=f mꜣʿ n ḏ.t*).[22] In Spalinger's view, the Canaanite chief is extolling Baal, his own god, as well as Ramesses. The dangling child, in Spalinger's opinion, thus represents a sacrifice to Canaanite Baal.

This interpretation has not been universally accepted. Responding to Derchain's argument that the Egyptian reliefs depict child sacrifice, O. Keel

19. *Syr. d.* 58. There is some question as to whether the children were "dropped," as the animals were, and thus would have probably died, or were "lowered," and thus would have only been "sacrificed" figuratively. The answer to this question hangs on the precise meaning of the verb κατάγνυμι. For a discussion of this question, see J. L. Lightfoot, *Lucian: On the Syrian Goddess* (New York: Oxford University Press, 2003), 523–28. Lightfoot himself doubts that the verb means "to drop" or that the child's death is intended.

20. *Praep. ev.* 1.10.44=4.16.11. See Attridge and Oden, *Philo of Byblos*, 60–62.

21. Spalinger, "A Canaanite Ritual Found in Egyptian Reliefs."

22. Ibid., 51 and 58 n. 23.

has offered a thorough survey of relevant Egyptian iconographic material and has convincingly demonstrated that the most natural interpretation of the relevant reliefs is that the besieged cities are attempting to pacify the pharaoh's wrath with offerings of incense and (living) children. Both sorts of gifts are widely attested in the Egyptian iconographic tradition as appropriate offerings when submitting to a pharaoh.[23] Keel rightly observes that Derchain's observation that children dropped some ten meters would make poor hostages does not take into account the fact that Egyptian art is thought-based, not visual-based ("Denk- und nicht Sehbilder"[24]); the artist no more wishes to depict a literal ten-meter drop than to indicate that the pharaoh is the same physical size as the city he is besieging, despite the reliefs' depicting him thus. Anticipating Spalinger's argument concerning the caption in which the city's inhabitants cry out to Baal,[25] Keel notes the common trope of likening the pharaoh to gods such as Montu and Baal; in the context of an Egyptian relief such as this one, "Baal" most naturally refers to the pharaoh himself.[26] The more obvious reading of these scenes, then, is that the people are submissively offering their children, as well as praise and incense, to assuage the pharaoh's wrath.[27] Although Keel does wonder whether the idea of pacifying the pharaoh's anger via (live) child offerings may eventually have led to the idea that the gods also might desire that children be offered to them, as human sacrifices,[28] he cogently demonstrates that the Egyptian iconographic record itself presents no evidence for such offerings during the second millennium. Thus, once again, what appeared to be solid material evidence for child sacrifice in the Levant disappears upon closer examination.[29]

The Punic Central Mediterranean

Probably the best-known archaeological evidence for the practice of child sacrifice in the ancient world comes from the Punic central Mediterranean. Excavations at the sacred precinct that would come to be known as the

---

23. O. Keel, "Kanaanäische Sühneriten auf ägyptischen Tempelreliefs," *VT* 25 (1975): 413–69.

24. Ibid., 437.

25. Spalinger, despite writing after Keel, does not seem to have been aware of Keel's work.

26. Keel, "Kanaanäische Sühneriten," 423.

27. So also M. Bauks, "Kinderopfer als Weihe oder Gabeopfer," 240–43.

28. Keel, "Kanaanäische Sühneriten," 462–63.

29. Recently, I. Ephʿal has rejected Keel's arguments in favor of Spalinger's (*The City Besieged: Siege and Its Manifestations in the Ancient Near East* [CHANE 36; Leiden: Brill, 2009], 158). Nonetheless, I continue to find Keel's arguments to be more convincing.

Carthaginian "tophet" took place already in the 1920s, but early excavators failed to publish their results adequately, making them of only limited use. It was clear at an early stage of research, however, that the site had numerous urns containing sheep, goat, and human infant remains.[30] It was not until after renewed excavations led by L. E. Stager in the 1970s that firm conclusions could be drawn. In the meantime, however, excavations at other Punic sites had revealed several other "tophets," identifiable by stelae that are distinctive to these installations. The stelae are characterized by iconographic elements such as the so-called "sign of Tanit" (which resembles an Egyptian *ankh* or a woman with raised arms), a symbol resembling a caduceus, a raised hand, a crescent-disk, and/or a sheep.[31] Urns containing the burned remains of children and/or animals have frequently been unearthed in the context of these stelae.[32] Relevant sites include North African Sousse/Hadrumetum (ca. seventh–first centuries BCE), Henchir el-Hami (second century BCE–second century CE), Thugga (second century BCE–second century CE), and Cirta (ca. third–second centuries BCE); Sicilian Motya (ca. eighth–fourth centuries BCE) and Lilybaeum (ca. fourth–third centuries BCE); and Sardinian Nora (ca. sixth–second centuries BCE), Tharros (ca. seventh–second centuries BCE), Sulcis (ca. eighth–second centuries BCE), Monte Sirai (ca. fourth–first centuries B.C.E.), and perhaps Cagliari (fifth–fourth centuries BCE),[33] in addition to possible evidence for a tophet on Malta (seventh century BCE?), which had already been discovered in the early nineteenth

30. P. Pallary, "Note sur les urnes funéraires trouvées à Salammbô près Carthage," *Revue Tunisienne* 152–54 (1922): 206–11. For a history of the excavation at Carthage prior to the 1970s, see Stager, "Carthage: A View from the Tophet," 155–57.

31. For a convenient collection and discussion of this iconographic material, see S. Brown, *Late Carthaginian Child Sacrifice and Sacrificial Monuments in their Mediterranean Context* (JSOT/ASOR Monograph Series 3; Sheffield: Sheffield Academic, 1991), 119–45 and 249–306.

32. The bibliography for each of these sites is extensive, and the references below are selective by necessity. For a more exhaustive bibliography, see V. Melchiorri, "Tophet: A Selected Bibliography," *SEL* 29–30 (2012–13): 283–312. For a very brief overview of the evidence, see M. E. Aubet, *The Phoenicians and the West: Politics, Colonies, and Trade* (2nd ed.; trans. M. Turton; Cambridge: Cambridge University Press, 2001), 250–56. For a discussion of the historical development of the various tophets and their role in the construction of Punic cultural identity, in addition to a brief overview of the evidence itself, see J. C. Quinn, "Tophets in the 'Punic World'," *SEL* 29–30 (2012–13): 23–48; as well as P. Bernardini, "Organized Settlements and Cult Places in the Phoenician Western Expansion between the 9th and 7th Centuries BCE: A Reflection on the Tophet," *SEL* 29–30 (2012–13): 1–22; and J. C. Quinn, "The Cultures of the Tophet: Identification and Identity in the Phoenician Diaspora," in *Cultural Identity in the Ancient Mediterranean* (ed. E. S. Gruen; Los Angeles: Getty Research Institute, 2011), 388–413.

33. For detailed references for each of these sites, see the Appendix to this chapter, pp. 69–71 below.

century but which was not subjected to thorough analysis of the sort that archaeologists of later generations would develop and employ.[34] Thus, the Punic evidence from Carthage, although frequently serving as the center of the discussion, is now also supported by evidence from several other Punic sites in the central Mediterranean.

Stager's reexamination of the evidence in the Carthaginian tophet leads him to conclude that there are at least eight identifiable phases of urn deposits at the site, dating from the seventh century to the second century BCE. He estimates that as many as 20,000 urns were deposited during the site's use, with the heaviest concentration dating to the fourth century. Although the urns contain both human and animal remains, the percentage of urns containing human remains increased significantly from the seventh/sixth centuries to the fourth century.[35] In Stager's opinion, these remains provide solid physical evidence for the reality of Carthaginian child sacrifice[36] and demonstrate that it increased in frequency over the course of time.[37]

Stager's conclusions have not gone undisputed, however. J. H. Schwartz argues, on the basis of his own analysis of the osteological data, that many of the infants found in the tophet were actually late third-trimester fetuses, not postnatal infants, which leads him to conclude that "most of the individuals in this sample had not been sacrificed in the sense of being victims of blood-killing."[38] In an even more recent study, Schwartz, along with F. Hough-

34. This evidence includes two stelae containing the phrase *mlk bʿl* "the *mlk* offering of a *bʿl*" and vases filled with small bones, interpreted by the excavators as either those of children or small animals. For an overview of these discoveries, see N. C. Vella, "Vases, Bones and Two Phoenician Inscriptions: An Assessment of a Discovery Made in Malta in 1816," in *Ritual, Religion and Reason: Studies in the Ancient World in Honour of Paolo Xella* (ed. O. Loretz et al.; Münster: Ugarit-Verlag, 2013), 589–99, as well as A. Bonanno and D. Cilia, *Malta: Phoenician, Punic and Roman* (Malta: Midsea, 2005), esp. 41–43; and C. Sagona, *The Archaeology of Punic Malta* (Ancient Near Eastern Studies 9; Leuven: Peeters, 2002), esp. 275–77.

35. Stager, "Carthage: A View from the Tophet," 157–61.

36. Ibid., 160–62. In a later study, Stager and S. R. Wolff further suggest that child sacrifice might have been a thinly veiled attempt at population control at Carthage ("Child Sacrifice at Carthage—Religious Rite or Population Control?" *BAR* 10:1 [1984]: 31–51).

37. For a more-recent convenient collection of the archaeological evidence, see H. Benichou-Safar, *Le tophet de Salammbô à Carthage: essai de reconstitution* (Rome: École française de Rome, 2004). It should be noted that Benichou-Safar herself remains skeptical that the remains from the tophet are evidence for infant sacrifice; she thinks that it is simply an infant cemetery (see especially pp. 159–63).

38. J. H. Schwartz, *What the Bones Tell Us* (New York: Holt, 1993), 52–53. Building on this conclusion, J. J. Azize challenges the idea that children were regularly sacrificed at all, opting for a non-sacrificial interpretation of the Punic epigraphic evidence and dismissing the Classical sources as defamatory propaganda ("Was There Regular Child Sacrifice in Phoenicia

ton, R. Macchiarelli, and L. Bonioli, conclude on the basis of a thorough reexamination of the bones that most of the infants buried in the tophet range in age from prenatal to five or six months in age. In their assessment, "Tophets were cemeteries for those who died shortly before or after birth, regardless of cause."[39] Because it seems unlikely that stillborn children would have been perceived as "sacrifices," unless the definition of "sacrifice" is expanded to eliminate the criterion of ritual killing, they conclude that the postnatal infants buried at the site could simply be children who had died of natural causes during infancy.[40] Thus, if Schwartz is correct, the Carthaginian tophet is in reality an infant cemetery and thus provides no evidence for the practice child sacrifice in the Punic colonies.

The debate does not end here. A more-recent osteological examination of the evidence by P. Smith, G. Avishai, J. A. Greene, and L. E. Stager contradicts Schwartz's conclusions and sets the infants' average age at death at one to one-and-one-half months, which is inconsistent with normal infant mortality and thus, contra Schwartz et al., points conclusively to the practice of child sacrifice.[41] But only a year after this study, Schwartz et al. published a rejoinder,[42] reasserting their interpretation of the osteological evidence. One year later, Smith et al. published further evidence in favor of their sacrificial interpretation.[43] Thus, the debate presently appears to be at an impasse, ultimately centering on the proper interpretation of the osteological remains.

In a convenient overview of this debate, V. Melchiorri comes to Stager et al.'s defense and criticizes Schwartz et al. for, among other things, confining their study to the Carthaginian remains and failing to take into account

and Carthage?" in *Gilgameš and the World of Assyria: Proceedings of the Conference Held at Mandelbaum House, The University of Sydney, 21–23 July 2004* [ed. J. Azize and N. Weeks; Ancient Near Eastern Studies Supplement 21; Leuven: Peeters, 2007], 185–206).

39. J. H. Schwartz et al., "Skeletal Remains from Punic Carthage Do Not Support Systematic Sacrifice of Infants," *PLoS ONE* 5 (2010): e9177.

40. It is not impossible, of course, following P. Xella, "'Tophet': An Overall Interpretation," *SEL* 29–30 (2012–2013): 171, that a stillborn child *could* have been offered as a sacrifice, in the specific case of an individual vowing to offer their next child to the gods in exchange for favor of some sort (as many of the stelae appear to indicate), but then the promised child is stillborn and then "sacrificed" without being killed. Of course, if the promised child were to have been born alive, then of necessity it would have been ritually killed in fulfillment of the vow.

41. P. Smith et al., "Aging Cremated Infants: The Problem of Sacrifice at the Tophet at Carthage," *Antiquity* 85 (2011): 859–74.

42. J. H. Schwartz et al., "Bones, Teeth, and Estimating Age of Perinates: Carthaginian Infant Sacrifice Revisited," *Antiquity* 86 (2012): 738–45.

43. P. Smith, et al, "Age Estimations Attest to the Practice of Infant Sacrifice at the Carthage Tophet," *Antiquity* 87 (2013): 1191–99.

the relevant evidence from Motya, Tharros, and elsewhere.[44] In their examination of the Tharros remains, for instance, F. Fedele and G. V. Foster concluded that they primarily represent children between the ages of zero and six months, not fetuses.[45] Likewise, in their examination of the remains from Motya, A. Ciasca et al. concluded that the victims are primarily newborns, and they make no mention of fetuses at all.[46] In Melchiorri's view, if Schwartz et al. wish to overturn the scholarly consensus concerning the archaeological evidence for Punic child sacrifice, they must take all of the evidence into consideration, not merely their specific sample set from Carthage. In addition, Melchiorri criticizes some of the more technical aspects of Schwartz et al.'s work, such as their failure to allow for bone-shrinkage during the cremation process.[47]

Perhaps even more significant is the fact that archaeological remains are only one piece of the evidence for Punic child sacrifice. If one considers the broader picture, including the textual evidence—both the accusations made by numerous Classical authors and the epigraphic material composed by the Punic colonists themselves—then it is more difficult to maintain that the practice of child sacrifice played no role in the religious cult of the Punic colonies. In a brief but incisive review of the combined textual and archaeological evidence, P. Xella et al. note that, despite the fact that the accusations of the Classical authors do not represent native testimony for the rites, they nonetheless show little evidence of being intentionally polemical. For instance, the (pseudo-?)Platonic *Minos* mentions Punic child sacrifice simply to demonstrate that various peoples have different conceptions of what is morally and religiously acceptable; there is no obvious attempt to excoriate or demonize the Carthaginians for the practice. Other Classical references also have a surprisingly clinical and nonjudgmental tone more often than not. Thus, although the Classical writers' claims should not be accepted uncritically, there is no real evidence to support the assertion that they simply manufactured their allegations in the service of anti-Carthaginian propaganda.[48]

---

44. V. Melchiorri, "Osteological Analysis in the Study of the Phoenician and Punic Tophet: A History of Research," *SEL* 29–30 (2012–13): 223–58.

45. F. Fedele and G. V. Foster, "Tharros: ovicaprini sacrificali e rituale del *tofet*," *RSF* 16 (1988): 29–46.

46. A. Ciasca et al., "Saggio preliminare sugli incinerati del 'tofet' di Mozia," *Vicino Oriente* 10 (1996): 317–46.

47. Melchiorri, "Osteological Analysis," 242–45.

48. P. Xella et al., "Phoenician Bones of Contention," *Antiquity* 87 (2013): 4–5.

This would be the case even if there were no native corroboration for the accusations. Corroboration does exist, though, in the form of the numerous stelae found at the various tophets, and the inscriptions on many of these stelae are difficult to interpret as referring to anything other than child sacrifice. As Xella et al. note, the tophet stelae frequently refer to vows that have been completed, often with the offering associated with the completion of the vow referred to as a "*mlk*," including the suggestive phrase *mlk ʾdm* "a *mlk* sacrifice of a human."[49] Although this could be understood as a "*mlk* sacrifice made *by* a human," this understanding is difficult to maintain in the face of the parallel phrase *mlk ʾmr* "a *mlk* sacrifice of a sheep." Since the latter obviously represents an objective genitive (unless one wishes to make the completely implausible suggestion that Punic sheep were themselves perceived as offering sacrifices), the former phrase naturally is understood as "a *mlk* sacrifice *of* a human"—that is, a human who has been sacrificed as a *mlk*. The fact that at least a few of the stelae depict a priest holding a child makes this understanding even more certain.[50] Finally, the biblical texts use similar terminology: children were also sacrificed in ancient Israel as part of rituals involving the identical root מלך.[51] Thus, although archaeological evidence must always be interpreted with caution, the combined data, both textual and archaeological, points to child sacrifice as having been a very real practice in the Punic colonies of the central Mediterranean.

One final, albeit problematic, piece of evidence that may support the claim that children were sacrificed in the Punic colonies is one of the reliefs preserved on a sepulcher from Pozo Moro, Spain, excavated by M. Almagro-Gorbea, dating to the beginning of the fifth century BCE.[52] The monument displays, in addition to Hellenistic and Iberian influences, clear Phoenician/Punic features[53] and thus may be helpful for the purposes of better understanding Punic religion. The relief depicts a two-headed monster sitting on a throne, grasping with one hand the leg of a boar and holding a bowl

49. For a convenient discussion of the formal structure of these inscriptions, see M. G. Amadasi Guzzo and J. Á. Zamora López, "The Epigraphy of the Tophet," *SEL* 29–30 (2012–13): 159–192.

50. Xella et al., "Phoenician Bones of Contention," 4–7.

51. Xella, "'Tophet': An Overall Interpretation," 263–65.

52. M. Almagro-Gorbea, "Pozo Moro, el monumento orientalizante, su contexto socio-cultural y sus paralelos en la arquitectura funeraria ibérica," *Madrider Mitteilungen* 24 (1983): 177–293.

53. Almagro-Gorbea, "Pozo Moro," 208–29. For a discussion of the relief's relationship to later Hellenistic mythology, see J. S. Rundin, "Pozo Moro, Child Sacrifice, and the Greek Legendary Tradition," *JBL* 123 (2004): 425–47.

containing what appears to be a human infant in the other. Almagro-Gorbea suggests that the scene depicts an infernal deity, perhaps influenced by the Kumarbi-Kronos myth.[54] A. Kempinski, however, suggests that this is a Punic depiction of Mot, the god of death attested at Ugarit, enjoying a feast in the underworld.[55] If Kempinski's interpretation is correct, the relief may indicate that children were understood as serving as food for some infernal deity and thus may present them as appropriate victims of sacrifice. Although the depiction of a monstrous deity about to consume a child is a tantalizing interpretation of the relief, especially given the fact that it shows clear influences from a culture repeatedly accused of sacrificing its children to Kronos, the mythological nature of the scene demands special caution in interpretation. Of particular signficance is the fact that the relief was found in the far western Mediterranean. Unlike Punic colonies of the central Mediterranean, where tophets are almost ubiquitous, there is at present no material evidence for tophets in the colonies farther west. It is interesting that the relief appears to depict a supernatural being consuming a human victim, but it would probably be unwise to base any conclusions on this somewhat slim evidence.

Even without the Pozo Moro relief, there is a significant amount of evidence pointing to the practice of child sacrifice in the Punic colonies of the central Mediterranean. Significantly, as Eissfeldt observed long ago, these sacrifices are referred to in the Punic epigraphic record with the term *mlk*, which bears a striking resemblance to the Hebrew term מלך, which was also associated with child sacrifice. Thus, it seems likely that the two rites are cognate in some way, although the precise relationship between them is not yet entirely clear.

More Evidence from the Levant? Tyre and Achziv

Given the convincing evidence for child sacrifice among the Punic colonists specifically linked to the term *mlk*, it is natural to assume some sort of connection with the biblical למלך sacrifices offered in the Jerusalem tophet. Because there is no reason to believe that Iron Age Judah and Carthage were in regular contact, however, it would be necessary to posit an intermediate connection between the two societies. The obvious candidate for this link

54. Almagro-Gorbea, "Pozo Moro," 197–200.

55. A. Kempinski, "Death and Resurrection: The Early Evidence," *BAR* 21:5 (1995): 38–49.

would be the Phoenician homeland, whence the Punic colonists originally embarked and with which Israel and Judah were in regular contact. Thus, if it could be convincingly established that the Punic colonists brought the practice of infant sacrifice with them from Phoenicia, a connection between biblical and Punic *mlk*-sacrifices of the sort that Eissfeldt suggested would be on a stronger footing. Because the Punic tophets all seem to have been founded at the same time as the colonies themselves, it is logical to conclude that the colonists brought the rites with them from their homeland and that the sacrifices are not a local development.[56]

The possibility nevertheless remains that the practice of child sacrifice was distinctively colonial and had no counterpart in Phoenicia proper. J. C. Quinn has suggested that, far from being a normal part of the Phoenician cult, "the settlers who practiced this particular and unusual form of cult came from a different and indeed dissident religious tradition and left at least in part for that reason." Quinn even compares the colonists at Carthage and elsewhere in the central Mediterranean with the dissenting Plymouth Brethren who settled in New England.[57] Thus, according his interpretation, the *mlk* sacrifices are a distinctively Punic, not Phoenician, rite. Without evidence from the Phoenician homeland itself, there is no data to refute this suggestion.

For a brief time, though, it appeared that there was such evidence. In 1990, just at the end of the Lebanese Civil War, "some people in Tyre" unearthed stelae, urns, and other pottery in the area. Some of the urns contained incinerated human remains, and the appearance of human remains in the context of stelae led some to conclude that evidence for a tophet in the Phoenician homeland had finally been found.[58] However, these claims did not remain unchallenged for long. The first and most obvious difficulty for identifying the remains as evidence of a "tophet" like those of the Punic central Mediterranean is the fact that the evidence comes from uncontrolled excavations, which only invites skepticism from the outset. Indeed, in her second publication on the stelae, H. Sader acknowledges that epigrapher P. Bordreuil, upon seeing the stelae, "had an immediate negative reaction

56. So Xella, "'Tophet': An Overall Interpretation," 367–68.

57. Quinn, "Tophets in the 'Punic World'," 33.

58. For a detailed presentation of this evidence, see H. Seeden, "A *Tophet* in Tyre?" *Berytus* 39 (1991): 39–82; J. Conheeny and A. Pipe, "Note on Some Cremated Bone from Tyrian Cinerary Urns," *Berytus* 39 (1991): 83–87; W. A. Ward, "The Scarabs, Scaraboid and Amulet-Plaque from Tyrian Cinerary Urns," *Berytus* 39 (1991): 89–99; and H. Sader, "Phoenician Stelae from Tyre," *Berytus* 39 (1991): 101–26.

concerning the inscriptions *only*: he declared them all fakes,"[59] although she herself disagrees with Bordreuil's assessment. Furthermore, S. Moscati disputes the claim that the remains should be understood as remains of a tophet, even if they are authentic, observing that none of the bones that could be assigned an age appear to have come from infants.[60] J. Conheeny and A. Pipe, the osteologists who examined the bones, observe: "On the whole, although there was little firm ageing data available from the bone fragments, their size was not consistent with them being the remains of small infants."[61] The primary characteristic of a tophet, however, is the presence of the bones of *children*. Not only are no infant remains present, but the presence of adult remains itself mitigates against the site's being identified as a tophet.[62] In addition, the stelae from the Tyrian "tophet" lack any of the distinctive characteristics, either iconographic or epigraphic, of those from the Punic tophets. Instead of describing vows to Baʿl Hammon and/or Tanit, the deities most associated with the Punic tophets, the stelae from the Tyrian "tophet" are inscribed only with personal names. As Moscati observes, these stelae, even if authentic (which remains questionable), could well be funerary, not sacrificial, in nature.[63] Furthermore, as Bartoloni observes, at least some of the pottery is particularly characteristic of adult cemeteries, but notably not of the Punic tophets.[64] In sum, the evidence for a tophet at Tyre has ultimately not held up to scholarly scrutiny.[65] This of course does not prove that there never was a tophet at Tyre, but it does mean that we do not yet have any archaeological evidence for one.

Another site that has received some attention as a possible tophet site on the Phoenician coast is Achziv, which lies approximately 20 miles south of Tyre.[66] The alleged "tophet" portion of the site has been published by E. Mazar.[67] The use of the term "tophet" in this context is misleading, however.

---

59. H. Sader, "Phoenician Stelae from Tyre," *SEL* 9 (1992): 53.

60. S. Moscati, "Non è un tofet a Tiro," *RSF* 21 (1993): 147–52.

61. Conheeny and Pipe, "Note on Some Cremated Bone," 85.

62. Moscati, "Non è un tofet a Tiro," 150.

63. Moscati, "Non è un tofet a Tiro,"151–52. See also M. G. Amadasi Guzzo, "Osservazioni sulle stele iscritte di Tiro," *RSF* 21 (1993): 157–63.

64. P. Bartoloni, "Considerazioni sul 'tofet' di Tiro," *RSF* 21 (1993): 143–56.

65. So also J. C. Quinn, "The Cultures of the Tophet," 406 n. 21.

66. J. A. Dearman, "The Tophet in Jerusalem: Archaeology and Cultural Profile," *JNSL* 22 (1996): 59–71.

67. E. Mazar, *The Northern Cemetery of Achziv (10th–6th Centuries BCE): The Tophet Site* (Cuadernos de Arqueología Mediterránnea 19–20; Barcelona: Publicaciones del Laboratorio de Arqueología, Universidad Pompeu Fabra de Barcelona, 2009–2010).

Although the site does appear to have served as a place for cremation, Mazar herself observes: "it is clear that the bodies of both men and women were cremated, though there is no evidence whatsoever of child cremation."[68] Likewise, although a variety of stelae have been found at the site,[69] unlike the stelae from the Punic central Mediterranean with their distinctive iconographic features, at Achziv "very few of the stelae at the site displayed any markings or symbols, and only one stele, not *in situ*, was discovered bearing an inscription (maybe 'Ashtoret')."[70] There is thus almost nothing to connect the tophets of the central Mediterranean with the cremation area at Achziv. Indeed, Mazar is only able to refer to the Achziv area as a "tophet" by making the (rather misleading) claim that "it is customary in Phoenician/Punic studies to identify sites that contained numerous cremation burials as *Tophet* sites," which is true enough, technically speaking. But the presence of cremated remains alone is not enough for a Punic/Phoenician installation to qualify as a "tophet." Other tophets are marked by the presence of *infant* remains, usually alongside the remains of sheep and often marked by stelae bearing distinctive iconographic and epigraphic elements. It is more accurate simply to refer to the Achziv "tophet" as a "cemetery," since it appears to have been used either primarily or exclusively for the burial of adults. Thus, the Achziv cemetery provides no evidence for a tophet in the Phoenician homeland.

The Nebi Yunis Inscription

Perhaps more promising is an inscription allegedly unearthed at Nebi Yunis, between Ashdod and Jaffa. The inscription appears to have been composed to commemorate a *mlk* offering, and it has much in common with similar Punic inscriptions from the central Mediterranean. If authentic, it would provide concrete evidence of a *mlk*-offering on the Levantine coast. The text of the inscription reads:[71]

68. Ibid., 207.

69. See ibid., 215–25.

70. Ibid., 214.

71. The reading here follows B. Delavault and A. Lemaire, "Une stèle 'molk' de Palestine dédiée à Eshmoun? RES 367 reconsidéré," *RB* 83 (1976): 574. The minor differences between their reading and that of Lidzbarski, *Ephemeris für semitische Epigraphik* 1, 285–87, in turn followed by Chabot, *RES* 367, are indicated in the notes. The inscription itself appears to have been lost: it was last accounted for at the Russian Consulate in Jerusalem prior to the First World War. Delavault and Lemaire, however, were able to locate four squeezes of the inscription: one at the Musée de l'École Biblique et Archéologique de Jérusalem and the other three at the Cabinet du Corpus des Inscriptions Sémitiques (Delavault and Lemaire, "Une stèle 'molk'

Col. 1
[n]ṣb mlk
ʾš ndr wytn hʿrkt ʾš ʿbdʾ bn ʿbdʾs [l]ʾdnnm lʾšmn šmʾdny bn ʿbdʾs wšmʿ bn šmʿ
wšlm bn bdʾ wʿbdmlk bn ʿbdʾšmn
tṭʾ wbʿlytn bn ysp wʿbdtwyn bn bʿlytn wbʿlṣlḥ bn ʿbdʾšmn ʿbdʾmn bn ʿbdʾbst
wmryḥy[72] *wytnbʿl bn ʿbdʾ wšlm*[73] *bn ʿbdʾšmn grʾmn bn bmʾ ʿbdṣpn*

Col. 2[74]
ʿbdyṣ[ ]ʾsytn bn
bn ʿbdʾšmn wʾbdʾ bn

Col. 3
ʾšmn [. . . wʿ]bdy bn
ʿbdy bn hgr wʿbdʾs bn hgr
šlmy bn mryḥy wʿbdʾsr

The inscription came to light when J. Germer-Durand presented a squeeze of the inscription to M.-J. Lagrange, who then published it in the first issue of *Revue biblique*.[75] It apparently may be translated something like "The stele of *mulk*[xxx?][76] which the men of ʿAbdoʾ son of ʿAbd-ʾis vowed — and they had paid the valuations — to their lord 'Ešmun. Šimu-'adōnay son of ʿAbd-ʾis and Šamoʿ son of Šamoʿ," [a long list of names follows].[77] If this interpretation is correct, then this is a concrete example of an inscription commemorating a *mlk* offering discovered in the Phoenician homeland and thus provides a key link between the Punic *mlk*-offerings and the Israelite למלך offerings.

de Palestine," 569). They provide black-and-white photographs of the best-preserved squeezes (pl. XLIV), which are fairly legible in the better-preserved portions of the inscription but which are not of high enough quality to provide much help in the more-difficult sections.

72. Lidzbarski and Chabot lack *w-*.

73. Lidzbarski and Chabot lack *w-*.

74. Lidzbarski and Chabot do not recognize Columns 2 and 3 as separate columns and thus read the names in a different order. In addition, Delavault and Lemaire are able to read more characters in this section than Lidzbarski was.

75. M.-J. Lagrange, "Une inscription phénicienne," *RB* 1 (1892): 275–81.

76. Gianto believes that an object of the *mlk*-offering, such as *ʾmr* "lamb," may have originally appeared after *nṣb mlk*, as is typical in other attested *mlk* inscriptions (see *CIS* 1 123a–b, 147, 194, 380, 2613, 5684, 5685).

77. So A. Gianto, "Some Notes on the Mulk Inscription from Nebi Yunis (*RES* 367)," *Bib* 68 (1987): 398.

Unfortunately, however, the inscription's authenticity is far from established and was already challenged by Lidzbarski on both grammatical and lexical grounds shortly after its initial publication.[78] Lidzbarski argued that the text presents several grammatical anomalies and that many of its terms and names appear to have been drawn from previously published inscriptions. Lidzbarski's opinion initially carried the day, and his arguments that the inscription is a forgery were approvingly cited when the text appeared as *RES* 367, after which it was largely ignored. It was not until Delavault and Lemaire,[79] followed by Gianto,[80] reasserted the inscription's authenticity that scholars again began to take it seriously. Contra Lidzbarski, they argued that the text as it stands is not necessarily grammatically impossible and that his suspicions of forgery are thus unfounded. Since their work on the inscription in the 1970s, the scholarly consensus has swung dramatically in favor of its authenticity. For instance, F. Stavrakopoulou states that the inscription "offers strong evidence suggesting that *mlk*-sacrifices were offered in mainland Phoenicia."[81] F. M. Cross likewise approvingly cited the text as evidence for *mlk* offerings in Phoenicia.[82] In his widely read *Early History of God*, M. Smith is a bit more circumspect, observing, "A *mlk* offering is perhaps attested once for Eshmun in the only *mlk* text from the Phoenician mainland."[83] Even G. C. Heider, whose primary project was to dispute Eissfeldt's thesis and to distance biblical מלך from Punic *mlk*, appears to concede the potential significance of the inscription, although he warns "against drawing overly-broad conclusions on the basis of this one, late text."[84] More recently, B. H. Reynolds has also pointed to the text as evidence for *mlk* offerings in the Phoenician homeland.[85]

As I have argued in detail elsewhere,[86] however, there remain several reasons for suspecting that the inscription is indeed a forgery as Lidzbarski originally suspected. In addition to the skepticism that must attend any inscription that appears via the antiquities market, there are several other signs

78. M. Lidzbarski, *Handbuch der nordsemitischen Epigraphik*, 131; idem, *Ephemeris für semitische Epigraphik* 1, 285–87.

79. Delavault and Lemaire, "Une stèle 'molk' de Palestine."

80. Gianto, "Some Notes on the Mulk Inscription."

81. Stavrakopoulou, *King Manasseh and Child Sacrifice*, 225.

82. Cross, "A Phoenician Inscription from Idalion," 236 n. 39.

83. M. S. Smith, *The Early History of God: Yahweh and the Other Deities in Ancient Israel* (2nd ed.; Grand Rapids, MI: Eerdmans, 2002), 172.

84. Heider, *The Cult of Molek*, 183–84.

85. Reynolds, "Molek: Dead or Alive?" 147.

86. H. D. Dewrell, "A 'Molek' Inscription from the Levant? Another Look at the Authenticity of *RES* 367," *RB* 123 (2016): 481–505.

that it is probably a modern forgery. First, Lidzbarski was more right than he knew about the suspicious correspondence between the contents of the Nebi Yunis inscription and Phoenician material that had already been published in both *CIS* and various Phoenician lexica and glossaries at the time of the inscription's appearance. Indeed, almost every word of the rather long inscription had already appeared in previously published material,[87] and a forger could easily have used already published material to compose his own inscription. Second—and even more damning, in my view—the inscription identifies the object on which it appears as a *nṣb mlk* "a *mlk* stele." This is interesting (and suspicious) because the item upon which the inscription appears is decidedly *not* a "stele"; it is an offering table. The inscription runs along one of the table's edges, and the item was clearly intended to be installed horizontally—as offering tables typically were—not vertically, as a stele (*nṣb*). It is especially noteworthy that several Punic inscriptions beginning *nṣb mlk* had already been published when the Nebi Yunis inscription appeared, and it is likely that a forger with access to these publications simply aped the language of previously published material. Our forger does not appear to have been entirely competent, though, and has mistakenly identified the offering table as a *nṣb*. Thus, both the circumstances of its discovery and the suspicious nature of its contents provide too much room for doubt to allow the Nebi Yunis inscription to serve as a secure basis for claiming evidence of *mlk* sacrifices in Phoenicia proper.

The Incirli Trilingual

A more recently discovered inscription likewise appears promising at first but is problematic for an entirely different reason: a trilingual inscription discovered in a secure context, at Incirli, during a survey of the Karamanmarash Valley (south-central Turkey) in 1993.[88] The stele bearing the inscription appears to have originally contained text in Akkadian, Luwian, and Phoenician, but only the latter has been preserved well enough to allow for an attempt at decipherment. In a preliminary publication, S. Kaufman has

87. For a list of lexemes and their correspondences in previously published inscriptions, see ibid., 493–96.

88. The circumstances of the stele's discovery along with a general description of the object and the text inscribed thereon, complete with photographs, is currently (March 2017) available at https://www.usc.edu/dept/LAS/arc/incirli/

worked through the Phoenician text, which itself is badly damaged.[89] Enough is preserved, however, to indicate that the stele was inscribed during the reign of Tiglath-pileser III and recounts a rebellion by Matiel of Arpad against his Assyrian suzerain. The inscription was commissioned by Awarikku, king of Que, and seems to indicate that Que did not participate in the revolt.[90] The relevant section for present purposes is contained in lines 11–15 on the front of the stele:[91]

> ***wkn*** *mrd* ***b****kl* ***mt*** *ḥ[t] wzbḥ* ***mlk*** *ʾrp****d***
> *lyʿn hdd* ***ml****k w****gzr mkpr k ʾrpd***
> *pḥd* ***mlk*** *ʾm/šr (ḥy)/(ʿl) wʿṣ* ***ḥkm*** *l/wʾmr*
> *km* ***ḥq*** *mlk* ***ʾrpd wḥlb ʾl tgzr****/l* ***ʾd[m]***
> [. . .]*ʾl tp****ḥd*** *kʾm kpr ʾš pḥtk* ***ʾl yḥr[b/m]***

(11) *There was a rebellion through the Hittite country*, and the King of Arpad *sacrificed* (12) *for the benefit of Hadad-Melek* (or: *for the purpose of a molk-offering for Hadad*), and redeemed [the human sacrifice] with butchered animal parts, because Arpad (13) *feared* (*a living molkomor*)/(*the King of Assyria. He* [*the wise man*] *arose*) and a wise man gave advice as follows: (14) "*According* to the law of the *King of*

89. S. Kaufman, "The Phoenician Inscription of the Incirli Trilingual: A Tentative Reconstruction and Translation," *Maarav* 14.2 (2007): 7–26. The inscription is cited as potential evidence for child sacrifice by M. S. Smith, "Child Sacrifice as the Extreme Case and Calculation," in *Not Sparing the Child: Human Sacrifice in the Ancient World and Beyond: Studies in Honor of Professor Paul* G. *Mosca* (ed. V. D. Arbel et al.; New York: Bloomsbury, 2015), 5–6.

90. Kaufman, "The Phoenician Inscription of the Incirli Trilingual," 9.

91. The transcription here attempts to reproduce Kaufman's helpful indications of how certain the reading of a given letter is. In lieu of solid and hollow Aramic block characters, the transcription here uses bold (= more confident) and non-bold (= less confident) italicized roman characters. Kaufman says:

> A solid black letter [here a bold character] is roughly 80%–100% certain. An underscored letter is similarly certain but admittedly only fragmentary, justified by definitive visible segments. A hollow letter [here a non-bold character] is much more uncertain, but reconstructed from available spacing and from context. A hollow letter with underscore is similarly uncertain, but is read based on substantive physical traces. Illegible letters are indicated with a period. Square brackets surround broken areas of text, and alternative readings are indicated by slashes. (Parentheses surround alternative readings longer than one letter.) ("The Phoenician Inscription of the Incirli Trilingual," 10.)

> Arpad and Aleppo, do not sacrifice a human-being (15) . . . *do not fear rather offer a substitute that your province* he not dest[roy . . .][92]

One can hardly fault Kaufman for his able attempt at reconstructing a badly damaged text, but it is nonetheless clear that any reconstruction must remain no more than tentative. Most suggestive in the text is the "Do not slaughter [Kaufman: 'sacrifice'] a man," since in that portion of the inscription (most of) the characters can be read with some confidence. This section may well refer to some sort of emergency human sacrifice similar to the one Mesha sacrificed during the Israelite-led invasion of Moab (2 Kgs 3; on which see chapter 4 below). Of course, given how poorly preserved the surrounding context is, it is possible to posit any number of other meanings for the phrase. Even less certain is any reference to a *mlk*-offering. As Kaufman himself suggests, in one case *mlk* could simply be the second part of a divine title "Hadad-Melek" and in another it could be the first word in the phrase *mlk ʾšr*, "King of Assyria." What is preserved is certainly suggestive, but not enough remains to say with much certainty what the text actually describes. If the inscription had followed a known formula, like the inscriptions attested on the stelae of the tophets of the Punic central Mediterranean,[93] then a reconstruction would be more certain. That this alleged *mlk*-offering appears in the context of what appears to be a historical narrative, however, makes it more difficult to reconstruct its contents. In short, the Incirli trilingual remains a potential source of information on human sacrifice in Syria-Palestine; continued work on the inscription may permit us to use it with more confidence in the future. At present, though, its readings are too uncertain to provide any definitive material evidence for child sacrifice.[94]

---

92. Kaufman, "The Phoenician Inscription of the Incirli Trilingual," 12, 15. Italics and brackets in the translation also reproduce Kaufman's markings.

93. For the standard formulae of the tophet stelae, see Amadasi Guzzo and Zamora López, "The Epigraphy of the Tophet," 159–92.

94. One other inscription from the Levantine coast that was once presented as evidence for child sacrifice is the Ugaritic text KTU^3 1.119. Line 31 contains the phrase [ ]*kr bʿl . n*[ ]*dš*, sometimes restored *bkr bʿl nqdš* "a firstborn, O Baʿl, we shall sanctify," which some have understood as referring to child sacrifice (so, e.g., B. Margalit, "Why King Mesha of Moab Sacrificed His Oldest Son," *BAR* 12:6 [1986]: 62). Many today, however, instead restore *dkr* "a male [animal]" instead of *bkr* "firstborn" (see, e.g., KTU^3). But even if *bkr* is restored here, there is no reason to suspect that a firstborn child is intended rather than a firstborn animal (so also D. Pardee, "Ugaritic Prayer for a City Under Siege (1.88)," *COS* 1, 285 n. 23). Thus, despite earlier suggestions, this text provides no evidence for child sacrifice.

The Deir ʿAllā Inscriptions

Turning our attention inland, some have found reference to child sacrifice east of the Jordan, in the Deir ʿAllā inscriptions.[95] Stavrakopoulou in particular draws far-reaching conclusions on the basis of Combination 2:4–15,[96] reproducing Hackett's edition,[97] which reads as follows:

---

95. The first photograph of these inscriptions was published by H. J. Franken, "Texts from the Persian Period from Deir ʿAllā," *VT* 17 (1967): 480–81. The *editio princeps* is J. Hoftijzer and G. van der Kooij, *Aramaic Texts from Deir ʿAlla* (Documenta et Monumenta Orientis Antiqui 19; Leiden: Brill, 1976). Important treatments include A. Caquot and A. Lemaire, "Les textes araméens de Deir ʿAlla," *Syria* 54 (1977): 189–208; J. A. Hackett, *The Balaam Text from Deir ʿAllā* (HSM 31; Chico, CA: Scholars Press, 1980); P. K. McCarter Jr., "The Balaam Texts from Deir ʿAllā: The First Combination," *BASOR* 239 (1980): 49–60; B. A. Levine, "The Deir ʿAlla Plaster Inscriptions," *JAOS* 101 (1981): 195–205; H.-P. Müller, "Die aramäische Inschrift von Deir ʿAllā und die älteren Bileamsprüche," *ZAW* 94 (1982): 214–44; H. Weippert and M. Weippert, "Die 'Bileam'-Inschrift von Tell Dēr ʿAllā," *ZDPV* 98 (1982): 77–103; E. Puech, "Le texte 'ammonite' de Deir ʿAlla: les admonitions de Balaam (première partie)," in *La vie de la Parole: De l'Ancien au Nouveau Testament* (Paris: Desclée, 1987), 13–30; J. Hoftijzer and G. van der Kooij, eds., *The Balaam Text from Deir ʿAlla Re-Evaluated: Proceedings of the International Symposium Held at Leiden, 21–24 August 1989* (Leiden: Brill, 1991); E. Lipiński, "The Plaster Inscription from Deir ʿAllā," in *Studies in Aramaic Inscriptions and Onomastics* (2 vols.; Leuven: Peeters, 1994), 2.103–70; M. Dijkstra, "Is Balaam Also Among the Prophets?" *JBL* 114 (1995): 43–64; B. A. Levine, *Numbers 21–36* (AB 4A; New York: Doubleday, 2000), 241–75; Stavrakopoulou, *King Manasseh and Child Sacrifice*, 261–72; E. Blum, "Die Kombination I der Wandinschrift vom Tell Deir ʿAlla: Vorschläge zur Rekonstruktion mit historisch-kritischen Anmerkungen," in *Berührungspunkte: Studien zur Sozial- und Religionsgeschichte Israels und seiner Umwelt* (ed. I. Kottsieper, R. Schmitt, and J. Wöhrle; AOAT 350; Münster: Ugarit-Verlag, 2008), 594–98; E. Blum, "'Verstehst du dich nicht auf die Schreibkunst. . . ?' Ein weisheitlicher Dialog über Vergänglichkeit und Verantwortung: Kombination II der Wandinschrift vom Tell Deir ʿAlla," in *Was ist Mensch, dass du seiner gedenkst? (Psalm 8,5)* (ed. M. Bauks, K. Liess, and P. Riede; Neukirchen-Vluyn: Neukirchener Verlag, 2008), 33–53; S. C. Russell, *Images of Egypt in Early Biblical Literature: Cisjordan-Israelite, Transjordan-Israelite, and Judahite Portrayals* (BZAW 403; Berlin: de Gruyter, 2009), 96–103.

96. Stavrakopoulou, *King Manasseh and Child Sacrifice*, 266–68.

97. Hackett, *The Balaam Text*, 26, 29–30. Underlined characters are noted as uncertain by Hackett. Significant variant readings and translations proposed by other scholars are indicated in the notes. No attempt is made to present every possible alternative reading or translation—a task that would swell the notes here well beyond the needs of the discussion. One should especially note, however, the different reconstruction of Blum, "Verstehst du dich nicht auf die Schreibkunst. . . ?" 34–40 and 52–53, who proposes new joins with some significant consequences for understanding the text. For the purpose of the lines cited here, however, Blum's new proposal is most significant for his suggestion that the five lines of Deir ʿAllā Combination VIIIb (see Hoftijzer and Van der Kooij, *Aramaic Texts from Deir ʿAlla*, 176) represent the ends of lines 4–8.

4 *ʿlmh. rwy. ddn . k— [*]
5 *lh. lm. nqr. wmdr. kl. rṭb [*]
6 *yrwy. ʾl. yʿbr. ʾl*[98]*. byt. ʿlmn. by[t*]
7 *byt. lyʿl. hlk. wlyʿl. ḥtn. šm. byt[.*]
8 *wrmh.*[99] *mn. gdš. mn. pḥzy. bny. ʾš. wmn. šqy- [*]
9 [ ] *ly. hl ʿṣh.* [bk] *lytʿṣ. ʾwlmlkh. lytmlk. yšb.- [*]
10 *n. m[ ]bn. tksn.*[100] *lbš. ḥd. hn. tšnʾn. yʾnš. hn. t[*]
11 *ʾšm[. .] tḥt. rʾšk. tškb. mškby. ʿlmyk. lḥlq. l- [*]
12 *ʾd-. rk[ ]h. blbbm. nʾnḥ. nqr. blbbẖ. nʾnḥ. [nqr?*]
13 *bt. šmh. mlkn. yḥzw. [ ]t. lyšbm[.] yqḥ. mwt. ʿl. rḥm. wʿl—[*]
14 *[ ] ʿl[ ]-r. mwt. šmh. kb-[ ]ḥ. ykn. lbb. nqr. šh*^{h} *. ky. ʾth. l-[*]
15 *lqṣh. š[ ] wzlp. gdr[.] tš [ ] šʾlt. mlk. ssh [.] wš[ʾ]l[t*]

4 his boy,[101] full of love [ ]
5 (?) "Why are/do the scion and the firepit containing foliage [. . . ?" ". . . *so that*][102]

98. Hoftijzer and Van der Kooij read *wybdʾl* and translate "El will make" (*Aramaic Texts from Deir ʿAlla*, 174). Similarly also G. Van der Kooij, "Book and Script at Deir ʿAlla," in *The Balaam Text from Deir ʿAlla Re-Evaluated: Proceedings of the International Symposium Held at Leiden, 21–24 August 1989* (ed. H. Hoftijzer and G. van der Kooij; Leiden: Brill, 1991), 260; Levine, "The Deir ʿAlla Plaster Inscriptions," 200; Lipiński, "The Plaster Inscription from Deir ʿAllā," 141; Dijkstra, "Is Balaam Also among the Prophets?" 49; Levine, *Numbers 21–36*, 255; and Müller, "Inschrift von Deir ʿAllā," 217–19. For his part, Blum concedes the reading but nonetheless considers *yʿbd* to be a scribal error for *yʾbr* (Blum, "Verstehst du dich nicht auf die Schreibkunst. . . ?" 36).

99. Levine reads *rmn* and translates "worm rot" (*Numbers 21–36*, 256–57).

100. Levine reads *mtksn* and translates "they cover themselves" ("The Deir ʿAlla Plaster Inscriptions," 200; *Numbers 21–36*, 256–57).

101. Others translate *ʿlmh* as "young woman" rather than "his young man." See Hoftijzer and Van der Kooij, *Aramaic Texts from Deir ʿAlla*, 180; Caquot and Lemaire, "Les textes araméens de Deir ʿAlla," 203. Lipiński translates "eternity" ("The Plaster Inscription from Deir ʿAllā," 142).

102. There is no consensus on the meaning of this line. Hackett's translation of "scion" for *nqr*, here and again in line 12, as well as "firepit" for *mdr*, both of which are important for finding any reference to child sacrifice in the inscription, are possible but not certain. Hackett's reading of the latter term is largely based on Isa 30:33, where מדרה refers to part of a tophet (*The Balaam Text from Deir ʿAllā*, 63). Hoftijzer and Van der Kooij, however, understand the terms as "blinded one" and "soil." In addition, they understand *rṭb* as "moist" rather than "foliage," a translation that is especially problematic in the context of a firepit (*Aramaic Texts from Deir ʿAlla*, 180). Lipiński agrees that *nqr* means "scion" but translates *mdr* "dwelling," based on מודר in Jewish Aramaic ("The Plaster Inscription from Deir ʿAllā," 142, 144). Blum, on the other hand, points to Isa 14:19, which may attest נצר II "putrefying matter" (so *DCH* 5.746) and

6 El will be satisified. Let him go (lit.: "cross over"[103]) to the House of Eternity, the hou[se]
7 the house where the traveler does not rise and the bridegroom does not rise, the house [. . ." ". . .]
8 and the worm from the tomb, from those who have arisen among human beings, and from the graves[104] of [. . ."]
9 [ ] "As for counsel, is it not you with whom he will take counsel; or for advice, will he not ask advice from one residing [. . . ?]
10 [ ] You will cover him with one garment. If you are unkind to him (lit.: "hate him"), he will falter. If you [. . .]
11 "I will put [ ] under your head. You will lie down on your eternal bed to perish [. . ."]
12 [ ] to themselves (lit.: "in their heart"). The scion sighs to himself (lit.: "in his heart"). [*The scion* (?)] sighs [ ]
13 [ ] Death will take the newborn child, the suckling [ ]
14 [ ] (?) [ ] (?) The heart of the scion is weak for he goes to [ ]
15 to his end [ ] (?) [ ]

Hackett somewhat cautiously suggests that this section may have to do with child sacrifice. Specifically, she notes that in the first Combination the Šaddayyin gods appear to declare the upheaval of the world. If Combinations 1 and 2 are two parts of a single narrative, then Combination 2 may describe an attempt to avert the calamity via the sacrifice of a royal child. The terms *nqr* "sprout/scion," *mdr* "firepit," and *yʿbr* "he will cause to pass over" all concentrated in the space of a few lines are the primary pieces of evidence for this interpretation. Hackett also notes the possibility that *mlkh. lytmlk* in line 9 has something to do with *mlk*-sacrifices but ultimately decides that proximity

on this basis translates *nqr* as "Verwesender" (Blum, "Verstehst du dich nicht auf die Schreibkunst. . . ?" 36, 42).

103. As noted above, others read *yʿbd* "he will do or make" rather than *yʿbr* "he will/let him cross over."

104. Another difficult word. Hackett links *šqy* to Syriac *šāqā* "mound of earth, sarcophagus" (*The Balaam Text from Deir ʿAllā*, 63). Hoftijzer and van der Kooij, on the other hand, understand the term as the common Aramaic term *šwq* "street, market," and cautiously translate "places (?)" (*Aramaic Texts from Deir ʿAlla*, 180 and 227). Lipiński understands this as Aramaic *šq* "thigh, leg" ("The Plaster Inscription from Deir ʿAllā," 142, 146); so also Blum, "Verstehst du dich nicht auf die Schreibkunst. . . ?" 37.

to terms having to do with "counsel" (*ʿṣh. lytʿṣ*) makes it more likely that the *mlk* terms here have to do with "advising" (see Akkadian *malāku*(*m*)). Furthermore, Hackett suggests that the *šdyn* in Combination 1:5–6 may have been particularly appropriate recipients of child sacrifices, since child sacrifice, Baal-Peor (in turn linked with Balaam in Num 31:16, a character who also appears prominently in Combination 1), and שדים (albeit vocalized in the MT as שֵׁדִים) all appear together in Ps 106. Thus, in her reconstruction, the Šaddayim, Balaam, and child sacrifice appear together in the Deir ʿAllā inscriptions just as they do in the Hebrew Bible.[105]

For her part, Stavrakopoulou accepts Hackett's interpretation but goes even further. She argues that the Šaddayin should be understood as related to El Šadday, one of Yahweh's epithets in the Hebrew Bible. She also proposes revocalizing שֵׁדִים "demons" in both Ps 106:37 and Deut 32:17 as שַׁדַּיִם, with the former in particular being a scribal distortion aimed at distancing Šadday from illicit offerings.[106] Stavrakopoulou also points to Ugaritic *šd*/*šdy* (depending on how one divides the words), a deity who appears in the same text as chthonic *rpu* (KTU³1.108), as well as the occurrence of *šd* possibly determined by the word *kbkb* "star" (KTU³ 1.179:11). On the basis of this Ugaritic evidence, Stavrakopoulou deduces a connection between *šd*/*šdy* and ancestor worship, and thus human fertility, and thus child sacrifice.[107] Finally, she notes that El Šadday is also linked to circumcision in Gen 17, which she in turn connects to child sacrifice, and she argues that this text "foreshadows" the (near) sacrifice of Isaac in Gen 22. Having laid out this evidence, Stavrakopoulou concludes: "This discussion has thus tentatively located a further tradition of child sacrifice that the biblical ideology has been unable to disguise fully: the sacrifice of children to the '*šadday*-gods'."[108]

Taken as a whole, this reconstruction presents an impressive picture, apparently supported by evidence from a variety of sources. However, when examined closely, the individual links of the chain of argument are not entirely solid. First, it is unclear whether Combination 1 and Combination 2 at Deir ʿAllā even belong together; this is possible but by no means certain. Second,

---

105. Hackett, *The Balaam Text from Deir ʿAllā*, 75–89. Hackett further develops this line of interpretation in her "Religious Traditions in Israelite Transjordan," in *Ancient Israelite Religion: Essays in Honor of Frank Moore Cross* (ed. P. D. Miller, P. D. Hanson, and S. D. McBride; Philadelphia: Fortress, 1987), 125–36.

106. Stavrakopoulou, *King Manasseh and Child Sacrifice*, 272–82.

107. Here she especially follows R. de Hoop, *Genesis* 49 in Its Literary and Historical Context (OTS 29; Leiden: Brill, 1999), 211.

108. Stavrakopoulou, *King Manasseh and Child Sacrifice*, 282.

even if they do belong together, it is unclear that Combination 2 refers to child sacrifice. The fragmentary state of the text makes any reconstruction difficult, but even the evidence that is preserved is problematic. As noted above, the verb *yʿbr* "pass over," a verb often associated with למלך sacrifices in the Hebrew Bible, should probably be read *yʿbd*. Likewise, *nqr* and *mdr* may indeed mean "scion" and "firepit" (although there is no consensus on this point, either), but even as reconstructed by Hackett there is no mention of putting the "scion" *into* the "firepit." Psalm 106 does contain references to Baal-Peor (and thus Balaam? see Num 31:16), child sacrifice, and שדים, but here too the connection is problematic. The psalm recounts the history of the Israelite people from the Exodus to the Exile. The sins at Baal-Peor (Ps 106:28) are separated from accusations of sacrificing children to שדים (Ps 106:37) by accounts of the sin at Meribah (Ps 106:32–33) and the conquest of Canaan (Ps 106:34–35). That is, despite appearing in the same psalm, the sacrifice of children to שדים does not appear in the specific context of the incident at Baal-Peor. Finally, although there does appear to be a reference to a dead child in line 13 of Combination 2, it is not clear that the infant is described as being sacrificed rather than having died due to other causes (perhaps, e.g., the end of the world described in Combination 1?). Thus, Hackett's interpretation of the text is certainly possible but by no means certain.

Stavrakopoulou's elaboration of the thesis is even more problematic. First, repointing שֵׁדִים to שָׂדַיִם in Ps 106:37 and Deut 32:17 is certainly possible but not obviously superior to MT. Next, Stavrakopoulou's Ugaritic evidence is especially problematic. It is true that both *šd*/*šdy* "Šaddayu"(?) and *rpu* "Rapiʾu" appear together in KTU[3] 1.108, but so do Athtartu, Anatu, Kotharu, and Baʿlu. The text is essentially a list of deities who are invited to drink(?) at a feast of Rapiʾu.[109] There is no indication that any of the other deities listed are chthonic in nature, and thus there is no reason to suspect that Šaddayu is either. Likewise, in KTU[3] 1.179:11, the determinative *kbkb* "star" does precede *šd* (or, more properly speaking, the apparent double name *ydd . w šd*), but in this same text *kbkb* also determines *šmm w thm* "the Sky and the Abyss," *bʿl . w pdry* "Baʿlu and Pidrayu," and [*kθ*]*r . w. y*[!]*ss* "Kotharu wa-Ḫasisu."[110] There is thus no reason to believe that *kbkb* "star" in this text serves to indicate divinized ancestors, as Stavrakopoulou suggests, much less child sacrifice as part of an ancestral cult associated with divinized ancestors.

109. See D. Pardee, *Ritual and Cult at Ugarit*, 192–95.

110. For a treatment of the text, see A. Caquot and A.-S. Dalix, "Un texte mythico-magique," in *Études ougaritiques I. Travaux 1985–1995* (ed. M. Yon and D. Arnaud; RSOu 14; Paris: Éditions Recherche sur les Civilisations, 2001), 393–405.

Stavrakopoulou is correct to note that Gen 17 does mention El Šadday in the context of Abraham's covenant of circumcision, but the epithet is notably absent in the obviously more relevant Gen 22. So, although it is hypothetically possible to forge a chain linking El Šaddai to child sacrifice, the connection ultimately rests on repointing שֵׁדִים to שָׂדַיִם in Ps 106:37 and Deut 32:17, the only basis for which is the Deir ʿAllā inscriptions, which themselves do not necessarily link child sacrifice to the *šdyn* gods, unless one assumes that Combinations 1 and 2 are part of the same narrative—a substantial string of assumptions. Furthermore, even granting all of these assumptions, it is still not clear that Combination 2 itself even mentions child sacrifice.

For all of these reasons, even though the Deir ʿAllā inscriptions offer tantalizing evidence that might indicate the practice of child sacrifice in the Transjordan, the nature of this evidence is highly problematic, and it is not possible to demonstrate conclusively that the inscription mentions child sacrifice. Even if Combination 2 does refer to child sacrifice, however, it remains unclear whether the rite is connected in any way to the *šdyn* of Combination 1. Finally, even if one finds child sacrifice in Combination 2 and connects this to the *šdyn* of Combination 1, there is no good evidence to link these *šdyn* beings to ancestor veneration and very little to connect either them or the El Šadday of the Hebrew Bible to child sacrifice.

The Idalion Inscription

One final inscription that allegedly refers to child sacrifice was unearthed at Idalion, Cyprus during archaeological excavations in 1974.[111] Cyprus is obviously not mainland Phoenicia, and thus any evidence of child sacrifice there could not provide a definitive link between Punic *mlk*-sacrifices and Israelite למלך offerings. Nonetheless, Cyprus lies much closer to the Levantine coast than does Carthage, and so evidence from Cyprus might prove suggestive, even if not conclusive. In addition to the Idalion inscription, there may be nontextual archaeological evidence of infant sacrifice at Amathus, although the data is ambiguous. It consists of a crematorium in which humans—infants, adolescents, and adults—are interred, sometimes along with animals.[112] While the obvious interpretation of this area is that it simply was

111. L. E. Stager, and A. Walker, eds., *American Expedition to Idalion, Cyprus 1973–1980* (OIC 24; Chicago: The Oriental Institute of the University of Chicago, 1989), 466.

112. D. Christou, "Cremations in the Western Necropolis of Amathus," in *Eastern Mediterranean: Cyprus-Dodecanese-Crete 16th–6th Cent. B.C.* (ed. V. Karageorghis and N. Stampolidis; Athens: University of Crete: 1998), 207–15; A. P. Agelarakis, A. Kanta, and N. Stampoli-

a cemetery, the fact that there is a concentration of infant remains in one section of the complex may suggest that the infants were interred under different circumstances than the adults and adolescents.[113] Of course, this conclusion can only be tentative: the possibility that infants were buried in a separate portion of the cemetery for entirely mundane reasons is just as likely.

In any case, the Idalion inscription itself is an ostracon inscribed with Phoenician characters and can be read:

[ ]*lbnrp*[ ]
[ ]*ltṣmḥ*[ ]
š
n

F. M. Cross dates the inscription on paleographic grounds to between 350 and 300 BCE and has reconstructed and interpreted it as follows[114]:

1. [ ]*l bn rp*[*'l* (?)]	1. [ ]l son of Rapa['il (?)]
2. [*ʿ*]*lt ṣmḥ*	2. [ho]locaust of a scion
3. *š*	3. Year
n	50

He bases his reconstruction of the crucial second line, "holocaust of a scion," on his reading of a fifth-century Cypro-Phoenician storage jar containing funerary remains, inscribed with an illegible Demotic inscription as well as a Phoenician inscription; the latter reads: *ʿlt / ṣmḥ*. The jar was discovered in Memphis, Egypt, and was first published by Spiegelberg, who translated the inscription as "oberhalb *Ṣmh*."[115] In his treatment of the text, Lidzbarski translated "für *Ṣmh*."[116] That is, both understand *ʿlt* as the preposition "over, to, for"[117] and *Ṣmh* as a proper name. Cross, however, argues that *ʿlt* here should instead be understood as a construct form of *ʿlh* "burnt offering," a

dis, "The Osseous Record in the Western Necropolis of Amathus: An Archaeo-Anthropological Investigation," in *Eastern Mediterranean: Cyprus-Dodecanese-Crete 16th–6th Cent. B.C.* (ed. V. Karageorghis and N. Stampolidis; Athens: University of Crete, 1998), 217–32.

113. The area is dubbed Context 1440 by the excavators. See Agelarakis, Kanta, and Stampolidis, "The Osseous Record," 220–24.

114. F. M. Cross, "A Phoenician Inscription from Idalion," 231–33. A photograph and a drawing of the inscription can be found on p. 232, figs. 33.1 and 33.2.

115. W. Spiegelberg, *Die demotischen Denkmäler, I: Die demotischen Inschriften* (Leipzig: Catalogue général des anitiquités égyptiennes du Musée du Caire, 1904), 89.

116. Lidzbarski, *Ephemeris für semitische Epigraphik*, 3, 123–25.

117. See *DNWSI*, 863–64.

term that appears frequently in the Hebrew Bible and occasionally in Punic inscriptions.[118] Furthermore, Cross suggests that, in both the Memphis and the Idalion inscriptions, *ṣmḥ* should be understood as the common noun "scion,"[119] not as a proper name. Here Cross leans especially heavily on his reading of two Neo-Punic texts, *KAI* 162 and 163. Departing from the readings of previous scholars in several important regards, Cross reads the first two lines of *KAI* 162:

1. *lʾyʾ*[120] *ʾdn ḥn*[121] *bʿl ḥmn bʿl*[122] *ʾdr bšrbl*[123]	To Ḥayyō (the Living [God], lord of grace, awesome lord: Bišširbaʿl
2. *bʿt tʿmt*[124] *bṣmḥ tḥbt*[125] *bšʾrm*	[has dedicated] a daughter without blemish, being a goodly scion, his own flesh (and blood).

And the first three lines of *KAI* 163:

1. *ʾtm ṭškʾ bntm*[126] *ltt lʾyʾ*[127] *bʿl*	Taškoʾ has fulfilled (his vow), with a whole heart, in giving to Ḥayyō Baʿl—
2. *ʾbmṣbt bnʾ ʾlm bdʿštrt*	together with a stele of the shades (lit., "sons of God")—Bod-ʿaštart,
3. *ʿl*[128] *trbt šqlt*[129] *kbl lʾ bṣmḥ šʾrm*	an infant, precious offpsring, a gift to him consisting of a scion of his flesh (and blood).

118. Cross, "A Phoenician Inscription from Idalion," 233–34. See *DNWSI*, 851.

119. Cross, "A Phoenician Inscription from Idalion," 234. See *DNWSI*, 970.

120. *KAI*^{5} and *HNPI* (Constantine N 50) read *lgdʾ*.

121. Read *ḃ. . .ṫ* by J. G. Février, "Un sacrifice d'enfant chez les Numides," in *Mélanges Isidore Lévy* (AIPHOS 13; Brussels: Secrétariat des Éditions de l'Institut, 1955), 162. *KAI*^{5} reads *wzn*, and *HNPI* reads *rzn*.

122. Février reads *ḃl*. *KAI*^{5} and *HNPI* read *pl*.

123. *KAI*^{5} and *HNPI* (Constantine N 50) read these two words as *ʿbdkšr*.

124. Février reads *tʿmṅ*.

125. Février and *KAI*^{5} read *t-spt*; *HNPI* reads *t*[ ]*spt*.

126. Février, *KAI*^{5}, and *HNPI* (Constantine N 51) all read *kntm*.

127. *HNPI* reads this as two words: *lʾ yʾ*.

128. Février, *KAI*^{5}, and *HNPI* all read *d/šl*.

129. Février, *KAI*^{5}, and *HNPI* all read this as two words, *š qlt*

In both inscriptions, Cross (notably contrary to previous treatments) locates the use of the term *ṣmḥ* in the context of the sacrifice of a child. Although Cross's interpretations of these two Neo-Punic texts may be accurate, it is nonetheless important to observe how disputed Cross's interpretation of each text is. If his understanding of the Neo-Punic inscriptions is incorrect, then any connection between the term *ṣmḥ* in the Idalion inscription (and the apparently identical inscription from Memphis) and child sacrifice disappears. As the many footnotes to the transcription of the inscriptions above demonstrate, there is significant divergence between the readings of Cross and those of others, and these differences have significant consequences for the interpretation of the text. For instance, Jongeling translates *KAI* 162 as "To Gidde, the lord, prince of Bal Amun, made (it) Abdkasher, citizen of / Bat Tamet . . ." Jongeling considers the penultimate word in line 2 illegible and thus leaves the remainder of the line untranslated.[130] In line 1, however, he understands *bʿt tʿmt* not as "a daughter without blemish" (i.e., the victim of the sacrifice) as Cross does, but as the name of the city from which the dedicant hails. Donner and Röllig, on the other hand, translate the lines, "Dem 'J', (dem) Herren . . . . . . Baʿal-Ḥammōn, Baʿal-Addir; BŠRBL / Tochter des TʿMN *im Austausch für ihr* (?) *Kind.*"[131] That is, they understand the stele as referring to an offering "in exchange for a scion" (*bṣmḥ*), not of the scion itself. In addition, unlike either Jongeling or Cross, they understand *bʿt tʿmt* as a patronymic, "the daughter of TʿMN," which they take as indicating the person who is making the sacrifice, not its victim. None of these readings is obviously superior to Cross's interpretation; the difficulties in the text are simply too great to form a confident judgment on the meaning of the inscription. In fact, the difficulties increase in the text's later lines, which is probably why Cross (wisely) chose not to treat them.[132]

The second Neo-Punic Inscription (*KAI* 163) is hardly any clearer. Indeed, Jongeling himself chooses not to translate it and opens his remarks, "It is impossible to give any coherent translation of this difficult text, as it deviates considerably from the customary formulae."[133] Février, and similarly Donner and Röllig after him, understands the stele as commemorating the offering of the "mute son Bodʿastart" (*bnʾ ʾlm bdʾštrt*).[134] Cross, however, prefers to understand *bnʾ ʾlm* as "the shades (lit., 'sons of God')," who are the

130. *HNPI*, 212–13.

131. *KAI* 2, 152–53.

132. See *HNPI*, 213 for a discussion of these difficulties.

133. Ibid.

134. Février, "Un sacrifice d'enfant," 166; *KAI* 2, 152–53.

recipients of the offering. This, however, leaves Cross without a sacrificial victim, which he then finds in *ʿl*, which he understands as "infant." In order to do this, he must reject the readings of earlier scholars, who read *šl* or *dl* rather than *ʿl*. Again, Cross may be correct on each of the points he makes, but the reading remains contested and far from certain.

In sum, in order to find evidence of child sacrifice on Cyprus, the phrase [ ]*lt ṣmḥ*[ ] must be reconstructed as *ʿlt ṣmḥ* and understood as "holocaust of a scion." The basis for this is two highly problematic Punic inscriptions from Algeria: *ṣmḥ* is not otherwise attested in the context of Punic child sacrifice. In addition, *ʿlt* has to be taken as a construct form of *ʿlh* "burnt offering," a term that, although common in Hebrew, is otherwise never used in the context of child sacrifice in Punic; indeed, to my knowledge, the term only occurs once in the entire corpus of Punic inscriptions (*KAI* 159:8). On the other hand, the preposition *ʿlt* "over, to, for" is quite common in both Punic and Phoenician.[135] A more straightforward reading of the Idalion inscription is either "on behalf of a scion" or "on behalf of [an individual named] *Ṣmḥ*." Neither possibility has anything to do with child sacrifice. Although it is not possible to prove Cross's reading wrong, this difficult and problematic inscription will probably not convince many skeptics that child sacrifice took place on Cyprus.

Summary and Conclusions

In this chapter, I have surveyed a wide variety of archaeological, iconographic, and epigraphic material, leading to the conclusion that the best evidence for child sacrifice in the Near East and Mediterranean during the first millennium BCE remains the Punic evidence, both archaeological and epigraphic, from the central Mediterranean. Although there have been many suggestions that some site or another, a relief, or an inscription may provide potential evidence for Syro-Palestinian child sacrifice, the survey above has demonstrated that none of this evidence is without problems. There is as yet no unambiguous material evidence from Syria-Palestine itself that corroborates the claims of the Hebrew Bible. The fact that the Punic evidence supports the conclusion that children were sacrificed as part of a *mlk* ritual makes it tempting to connect these sacrifices with Hebrew מֹלֶךְ sacrifices, as Eissfeldt did nearly a century ago, but making this connection probably requires assuming that the rite also took place on the Phoenician mainland

135. See *DNSWI*, 863–64.

itself in order to provide the necessary link between Judah and Carthage. Unfortunately, there is as yet no strong material evidence for child sacrifice in Phoenicia proper, or Syria-Palestine in general, apart from the possible exception of the third-millennium equid burials at Umm el-Marra, which are largely irrelevant to this discussion, given their early date and specific connection with equid funerary rites. Thus, in order to maintain a connection between Punic *mlk* and Hebrew מֹלֶךְ, as I do, circumstantial evidence remains, for now, the only basis. Although I think that Phoenicia was probably the source for both Israelite and Punic *mlk* rites (see chapter 4 below), I nonetheless acknowledge that there is as yet no concrete material evidence supporting (or refuting) this hypothesis. It can only be supported by noting the presence of an apparently identical child sacrifice rite both in Carthage and in Judah and by positing Phoenicia as the most likely link between the two. I hope that future archaeological discoveries will remedy this unfortunate gap in our evidence and either confirm or deny this working hypothesis.

Appendix: Documentation of Sites with Tophets

Sousse/Hadrametum: P. Cintas, "Le sanctuaire punique de Sousse," *Revue africaine* 91 (1947): 1–80; L. Foucher, *Hadrumetum* (Paris: Publications de l'Université de Tunis), esp. 33–57; S. Brown, *Late Carthaginian Child Sacrifice*, 58–61; M. M. McCarty, "Representation and the 'Meanings of Ritual Change': The Case of Hadrumetum," in *Ritual Dynamics in the Ancient Mediterranean: Agency, Emotion, Gender, Representation* (ed. A. Chaniotis; Heidelberger althistorische Beiträge und epigraphische Studien 49; Stuttgart: Steiner, 2011), 197–228.

Henchir el-Hami: A. Ferjaoui, *Le sanctuaire de Henchir el-Hami: de Baʿal Hammon au Saturne africain: Ier s. av. J.-C.-IVe s. ap. J.-C.* (Tunis: Institut national du patrimoine, 2007); M. M. McCarty, "Continuities and Contexts: The Tophets of Roman Imperial-Period Africa," *SEL* 29–30 (2012–13): 93–118.

Thugga: L. B. C. Carton, *Le sanctuaire de Baal-Saturne à Dougga: rapport sur les fouilles exécutées à Dougga en 1893* (Nouvelles archives des missions scientifiques 7; Paris: Imprimerie nationale, 1896), 35–53; S. Saint-Amans, *Topographie religieuse de Thugga (Dougga): Ville romaine d'Afrique proconsulaire (Tunisie)* (Pessac: Ausonius, 2004), 354–56; A. Krandel-Ben Younès, *La présence punique en pays numide* (Tunis: République Tunisienne, Ministère de la culture, Institut national du patrimoine, 2002); R. Lantier and L. Poinssot, "Les stèles découvertes dans une favissa du temple de Saturne à Dougga," *Bulletin archéologique du Comité des travaux historiques et scientifiques* (1942): xii–xxviii; C. Poinssot, *Les ruines de Dougga* (2nd ed.; Tunis: Ministère des affaires culturelles, Institut national d'archéologie et d'arts, 1983), esp. 65–66, pl. xix; McCarty, "Continuities and Contexts," 93–118.

Cirta: J.-B. Chabot, "Punica XVIII. Stèles puniques de Constantine," *JA* 11:10 (1917): 38–79; A. Berthier and R. Charlier, *Le sanctuaire punique d'El Hofra à Constantine* (2 vols.; Paris: Arts et métiers graphiques, 1952–1955); Brown, *Late Carthaginian Child Sacrifice*, 62–63, 294–96.

Motya: J. I. S. Whitaker, *Motya: A Phœnician Colony in Sicily* (London: G. Bell and Sons, 1921); A. Ciasca et al., *Mozia – I: Rapporto preliminare della Missione archeologica della Soprintendenza alle Antichità della Sicilia occidentale e dell'Università di Roma* (Studi semitici 12; Rome: Istituto di studi del vicino Oriente, 1964), esp. 41–104; A. Ciasca et al., *Mozia – II: Rapporto preliminare della Missione archeologica della Soprintendenza alle Antichità della Sicilia occidentale e dell'Università di Roma* (Studi semitici 19; Rome: Istituto di studi del vicino Oriente, 1966), esp. 25–117; I. A. Brancoli et al., *Mozia – III: Rapporto preliminare della Missione archeologica della Soprintendenza alle Antichità della Sicilia occidentale e dell'Università di Roma* (Studi semitici 24; Rome: Istituto di studi del vicino Oriente, 1967), esp. 11–81; A. Ciasca et al., *Mozia – IV: Rapporto preliminare della Missione archeologica della Soprintendenza alle Antichità della Sicilia occidentale e dell'Università di Roma* (Studi semitici 29; Rome: Istituto di studi del vicino Oriente, 1968), esp. 25–102; A. Ciasca et al., *Mozia – V: Rapporto preliminare della Missione congiunta con la Soprintendenza alle Antichità della Sicilia Occidentale* (Studi semitici 31; Pubblicazioni del Centro di studio per la civiltà fenicia e punica 1; Rome: Consiglio nazionale delle ricerche, 1969), esp. 35–116; A. Ciasca et al., *Mozia – VI: Rapporto preliminare della Missione congiunta con la Soprintendenza alle Antichità della Sicilia Occidentale* (Studi semitici 37; Pubblicazioni del Centro di studio per la civiltà fenicia e punica 7; Rome: Consiglio nazionale delle ricerche, 1970), esp. 63–93; F. Bevilacqua et al., *Mozia – VII: Rapporto preliminare della Missione congiunta con la Soprintendenza alle Antichità della Sicilia Occidentale* (Studi semitici 40; Pubblicazioni del Centro di studio per la civiltà fenicia e punica 10; Rome: Consiglio nazionale delle ricerche, 1972), esp. 87–117; A. Ciasca et al., *Mozia VIII: Rapporto preliminare della Missione congiunta con la Soprintendenza alle Antichità della Sicilia Occidentale* (Studi semitici 45; Pubblicazioni del Centro di studio per la civiltà fenicia e punica 14; Rome: Consiglio nazionale delle ricerche, 1973), esp. 57–91; A. Ciasca et al., *Mozia IX: Rapporto preliminare della Missione congiunta con la Soprintendenza alle Antichità della Sicilia Occidentale* (Studi semitici 50; Pubblicazioni del Centro di studio per la civiltà fenicia e punica 18; Rome: Consiglio nazionale delle ricerche, 1978), esp. 123–59; M. P. Toti, "Gli scavi al Tofet di Giuseppe Whitaker," in *Mozia X: Zona C. Il Kothon, Zona D. Le pendici occidentali dell'Acropoli, Zona F. La Porta Ovest* (ed. L. Nigro; Studi semitici 50; Pubblicazioni del Centro di studio per la civiltà fenicia e punica 18; Rome: Consiglio nazionale delle ricerche, 1978), 499–509; A. Ciasca, "Mozia, sguardo d'insieme sul *tofet*," *Vicino Oriente* 8 (1992): 113–55; A. Ciasca et al., "Saggio preliminare sugli incinerati del 'tofet' di Mozia," *Vicino Oriente* 10 (1996): 317–46; S. Moscati, *Italia archeologica: Centri greci, punici, etruschi, italici* (vol. 1; Novara: Istituto geografico di Agostini, 1973), 160–67; Brown, *Late Carthaginian Child Sacrifice*, 63–65; P. Bernardini, "Per una rilettura del santurario tofet – I: il caso di Mozia," *Sardinia, Corsica et Baleares Antiquae* 3 (2005): 55–75.

Lilybaeum: A. M. Bisi, *Le stele puniche* (Studi semitici 27; Rome: Istituto di studi del vicino Oriente, Università di Roma, 1967), 149–156, fig. 112, pl. XLIII–XLV; S. Moscati, *Italia archeologica*, 168–69; Brown, *Late Carthaginian Child Sacrifice*, 65, 300. C. A. Di Stefano, *Lilibeo Punica* (Rome: Libreria dello Stato: Istituto Poligrafico e Zecca dello Stato, 1993), esp. 35–36, 58.

Nora: G. Patroni, "Nora, colonia fenicia in Sardegna," *Monumenti antichi* 14 (1904): 109–268; S. Moscati and M. L. Uberti, *Le stele puniche di Nora nel Museo nazionale die Cagliari* (Studi semitici 35; Rome: Consiglio nazionale delle ricerche, 1970); Moscati, *Italia archaeologica*, 186–89; idem, *Il santuario dei bambini (tofet)* (Rome: Istituto Poligrafico e Zecca dello Stato, 1992), 23–25, figs. 16–19; G. Chiera, *Testimonianze su Nora* (Collezione di studi fenici 11; Rome: Consiglio nazionale delle ricerche, 1978); Brown, *Late Carthaginian Child Sacrifice*, 65–66.

Tharros: G. Pesce, *Tharros* (Cagliari: Editrice Sarda Fratelli Fossataro, 1966); Moscati, *Italia archeologica*, 212–19; E. Acquaro et al., "Tharros – I," *RSF* 3 (1975): 89–119; E. Acquaro and M. L. Uberti, "Tharros – II," *RSF* 3 (1975): 213–25; E. Acquaro et al., "Tharros – III," *RSF*

4 (1976): 197–228; E. Acquaro et al., "Tharros – IV," *RSF* 6 (1978): 63–99; E. Acquaro et al., E. Acquaro et al., "Tharros – V," *RSF* 7 (1979): 49–124; E. Acquaro et al., "Tharros – VI," *RSF* 8 (1980): 79–142; E. Acquaro et al., "Tharros – VII," *RSF* 9 (1981): 29–119; E. Acquaro et al., "Tharros – VIII," *RSF* 10 (1982): 37–102; E. Acquaro et al., "Tharros – IX," *RSF* 11 (1983): 49–111; E. Acquaro et al., "Tharros – X," *RSF* 12 (1984): 47–75; E. Acquaro et al., "Tharros – XI," *RSF* 13 (1985): 11–147; E. Acquaro et al., "Tharros – XII," *RSF* 14 (1986): 95–107; E. Acquaro et al., "Tharros – XIII," *RSF* 15 (1987): 75–102; E. Acquaro et al., "Tharros – XIV," *RSF* 16 (1988): 207–52; E. Acquaro et al., "Tharros – XV–XVI," *RSF* 17 (1989): 249–306; E. Acquaro, "Il tofet di Tharros: note di lettura," in *Riti funerari e di olocausto nella Sardegna fenicia e punica* (Quaderni della Soprintendza Archeologica per le Province di Cagliari e Oristano 6/1989, Supplemento; Cagliari: Edizioni della Torre, 1990), 13–22; Brown, *Late Carthaginian Child Sacrifice*, 68–70.

Sulcis: P. Bartoloni, "Urne cinerarie arcaiche a Sulcis," *RSF* 16 (1988): 165–79; P. Bernardini, "Recenti indagini nel santuario tofet di Sulci," in *Atti del V Congresso internazionale di studi fenici e punici: Marsala-Palermo, 2–8 ottobre 2000* (Palermo: Università degli Studi di Palermo. Facoltà di Lettere e Filosofia, 2005), 1059–69; Brown, *Late Carthaginian Child Sacrifice*, 66–67; V. Melchiorri, "Le *tophet* de Sulci (S. Antioco, Sardaigne): État des études et perspectives de la recherche," *UF* 41 (2009): 509–24; eadem, "Osteological Analysis in the Study of the Phoenician and Punic Tophet: A History of Research," *SEL* 29–30 (2012–2013): 236–38.

Monte Sirai: F. Barreca et al., *Monte Sirai–I: Rapporto preliminare della Missione archeologica dell'Università di Roma e della Soprintendenza alle Antichità di Cagliari* (Studi semitici 11; Rome: Centro di studi semitici, Istituto de studi del vicino Oriente–Università, 1964), esp. 21–23, 65–93, and pls. X–XI and XXXI–XLVII; M. G. Amadasi et al., *Monte Sirai–II: Rapporto preliminare della Missione archeologica dell'Università di Roma e della Soprintendenza alle Antichità di Cagliari* (Studi semitici 14; Rome: Centro di studi semitici, Istituto de studi del vicino Oriente–Università, 1965), esp. 123–33, fig. 8, and pls. L–LVI; S. Moscati, *Italia archeologica,* 202–9; P. Bartoloni, "Monte Sirai 1981: La ceramica del *tofet*," *RSF* 10 (1982): 283–94; S. F. Bondì, "Monte Sirai 1985. Lo scavo del tofet," *RSF* 15 (1987): 179–90; idem, "Nuovi dati sul tofet di Monte Sirai," in *Riti funerari e di olocausto nella Sardegna fenicia e punica* (Quaderni della Soprintendeza Archeologica per le province di Cagliari e Oristano 6/1989, Supplemento; Cagliari: Edizioni della Torre), 23–43; "Il tofet di Monte Sirai," in *Carbonia e il Sulcis: Archeologia e territorio* (ed. V. Santoni; Oristano: Editrice S'Alvure, 1995), 225–38; P. Bartoloni, *La necropoli di Monte Sirai – I* (Collenzione di Studi Fenici 41; Rome: Consiglio Nazionale delle Ricerche, 2000), esp. 79–80.

Cagliari: S. Puglisi, "Cagliari. Necropoli punica a incinerazione," *Notizie degli scavi antichità* 7:3 (1942): 104–6; C. Tronchetti, *Cagliari fenicia e punica* (Sardò 5: Sassari; Chiarella, 1990), 13; Moscati, *Il santuario dei bambini (tofet)*, 23–25; and J. C. Quinn, "Tophets in the 'Punic World,'" 33.

CHAPTER 3

A General Sacrifice of Firstborn Israelite Children?

In many ways, the debate surrounding the possibility that the Israelites sacrificed firstborn children is more straightforward than the debate surrounding the למלך ritual. It centers on the proper interpretation of the "Law of the Firstborn," variations of which appear in Exod 13:2, 11–13; 22:28b–29; 34:19–20; Lev 27:26–27; Num 3:11–13; 8:1–20; 18:13–18; and Deut 15:19–23. Of these, Lev 27:26–27 and Deut 15:19–23 make no mention of human firstborn and are thus not directly germane to the present question. All of the other texts, however, state that the firstborn of both humans and animals belong to Yahweh. But nearly every version of the law also allows for human firstborn children to be "redeemed" (√פדה), either by offering a sheep or monetary support for the temple (Exod 13:11–13; 34:19–20; Num 18:13–18) or by the devotion of the Levites to the service of Yahweh instead of offering Israelite firstborn children (תחת כל בכור פטר רחם מבני ישראל; Num 3:11–13). Only Exod 13:2 and 22:28b–29 [Eng. 22:29b–30] declare that the firstborn of both humans and animals belong to Yahweh, without any mention of redemption. The former is problematic, however, since it serves as the preface to Yahweh's instructions to Moses regarding the commemoration of the Passover, and in its present context redemption is probably assumed. Indeed, later in the same chapter (13:11–13) redemption is explicitly commanded.

This leaves Exod 22:28b: "The firstborn of your sons you shall give (תתן) to me"; no redemption clause accompanies this statement. It is this version of the law that has been the center of the debate regarding whether or not firstborn children were actually sacrificed in ancient Israel. Does it indicate that all firstborn children were to be sacrificed to Yahweh? Or does it assume the same type of redemption clause found with other forms of the law? The most obvious difficulty with claiming that it indeed requires that all firstborn children be sacrificed to Yahweh is that there are many children mentioned in the Hebrew Bible who are explicitly referred to as "firstborn" (בכר)—Esau (Gen 27:19), Reuben (Gen 35:23), Manasseh (Gen 41:51), Nadab (Num 3:2), Amnon (2 Sam 3:2), etc.—and none of them were sacrificed. If there ever were an Israelite custom that all firstborn children were to be sacrificed on the eighth day, then it is remarkable that not a single biblical narrative alludes to the practice. Thus, whatever Exod 22:28b appears to mean, the argument goes, it must actually mean something else. It is possible to imagine a number of ways that a child could be "given" to Yahweh, perhaps in service at the temple (see 1 Sam 1:11).[1] This view finds some support in the version of the law of the firstborn in which the Levites are accepted in place of the Israelite firstborn (see Num 3:12). This version of the law may reflect the idea that Israelite firstborn children were owed to Yahweh at an earlier period, but now their place has been filled by the Levites. Since the Levites were devoted to cultic service, it might be that firstborn children also once were similarly devoted to serve in a cultic capacity.

The precise phrasing of the version of the law in question, however, read most naturally, seems to stipulate that children ought to be sacrificed. The full text of the law (Exod 22:28b–29 [Eng. 29b–30]) reads:

> בכור בניך תתן לי כן תעשה לשרך לצאנך שבעת ימים יהיה עם אמו ביום השמיני תתנו לי
>
> The firstborn of your children/sons you shall give to me. Thus you shall do with your cattle and your sheep. Seven days he/it will be with his/its mother. On the eighth day you will give him/it to me.

Especially problematic is the כן "thus" of Exod 22:29. Elsewhere, when first-born animals are "given" to Yahweh, they are explicitly said to be offered as

1. This is a suggestion that has been raised by several scholars, with varying degrees of confidence. W. C. H. Propp, for instance, posits that "in some cases, [the child] is destined to become a sacrifice. Perhaps in other situations, he will be donated to a shrine like the young Samuel. . . . Most often, however, his life would be redeemed with an animal sacrifice" (*Exodus 19–40*: A New Translation with Introduction and Commentary [AB 2A; New York: Doubleday, 2006], 270). Likewise, G. Brin argues that "The first-born had always been understood as responsible for conducting the family cult in memory of the familial ancestors, and other similar functions. It is therefore reasonable to assume that, during that stage that preceded the establishment of the tribe of Levi as the priestly tribe, they would have been seen as most suitable to serve the holy." Brin argues further that although Exod 22:28b–29 does refer to service at the cult, even there it was a "theoretical law that was not carried out in fact" (*Studies in Biblical Law: From the Hebrew Bible to the Dead Sea Scrolls* [trans. J. Chipman; JSOTSup 176; Sheffield: JSOT Press, 1994], 221–22).

sacrifices (see Num 18:17).[2] The "thus" in Exod 22:29 would indicate that the children of 22:28b are to be given in the same way as the animals in 22:29. Thus if "giving" an animal to Yahweh indicates sacrifice, then the "giving" of children should as well.

Further complicating the dedicatory hypothesis are the two concluding clauses: "Seven days he/it will be with his/its mother. On the eighth day you will give him/it to me." Whatever "giving" a child or an animal to Yahweh means, it stands in direct contrast to "being with its mother." That is, once it is given to Yahweh, the child or animal will no longer be with its mother. If temple service or some other form of "giving" was envisioned, then these instructions would be highly impractical. An eight-day-old child could hardly survive apart from its mother for very long, unless we are to envision a staff of wet nurses in the employ of the shrine, responsible for caring for dedicated firstborn children until they were weaned. Surely it would be more practical for a dedicated child to simply remain with its mother until it was weaned, as in the case of Samuel (1 Sam 1:24), but the phrase "on the eighth day" precludes this possibility. Again, a more straightforward explanation of the meaning of this clause is that both the child and the animal were to be "given" on the eighth day and that it would no longer need to be "with its mother" because the "giving" implies sacrificial killing.

2. Contra J. B. Segal, who suggests that firstborn animals were "dedicated," which in his view might involve sacrifice but could also involve selling the animal and giving the proceeds to the temple. Segal's reconstruction is based on a creative but ultimately unconvincing harmonization of the various laws of the firstborn (i.e., Exod 13:15; Deut 12:6–7; 14:24–26; and Num 18:15–18; *The Hebrew Passover from the Earliest Times to A.D. 70* [London Oriental Series 12; London: Oxford University Press, 1963], 181–82). In this he is followed by Propp, *Exodus 19–40*, 270. The suggestion that √נתן in these verses was intended to encompass all of these possibilities is unlikely; even the versions that do allow for alternatives to sacrifice appear to assume sacrifice as the norm. For instance, Exod 34:19–20 contains a redemption clause for donkeys (and children), but that clause only makes sense in light of the assumption that an unredeemed animal would have otherwise been sacrificed. Likewise, Deut 14:24–26 allows for selling firstborn animals and bringing the proceeds to the temple. This, however, is only allowed in cases in which "the road is long for you." Again, the normal way one gives a firstborn animal is sacrifice, and Deuteronomy only offers an exception to this norm to mitigate the difficulty that the centralization of the cult presented for the regular offering of firstborn livestock. Underlying all versions of the law of the firstborn is the assumption that "giving" an animal to Yahweh involved sacrifice (or eating it as part of a sacrificial meal, in the case of Deut 12:6–7). It was not the case that one could "give" an animal to Yahweh in a variety of ways; instead, "giving" an animal to Yahweh involved sacrifice even if some traditions permitted this requirement to be mitigated or modified. In any version of the law that did not include a mitigating clause, such as Exod 22:29, "give" most naturally should be understood as "sacrifice."

These clauses are equally problematic for Levenson's argument; he claims that "Exodus 22:28b articulates a theological ideal about the special place of the firstborn son, an ideal whose realization could range from literal to non-literal implementation, that is, from sacrifice to redemption, or even to mere intellectual assent without any cultic act whatsoever."[3] Obviously, it is wise to be wary of viewing the "laws" of the Hebrew Bible as apodictic in nature rather than as descriptive attempts to codify the practices of a particular community; these descriptions may better represent how a scribe thought things ought to be than how they actually were. Nonetheless, even if Exod 22:28b–29 represents an "ideal," the literal wording of this ideal unambiguously demands child sacrifice, and it does not allow for a range of options. The fact that Exod 22:28b–29 elaborates that "giving" involves separation from the child's mother narrows the range of interpretive possibilities considerably. It is difficult to imagine what might be intended other than sacrifice if the act involves separating an eight-day-old child from its mother. Even if this version of the law of the firstborn represents an "ideal," then this ideal involved child sacrifice and does not envision other means of fulfilling it.

Others attempt to avoid the conclusion that the plain meaning of the text demands child sacrifice by asserting from the outset that a command to sacrifice all firstborn children is simply ridiculous on its face. W. R. Smith long ago argued: "To conclude from [Exod 22:28b–29] that at one time the Israelites actually sacrificed all their first born sons is *absurd*; but, on the other hand, there must have been some point of attachment in ancient custom for the belief that the deity asked for such a sacrifice" [emphasis mine]. He goes on to suggest that the command only concerns the special "sanctity" of firstborn children, and certainly did not involve their actual sacrifice: "all the prerogatives of the firstborn among Semitic peoples are originally prerogatives of sanctity; the sacred blood of the kin flows purest and strongest in him (Gen. xlix. 3)."[4] Smith's objection to understanding Exod 22:28b–29 as referring to child sacrifice is thus not grounded on interpreting the text but on the alleged absurdity of any interpretation that concludes that it requires the general sacrifice of firstborn children.

Smith is not alone in allowing his judgment of what does and does not constitute the "absurd" to settle the matter. R. de Vaux similarly concludes: "It would be *absurd* to suppose that there could have been in Israel or among

3. Levenson, *Death and Resurrection*, 9.

4. W. R. Smith, *Lectures on the Religion of the Semites* (New York: D. Appleton & Company, 1889), 445–46.

any other people, at any moment in their history, a constant, general law, compelling the suppression of the first-born, who are the hope of the race"[5] [emphasis mine]. Notably, this last clause, "who are the hope of the race," reveals an important underlying assumption concerning the nature of the alleged absurdity of the practice: if any people were to sacrifice all of their firstborn children, then "the race" would soon cease to exist. This assumption is made even more explicit by W. H. C. Propp, who takes it "as axiomatic that a kind of natural selection weeds out customs inimical to the survival of the family and the society. . . . And killing every male firstborn would be no less than Darwinian suicide."[6] So the argument goes: no matter what the most natural reading of the text is, the idea that it requires all firstborn children to be sacrificed must be rejected because such a command would be "absurd" and would have a detrimental effect on the Israelite population.

It is surprising, when considering the second objection, how *little* effect the general sacrifice of firstborn children would have on the population of an ancient society. In the ancient world, infant mortality rates were significantly higher than in modern industrialized societies. In their survey of the data from a variety of historical periods and locales, Garnand, Stager, and Greene observe that a mortality rate as high as 50–60% during a child's first year can be assumed, which would require a replacement fertility rate of somewhere between 3.5 and 7.0.[7] Thus, although firstborn children make up approximately one-half of the total children born to a modern Western household, with our fertility rate of around 2.0, the same child would only make up about one-quarter to one-seventh of the children born to an ancient household.[8]

---

5. R. de Vaux, *Studies in Old Testament Sacrifice* (Cardiff: University of Wales Press, 1964), 71. Similarly, Mosca, who is more concerned to demonstrate that whatever the law of the firstborn was it was *not* the same as the למלך sacrifices (his work is primarily concerned with the latter), approvingly quotes de Vaux and concludes, "Redemption must have been allowed from the first, despite the silence of Ex. 22" ("Child Sacrifice," 237).

6. Propp, *Exodus 19–40*, 268.

7. B. K. Garnand, L. E. Stager, and J. A. Greene, "Infants as Offerings: Palaeodemographic Patterns and Tophet Burial," *SEL* 29–30 (2012–13): 208–9, 220. Similarly, C. Meyers estimates that the average Israelite house would have had nearly two childbirths for every child who survived to age five ("The Family in Early Israel," in *Families in Ancient Israel* [ed. L. G. Perdue et al.; Louisville: Westminster John Knox, 1997], 28); and G. Galil, who notes a mortality rate for children under five years of age in Africa and the Middle East during the seventeenth and eighteenth centuries CE of 17–28% (*The Lower Stratum Families in the Neo-Assyrian Period* [Leiden: Brill, 2007], 310 n. 3.

8. The World Bank's database of global fertility rates puts France at 2.0, the United States and United Kingdom at 1.9, and Germany at only 1.4 as of 2013 (World Bank, "Fertility rate, total [births per woman]," http://data.worldbank.org/indicator/SP.DYN.TFRT.IN).

Thus, were a modern Western society, with our relatively low fertility rates, to sacrifice every firstborn child, it certainly could constitute something akin to "Darwinian suicide," as Propp asserts. In a society without any reliable means of birth control, however, and in which a woman might easily bear as many as seven or eight children, on average, during the course of her life,[9] the demographic calculations look a little less precarious. In addition, infant mortality is particularly high in the case of first births to young mothers, as we can assume most first-time mothers were in ancient times.[10] That is, Israelite firstborn children, statistically speaking, would have already been the least likely to survive in the first place. Finally, the sacrifice of a firstborn child would have had the obvious side-effect that the mother would not nurse the child beyond its eighth day, and she would therefore not experience the decrease in fertility normally associated with nursing mothers. Taking all of these factors into account, Garnand, Stager, and Greene conclude, "If a fifteen-year-old mother survived giving birth, and if she had another child in the following year, the net demographic effect of losing her firstborn would be the same as postponing marriage for a year."[11] Thus, while sacrificing firstborn children would have a modest effect on the growth rate of a community's population, there is no reason to think that this reduction would seriously threaten the existence of the community itself. There is no demographic reason why all firstborn children could not have been sacrificed; doing so certainly would not have sacrificed the "hope of the race" or resulted in "Darwinian suicide."

It is likely, however, that de Vaux thinks that the negative demographic implications are not the only "absurd" thing about the general sacrifice of firstborn children. A common assumption in most modern Western societies is that parents have a strong biologically ingrained attachment to children from the moment of their birth and that it is impossible for parents ever to imagine sacrificing a child, except perhaps in the most dire and hopeless of circumstances. But this modern construction of parenthood is, like all social constructions, closely bound up with our own time and place. As J. F. Parker has observed in her thorough exploration of the depiction of children in the Hebrew Bible, "Concepts of children as coddled innocents and romantic notions of childhood as a period of entitlement are anachronistic, ethnocentric,

9. So Meyers, "The Family in Early Israel," 28.

10. Garnand, Stager, and Greene, "Infants as Offerings," 209, following J. E. Finlay, E. Özaltin, and D. Canning, "The Association of Maternal Age with Infant Mortality, Child Anthropometric Failure, Diarrhoea and Anaemia for First Births: Evidence from 55 Low- and Middle-Income Countries," *BMJ Open* 2011;1:e000226 doi:10.1136/bmjopen-2011–000226.

11. Garnand, Stager, and Greene, "Infants as Offerings," 209.

and inappropriate for biblical understanding."[12] Especially in the wake of the work of P. Ariès,[13] scholars have been acutely aware that the modern construction of childhood and modern attitudes toward children are indeed nothing more than modern constructions. Even if one is not entirely convinced by Ariès's bold conclusion that "[i]n medieval society the concept of childhood did not exist,"[14] his observations about the effects of a high infant mortality rate and its impact on the ability of parents to become attached to their children remain perceptive. At a time when one of every two children was expected to die before adulthood, "People could not allow themselves to become too attached to something that was regarded as a probable loss."[15] In the privileged upper-middle class positions that most Western academics occupy—a world in which parenthood is constructed as a carefully planned event that involves prenatal vitamins; multiple obstetrician appointments, complete with ultrasounds; maternal abstention from alcohol, caffeine, sushi, deli meat and whatever other consumables contemporary parenting literature warns may present a dire threat to the well-being of the child; refurnishing an entire room to serve as a nursery; and often purchasing an automobile that will more amply accommodate the child's needs—it is natural to expect that parents would be strongly attached to their children from the moment of their birth, and even before birth. Each child is individually planned and prepared for, and the investment in each child often begins well more than a year before the child's birth. With so much already invested in a child at the moment of birth, an immediate attachment to the child seems natural and expected.[16]

---

12. J. F. Parker, *Valuable and Vulnerable: Children in the Hebrew Bible, Especially the Elisha Cycle* (BJS 355; Providence: Brown University, 2013), 199. Other recent work on the construction of the concepts of "children" and "childhood" and how the conceptions of ancient Israelites varied significantly from our own include L. W. Koepf-Taylor, *Give Me Children or I Shall Die: Children and Communal Survival in Biblical Literature* (ES; Minneapolis: Fortress, 2013); N. Steinberg, *The World of the Child in the Hebrew Bible* (HBM 51; Sheffield: Sheffield Phoenix, 2013); and K. H. Garroway, *Children in the Ancient Near Eastern Household* (EANEC 3; Winona Lake, IN: Eisenbrauns, 2014).

13. P. Ariès, *Centuries of Childhood: A Social History of Family Life* (trans. R. Baldick; New York: Knopf, 1962). For a helpful and concise overview of Ariès's work and work on the topic since, see Parker, *Valuable and Vulnerable*, 31–39.

14. Ariès, *Centuries of Childhood*, 128. For a rebuttal to Ariès's arguments, see N. Orme, *Medieval Children* (New Haven: Yale University Press, 2001).

15. Ariès, *Centuries of Childhood*, 38.

16. Even so, the persistence of "bonding disorders"—that is, the failure of "natural" maternal affection to manifest toward the child (see R. C. Kumar, "'Anybody's Child': Severe Disorders of Mother Infant Bonding," *British Journal of Psychiatry* 171 [1997]: 175–81; I. F. Brock-

It is interesting to observe, however, that in those societies that continue to suffer from relatively high infant mortality rates, immediate attachment to infants is *not* necessarily the norm. For instance, N. Scheper-Hughes observed a striking "indifference" to infant death in a shantytown in northeast Brazil, where rampant malnutrition took the lives of a tragically high number of infants.[17] Scheper-Hughes recounts a particularly heart-wrenching scene that she encountered firsthand:

> Within the first month of my arrival in Bom Jesus, a young mother came to me with a very sick and wasted baby. Seeing that the child's condition was precarious, I rushed with him to the local hospital, where he died soon after, the desperate efforts of myself and the two clinic attendants notwithstanding. I was devastated and frightened. I had come from a society in which (at least to my limited knowledge and experience) babies didn't die, or if they did, where it was a great human tragedy for all concerned. How could I break the news to the child's mother? Would she hold me responsible for the death? Would I be forced to leave my post of duty so soon after my arrival? Selfish concerns, mind you. Meanwhile, I had to trek all the way through town and climb the Alto with the tiny, yet strangely heavy, dead weight in my arms. It was almost more than I could bear, and I wept bitter and angry tears all along the way. To my great wonder and perplexity, however, the young woman took the news and the bundle from my arms placidly, almost casually and indifferently. Noting my red eyes and tear-stained face, the woman turned to comment to a neighbor woman standing by, "*Hein, hein, coitada! Engraçada, não é*; Tsk! Tsk! Poor thing! Funny, isn't she?" What was funny or amusing seemed to be my inappropriate display of grief and my concern over a matter of so little consequence. No one, least of all the mother, had expected the little tyke to live in any case.[18]

ington et al., "A Screening Questionnaire for Mother-Infant Bonding Disorders," *Archives of Women's Mental Health* 3:4 [2001]: 133–40; I. F. Brockington, *Motherhood and Mental Health* [Oxford: Oxford University Press, 1996], 347–60]), indicates that, even with all of this prenatal investment, cases in which this "natural" affection is nonetheless absent are not uncommon.

17. N. Scheper-Hughes, *Death Without Weeping: The Violence of Everyday Life in Brazil* (Berkeley: University of California Press, 1993); eadem, "Social Indifference to Child Death," *The Lancet* 337:8750 (1991): 1144–47; eadem, "Death Without Weeping: Has Poverty Ravaged Mother Love in the Shantytowns of Brazil?" *Natural History* 10 (1989): 8–16. Thankfully, during the years since Scheper-Hughes's fieldwork in the 1980s, a general improvement in living conditions has seen an accompanying decline in infant mortality rates. As one might expect, this decline in infant mortality rates has also been accompanied by an increased degree of grief experienced by bereaved parents. See N. Scheper-Hughes, "No More Angel Babies on the Alto," *Berkeley Review of Latin American Studies* (Spring 2013): 25–31.

18. Scheper-Hughes, *Death Without Weeping*, 270–71.

This detached and indifferent response to the death of a child seems extraordinarily callous and even inhumane to those of us who are privileged enough to inhabit social spaces in which infant death is a relatively uncommon experience, and it may be tempting at first to view the inhabitants of the Alto as heartless. As Scheper-Hughes observes, however, although infants were not mourned on the Alto, motherhood and mother love (of older children) were among the chief and most celebrated virtues.[19] Mothers simply could not afford the emotional trauma of becoming attached to an infant from the time of its birth; instead, as Scheper-Hughes puts it, "mother love grows slowly, tentatively, and fearfully."[20] In addition, from a purely pragmatic standpoint, selective neglect of sickly infants, also widely practiced on the Alto, allowed scarce food and resources to be consumed by children who were seen as more likely to survive. Scheper-Hughes notes that this is an "old" reproductive strategy: "to give birth to many children and, on the expectation that only a few will survive infancy, to invest selectively in those considered the 'best bets' for survival in terms of preferred sex, birth order, appearance, health, or perceived viability."[21] It is significant that the conditions that Scheper-Hughes observed in northeast Brazil, with its high infant mortality rates, match well those of antiquity. The resulting strategy of maintaining an emotional distance from infants until a certain age therefore also makes sense under similar conditions. The death of an infant was not heart-wrenchingly tragic, as it is in modern industrialized Western societies, because it was so very common. In this regard, it is also worth observing Jewish prohibitions against mourning infants who die before their thirty-first day,[22] which probably have their origin and basis in similar demographic realities.

All this still leaves aside the most obvious piece of evidence against the idea that parents could never regularly kill their own children: the extraordinarily common cross-cultural evidence for the practice of infanticide.[23] Although infanticide can be difficult to detect directly, since it is also common for societies that practice some form of regular infanticide to conceal or deny

19. Ibid., 357–59.

20. Ibid., 359.

21. Ibid., 402.

22. *Shulkhan Arukh, Yoreh De'ah* 374:8 and Maimonides, *Mishneh Torah, Hilkhot Aveilut* 1:6.

23. S. Mays, "The Bioarchaeology of the Homicide of Infants and Children," in *Tracing Childhood: Bioarchaeological Investigations of Early Lives in Antiquity* (ed. J. L. Thompson, M. P. Alfonso-Durruty, and J. J. Crandall; Gainesville, FL: University Press of Florida), 99–122; L. Williamson, "Infanticide: An Anthropological Analysis," in *Infanticide and the Value of Life* (ed. M. Kohl; Buffalo, NY: Prometheus, 1978), 61–75.

the practice, anthropologists have observed at least one form of infanticide—the preference for male children, which results in the killing of female infants—via a society's ratio of male to female children. Examining nineteenth and twentieth-century censuses of 393 populations from Asia, Africa, North America, South America, and Oceania, W. T. Divale and M. Harris conclude that 179 of these societies (45.5%) regularly engaged in sex-selective infanticide, and another 29 (7.4%) at least occasionally did.[24] Sex-selective infanticide is only one form of the practice, however. There is evidence of infanticide as a form of "birth control" from ancient to modern times. At Ashkelon, for example, the sewers beneath a Roman-era brothel reveal evidence of infanticide, in this case disproportionally boys, who had been killed and their bodies discarded.[25] Evidence for infanticide has also been discovered on the other end of the empire, in Roman-era Britain.[26] Likewise, the evidence for the exposure of unwanted infants in ancient Greece is well known, although the prevalence of the practice, which likely varied over the course of time, is difficult to determine with much confidence.[27] The description of the abandoned infant girl in Ezekiel 16 may also be evidence that the practice of exposing infants was not unknown within Israel itself.[28] Infanticide, as well as the related practice of infant abandonment, even appears to have occurred

---

24. W. T. Divale and M. Harris, "Population, Warfare, and the Male Supremacist Complex," *American Anthropologist* 78 (1976): 525–26. The practice of female infanticide has been well documented in India and China. See R. D. Bhatnagar, R. Dube, and R. Dube, *Female Infanticide in India: A Feminist Cultural History* (New York: State University of New York Press, 2005); D. E. Mungello, *Drowning Girls in China: Female Infanticide since 1650* (New York: Rowman & Littlefield, 2008); and A. M. den Boer and V. M. Hudson, "Sex-Selective Infanticide and the 'Missing Females' in China and India," in *Killing Infants: Studies in the Worldwide Practice of Infanticide* (ed. B. H. Bechtold and D. C. Graves; Lewiston, NY: Mellen, 2006), 337–71.

25. P. Smith and G. Kahila, "Identification of Infanticide in Archaeological Sites: A Case Study from the Late Roman–Early Byzantine Periods at Ashkelon, Israel," *Journal of Archaeological Science* 19 (1992): 667–75; M. Faerman et al., "DNA Analysis Reveals the Sex of Infanticide Victims," *Nature* 385 (1997): 212–13; and M. Faerman et al., "Determining the Sex of Infanticide Victims from the Late Roman Era through Ancient DNA Analysis," *Journal of Archaeological Science* 25 (1998): 861–65.

26. S. Mays and J. Eyers, "Perinatal Infant Death at the Roman Villa Site at Hambleden, Buckinghamshire, England," *Journal of Archaeological Science* 38 (2011): 1931–38; and S. Mays, "Infanticide in Roman Britain," *Antiquity* 67 (1993): 883–88.

27. M. Golden, *Children and Childhood in Classical Athens* (2nd ed.; Baltimore: Johns Hopkins University Press, 2015), 144–48; and L. A Beaumont, *Childhood in Ancient Athens: Iconography and Social History* (New York: Routledge, 2012), 90–92.

28. B. A. Nakhai, "Female Infanticide in Iron II Israel and Judah," in *Sacred History, Sacred Literature: Essays on Ancient Israel, the Bible, and Religion in Honor of R. E. Friedman on His Sixtieth Birthday* (ed. S. Dolansky; Winona Lake, IN: Eisenbrauns, 2008), 257–72.

to one degree or another in medieval Europe, although again it is difficult to determine how widespread the practice was.[29] Thus, while the concept of infanticide is horrifying to modern Western observers, the evidence is that the practice is well attested across time and space.

If there is no real demographic impediment and there is no reason to assume that widespread infanticide is somehow "absurd" on its face, then there is nothing a priori to militate against a literal understanding of the version of the law of the firstborn in Exod 22:28b–29. Indeed, it is possible even to argue, somewhat counterintuitively, that infant sacrifices given in response to Yahweh's claim to all firstborn children and animals actually demonstrates how children were strongly *desired* among the Israelites. A strong desire for progeny is expressed throughout the Hebrew Bible. In the patriarchal narratives, for instance, infertility is a repeated problem to be overcome, one that often serves as the driving force of the narrative (Gen 11:30; 25:21;

29. For arguments that the practice of infanticide was quite common in medieval Europe, see R. C. Trexler, "Infanticide in Florence: New Sources and Results," *History of Childhood Quarterly* 1 (1973): 98–116; B. A. Kellum, "Infanticide in England in the Later Middle Ages," *History of Childhood Quarterly* 1 (1974): 367–88; R. H. Helmholz, "Infanticide in the Province of Canterbury During the Fifteenth Century," *History of Childhood Quarterly* 2 (1975): 379–90. In a notable departure from the consensus established by Trexler, Kellum, and Helmholz, S. M. Butler, although not denying the existence of infanticide, pushes back against the claims both that it was commonly employed as a "means of belated contraception" in medieval England and that the courts had a generally lenient attitude toward the practice ("A Case of Indifference? Child Murder in Later Medieval England," *Journal of Women's History* 19 [2007]: 59–82). Orme similarly argues, "We have no means of reckoning how many infants were deliberately destroyed in medieval England, but it is likely that (as today) the events were abnormal not normal. The disapproval of such killings by the Church and the crown is likely to have harmonised with the feelings of most people" (*Medieval Children*, 96). B. A. Hanawalt is also skeptical concerning how widespread infanticide was, as opposed to the mere (albeit still often fatal) practice of infant neglect (*Growing Up in Medieval London* [Oxford: Oxford University Press, 1993], 44–45; eadem, "Medievalists and the Study of Childhood," *Speculum* 77 [2002]: 450–53). Finally, in his *The Kindness of Strangers: The Abandonment of Children in Western Europe from Late Antiquity to the Renaissance* (New York: Pantheon, 1988), J. Boswell argues that, though child abandonment was widespread in pre-modern Europe, it would have only rarely resulted in the child's dying as a result, since the child would have usually been adopted by someone. His conclusions have not met universal acceptance, however; as one reviewer quips, "We are asked to believe that, even though the children were sold into slavery, left on the street, deposited on garbage piles and dung heaps, the kindness of strangers rescued them and brought them through these traumas unscathed" (D. L. Ransel, review of J. Boswell, *The Kindness of Strangers*, *History of Education Quarterly* 30 [1990]: 227). Despite some disagreement concerning how common the practice of infanticide was and how detrimental the related practice of abandonment was to a child's survival, it does seem clear that, at the very least, parents of medieval Europe had strikingly different attitudes toward their infant children than most contemporary parents in the industrialized West.

29:31; 30:22). Likewise, Hannah bitterly laments her inability to have children (1 Sam 1). A demonstration of Solomon's great wisdom hinges on the assumption that a mother would rather allow someone else to have her child than see it perish (1 Kgs 3:16–28). An entire psalm (Ps 127) is devoted to extolling the joys of having an abundance of children, and the suffering and death of infants and children is presented as among the worst possible calamities (see, e.g., Lam 2:11–12, 20–22). In short, there is ample evidence that Israelites were no different from most other societies: all things being equal, children were a blessing, and the more the merrier.

How can one square this with a command to sacrifice all firstborn children? To make sense of the apparent contradiction, it is necessary to examine the "logic" of the laws of firstfruits and firstborn. All firstfruits and firstborn are owed to Yahweh as his portion of Israel's produce, and thus to deprive Yahweh of firstfruits would be to deprive him of his due. The offering of firstlings and firstfruits was understood to benefit not only Yahweh, however. Rendering Yahweh his portion was seen as also bestowing a blessing on all the *remainder* of the crops, livestock, and (presumably) children. One of the most explicit presentations of the logic behind the giving of firstfruits is found in Prov 3:9–10: "Honor Yahweh with your wealth, with the firstfruits of all your harvest, and your silos will be full with plenty, and your vats will burst with wine." The theme appears again in Jer 2:3, where the nation of Israel is described as Yahweh's firstfruits: "Israel was holy to Yahweh, the firstfruits of his harvest. All who ate of it were guilty; evil came upon them—an utterance of Yahweh." Thus, while Proverbs promises prosperity for those who give Yahweh his due, Jeremiah declares disaster for those who would rob Yahweh by consuming the firstfruits (here, metaphorically, the people Israel). Deuteronomy's tithe functions similarly; at the end of the instructions concerning bringing in the tithes, it provides the reason for doing so: "in order that Yahweh your God will bless you in every deed of your hand that you do" (Deut 14:29). Yet again, the result of setting apart for Yahweh his portion is that Yahweh in turn will cause the remainder to prosper.

Including children among firstlings and firstfruits means that the logic of the firstfruit offerings applied to them as well: giving Yahweh the first of one's children would result in a large number of healthy children in return. In a society in which infant mortality rates probably approached 50%, it is easy to imagine that the Israelites would have sought any available means of increasing the number of children who survived to adulthood. If one sincerely believed that the sacrifice of one's firstborn child would result in an increased likelihood of survival for the rest of one's children, then it would be entirely "rational" to sacrifice that child. This gruesome "rationality" would have been bolstered by the fact that there was only around a 50% chance that the sacrificed child would have survived anyway. In sum, the act of sacrificing a firstborn child may well have been carried out for the purpose of *preserving* the lives of one's (future) children. Far from demonstrating a lack of parental sentiment, these sacrifices would have exhibited the parents' willingness to lose the life of one child in exchange for the lives of one's future children.

This line of reasoning is not very different from the motives that Polybius gives for "limiting" the size of one's household (= exposing unwanted infants) in ancient Greece. With fewer surviving children, parents could hope that the few who did survive would live more affluent lives—a practice that Polybius himself judges to be short-sighted:

> τῶν γὰρ ἀνθρώπων εἰς ἀλαζονείαν καὶ φιλοχρημοσύνην, ἔτι δὲ ῥᾳθυμίαν ἐκτετραμμένων καὶ μὴ βουλομένων μήτε γαμεῖν μήτ', ἐὰν γήμωσι, τὰ γινόμενα τέκνα τρέφειν, ἀλλὰ μόλις ἓν τῶν πλείστων ἢ δύο χάριν τοῦ πλουσίους τούτους καταλιπεῖν καὶ σπαταλῶντας θρέψαι, ταχέως ἔλαθε τὸ κακὸν αὐξηθέν.
>
> For people, having turned aside into pretension, greed, and laziness and not desiring either to marry or, if they should marry, to rear children who are born—but only one or at most two in order to bequeath wealth to these and to raise pleasure-seekers—the evil escaped notice and rapidly increased.[30]

Despite Polybius's ungenerous description of his contemporaries' parenting strategies, it is clear even in his invective that children were not exposed because they were not wanted. Instead, some children were exposed to allow parents to maximize their investment in the children whom they chose to keep. The goal was not to kill one's own child or even to avoid having children. Instead, facing the reality that some could hardly afford to provide all the children that they would naturally produce with their preferred standard of living, some children were kept and others abandoned. Although the mechanism is obviously quite different, the motivation here is little different from that of present-day parents who artificially limit the size of their family in order to maximize their investment in a smaller number of children than they would naturally produce. Of course, with the advent of reliable contra-

30. Polybius, *Histories* 36.17.7. On the significance of this passage, see Golden, *Children and Childhood in Classical Athens*, 145.

ception, infanticide and infant abandonment become less attractive methods of birth control, but the underlying logic nonetheless remains the same.

Even if there is no good reason to doubt that Exod 22:28b–29 means precisely what it appears to say, this is still some distance from proving that any significant number of ancient Israelites actually sacrificed their firstborn children on the eighth day. That is, showing that the regular sacrifice of firstborn children would have been neither detrimental to the Israelite population nor particular shocking, given cross-cultural comparative evidence, is not enough to demonstrate that the sacrifice of firstborn children was widely practiced in ancient Israel. As observed above, there is still no evidence from any biblical narrative that any firstborn child was actually sacrificed on the eighth day. Although there are several narratives in which children are sacrificed in the Hebrew Bible (on which, see the following chapter), in none of these instances is the child specifically offered on the eighth day as part of a common sacrificial rite.

What should we make of all this evidence? The problem may lie in a mistaken assumption that the Covenant Code ever reflected the religious practices of all Israel, rather than merely representing a scribal attempt to codify the traditions of a particular Israelite community. There is no reason to believe that there was any such thing as "pan-Israelite" Yahwism; even the Hebrew Bible itself presents a diversity of Yahwistic belief and practice. Whatever the identity of the particular Israelite group whose practices more or less approximate those described in the Covenant Code, they probably did fulfill the obligation to "give" Yahweh the firstborn of their children, as well as of their cattle, via sacrifice. That there are several other traditions in the Hebrew Bible that did not advocate following the law of the firstborn as applied to children literally is evidence that the "Covenant Code group" represented only one subset of the Israelite population.

Several factors may have contributed to a literal interpretation of Yahweh's claim to firstborn children among some Israelites. First, it is clear that a belief that firstborn children were in someway "owed" to Yahweh was quite widespread, a belief that is evident even in versions of the law of the firstborn that do not demand sacrifice to fulfill this obligation (Exod 13:2, 11–13; 22:28b–29; 34:19–20; Num 3:11–13; 8; 18:13–18). Add to this the cross-cultural evidence presented above that parents in societies with high infant mortality rates tend not to become deeply attached to their children until some time after birth, and it is not surprising that in some cases belief concerning Yahweh's claim to the firstborn led to the logical conclusion that firstborn infants were to be sacrificed. It is clear from variant biblical traditions that other Israelite Yahwists found different, often creative, means of fulfilling this obligation without actually sacrificing their children. The evidence of the Covenant Code nonetheless suggests that at least some Yahwists did practice child sacrifice.

If this group did exist, then what else can be said about them? Who were these people and when did they live? For the most part, those scholars who have argued that firstborn children were sacrificed during some era or other have tended to set the practice at a very early historical, or even prehistorical, period of Israelite history. For instance, nearly a century ago, one of H. Gressmann's key arguments for dating the Covenant Code early is the presence of the command to sacrifice children, while in other portions of the Hebrew Bible a redemption clause is found.[31] Likewise, P. Volz argues that, although firstborn children were originally sacrificed, already at a very early period the Israelites began substituting animals in their stead. He attributes this development to the "Fortschritt der Erkenntnis und der Zivilisation."[32] R. Dussaud ascribed the practice of child sacrifice "à haute époque," and said that substitution later triumphed over "des rigeurs du rituel."[33] G. Hölscher attributed the sacrifice of firstfruits and firstlings, including human firstlings, to an early state of religion that was characterized by "Mythus und Zauberglaube."[34] At a later period, however, with "zunehmender Zivilisation," substitutes came to replace humans as offerings.[35] Thus, one common view is that firstborn sacrifice was an archaic practice that the Israelites came to "outgrow," and the Covenant Code's version of the law of the firstborn represents the practice of early worshipers of Yahweh.

More recently, a similar reconstruction has been posited by M. Fishbane, who traces the rite through its various permutations in the Pentateuch, from actual sacrifice of children (Num 18:15a; Fishbane views the redemption clause of 15b as secondary), through an intermediate phase during which

31. H. Gressmann, *Die älteste Geschichtsschreibung und Prophetie Israels (von Samuel bis Amos und Hosea)* (Schriften des Alten Testaments 2:1; 2nd ed.; Göttingen: Vandenhoeck & Ruprecht, 1921), 232.

32. P. Volz, *Die biblischen Altertümer* (Calw & Stuttgart: Verlag der Vereinsbuchhandlung, 1914), 178–79.

33. R. Dussaud, *Les origines cananéennes du sacrifice israélite* (Paris: Leroux, 1921), 167- 73.

34. G. Hölscher, *Geschichte der israelitischen und jüdischen Religion* (Giessen: Töpelmann, 1922), 12, 28–29.

35. Ibid., 49. Similarly C. Steuernagel, *Das Deuteronomium* (2nd ed.; HKAT 1:3,1; Göttingen: Vandenhoeck & Ruprecht, 1923), 100; D. O. Procksch, *Die Genesis* (KAT 1; 2nd/3rd ed.; Leipzig: Deichertsche, 1924), 320–21; and A. Wendel, *Das Opfer in der altisraelitischen Religion* (Leipzig: Pfeiffer, 1927), 153–55.

redemption may have been allowed (evidenced by the potential ambiguity of נתן in Exod 22:28), and finally to a stage in which various forms of redemption were officially instituted, thereby avoiding either the sacrifice or the dedication of children (e.g., Exod 13:13; 34:20; Num 3:12–13; 8:16–19; 18:15b–16).[36] Fishbane acknowledges that references to the sacrifice of firstborns in Ezekiel (16:21; 20:25–26; 23:39) imply that children were still being sacrificed in the final days of the Judahite monarchy, but he considers this late practice of the rite to be only "hints of vestigial cultic practices," possibly encouraged by "noticeable contamination from local Canaanite practices . . . and from the neighbouring Aramaean states."[37] In this way, Fishbane manages to thread the needle of acknowledging that firstborn sacrifice is alleged to have occurred as late as the end of the monarchy but at the same time denying that it was a legitimate part of the Judahite cult at this late date. This in turn allows him to construct a general narrative in which an archaic rite of child sacrifice was gradually replaced by more humane alternatives, which Fishbane attributes to "strong theological motivations" and "socio-economic considerations."[38]

K. Finstberbusch has likewise attempted to trace the history of the offering of firstborn children in ancient Israel. In her view, the earliest version is preserved in Exod 22:28–29. She does not go so far as to argue that this version demands the sacrifice of all firstborn children, but she does acknowledge that the wording at least "implies their sacrifice" and "includes the possibility that the verse can be understood such that YHWH requires the sacrifice of the first-born child."[39] Exod 34:19–20, on the other hand, introduces several innovations: human firstborn are to be redeemed, the law of the firstborn only applies to males, and all firstborn are depicted as already belonging to Yahweh, not "given" to him as in Exod 22:28–29.[40] Next comes Deut 15:19–23, which unlike the previous two versions of the law, has nothing to say about firstborn children. Instead, its focus is on firstborn animals, which are commanded not to be used for labor but rather to be eaten before Yahweh, probably at the Feast of Booths. Finsterbusch believes that this version of the law expresses a

36. M. Fishbane, *Biblical Interpretation in Ancient Israel* (Oxford: Oxford University Press, 1985), 181–87.

37. Ibid., 186.

38. Ibid., 187.

39. K. Finsterbusch, "The First-Born between Sacrifice and Redemption in the Hebrew Bible," in *Human Sacrifice in the Jewish and Christian Tradition* (ed. K. Finsterbusch, A. Lange, and K. F. D. Römheld; SHR 112; Leiden: Brill, 2007), 95.

40. Ibid., 95–97.

"'farmer-friendly' tendency," in that unlike the previous versions of the law it mandates "giving" neither children nor donkeys, which in turn "would mean a considerable material relief for the Israelite families."[41] The next version of the law is Num 18:15–18, which apparently applies to all firstborn animals and children, male and female,[42] clean and unclean. Clean animals are to be sacrificed, and unclean animals and humans are to be redeemed, with the redemption price given to the priest. Finsterbusch considers this version of the law to be "priest friendly," in that it exhibits an "intention to impose as many offerings of first-born as possible on the Israelite, since these offerings were intended as part of the living support of the priests."[43]

Finally, there is Exod 13:1–2 and 11–16. This version of the law stands in the midst of instructions concerning the original Passover night, when Moses is commanded to consecrate every firstborn of the Israelites. In Finsterbusch's view, this command assumes the claim of Num 3 that the Levites serve as substitutes for the Israelite firstborn. It thus ties Yahweh's claim to the Israelite firstborn to the original Passover night and, indirectly, supports his claim to the Levites. In Finsterbusch's view, the Exod 13 version also assumes redemption, presumably via cash payment along the same lines as Num 18:16.[44] Ultimately, then, Finsterbusch believes that firstborn children may have been sacrificed at an early period of Israelite history but that "all later laws are unmistakably clear" that "the first-born child or first-born son is to be redeemed."[45] Like Fishbane, she breaks from the majority of scholars in allowing for the possibility of child sacrifice in compliance with Yahweh's claim to firstborn children, but she too pushes it back into the early days of Israel and presents an overarching narrative in which the practice came to be replaced in various ways over time.

Despite the widespread assumption that the differences in the various forms of the law of the firstborn can be attributed to some kind of diachronic development, I remain skeptical. In particular, there is no reason to assume that the sacrifice of firstborn children was limited to an early period of Israelite history and then fell out of use with the "progress of civilization" or some such. Although it is true that the version of the law that mandates these sacrifices, Exod 22:28b–29, appears in the Covenant Code, which is considered

41. Ibid., 99.

42. Finsterbusch believes that 18:16 is a secondary addition that may assume that only males were subject to this version of the law (ibid., 101).

43. Ibid., 102.

44. Ibid., 102–7.

45. Ibid., 108.

by most to be the earliest of the biblical legal collections,[46] these firstborn sacrifices are most clearly and explicitly condemned in Ezekiel's oracles (Ezek 20:25–26), which date at the earliest to the late monarchic period. Thus, it is not possible to assume that the sacrifice of firstborn children represents a primitive form of the rite that gradually gave way to redemption. Instead, it appears that sacrifice of firstborn children was practiced in some circles both in a relatively early period as well as during the last days of the monarchy. Although it is theoretically possible to argue, like Fishbane, that child sacrifice was an early rite that fell out of general practice but then again arose under the influence of Israel's neighbors, it seems equally likely that the ritual simply continued to exist throughout a relatively long period of Israel's history, only finally falling out of practice during the exile.

On the other hand, that child sacrifice was probably never a universal means of fulfilling the firstborn requirement in ancient Israel is demonstrated both by the paucity of evidence for the rite in biblical narrative and by the very existence of other versions of the law (on which, see chapter 5 below). Why did several different procedures for satisfying Yahweh's claim to firstborn children apparently coexist? Stavrakopoulou suggests that various forms of the rite "would give families the option of sacrificing either a firstborn child or an animal, presumably depending upon the circumstances of the (extended) family."[47] Although it is appropriate to emphasize the lack of uniformity of religious practice in ancient Israel, this explanation seems to put more emphasis on the individual family than would likely have obtained in an ancient society. It is unlikely that parents, even in consultation with their extended family, would have had the "option" of choosing whether to sacrifice the child, as prescribed in the Covenant Code, or to redeem the child with either an animal sacrifice or a donation to the temple, as prescribed in other versions of the law. More likely, in my opinion, is Ackerman's suggestion that

46. *Pace* the notable and radical departure from the scholarly consensus by J. Van Seters, who dates the Covenant Code to the exilic period, after the code of Deuteronomy (*A Law Book for the Diaspora: Revision in the Study of the Covenant Code* [Oxford: Oxford University Press, 2003]). For a rebuttal to Van Seters's arguments, see B. M. Levinson, "Is the Covenant Code an Exilic Composition? A Response to John Van Seters," in *In Search of Pre-Exilic Israel: Proceedings of the Oxford Old Testament Seminar* (ed. J. Day; JSOTSup 406; New York: T. & T. Clark, 2004), 272–325; E. Otto, review of J. Van Seters, *A Law Book for the Diaspora: Revision in the Study of the Covenant Code*, *RBL* 7 (2004). For Van Seters's response to these criticisms, see J. Van Seters, "Revision in the Study of the Covenant Code and a Response to My Critics," *SJOT* 21 (2007): 5–28.

47. Stavrakopoulou, *King Manasseh and Child Sacrifice*, 285.

sacrifice of the firstborn was "possible *within some circles* of Yahwism" [emphasis mine].[48] These circles were probably geographically delineated, at least to a degree, as J. Hutton argues; he concludes that "child sacrifice was in fact a legitimate feature of at least *some forms* of Judahite, if not pan-Israelite, cultic expression" [emphasis mine].[49] Even though there is unfortunately little evidence for identifying the specific geographic locations(s) of the group(s) that practiced firstborn sacrifice, there does seem to be evidence for the existence of these groups both at a relatively early period (Exod 22:28b–29) and during a relatively late time (Ezek 20:25–26). At present, however, we can say little more about these groups other than they do seem to have existed.

Thus, in addition to the so-called למלך sacrifices discussed in the previous chapters, there also was another form of Israelite child sacrifice: the general sacrifice of firstborn children. It is impossible to say how extensive either practice was, but it is likely that those who actually sacrificed their firstborn children consisted only of a small "ultra-pious" or "literalist" group of Yahwists, a group that probably perpetually remained a minority of the Israelite population at large. This minority status explains why no trace of this rite is evident in the narrative material of the Hebrew Bible. I must admit, however, that it may well be the case that my affection for the people of ancient Israel and the literature that they produced has influenced my optimism about the frequency of firstborn sacrifice.

48. Ackerman, *Under Every Green Tree*, 119.

49. J. Hutton, "Southern, Northern, and Transjordanian Perspectives," in *Religious Diversity in Ancient Israel and Judah* (ed. F. Stavrakopoulou and J. Barton; New York, T. & T. Clark, 2010), 164.

Chapter 4

Varieties of Child Sacrifice in Ancient Israel

The preceding chapters focused on questions regarding the historical reality of two particular forms of Yahwistic child sacrifice: (a) the למלך sacrifices and (b) the general sacrifice of firstborn children. Demonstrating the existence of these two particular rites, however, is only the first step in our project; other important questions remain. Not least of these is whether these were the only two rites involving Israelite child sacrifice or whether we have evidence for others. As the following examination will reveal, the למלך sacrifices and the general sacrifice of firstborn children do not in fact appear to be the only forms of child sacrifice described in the Hebrew Bible. Furthermore, although the logic of firstborn offerings was an important consideration in the discussion above concerning the plausibility of their historical reality, relatively little has been said thus far about the purpose and function of the למלך sacrifices. This chapter explores other potential examples of Israelite child sacrifice, examining biblical texts that appear to refer to the sacrifice of children and assessing their historical value. In addition, as far as the evidence will permit, this chapter will focus on the apparent purpose, function, and historical development the various forms of Israelite child sacrifice. Finally, it will conclude by returning to the למלך sacrifices, comparing their apparent historical development, significance, and ritual function to other forms of Israelite child sacrifice.

Mesha's Sacrifice of His Firstborn Son

First, there is an account that King Mesha of Moab sacrificed his firstborn son narrated in 2 Kings 3. The sacrifice takes place in the context of a revolt against the king of Israel, Mesha's suzerain. As was often the case, the occasion for Mesha's revolt appears to have been the death of his suzerain, in this case, King Ahab of Israel, and the accession of his successor, King Jehoram

(3:5). Other than the Deuteronomistic introduction to Jehoram's reign (3:1–2), the chapter has traditionally been ascribed to a "northern collection of prophetic stories about Elisha,"[1] even though there has been some debate about whether 2 Kgs 3 was indeed originally part of this cycle of stories or instead was only secondarily connected with Elisha.[2] The relationship of this collection of tales itself to the rest of the Deuteromistic History has also been debated.[3] Furthermore, the historical veracity of the story, and especially its relationship to the campaign described in the Mesha stele, is also a matter of contention.[4] Ultimately, questions concerning the historical reality behind the accounts of the war(s) between Moab and Israel are of only secondary importance for our discussion. What matters here is the way in which child sacrifice is depicted in the tale, since it is this depiction itself that reveals the beliefs and perhaps practices of the community within which the story circulated. That is, whether or not the historical King Mesha of Moab ever actually sacrificed his son, if the story realistically presents this sacrifice as effective and legitimate, then the implication is that child sacrifice did in fact have some historical basis in the cult of the group(s) that preserved the tale.

The outline of the story is as follows: Mesha's revolt leads Jehoram, the new Israelite king, to respond by making preparations to invade Moab in order to bring his rebellious vassal back under control. For assistance in the task, he calls on King Jehoshaphat of Judah and an unnamed king of Edom

1. M. Cogan and H. Tadmor, *II Kings: A New Translation with Introduction and Commentary* (AB 11; Garden City, NY: Doubleday, 1988), 48. So also, M. Noth, *The Deuteronomistic History* (trans. J. Doull, J. Barton, and M. D. Rutter; JSOTSup 15; Sheffield: JSOT Press, 1981), 68, 71–72.

2. The latter position is argued by J. M. Miller, "The Elisha Cycle and the Accounts of the Omride Wars," *JBL* 85 (1966): 441–54; and followed by J. Van Seters, *In Search of History: Historiography in the Ancient World and the Origins of Biblical History* (New Haven: Yale University Press, 1983; reprinted: Winona Lake, IN: Eisenbrauns, 1997), 305.

3. Noth has considered them to be sources for the Deuteronomistic historian (*The Deuteronomistic History*, 68, 71–72), while Miller viewed them as later insertions ("The Elisha Cycle," 441–54). Here Miller is followed by most recent scholarly treatments, including H.-J. Stipp, *Elischa–Propheten–Gottesmänner* (Arbeiten zu Text und Sprache im Alten Testament 24; St. Ottilien: EOS, 1987), 463–80; S. L. McKenzie, *The Trouble with Kings: The Composition of the Book of Kings in the Deuteronomistic History* (VTSup 42; Leiden: Brill, 1991), 95–98; and S. Otto, "The Composition of the Elijah-Elisha Stories and the Deuteronomistic History," *JSOT* 27 (2003): 494–97.

4. See A. Lemaire, "The Mesha Stele and the Omri Dynasty," in *Ahab Agonistes: The Rise and Fall of the Omri Dynasty* (ed. L. L. Grabbe; LHBOTS 421; New York: T. & T. Clark, 2007), 135–44; and N. Naʾaman, "Royal Inscriptions versus Prophetic Story: Mesha's Rebellion according to Biblical and Moabite Historiography," in *Ahab Agonistes: The Rise and Fall of the Omri Dynasty* (ed. L. L. Grabbe; LHBOTS 421; New York: T. & T. Clark, 2007), 145–83.

(3:7–9). The coalition of kings encounters a crisis along the way when they take a roundabout path through the wilderness, probably in order to gain the advantage of a surprise attack from an unexpected direction (3:9), in that the seven-day journey that this roundabout path involves exhausts the water supply of the three kings' troops, risking defeat before they even come within sight of Moab (3:10). Jehoshaphat, the king of Judah, suggests seeking an oracle from a prophet of Yahweh, and when it is noted that Elisha lives nearby, Jehoshaphat approves of consulting him (3:11–12). After some initial resistance, and with the aid of a musician, Elisha offers a positive oracle: the wadi will be miraculously filled with water, Yahweh will hand over Moab to the Israelite coalition, and they will "strike" (√נכה Hiphil) every fortified Moabite city and devastate the surrounding countryside (3:15–19). After the water miraculously appears as predicted, the Moabites are deceived by what appear to be vast pools of blood in the light of morning. This in turn leads the Moabites to assume that the Israelites, Judahites, and Edomites have slaughtered one another (3:20–23). As they rush out to take spoil from the supposed carnage, the Moabites are surprised by a counter-offensive. The Israelite coalition, as Elisha predicted, devastates the countryside and drives the Moabites back into the stronghold of Kir-hareseth, whereupon the slingers strike (√נכה Hiphil) the walls (3:24–25). After one final but unsuccessful defensive attack, the Moabite King Mesha, in an apparent act of desperation, sacrifices his firstborn son on the wall of Kir-hareseth as a burnt offering (עלה), which brings wrath (קצף) against/upon (על) the Israelites and prompts them to withdraw (3:26–27).

There is much that could be said about this fascinating narrative. Although the sacrifice of Mesha's firstborn son is obviously the most pertinent aspect of the narrative for our purposes, there are two important preliminary questions to be addressed. First, does the narrative intend to portray Elisha's prophecy as having gone unfulfilled? He predicted that the Israelite alliance would utterly defeat the Moabites, but in the end it is the Israelite coalition that retreated. Second, what does it mean that "wrath" (קצף) came against/upon Israel? Who is the subject and who or what is the object of this wrath? As will become clear below, these two issues cannot be treated independently from each other.

The problem of the unfulfilled prophecy could easily be solved by simply positing that 3:26–27 is secondary. If this is the case, the prophetic narrative originally ended after 3:25, with the Israelites victorious over the Moabites, having devastated their land. A contradictory historical tradition, however, may have presented Mesha as having survived the ordeal, so an epilogue was tacked on to resolve the discrepancy. This is the solution of Cogan and Tadmor, who argue that the editor took refuge in the ambiguous "wrath" to explain why events did not unfold as Elisha predicted.[5] This solution, however, requires assuming that our scribe suffered from a serious lack of rhetorical sophistication. Surely an editor could have instead simply ascribed some sin or other to the Israelites (so, e.g., Josh 7) or repentance to King Mesha (as in the case of Ahab; 1 Kgs 21:27–29) to explain the failure of the event to come to pass as Elisha predicted, instead of introducing an unexplained "wrath" that turns the tide of battle and expecting readers to accept this as a legitimate explanation for the failure of a prophecy. In short, viewing 3:26–27 as an editorial addition solves no problems but actually creates new ones. Even Cogan and Tadmor admit that the explanation "may have satisfied the ancient editor, but it has been an embarrassment to all his readers."[6]

If we assume that these verses were original to the narrative, then what precisely is this "wrath" and how does it serve to counteract Elisha's prophecy? Some take the wrath to be an emotion felt by the Israelites: upon seeing the human sacrifice, the Israelites either "became angry,"[7] "lost all heart,"[8] or had a "psychological breakdown."[9] This view assumes that the prophecy only failed because the Israelites failed to grasp the victory that Yahweh had given them; it was their outrage at seeing the gruesome act of human sacrifice that cost them the victory.[10] This solution is problematic, however, since the natural reaction to "wrath" (*pace* Montgomery, קֶצֶף certainly does not refer to "losing heart") is to fight all the harder, not to retreat. Furthermore, the phrase "a (great) wrath came upon" elsewhere in the Hebrew Bible is exclusively used of divine anger against human beings, which tilts the balance in favor of viewing the "wrath" here as divine, not human.[11] If then the "wrath"

5. Cogan and Tadmor, *II Kings*, 48–52.

6. Ibid., 52.

7. M. A. Sweeney, *I & II Kings: A Commentary* (OTL; Louisville: Westminster John Knox, 2007), 284.

8. J. A. Montgomery, *A Critical and Exegetical Commentary on the Books of Kings* (ed. H. S. Gehman; ICC; New York: Charles Scribner's Sons, 1951), 364.

9. B. Margalit, "Why King Mesha of Moab Sacrificed His Oldest Son," *BAR* 12:6 (1986): 63.

10. This is argued most explicitly by R. B. Chisholm Jr. "Israel's Retreat and the Failure of Prophecy in 2 Kings 3," *Bib* 92 (2011): 70–80. In a somewhat similar vein, J. Sprinkle, "Deuteronomic 'Just War' (Deut 20,10–20) and 1 Kings 2,27," *ZABR* 6 (2000): 285–301, suggests that Elisha's prophecy failed because Israel violated the rules of war as outlined in Deut 20:10–20. The narrative under discussion makes no mention of these rules, however, and introducing them here seems forced.

11. So R. G. Kratz, "Chemosh's Wrath and Yahweh's No: Ideas of Divine Wrath in Moab and Israel," in *Divine Wrath and Divine Mercy in the World of Antiquity* (ed. R. G. Kratz and

is something that goes out *against* Israel rather than something felt *by* them, it appears that Mesha's sacrifice called down a divine "wrath" that effectively countered the oracle of the prophet Elisha.

This is the interpretation of L.-S. Tiemeyer, who argues that the Mesha story represents one of several biblical narratives in which prophecy is counteracted by a more powerful ritual. Although the Israelite alliance was indeed promised certain victory against the Moabites, the power of King Mesha's drastic measures outweighed the power of Elisha's prophecy.[12] Tiemeyer especially points to the Mesopotamian *namburbi* rituals, which were designed to cancel undesired predictions.[13] Why would the sacrifice of a firstborn child be an appropriate and effective means of counteracting an oracle? Tiemeyer suggests that Mesha employed probably the "most powerful ritual act he [could] imagine."[14] It nonetheless remains surprising that Israelite scribes would compose and preserve a tale that tells of a foreign king counteracting an oracle of Yahweh via a human sacrifice, presumably to the Moabite god Chemosh (despite the fact that the divine recipient is conspicuously unnamed).[15] That the text reports this act without any expression of judgment concerning the act is all the more striking.

R. Westbrook situates the tale in the context of ancient suzerain-vassal relationships. Typically, vassals were bound to their suzerains via treaties that

H. Spieckermann; FAT 2 33; Tübingen: Mohr Siebeck, 2008), 107. See Num 1:53; 18:5; Josh 9:20; 22:20; Isa 34:2; Zech 1:15; Ezra 7:23 (Aramaic); 1 Chr 27:24; 2 Chr 19:2, 10; 24:18; 29:8; 32:25–26. In addition, in other syntactical constructions the noun קצף specifically refers to divine wrath in Num 17:11 [Eng. 16:46]; Deut 29:27; Isa 54:8; 60:10; Jer 21:5; 32:37; 50:13; Zech 1:2; 7:12; Ps 38:2 [Eng. 38:1]; 102:11 [Eng. 102:10]. Instances, on the other hand, in which human beings are depicted as the source of the noun קצף are rare, and all are late: Eccl 5:16 [Eng. 5:17]; Esth 1:18. Looking more broadly, it is true that humans often do appear as the subject of the cognate verb √קצף: the pharaoh (Gen 40:2; 41:10); Moses (Exod 16:20; Lev 10:16; Num 31:14); the princes of the Philistines (1 Sam 29:4); Naaman (2 Kgs 5:11); the man of God (2 Kgs 13:19); the Israelite people (Isa 8:21); the officials in Jerusalem (Jer 37:15); the king of Persia (Esth 1:12; Dan 2:12 [Aramaic]); and two Persian eunuchs (Esth 2:21). Nonetheless, the verb most often appears in the context of divine anger (Lev 10:6; Num 16:22; Deut 1:34; 9:7–8, 19, 22; Josh 22:18; Isa 47:6; 54:9; 57:17; 64:4, 8 [Eng 64:5, 9]; Zech 1:2, 15 (2×); 8:14; Ps 106:52; Lam 5:22; Eccl 5:15). Finally, the occurrence of the noun קצף in Hos 10:7 is probably not "wrath" but rather a homonym meaning "foam" (see C. Cohen, "Foam in Hosea 10:7," *JANES* 2 (1969): 25–29).

12. L.-S. Tiemeyer, "Prophecy as a Way of Cancelling Prophecy: The Strategic Uses of Foreknowledge," *ZAW* 117 (2005): 345–46.

13. Ibid., 333, 345–46.

14. Ibid., 346.

15. So also Levenson, *Death and Resurrection*, 15; and Tatlock, "How in Ancient Times," 202.

involved oaths to the gods of both parties.[16] In violating his treaty, Mesha was sinning against his own god, Chemosh. Mesha's sacrifice of his firstborn son served to assuage the anger (קצף) of Chemosh. Westbrook posits that the public nature of the sacrifice served to indicate to the Israelites that Mesha had repented of his treaty violation and desired to reestablish his relationship as Israel's vassal. When the Israelites refused to relent, despite Mesha's indication of his submission, Chemosh's wrath, formerly directed toward the Moabites, now turned toward the Israelites.[17] Although Westbrook's solution is speculative in some of its details, it is likely that Mesha's sacrifice was understood, among other things, to expiate whatever wrongdoing led to Moab's current predicament. Once Mesha demonstrated his contrition, Chemosh returned to fight on the side of the Moabites and drove off the Israelite coalition.

In the matter of unfulfilled prophecy, Westbrook elsewhere[18] has suggested that Elisha's prophecy was intentionally ambiguous and deceptive—that is, that Elisha never actually predicted that the Israelites would *win*. Westbrook notes that by using the word √נכה (Hiphil), which can mean "to destroy" but which also has the more basic meaning "to strike," Elisha let Jehoram believe that he would "destroy" (√נכה 3:19) all of the fortified cities of Moab. But the king was surprised to find that his slingers were ineffectually "striking" (√נכה) the walls of Kir-hareseth with stones (3:25). Thus, Elisha's prophecy was technically fulfilled, albeit contrary to the reasonable expectations of the Israelite coalition. Westbrook points to a similar tale preserved by Herodotus concerning King Croesus of Lydia. When Croesus consulted the oracle at Delphi about whether he should attack the Persians, the reply of the oracle was: "If he attacks the Persians, he will destroy a great empire" (ἢν στρατεύηται ἐπὶ Πέρσας, μεγάλην ἀρχὴν μιν καταλύσειν; *Hist.* 1.53). What the oracle said was literally true in that a great empire was destroyed—that of Croesus!—but this is obviously not how Croesus understood the oracle. Westbrook's suggestion is quite clever, but it does suffer from some difficul-

16. See, for instance, the long lists of deities, both Assyrian and Syro-Palestinian, in the Aramaic inscription Sefire 1 (*KAI* 222A:7–14), in the treaty between Aššur-nerari V of Assyria and Matiʾilu of Arpad (SAA 2 2.vi:6–26), and in the treaty between Esarhaddon of Assyria and Baal of Tyre (SAA 2 5.iv:1–19).

17. R. Westbrook, "Laws in Kings," in *The Books of Kings: Sources, Composition, Historiography and Reception* (ed. B. Halpern and A. Lemaire; Leiden: Brill, 2010), 464–66. Similarly, Tatlock suggests that the sacrifice was intended to atone for sins against Chemosh that had aroused his ire ("How in Ancient Times," 203).

18. R. Westbrook, "Elisha's True Prophecy in 2 Kings 3," *JBL* 124 (2005): 530–32. Similarly, I. W. Provan, *1 and 2 Kings* (NIBCOT; Peabody, MA: Hendrickson, 1995), 183–84.

ties. As Chisholm rightly notes, this reading has to ignore Elisha's claim in 3:18 that Yahweh would "give Moab into your hand" (ונתן את מואב בידכם). Although √נכה (Hiphil) might be ambiguous, this statement is certainly not.[19] Furthermore, although Westbrook's account solves the difficulty of Elisha's unfulfilled oracle, it provides no explanation for the necessity of Mesha's sacrifice. In the narrative, the immediate occasion for the Israelite retreat is the קצף, and the immediate occasion for the קצף is the sacrifice of Mesha's firstborn son. If the narrative hung only on a cleverly and ambiguously worded oracle, then neither of these events would be necessary for the development of the plot. Indeed, they would obfuscate the role of the allegedly ambiguous oracle in the first place. Why would Mesha need to sacrifice his son in order to invite the קצף that would drive back the Israelites if the Israelites were already fated only to "strike" but not to defeat the Moabites?

Despite these difficulties, however, it does seem clear that Mesha's sacrifice of his firstborn son was carried out in response to a dire situation in which he needed divine help. Just as importantly, the sacrifice is depicted as efficacious—that is, Mesha's sacrifice of his firstborn son is presented as an effective means of propitiating a deity. There is no indication in the narrative that the sacrifice was illegitimate or even surprising. At the very least, such sacrifices were within the conceptual realm of the communities among whom this tale circulated. The matter-of-fact way in which the sacrifice is reported, without a word of explanation or elaboration, also indicates that the ancient audience was acquainted with the possibility of sacrificing one's firstborn child in desperate circumstances and found it plausible that child sacrifices would persuade one's god(s) to intervene.

It is equally important for present purposes to observe that this particular firstborn sacrifice is a fundamentally different sort of sacrifice from the sacrifice of firstborn children as discussed in the previous chapter. Those sacrifices were general in nature: every firstborn was to be given to Yahweh, just as the firstlings of all cattle and flocks and the firstfruits of all produce rightfully belonged to him. To hand these over was not to make an extraordinary gift that might invite some special form of divine intervention. Instead, they were simply owed to Yahweh, and to withhold them was an act of theft. The benefit of giving Yahweh all firstborn/firstlings/firstfruits was the resulting general fecundity of land, animals, and humans (or at least a lack of divine intervention in the form of famine and bereavement). Mesha's sacrifice, on the other hand, was clearly exceptional, offered during a crisis.

19. Chisholm, "Israel's Retreat and the Failure of Prophecy," 75.

Indeed, even as a purely practical matter, Mesha's sacrifice of his firstborn son is entirely incompatible with a general sacrifice of firstborn children. If Mesha *had* sacrificed his son on the eighth day, as the Covenant Code's version of the law of the firstborn stipulates, then he could not very well have *also* sacrificed the child during the Israelite siege—barring, of course, the unlikely coincidence that the Israelite siege began precisely seven days after the birth of Mesha's firstborn son. Whether Mesha's sacrifice of his firstborn son was a ritual intended to counteract a negative oracle, a rite of atonement for his violation of his treaty with his Israelite suzerain, or some combination of the two, it remains fundamentally different from the sacrifice of firstborn children in compliance with Yahweh's claim to firstlings and firstfruits. The two rites are distinct conceptually and incompatible practically; one cannot be subsumed to the other, nor are they variations of a single ritual.

Is this a distinction between Israelite and Moabite religious practice? The fact that the Moabites may have sacrificed their firstborn children during times of distress does not necessarily mean that the Israelites did the same. Indeed, the "foreign" nature of child sacrifice is repeatedly alleged in the Hebrew Bible, especially in Deuteronomistic material (see Deut 12:31; 18:9–11; 2 Kgs 16:3; as well as Ps 106:28; on all of these, see the following chapter), and one cannot rule out the possibility that some truth might lie behind these polemics. Could Mesha's sacrifice be a rare glimpse at alleged "foreign" child sacrifices? This is of course possible, but there are reasons to suspect that Moabite and Israelite religion were rather similar in many regards, and although we must be careful not to go too far in leveling the religious practices of Iron Age Syria-Palestine, there are several reasons to suspect that Mesha's sacrifice would not have been out of place in Israelite practice.

First, the Mesha Stele (*KAI* 181), the best extant source of information about Moabite religion during the Iron Age, provides substantial evidence that Israelite and Moabite religion, although not identical, shared much in common. This inscription records Mesha's victory over an Israelite successor to King Omri, who had previously subjugated the Moabites (181:4–9). Mesha attributes the Moabites' deliverance (√*yšʿ* C-stem; 181:4) to Chemosh, the god of the Moabites, in the same way that the Hebrew Bible frequently attributes Israelite victories over their enemies to the "deliverance" (√ישע Hiphil) of Yahweh.[20] Mesha also indicates that he built Chemosh a "high place" (*bmt*; 181:3, 27), parallel to the shrines (במות) commonly built in

20. See, e.g., Deut 20:4; Judg 3:9; 6:36–37; 7:7; 1 Sam 14:23, 39; 2 Kgs 14:27; 19:34; Isa 25:9; 33:22; 35:4; 37:35; 43:12; 49:25; 63:9; Jer 31:7; Ezek 34:22; Hos 1:7; Hab 1:2; Zeph 3:17, 19; Zech 8:7, 13; 9:16; 10:6; 12:7; Ps 28:9; 69:36 [Eng. 69:35]; 106:8 118:25; 2 Chr 20:9.

both Israel and Judah[21] (despite the frequent condemnation of these sites by some of the biblical writers, especially the Deuteronomists). Likewise, upon his victory over the Israelites, Mesha records that he "ritually devoted" (√*ḥrm* C-stem; 181:17) his captives to Ashtar-Chemosh, just as the Bible describes the Israelites devoting spoils of war to Yahweh.[22]

Of course, we should be careful not to assume that because there are some clear similarities between Israelite and Moabite religious practice we can claim that any religious practice attributed to the Moabites also had its counterpart in Israel. Furthermore, it is not entirely clear that Mesha's sacrifice of his firstborn son represents authentic Moabite practice rather than the projection of Israelite beliefs and practices onto a Moabite person in an Israelite tale. Nonetheless, the similarities are striking, and it seems appropriate tentatively to take this report of Moabite firstborn sacrifice as circumstantial evidence that a parallel Israelite rite existed. Additionally, there is at least one instance in the Hebrew Bible that appears to support the idea that some Israelites themselves considered firstborn children to be appropriate offerings during periods of distress. The text in question is the oft-cited and much disputed Micah 6:1–8, which presents an Israelite audience as wondering whether Yahweh would listen if they were to go to the extreme of offering up their firstborn children.

Firstborn Offerings in Micah 6:1–8

The oracle contained in Mic 6:1–8 begins with the prophet's announcment of a dispute (ריב) between Yahweh and Israel (6:1–2):[23]

21. See, e.g., 1 Sam 9:12–13; 1 Kgs 3:2–4; 2 Kgs 12:3; 14:4; 15:4; 23:15; 1 Chr 16:39; 21:29; 2 Chr 1:3, 13.

22. See, e.g., Num 21:2; Deut 2:34; 3:6; 7:2; 20:17; Josh 6:21; 8:26; 10:28, 35, 37, 39, 40; 11:11, 12, 20, 21; 1 Sam 15:3, 8, 9, 15, 18, 20.

23. The literature on the nature of the ריב genre employed by several prophets is extensive, although the existence and scope of the genre itself is disputed. Important studies on the topic include C. Westermann, *Basic Forms of Prophetic Speech* (trans. H. C. White; Philadelphia: Westminster, 1967), 199–200; J. Limburg, "The Root ריב and the Prophetic Lawsuit Speeches," *JBL* 88 (1969): 291–304; G. W. Ramsey, "Speech-forms in Hebrew Law and Prophetic Oracles," *JBL* 96 (1977): 45–58; K. Nielsen, *Yahweh as Prosecutor and Judge: An Investigation of the Prophetic Lawsuit (Rîb-Pattern)* (JSOTSup 9; Sheffield: JSOT Press, 1978); M. de Roche, "Yahweh's *Rîb* against Israel: A Reassessment of the So-Called "Prophetic Lawsuit" in the Preexilic Prophets," *JBL* 102 (1983): 563–74; D. R. Daniels, "Is There a 'Prophetic Lawsuit' Genre?" *ZAW* 99 (1987): 339–60; T. M. Milinovich, "Form Criticism and the *rîb* in Isaiah 41,21–42,4," *BN* 136 (2008): 45–57. In the case of Micah 6, it is helpful that, however extensive this genre might be in the biblical prophetic corpus as a whole, this oracle identifies itself as a ריב three times at its outset (Mic 6:1–2).

Hear Yahweh speaking,	שמעו נא את יהוה אמר
"Arise, dispute with the mountains,	קום ריב את ההרים
and let the hills hear your voice."	ותשמענה הגבעות קולך
Hear, mountains, the dispute of Yahweh,	שמעו הרים את ריב יהוה
strong foundations of the earth.	והאתנים מסדי ארץ
For Yahweh has a dispute with his people,	כי ריב ליהוה עם עמו
and with Israel he will argue.	ועם ישראל יתוכח

Then the oracle shifts, with Yahweh speaking in the first person and asking what he has failed to do for the Israelites during the history of their existence as a people (6:3–5):

My people, what did I do to you?	עמי מה עשיתי לך
And how have I wearied you? Answer me!	ומה הלאתיך ענה בי
For I brought you up from the land of Egypt;	כי העלתיך מארץ מצרים
and from a house of slaves I ransomed you.	ומבית עבדים פדיתיך
I sent before you Moses, Aaron, and Miriam.	ואשלח לפניך את משה אהרן ומרים
My people, remember what Balak, king of Moab, plotted,	עמי זכר נא מה יעץ בלק מלך מואב
and how Balaam, son of Beor, answered him,	ומה ענה אתו בלעם בן בעור
from Shittim to Gilgal,	מן השטים עד הגלגל
in order to know the justice of Yahweh.	למען דעת צדקות יהוה

Next, with another shift in speaker, the Israelites themselves reply, asking what they must do to get Yahweh to act in the present (6:6–7):

With what should I approach Yahweh	במה אקדם יהוה
and bow to the exalted God?	אכף לאלהי מרום
Will I approach him with burnt offerings,	האקדמנו בעולות
with one-year-old calves?	בעגלים בני שנה
Will Yahweh be pleased with thousands of rams	הירצה יהוה באלפי אילים
or with tens of thousands of rivers of oil?	ברבבות נחלי שמן
Will I give my firstborn for my transgression,	האתן בכורי פשעי
the fruit of my belly for the sin of my self?[24]	פרי בטני חטאת נפשי

24. נפשי, originally and most literally "my throat," parallel to בטני "my belly," earlier in the line. Unfortunately, the pun does not translate well into English.

Finally, the oracle shifts back to where it began, with the prophet speaking on Yahweh's behalf (6:8):

He has told you, human, what is good	הגיד לך אדם מה טוב
and what Yahweh seeks from you:	ומה יהוה דורש ממך
only doing justice	כי אם עשות משפט
and loving faithfulness	ואהבת חסד
and humbly walking with your God.	והצנע לכת עם אלהיך

While this conclusion makes clear that Yahweh does not desire any of the offerings listed, the fact that the supplicant assumes that Yahweh would be induced to act by means of a human sacrifice, "my firstborn" or "the fruit of my belly," is striking. That is, Micah implies that his listeners believed that Yahweh could potentially be persuaded to act by the sacrifice of a firstborn child. Complicating matters, however, are two major objections to understanding the passage as referring to firstborn sacrifice as a legitimate Yahwistic rite.

The first is that the people's ostensible question concerning whether Yahweh would be pleased with the sacrifice of one's child is answered with an unambiguous "no": Yahweh replies that he does *not* desire a firstborn son. How could one infer that Yahweh desired child sacrifice based on a text that explicitly states that he does not? This objection is less difficult than it might at first appear, however, since Yahweh also states that he does not desire calves or oil, and other biblical texts make it abundantly clear that (at least some) Yahwists perceived these as perfectly acceptable, even mandatory, offerings to Yahweh. The more pertinent question, then, is whether one can infer from this oracle that, just as Yahweh was perceived as enjoying sacrifices of calves,[25] rams,[26] and oil,[27] he was also sometimes understood as being pleased with the offering of a firstborn child.

Many scholars reject this conclusion. J. L. Mays argues: "The proposal is not drawn from the recognized range of possibilities in the cult of Israel. It is rather a function of the escalation of the list and reaches beyond the options available in Israel's cult to exhaust the total cultic enterprise by citing

25. Lev 9:1–8.

26. Gen 22:13; Exod 29:15–32; Lev 5:15–18, 25 [Eng. 6:6]; 8:2, 18–29; 9:2–4, 18–19; 16:3–5; 19:21–22; 23:18; Num 6:14–19; 7:15–88; 15:6; 23:1–4, 14, 29–30; 28:19–20, 27–28; 29:1–37; Isa 60:7; Ezek 43:23–25; 45:23–24; 46:4–7, 11; Ps 66:15; Job 42:8; Ezra 8:35; 10:19; 1 Chr 15:26; 29:21; 2 Chr 13:9; 17:11; 29:21–22, 32.

27. Gen 35:14; Lev 2:1–9; 6:14; 7:12; 9:4; 14:10–12, 21–24; 23:13; Num 6:15; 7:13, 19, 25, 31, 37, 43, 49, 55, 61, 67, 73, 79; 8:8; 15:6, 9; 28:5, 9, 12–13, 20, 28; 29:3, 9, 14; Ezek 45:24–25; 46:5, 7, 11, 14–15.

its most desperate measure."[28] Likewise, H. W. Wolff claims that "the teacher exaggerates in the extreme by pushing his examples of boundless sacrifices toward what is plainly frivolous. He portrays the sheer despair of the intention to give oneself fully to acts of propitiation; going beyond all legal possibilities provided by the Yahwistic cult, he offers to *sacrifice his firstborn*" [italics in the original].[29] It is important to observe that both Mays and Wolff assume (1) that there was an established "range" of "legal possibilities" characteristic of Yahwism in Iron Age Israel and Judah and (2) that this alleged range excluded child sacrifice. Furthermore, both seem to assume that the "legal possibilities" that constituted the (apparently monolithic) "Yahwistic cult" are essentially circumscribed by the writings contained in the Hebrew Bible.

The Hebrew Bible, however, certainly does not encompass the full range of cultic activity that was viewed as legitimate in ancient Israel. Indeed, the Hebrew Bible itself is full of condemnations of religious practices carried out by Yahwists, even some Yahwists at the temple itself, and it is hard to imagine a more "legitimate" (whatever one means by that) version of Yahwism than the one endorsed by the functionaries at the Jerusalem temple. Indeed, much of the Deuteronomistic History and several of the prophetic books are primarily devoted to the fact that the standard Jerusalem cult did not conform to their idea of legitimate Yahwistic practice. This fact should warn us against basing one's reconstruction of actual (in contrast to biblically ideal) Israelite religious practice on the "legal possibilities" presented in the Hebrew Bible. That is, even if the texts of Hebrew Bible do absolutely and unanimously reject child sacrifice (a dubious claim to begin with, given Exod 22:28b–29), they would still provide little evidence that all, or even most, Israelite Yahwists agreed.

Furthermore, there is no indication in the text of Mic 6:1–8 that firstborn sacrifice was understood as qualitatively different from the sacrifice of calves, rams, or oil. Indeed, the logic of the oracle seems to proceed from sacrifices that would have been perceived as acceptable (burnt offerings and calves) to those that would have been viewed as even more effective (thousands of rams and myriads of oil), finally culminating in the most precious of all possible sacrifices—the offering of a firstborn child. The rhetoric of the oracle demands that Yahweh be understood as viewing such a sacrifice as not only pleasing but as even more pleasing than untold quantities of other, less pre-

28. J. L. Mays, *Micah: A Commentary* (OTL; Philadelphia: Westminster, 1990), 140.
29. H. W. Wolff, *Micah: A Commentary* (trans. G. Stansell; CC; Minneapolis: Augsburg, 1990), 178–79.

cious offerings. The sacrifice of one's firstborn child is depicted as extraordinary, but there is no indication that the oracle is presenting the sacrifice as in any way intrinsically unsuitable. Thus, the context of the oracle implies that all of the offerings are extremely valuable and, at least in theory, acceptable,[30] even if current circumstances had caused Yahweh to reject *all* sacrifices as ineffective.

A second potential objection to using Micah 6:1–8 as a source of information about child sacrifice specifically among Iron Age Yahwists is that the oracle's date of composition has been debated. Setting aside the wide diversity of proposals concerning the unity of the various oracles contained in the present book of Micah and the variety of dates that have been assigned to each of them,[31] the date of 6:1–8 is our only important consideration. H. Ewald, whose research on the composition of the book of Micah has set the tone for discussion on the topic ever since, dates the oracle to the seventh century BCE, to the time of Manasseh, some time later than a "historical Micah" would have lived but still prior to the exile.[32] Wolff, on the other hand, dates our oracle along with the rest of 6:2–7:7 to the postexilic period on the basis of the presence of what he perceives to be Deuteronomic and Deuteronomistic language and themes.[33] Mays divides the oracle into four sections: an introduction (6:1a); a call for Yahweh's "*rîb*-saying" (6:1b); a Deuteronomic address to "an Israel that is weary with YHWH's way" (6:2–5); and a look back "on the prophetic insistence on justice and loyalty as a revelation which has long since settled the question of what Yahweh requires" (6:6–8). Mays dates these various sections from the late-preexilic/exilic period to the postexilic period.[34] W. McKane likewise views chapters 6–7 as exilic or postexilic additions to the book, intended to provide reassurance that the community

30. So also Mosca, "Child Sacrifice," 225; D. R. Hillers, *Micah: A Commentary on the Book of the Prophet Micah* (ed. P. D. Hanson; Hermeneia; Philadelphia: Fortress, 1984), 78–79; F. I. Andersen and D. N. Freedman, *Micah: A New Translation with Introduction and Commentary* (AB 24E; New York: Doubleday, 2000), 538; Levenson, *Death and Resurrection*, 10–11; Stavrakopoulou, *King Manasseh and Child Sacrifice*, 189–91; and *pace* the notable objection of de Vaux (*Studies in Old Testament Sacrifice*, 68–69), who argues that the suggestion is to be understood as an "impossible" offering.

31. For a convenient overview of various opinions on these matters, see M. R. Jacobs, *The Conceptual Coherence of the Book of Micah* (JSOTSup 322; Sheffield: Sheffield Academic, 2001), 14–45.

32. H. Ewald, *Die Propheten des Alten Bundes* (2nd ed.; Göttingen: Vandenhoeck & Ruprecht, 1867), 525–27.

33. Wolff, *Micah*, 22–24, 171–72.

34. Mays, *Micah*, 30–31.

is "not marooned, doomed to stagnation, and they have a future into which [Yahweh] will lead them and a destination that they will reach."[35]

On the other hand, D. R. Hillers notes that the exile is not the only historical setting during which the Israelites might have needed reassurance. He sees the oracles of doom followed by a series of oracles of hope as reflecting a "millennial protest" that calls for a "revitalization" and reflects "a deliberate, organized, conscious effort by members of a society to construct a more satisfying culture." He further argues that the fall of the Northern Kingdom during the late eighth century BCE created a socioeconomic situation ripe for such millenarianism and sees no reason to divide the book into disparate pieces (other than a few editorial additions) and to date them to diverse periods. Instead, he views the book as essentially a unified whole.[36] Likewise, although Andersen and Freedman are generally cautious about assigning specific dates to the various oracles in Micah, they confidently assign 6:1–8 to the reign of Ahaz, albeit largely due to the fact that he was the king who "revived human sacrifice" (2 Kgs 16:2–3), and it is to this revival that they believe 6:7 alludes.[37]

Without weighing in on any particular theory of composition here, I believe that a preexilic date for this particular oracle is more plausible than an exilic or postexilic context. The two primary internal arguments for a postexilic date presented by Wolff are the "juxtaposition of the critique of the cult (indirect in Mic. 6:6f.) with the requirement of obedience (v. 8)," which is "one of the particular characteristics of Deuteronomistic interpretation of the prophets," and the mention of Miriam alongside Moses and Aaron (6:4), a trio that otherwise only appears together in relatively late texts (1 Chr 5:29; Num 12; 26:59).[38] The "critique of the cult" here, however, is rather qualified and "indirect" indeed. There is no indication that the cult itself is the object of criticism. Instead, cultic offerings are simply described as not the means of convincing Yahweh to act under current circumstances. The neglect of justice and faithfulness have rendered sacrifices ineffective, but there is no indication in the oracle that sacrifices are generally undesirable. With regard to Moses, Miriam, and Aaron appearing together, as Andersen and Freedman point out, the only Pentateuchal narrative in which all three appear is one in which the three are in conflict. Micah, however, portrays the three characters

35. W. McKane, *The Book of Micah: Introduction and Commentary* (ICC; Edinburgh: T. & T. Clark, 1998), 14–15.

36. Hillers, *Micah*, 4–8.

37. Andersen and Freedman, *Micah*, 530–32.

38. Wolff, *Micah*, 170–72.

as co-leaders of the people during the exodus, which is at odds with anything presented elsewhere in the Hebrew Bible, either early or late.[39] It would be naïve, however, to think that all of the stories about the three figures have been preserved in the biblical exodus narrative, and it is possible that Micah is drawing on a no-longer-preserved tradition that diverges somewhat from the canonical version of the story. Because no such tradition is extant, it is impossible to use it as an anchor for dating the oracle. Furthermore, Mays's contention that the passage probably dates to a late period because it uses Deuteronomistic vocabulary (e.g., 6:4, "ransom" [√פדה; see Deut 7:8; 9:26; 13:6; 15:15; 21:8; 24:18; 2 Sam 7:23] and "house of slaves" [בית עבדים] as an epithet of Egypt [see Deut 6:12; 8:14; 13:11])[40] is suggestive but not definitive. Although Hillers acknowledges that these terms could point to a late date, he suggests they could just as easily "indicate the influence of an early form of Deuteronomy or a source of Deuteronomy."[41] Indeed, it may even be that the influence went the other way and that Micah's vocabulary influenced Deuteronomy's.

Examination of the content of the oracle itself might assist us in positing a date for the oracle. The oracle's claim that Yahweh does not desire offerings but ethical behavior has close parallels with oracles found in other collections attributed to eighth-century prophets. For instance, Isa 1:10–17; Hos 6:6; 8:13; and Amos 4:1–5; 5:21–24 all contain a rejection of cultic acts and call instead for ethical behavior. Admittedly, the same theme continues to appear in later material,[42] but it is not at all exclusive to late texts. Thus,

39. Andersen and Freedman, *Micah*, 519.

40. Mays, *Micah*, 130.

41. Hillers, *Micah*, 79.

42. See Isa 43:24; 66:3; Jer 6:19–20; 7:8–10, 21–23; Ezek 20:39; Zech 7:5–14; Mal 1:10–13; 2:13–14; as well outside the prophetic corpus in 1 Sam 15:22; Ps 40:7–9 [Eng. 40:6–8]; 50:7–23; 51:18–19 [Eng. 51:16–17]; Prov 15:8, 29; 21:3, 27; 28:9; Eccl 4:17. There has been much recent work on prophetic critique of the cult, including A. B. Ernst, *Weisheitliche Kultkritik: zu Theologie und Ethik des Sprüchbuchs und der Prophetie des 8. Jahrhunderts* (Biblisch-Theologische Studien 23; Neukirchen-Vluyn: Neukirchener Verlag, 1994); R. S. Hendel, "Prophets, Priests, and the Efficacy of Ritual," in *Pomegranates & Golden Bells: Studies in Biblical, Jewish, and Near Eastern Ritual, Law, and Literature in Honor of Jacob Milgrom* (ed. D. P. Wright, D. N. Freedman, and A. Hurvitz; Winona Lake, IN: Eisenbrauns, 1995), 185–98; M. Weiss, "Concerning Amos' Repudiation of the Cult," in *Pomegranates & Golden Bells: Studies in Biblical, Jewish, and Near Eastern Ritual, Law, and Literature in Honor of Jacob Milgrom* (ed. D. P. Wright, D. N. Freedman, and A. Hurvitz; Winona Lake, IN: Eisenbrauns, 1995), 199–214; J. Barton, "The Prophets and the Cult," in *Temple and Worship in Biblical Israel* (ed. J. Day; LHBOTS 422; New York: T. & T. Clark, 2005), 111–22; T. Krüger, "Erwägungen zur prophetischen Kultkritik," in *Die unwiderstehliche Wahrheit: Studien zur alttestamentlichen Prophetie* (ed. R. Lux and E.-J. Waschke;

even if one were inclined to date the oracle on the basis of its message and rhetoric (already a precarious undertaking[43]), one could argue either that it fits in nicely with other oracles ascribed to eighth-century prophets such as Amos, Hosea, and Isaiah, or one could suggest that it merely participates in a long tradition of prophetic critique of cultic activity absent ethical rectitude. Thus, a preexilic date for the oracle is entirely possible on the basis of the its message and rhetoric, although this early date is admittedly not required on this basis.

Perhaps the greatest objection to dating Mic 6:1–8 to a late period, however, is the very mention of child sacrifice in an apparently positive, or at the very least ambivalent, context. As will be observed below in chapter 5, from the late monarchic period onward, child sacrifice is vociferously condemned by every biblical writer who addresses the issue. Given such vehement opposition to the practice during later periods, it seems unlikely that a postexilic redactor would compose an oracle that implies that Yahweh could be pleased with child sacrifice, even if only in extraordinary cases. Indeed, probably the only reasons that this oracle was preserved were the general tendency not to delete oracles perceived to be divinely inspired[44] and the fact that the reference to child sacrifice is ambiguous enough that the reader can assume that Yahweh did not accept child sacrifice under any circumstances. In any case, it seems unlikely that a postexilic scribe would compose an oracle that presents child sacrifice in a potentially positive way, although the preservation of an older oracle of this sort is understandable.

Arbeiten zur Bibel und ihrer Geschichte 23; Leipzig: Evangelische Verlagsanstalt, 2006), 37–55; J. Klawans, "Rethinking the Prophetic Critique," in *Purity, Sacrifice, and the Temple* (New York: Oxford University Press, 2006), 75–100; R. Hendel, "Away from Ritual: The Prophetic Critique," in *Social Theory and the Study of Israelite Religion: Essays in Retrospect and Prospect* (ed. S. Olyan; RBS 71; Atlanta: Society of Biblical Literature, 2012), 59–70; T. V. Lafferty, *The Prophetic Critique of the Priority of the Cult: A Study of Amos 5:21–24 and Isaiah 1:10–17* (Eugene, OR: Pickwick, 2012); and P. N. de Andrado, "*Ḥesed* and Sacrifice: The Prophetic Critique in Hosea," CBQ 78 (2016): 47–67.

43. See the perceptive essay by B. J. Sommer, "Dating Pentateuchal Texts and the Perils of Pseudo-Historicism," in *The Pentateuch: International Perspectives on Current Research* (ed. T. B. Dozeman, K. Schmid, and B. J. Schwartz; FAT 78; Tübingen: Mohr Siebeck, 2011), 85–108. Particularly astute is his observation that trying to date Henry David Thoreau's "Civil Disobedience" on such criteria could easily place it contemporaneous with Gandhi or Martin Luther King, rather than correctly identifying it as an earlier composition that served as a source of inspiration for their words and actions.

44. Observe, for instance, the fact that unfulfilled prophecies, such as the claim that Nebuchadnezzar would conquer Tyre (Ezek 26:7–14) or Egypt (Ezek 29:8–15; Jer 43:8–13), continued to be preserved and transmitted, despite the fact that their lack of fulfillment must have been at least a bit embarrassing.

Thus, the weight of the evidence is that Mic 6:1–8 reflects a preexilic practice of sacrificing firstborn children in particularly dire circumstances. This sacrifice would be essentially the same sort of offering as Mesha's sacrifice discussed above. Both sacrifices are presented as offered during times of distress, and in each case the sacrifice of a firstborn child appears to have been perceived as a particularly valuable, and presumably particularly effective, offering. The sacrifice of a firstborn child in each case is an act of sheer desperation, when all other avenues of appeal have been exhausted. Mesha only offered his firstborn son once his last line of defense had proved ineffective (2 Kgs 3:26–27), and Micah's oracle includes the possibility of firstborn sacrifice at the end of the text's list of extravagant offerings.

One final observation: as in the case of Mesha's offering, the type of firstborn sacrifice described in Micah's oracle cannot be the same type of firstborn sacrifice described in Exod 22:28b–29. In the Exodus text, the assumption is that firstborn children are *all* due to Yahweh and that they are due to him simply by virtue of their being firstborn children. In the case of Mesha and Micah, however, firstborn children are presented as precious, extravagant sacrifices, worth more than "rivers of oil" and only offered in the direst of circumstances. Furthermore, the general law of firstborn sacrifice was linked to the fecundity and prosperity of one's harvest, herds, and family. The sacrifices of both Mesha and Micah, on the other hand, are offered in situations of distress requiring extraordinary divine intervention. Thus, although some have sought to connect the two,[45] the only characteristic shared by these two types of offerings is that both involved the sacrifice of firstborn children. The function, purpose, and conception of the two types of firstborn sacrifices were entirely different. Tatlock rightly observes that "firstborn animals were not sacrificed for a single purpose. This is also the case with the slaying of firstborn children as burnt-sacrifices."[46] One can no more conflate the firstborn sacrifice of Exod 22:28b–29 with the sacrifices of Micah and Mesha than one can conflate the sacrifice of the year-old male Passover lamb (Exod 12:5) with the sacrifice of a year-old male lamb offered when a Nazirite inadvertently came in contact with a corpse (Num 6:9–12) simply because the

45. See, e.g., Levenson, *Death and Resurrection*, 10–11; Z. Zevit, *The Religions of Ancient Israel: A Synthesis of Parallactic Approaches* (New York: Continuum, 2001), 578–79; Stavrakopoulou, *King Manasseh and Child Sacrifice*, 190–91.

46. J. Tatlock, "The Place of Human Sacrifice in the Israelite Cult," in *Ritual and Metaphor: Sacrifice in the Bible* (ed. C. A. Eberhart; RBS 68; Atlanta: Society of Biblical Literature, 2011), 36. Elsewhere, Tatlock stresses the connection between sacrificing firstborn children and atoning for sin in both the Mesha narrative and the Micah oracle ("How in Ancient Times," 222–23, 228–29).

same type of victim was offered in both instances. Indeed, if any subset of Israelite Yahwists did engage in a general sacrifice of firstborn children, it would have been among the most common forms of child sacrifice that they practiced. Alternatively, among those who only offered firstborn children during desperate circumstances, these extraordinary sacrifices by definition would have been exceedingly rare. Thus, these two different forms of firstborn sacrifice vary with regard to intended function, presumed frequency, and timing (eighth day versus when an emergency should arise) and cannot be viewed as identical.

Jephthah

Another case, and a particularly difficult one to assess, is the story of Jephthah's sacrifice of his daughter recounted in Judges 11. The story is set in premonarchic Gilead at a time when the Israelites are said to have been oppressed by the Ammonites. The Israelites were looking for someone to deliver them from this situation and to rule over them afterward (Judg 10:17–18). Jephthah had been born to Gilead (apparently the name both of his father and of his homeland[47]) by a prostitute. He was driven away from his father's estate by his brothers, the legitimate sons of their father's wife (Judg 11:2). Making the best of a bad situation, Jephthah rallied a band of warriors around him and led them on raiding expeditions (11:3). Thanks to the military prowess that he exhibited during his career as a marauder, the elders of Gilead called on Jephthah to deliver them from the Ammonites, an offer Jephthah accepted on the condition that he be made their chief should he successfully defeat the Ammonites—a condition that the elders of Gilead accepted (11:5–10). After an unsuccessful round of negotiations between Jephthah and the king of the Ammonites, negotiations centering on disputes concerning historical acts of aggression between the Israelites and the Ammonites and on which party bore the blame for these hostilities (11:11–28), Jephthah prepared for battle. Before commencing the fight, Jephthah made his fatal vow:

> אם נתון תתן את בני עמון בידי והיה היוצא אשר יצא מדלתי ביתי לקראתי
> בשובי בשלום מבני עמון והיה ליהוה והעליתהו עולה

47. Or, perhaps, "so uncertain was Jephthah's lineage that only the personified district of Gilead could qualify as his sire," P. Trible, *Texts of Terror: Literary-Feminist Readings of Biblical Narratives* (Philadelphia: Fortress, 1984), 94; following C. F. Burney, *The Book of Judges* (London: Rivingtons, 1918), 308; and R. G. Boling, *Judges: Introduction, Translation, and Commentary* (AB 6; Garden City, NY: Doubleday, 1975), 197.

> If you will give the Ammonites into my hand, then that which comes out from the doors of my house to meet me when I return in peace from the Ammonites will be Yahweh's. I will sacrifice it as a burnt offering. (Judg 11:30b–31)

After Jepthah's convincing victory (11:32–33), upon returning home, the first person to greet him is his daughter, tragically described:

> ורק היא יחידה אין לו ממנו בן או בת
>
> She was his one and only child. He did not have a son or daughter apart from her. (Judg 11:34c)

Jephthah, realizing the rashness and irrevocability of his oath, tore his clothes in grief, but his daughter stoically advised him that his vow must be fulfilled, only asking for two months to go into the hills so that "she may weep over her youth"[48] (תבך על בתוליה). After the allotted time, she returned to her father, who fulfilled his vow to sacrifice her (11:35–39). The narrative concludes with a notice that she had never known a man sexually and an etiology for an otherwise unknown custom in which the daughters of Israel weep for the daughter of Jephthah for four days each year (11:39–40).[49]

Much could be, and has been, said about this brief but fascinating tale.[50] For the purposes of the present examination, however, it is Jephthah's vow and sacrifice, and especially what can be gleaned from them concerning the

---

48. בתולים, *pace* BDB and *HALOT*, does not necessarily mean "virginity," or at least not unambiguously so. See Joel 1:8, where a בתולה is said to mourn her "husband" (בעל) and the discussions in G. J. Wenham, "Betûlāh 'A Girl of Marriageable Age,'" *VT* 22 (1972): 326–48; M. Tsevat, בְּתוּלָה *bᵉthûlāh*; בְּתוּלִים *bᵉthûlîm*, *TDOT* 2, 338–43; and P. L. Day, "From the Child Is Born the Woman: The Story of Jephthah's Daughter," in *Gender and Difference in Ancient Israel* (ed. P. L. Day; Minneapolis: Fortress, 1989), 59–60. As Day concludes, "it refers to a particular stage in the female life cycle and, like the word 'adolescence,' is best understood as a social recognition of puberty. More precisely [Day] would define a *bĕtûlâ* as a female who had reached puberty and was therefore potentially fertile, but who had not yet given birth to her first child." In several of its attestations, however, it does seem to have at least an implication of virginity (see Gen 24:16; Lev 21:3, 14; 21:12; 2 Sam 13:18–19). Nonetheless, I prefer to err on the side of caution and translate the word "youth."

49. On the possible nature of this festival, see Day ("From the Child Is Born the Woman," 58–74) who, drawing on the Classical parallels of Iphigenia and Kore/Persephone, suggests that it represented a rite of passage for young Israelite women.

50. See especially the careful and seminal reading of Trible, *Texts of Terror*, 93–116; and the detailed examination of the tale in J. Sasson, *Judges 1–12*: A New Translation with Introduction and Commentary (AYB 6D; New Haven: Yale University Press, 2014), 416–58.

historical reality of such sacrifices, that are most pertinent. The first question has to do with what, precisely, Jephthah is depicted as promising in his vow. Is the audience to conclude that Jephthah intended to promise to sacrifice a human being to Yahweh if his campaign against the Ammonites proved successful? Although creative, and sometimes ingenious, arguments have been put forward claiming that he did not—for example, the suggestion that Jephthah was envisioning an animal coming out to meet him rather than a human[51] or that Jephthah intended (and then carried out) a "figurative" human offering via a dedication to celibacy[52]—nearly all agree that the most natural reading of the narrative is that Jephthah in fact vowed to sacrifice the first thing coming out to meet him, that he knew it was possible or even probable that this would be a human being, and that Jephthah literally sacrificed his daughter as a result.[53] This near consensus is unsurprising, since it is difficult to understand "I will offer up a burnt offering" (והעליתהו עולה) as meaning anything other than sacrifice.

---

51. This possibility is entertained by Boling, *Judges*, 208; and argued by Y. Kaufmann, *The Book of Judges* (Jerusalem: Kiryat Sepher, 1968), 226 [Hebrew]. For a summary of Kaufmann's arguments in English, see D. Marcus, *Jephthah and His Vow* (Lubbock, TX: Texas Tech Press, 1986), 16. N. Steinberg, on the other hand, suggests that Jephthah may have hoped that one of his daughter's companions (Judg 11:37–38) would be the first to greet him ("The Problem of Human Sacrifice in War: An Analysis of Judges 11," in *On the Way to Nineveh: Studies in Honor of George M. Landes* [ed. S. L. Cook and S. C. Winter; ASOR Books 4; Atlanta: Scholars Press, 1999], 125).

52. So, tentatively, Marcus, *Jephthah and His Vow*, esp. 50–52, who helpfully collects and lays out the arguments both in favor of and against understanding Jephthah's vow as involving a literal sacrifice, and similarly, P. T. Reis, *Reading the Lines: A Fresh Look at the Hebrew Bible* (Peabody, MA: Hendrickson, 2002), 105–30. Reis argues, via a highly synchronic reading of the Hebrew Bible, that Jephthah would have known the stipulations for redeeming vowed human beings in Lev 27:1–8 as well as the many biblical laws against murder in general and human sacrifice in particular. Thus, according to Reis, Jephthah would have assumed all these regulations when making his vow, and for this reason the vow must be understood in that context. Reis argues that just as a monetarily redeemed animal was forbidden to be worked (Lev 27:9–10), so also a redeemed woman would not have been allowed to bear children. Thus, Reis concludes, Jephthah's vow was a promise to dedicate her to celibacy.

53. So, e.g., J. A. Soggin, *Judges: A Commentary* (OTL; Philadelphia: Westminster, 1981), 215; Levenson, *Death and Resurrection*, 14; Day, *Molech*, 69; S. Ackerman, *Under Every Green Tree*, 129; Stavrakopoulou, *King Manasseh and Child Sacrifice*, 194; Tatlock, "How in Ancient Times," 187–95; idem, "Place of Human Sacrifice," 35–37; A. Lange, "They Burn their Sons and Daughters—That Was No Command of Mine (Jer 7:31): Child Sacrifice in the Hebrew Bible and in the Deuteronomic Jeremiah Redaction," in *Human Sacrifice in the Jewish and Christian Tradition* (ed. K. Finsterbusch, A. Lange, and K. F. D. Römheld; SHR 112; Leiden: Brill, 2007), 118–19; S. Niditch, *Judges: A Commentary* (OTL; Louisville: Westminister John Knox, 2008), 133–35; Smith, "Child Sacrifice," 12–17; T. C. Butler, *Judges* (WBC 8; Nashville: Nelson, 2008), 290–93; Sasson, *Judges 1–12*, 444–51, 457–58.

Thus, accepting the conclusion that an actual human sacrifice is described in Judg 11, is it possible to argue that it is yet another example of firstborn sacrifice during a time of crisis, like the sacrifices of Mesha and Micah? This case certainly can be made, since 11:34c goes to such great lengths to state that Jephthah's daughter was his only child, thus a "firstborn" (assuming that a child of either sex can be considered "firstborn"[54]). The result of Jephthah's firstborn sacrifice is a military victory, just as in the case of Mesha's firstborn sacrifice. Thus, both the victim and the result appear to be analogous in these two cases. Finally, both Mesha's sacrifice (2 Kgs 3:27) and Jephthah's (Judg 11:31) are referred to by the term עלה/עולה, and identical terminology may suggest an identical rite. Despite these similarities, however, some significant differences are worth considering.

First, in the case of Mesha's firstborn sacrifice, and probably also in the case of the firstborn sacrifice mentioned in Micah, the sacrifice precedes the act of divine favor. Mesha recognized his desperate circumstances and offered up his son as a burnt offering, which then successfully invoked divine action on Mesha's behalf. Jephthah's sacrifice, however, was not made until after he had already been granted divine aid in his war against the Ammonites. His sacrifice was in fulfillment of a vow that he made prior to the battle, while in Mesha's case there is no mention of a vow at all. By offering his firstborn son prior to receiving divine aid, Mesha made an offering that was not contingent upon help ever actually materializing. Even if Kir-hareseth had fallen, Mesha's son would still have been offered up. Jephtah's vow, on the other hand, only required that Jephthah fulfill it if Yahweh first held up his end of the bargain.

Second, and more importantly in my view, Mesha's firstborn sacrifice involves him *intentionally* offering his firstborn son. The fact that Mesha's offspring is explicitly identified as "his son" (בנו), "the firstborn" (הבכור), and "who was to rule after him" (אשר ימלך תחתיו; 2 Kgs 3:27) makes it clear that the identity of the victim was an important part of the ritual. Likewise, the fact that Mic 6:7 specifically names "my firstborn" (בכורי) as the proposed offering indicates that the victim's identity as a firstborn child is significant in this text as well. Jephthah's sacrifice of his firstborn child, however, came about purely by chance (or perhaps by fate?). Jephthah did not promise to

54. At least with regard to the law of the firstborn, the evidence is mixed. In some instances, only firstborn males are subject to the law (Exod 13:13; 34:19 [LXX]), but in other cases it appears that either sex may have been intended (Exod 13:2; 22:28b [Eng 22:29b]). On the role of gender in the various versions of the law of the firstborn, see Finsterbusch, "The First-Born between Sacrifice and Redemption."

sacrifice his firstborn child. Instead, he vowed to offer up as a burnt offering "that which comes out of the doors of my house to meet me" (היוצא אשר יצא מדלתי ביתי לקראתי; Judg 11:31). Jephthah's vow leaves the identity of the victim indeterminate, and there is no indication that he intended this vow to result in the sacrifice of his firstborn child. On the contrary, when Jephthah's daughter came out to greet him upon his successful return, his reaction was one of shock and despair. Once he realized what the vow actually entailed, he bitterly lamented the outcome (Judg 11:35). He clearly had not expected his vow to involve sacrificing his firstborn child. Thus, while Jephthah's sacrifice of his firstborn daughter has the same victim, the same result, and the text uses the same sacrificial terminology, there is a key difference in that in Jephthah's case there is a lack of intention. Therefore, Jephthah's vow should be considered distinct from the other two cases, Mesha's sacrifice and Micah 6, even if conceptually all three may be grouped together under the broader rubric of *do ut des* offerings.

One final difficulty for using the Jephthah story to reconstruct historical child sacrifice in ancient Israel is the legendary and etiological nature of the tale. As the story currently stands, the sacrifice of Jephthah's daughter serves to explain the origin of an annual custom of the "daughters of Israel" (Judg 11:39–40), and it is not difficult to find fantastical etiology stories elsewhere in the Hebrew Bible. The custom of keeping the Sabbath is explained on the basis of God's having rested on the seventh day of creation (Gen 2:2–3; Exod 20:11); the diversity of world languages is explained as the result of human disobedience at Babel (Gen 11:9); the Israelites are said not to eat a certain portion of the thigh because their ancestor Jacob was injured in that area during a supernatural wrestling match (Gen 32:32); both Yahweh's claim to the firstborn and the Passover meal are traced back to the tenth plague against the Egyptians (Exod 13); and the social location of the Gibeonites within Israelite society is traced to their having deceived Joshua and extracted an unwitting vow from him during his conquest of the Promised Land (Josh 13). Few historians today draw historical reality from any of these etiological tales, since the primary purpose of such stories is to provide an entertaining account of why people today do the things that they do, and historical veracity is at best only of secondary importance.

Further complicating matters, the story of Jephthah's vow is presented in the context of a folktale, an observation made well over a century ago by Gunkel.[55] It was Baumgartner, however, who fully presented the key features

55. H. Gunkel, "Die israelitische Literatur," in *Die orientalischen Literaturen* (ed. P. Hinneberg; *Die Kultur der Gegenwart: ihre Entwicklung und ihre Ziele* 1:7; Berlin: Teubner, 1906), 56.

of the *Märchenmotiv* of which the story of Jephthah and his daughter is only one example:[56] a man—rarely a woman—promises his child to a stranger, a demon, a sorcerer, a wild animal, etc. in return for help during some sort of crisis. The child is either his only child or his most beloved, sometimes a son and sometimes a daughter. Often, the child is explicitly and directly requested, but often in dark and concealed terms—usually in the form "the first to meet him upon his arrival home"—and thus the father only belatedly understands the full significance of his promise. In most fairytales, this *Märchenmotiv* occurs at the beginning of a longer tale, one that usually involves the adventures of the child who had been promised and handed over, typically with a happy ending. Baumgartner points to various tales collected by the Brothers Grimm: Mary's Child (KHM 3), Rapunzel (KHM 12), the Handless Maiden (KHM 31), the Singing, Springing Lark (KHM 88), the King of the Gold Mountain (KHM 92), and the Nixie of the Mill-Pond (KHM 181). Such tales are hardly confined to this corpus, however, as Baumgartner notes other examples of the motif in legends from Germany, Lorraine, Austria, Sweden, Scandinavia, Iceland, Lithuania, Russia, Arabia, and even China.[57]

Baumgartner finds two Greek parallels to be most relevant: the story of Idomeneus as told by Servius[58] and the tale of Maeander as told by Pseudo-Plutarch.[59] In the former, King Idomeneus of Crete promised to sacrifice to Neptune the first thing to meet him upon his return home should he survive a storm at sea. The "first to meet him" turned out to be his son, but Servius observes that his sources are divided on whether Idomeneus actually went through with the sacrifice. Either way, shortly thereafter a plague broke out and Idomeneus was driven from Crete. Similarly, in the tale of Maeander, the protagonist made an identical vow to the Mother of the Gods in return for victory in a battle. He was horrified when his son, his wife, and his sister *all* ran out to meet him upon his return home. After fulfilling his vow and sacrificing his family, in despair he drowned himself in a river, which was subsequently named "Maeander" after him. To these two stories, Sasson[60] adds a tale told by Pausanias[61] about a ruler of Haliartus who inquired at Delphi concerning how to provide his land with water. The Pythian priestess there

56. W. Baumgartner, "Jephtas Gelübde: Jud. 11 30–40," *AR* (1915): 240–49. The summary of the key features of the *Märchenmotiv* that follows is essentially my English paraphrase of Baumgartner's outline.

57. See also Marcus, *Jephthah and His Vow*, 40–41.

58. *Commentary on the Aeneid of Vergil* 3.121, 11.264

59. *De fluviis* 9

60. Sasson, *Judges 1–12*, 445.

61. *Description of Greece* 9.33.4

instructed him to kill the first man he should meet. This turned out to be the ruler's son Lophis. He struck the boy with his sword, and despite a rather serious head wound, the boy survived long enough to run about bleeding all over the ground. The blood caused water to spring up from the land, and the resulting river was named "Lophis" after him.[62] Thus, there is a well-attested literary motif in which a father agrees to sacrifice the first person to meet him in order to obtain some benefit and is surprised to discover that the fated victim turns out to be his own child.[63] The similarities to the Jephthah story are obvious.[64] Finally, the commonly cited version of the story of Iphigenia's (sometimes only near) sacrifice may be cited,[65] especially the version contained at the beginning of Euripides's *Iphigenia in Tauris*. Euripides's version is unique in that Artemis refuses to allow Agamemnon to set sail for Troy until he has sacrificed his daughter Iphigenia in fulfillment of a vow: he had sworn that he would sacrifice the most beautiful creature that was born that

62. For these, as well as other less obviously related tales of human sacrifice recounted in Classical sources, see D. D. Hughes, *Human Sacrifice in Ancient Greece* (New York: Routledge, 1991), 71–138.

63. This motif appears as "S241. Child Unwittingly Promised: 'first thing you meet,'" in S. Thompson, *Motif-Index of Folk-Literature* (vol. 5; revised edition; Bloomington, IN: Indiana University Press, 1957), 317; and the story itself is presented as an example of "425H. Short form of the tale. Girl promised to an animal," in A. Aarne, *The Types of the Folktale: A Classification and Bibliography* (trans. S. Thompson; 2nd. ed.; FFC 184; Helsinki: Suomalainen Tiedeakatemia, 1964), 144; and as a variant of "1191. Sacrifice on the Bridge" in H.-J. Uther, *Tales of the Stupid Ogre, Anecdotes and Jokes and Formula Tales* (Part 2 of *The Types of International Folktales: A Classification and Bibliography Based on the System of Antti Aarne and Stith Thompson*; FFC 285; Helsinki: Suomalainen Tiedeakatemia, 2004), 69. In this regard, Niditch perceptively connects the tale with European folktales, especially "Beauty and the Beast," which shares with the tale of Jephthah's daughter the trope of a father's handing over a daughter of marriageable age in order to preserve his own life (*Judges*, 134–35).

64. Indeed, T. C. Römer has attributed this similarity to literary dependence on the part of the author of the Jephthah story. In his view, the story of Jephthah's vow and sacrifice is a post-Dtr, Persian-period addition that takes its point of departure from similar Greek stories, especially the Iphigenia tale(s), and the Aqedah of Gen 22 ("Why Would the Deuteronomists Tell about the Sacrifice of Jephthah's Daughter?" *JSOT* 77 [1998]: 27–38; so also I. Finkelstein, "The Old Jephthah Tale in Judges: Geographical and Historical Considerations," *Bib* 97 [2016]: 7). Although I find the similarity among the Classical stories and the Jephthah tale to be undeniable, I do not find Römer's arguments that the story is a late addition as convincing as the traditional argument that it represents an earlier version of a fairly ubiquitous folktale incorporated into their larger work by the Deuteronomistic historian(s).

65. This is perhaps the most frequently cited parallel to the Jephthah story, although scholars disagree on how close the parallel is. See, e.g., Day, "From the Child Is Born the Woman," 60–62; Burney, *Judges*, 332; Niditch, *Judges*, 134; Sasson, *Judges 1–12*, 447.

year, unaware that this creature would be his own daughter, Iphigenia.[66] As in the Jephthah tale, here is a vow to sacrifice an indeterminate victim who later turns out to be the person's own child; the only difference is that in the case of the Iphigenia tale the common motif of "the first person one meets" is absent.

The significance of this comparative material is that it marks the Jephthah story unambiguously as a folktale, and attempting to draw historical reality from folktales is a methodologically dubious endeavor—one that could easily result, for example, in portraying early nineteenth-century Germany as a place where cannibal witches lived in houses made of cakes and candies. This is different from the cases of Mesha and Micah. In both of these cases, the practice of sacrificing firstborn children during times of emergency is *assumed* by both author and audience. The reality of the potential for child sacrifice in times of extraordinary distress provides the necessary background for making sense of the mention of child sacrifice in the Mesha narrative and Micah oracle. On the other hand, the arc of the tale of Jephthah's vow turns on explaining how Jephthah inadvertently and *unexpectedly* came to sacrifice his daughter. The audience shares Jephthah's surprise at its tragic outcome, although a sense of foreboding disaster is already established by the ambiguous nature of the vow. Although the audience is expected to acknowledge that such a vow might be made and could theoretically result in the sacrifice of one's own child, the sacrifice of Jephthah's only daughter is presented as a tragic and at least somewhat surprising outcome.

That the story of Jephthah's vow is judged ahistorical does not mean that Israelite children were never actually sacrificed in fulfillment of vows. I have argued at length above that the evidence that Israelite children served as the victims of other forms of sacrifice is substantial. Establishing that there existed in ancient Israel a rite by which children were vowed and then sacrificed solely on the basis of the Jephthah story, however, puts more historical weight on the folktale than it can bear. It is possible to conclude that sacrifice of a firstborn child in fulfillment of an ambiguous vow was at least conceptually and theoretically possible, although how often this theoretical possibility played out in actual practice remains uncertain.

66. *Iphigenia in Tauris* 25–31. In other versions of the story, the obligation to sacrifice Iphigenia is due to a boast Agamemnon made after shooting a stag, which appears to have angered Artemis badly enough to prevent his voyage (see Sophocles, *Electra* 664–77, and Apollodorus, *Epitome* 21–22). Whether Iphigenia is actually sacrificed in the end varies among the different versions of the tale.

Hiel's Firstborn and Youngest Sons?

Some scholars find another instance of child sacrifice in the notice: "In his [= Ahab's] days, Hiel of Bethel built Jericho. By Abiram, his firstborn, he laid its foundations, and by Segub, his youngest, he set up its gates, according to the word of Yahweh which he spoke to Joshua son of Nun" (1 Kgs 16:34). The final clause is a reference to Joshua's curse on anyone who should rebuild the city of Jericho in the immediate aftermath of its destruction: "And Joshua swore in that time, 'Cursed is the man before Yahweh who arises and builds this city Jericho. By his firstborn he will lay its foundations and by his youngest he will set up its gates'" (Josh 6:26). This combination of the report of a prophecy followed later by a notice of its fulfillment is one of several such instances that appears in the Deuteronomistic history, all of which, according to W. Dietrich, make up a post-DtrH/DtrG redactional layer that he dubs "DtrP." More specifically, in Dietrich's view, 1 Kgs 16:34a can be traced to a historical report of some kind, and the notice that this all happened "according to the word of Yahweh, etc." has been appended to that notice. According to Dietrich, this same hand then also composed and added Joshua's curse in Josh 6:26, creating the prophecy–fulfillment dynamic.[67] Whether or not one accepts Dietrich's conclusions concerning a DtrP redactor of the Deuteronomistic history, the important question for us is whether the text presents Hiel as offering his children as sacrifices.

What does it mean that, when Hiel built Jericho, "he laid its foundations *by* Abiram (באבירם), his firstborn" and that he set up its gates "*by* Segub (K בשגיב; Q בשגוב), his youngest"? The fact that Josh 6:26 reads "Cursed is the man before Yahweh" (ארור האיש לפני יהוה) makes it clear that, whatever it means to found a city "by" one's children, it is an undesirable thing, probably involving their death. In a previous generation of scholars, it was sometimes suggested that Hiel's children were offered as "foundation sacrifices," and archaeological evidence—specifically, the presence of infants buried under the floors of houses—was proffered as support for this interpretation.[68]

67. W. Dietrich, *Prophetie und Geschichte: Eine redaktionsgeschichtliche Untersuchung zum deuteronomistischen Geschichtswerk* (FRLANT 108; Göttingen: Vandenhoeck & Ruprecht, 1972), 111–12. Noth attributed the insertion of the two notices to the Deuteronomistic historian, who expanded a report that he drew from the "Books of the Chronicles" (*The Deuteronomistic History*, 37 and 65). Nonetheless, it is ultimately unimportant for present purposes to determine at what stage the material was incorporated into the Deuteronomistic history. What is important here is specifically what the notice claims concerning the fate of Hiel's sons.

68. H. C. Trumbull, *The Threshold Covenant* (2nd ed.; New York: Charles Scribner's Sons, 1896), 46–47; S. A. Cook, *The Religion of Ancient Palestine in the Second Millennium in the Light*

The problem, however, is that these infant burials need not be interpreted as sacrifices, and the only textual evidence offered in support of interpreting them as such was this notice concerning Hiel.[69] Absent this notice, the very existence of a custom in which children were offered as foundation sacrifices is debatable. Even if one could demonstrate that children were offered as foundation sacrifices in the ancient Near East in general and in ancient Israel in particular, however, the context of the biblical notice makes more sense if one understands the death of Hiel's sons as non-sacrificial. After all, if Hiel had sacrificed his children during the reestablishment of Jericho, then their deaths would have been an intentional choice. What would be the nature of the "curse," if he offered his children willingly? If the death of Hiel's sons was something that he did not anticipate but that came about as an unintentional result of (or as divine punishment for) his rebuilding the city, on the other hand, then the curse oracle and its fulfillment notice make much more sense. Thus, despite the ongoing claims by some that the story of Hiel's refounding of Jericho provides evidence for yet another instance of Israelite child sacrifice,[70] it is more likely that the mention of Hiel's children is simply a recounting of their deaths, which occurred as a consequence of and as retribution for violating Joshua's prohibition against rebuilding the city.

Child Sacrifice in Assyrian Samerina?

One final possible example of child sacrifice in ancient Israel to be explored before returning to the למלך sacrifices is the brief but tantalizing notice that the "Sepharvim burned their children in fire to Adrammelech and Anammelech, the gods of Sepharvaim" (2 Kgs 17:31b). This notice appears in the context of the Neo-Assyrian settlement of foreign populations in the territory of the conquered Northern Kingdom, reorganized as the Assyrian province of Samerina. On the one hand, this brief notice provides a remarkable amount of information: by using the verb "to burn" (√שרף) rather than something more ambiguous such as "to give" (√נתן) or "to cause to pass over" (√עבר Hiphil), there can be little doubt that the actual killing of children is described. Likewise, by explicitly identifying Adrammelech and Anammelech

---

of Archæology and the Inscriptions (London: Constable & Company, 1921), 38–41; W. C. Graham and H. G. May, *Culture and Conscience: An Archaeological Study of the New Religious Past in Ancient Palestine* (Chicago: University of Chicago Press, 1936), 77–78.

69. Green, *The Role of Human Sacrifice in the Ancient Near East*, 169.

70. Cf. Tatlock, "How in Ancient Times," 198–200; and Stavrakopoulou, *King Manasseh and Child Sacrifice*, 186–87.

as "the god(s) of Sepharvaim" (K אלה ספרים; Q אלהי ספרוים), there can be no doubt that these terms refer to the divine recipients of the sacrifices. Finally, the individuals who made these offerings are also explicitly identified as the "Sepharvim" (הספרוים). This, then, is one of the most explicit descriptions of child sacrifice in the Hebrew Bible: children are sacrificed to specific, named deities by explicitly identified people.

Unfortunately, however, despite the clarity of the text's language, it is difficult to draw any firm historical conclusions from this notice. First, both the location of "Sepharvaim" and the identity of its people, the "Sepharvim," are unknown. The place-name also appears in 2 Kgs 18:34 and 19:13 (//Isa 39:16 and 37:13), but the only information provided there is that it was among the places conquered by the Assyrians. Likewise, the deities "Adrammelech" and "Anammelech" are unattested anywhere outside this notice, although they do appear to be West Semitic in origin.[71] Thus we are presented with an unknown people from an unknown land accused of sacrificing their children to unknown gods. Furthermore, it is possible that the divine names are merely "artificial creations" of the Deuteronomistic historian(s) intended to add a sense of veracity to their description of the religious practices of the postmonarchic North,[72] and if we take this possibility seriously, we may well be attempting to derive historical reality from polemical invention. After all, Deuteronomy and the Deuteronomistic History are hardly interested in presenting an objective, unbiased account of the religious practice of Israel and Judah; Stavrakopoulou rightly observes that the Deuteronomists demonstrate a clear tendency to depict child sacrifice as foreign and foreigners as child-sacrificers.[73] Thus, because of the uncertainty about the identities of the people who are said to sacrifice their children and the gods to whom they were allegedly sacrificed, along with the suspect nature of the accusation itself, it is best not to lean too heavily on the brief notice in 2 Kgs 17:31b when creating a historical reconstruction of Israelite child sacrifice. At most,

---

71. For an overview of the problems concerning the identities of the Sepharvim and their gods, see M. Nissinen, "Adrammelech (Deity)," *EBR* 1, 442; A. R. Millard, "Adrammelech אדרמלך," *DDD*[2], 10–11; A. R. Millard, "Anammelech ענמלך," *DDD*[2], 34–35; A. K. Grayson, "Adrammelech (Deity)," *ABD* 1, 79; W. J. Fulco, "Anammelech," *ABD* 1, 223; H. Avalos, "Sepharvaim," *ABD* 5, 1091; B. Becking, *The Fall of Samaria: An Historical and Archaeological Study* (SHANE 2; Leiden: Brill, 1992), 99–102; R. Zadok, "Geographical and Onomastic Notes," *JANES* 8 (1976): 115–17.

72. So Stavrakopoulou, *King Manasseh and Child Sacrifice*, 154–55; following V. Fritz, *1 & 2 Kings* (trans. A. Hagedorn; CC; Minneapolis: Fortress, 2003), 355–56.

73. Stavrakopoulou, *King Manasseh and Child Sacrifice*, 155.

it is possible to argue that the Israelite Yahwists may not have been the only groups sacrificing children in the region, but even this conclusion may exceed our evidence.

Molek Revisited: The History and Nature of Israelite למלך Sacrifices

Chapter 1 was primarily devoted to questions concerning whether children were actually sacrificed as part of a למלך rite in ancient Israel and, more specifically, whether such sacrifices were offered to Yahweh, the god of Israel. Both of these questions were answered in the affirmative, but this conclusion hardly exhausts an exploration of the nature of these sacrifices. Other important questions concerning the rite include: Were they a "native" part of Israelite Yahwistic practice, or were they a syncretistic borrowing from elsewhere? In either case, what was the intended purpose and cultic function of these sacrifices?

Regarding the first question, those like Heider and Day who view "Molek" as the name or epithet of a deity might naturally assume that such rites were syncretistic, a result of borrowing from a foreign source,[74] since if "Molek" was a non-Yahwistic deity, then offerings to him would also be non-Yahwistic by definition. On the other hand, if למלך was a type of sacrifice offered to Yahweh, then one might naturally conclude that this sacrifice was "native" to Yahwism. Eissfeldt himself, the first to suggest that למלך sacrifices were offered to Yahweh rather than being sacrifices to a "Molek" deity, pointed to biblical evidence that various forms of child sacrifice existed during early periods of Israelite history (see e.g., Gen 22; Mic 6:7; 2 Kgs 3; Exod 22:28–29); he used this evidence to support his conclusion that child sacrifice in the form of למלך offerings in the eighth and seventh centuries, during the reigns of Ahaz (2 Kgs 17:31) and Manasseh (2 Kgs 21:6), need not be attributed to religious syncretism. Instead, he argued that child sacrifice had always had a

74. Heider, on the basis of texts such as Isa 30:33 and 2 Kgs 16:3 (on which see below), believes that the "Molek" cult was well established in Jerusalem at a fairly early date. Nevertheless, despite its long history in Jerusalem, he argues that it was originally "imported," not original to Yahwism. He suggests that it is not possible to know "whether the cult of Molek was imported (presumably from Phoenicia) under Solomon, or was taken up directly during the conquest/settlement from the Canaanite inhabitants (as we think more likely)" (*Cult of Molek*, 327). Interestingly, Day believes that "Molek" was an old Jebusite underworld deity (*Molech*, 55), which has the interesting consequence of making Molek native to Jerusalem but nonetheless foreign to Israelite Yahwism (*Molech*, 82–85).

place among Israelite Yahwists, and he posited that the absence of evidence for למלך sacrifices at the official ("staatlichen") level during earlier periods is simply due to the limitations of our sources—that is, the "Nicht-Erwähnung" of child sacrifice does not necessarily imply its "Nicht-Vorkommen."[75]

Similarly, Mosca points to Deut 12:31, 2 Kgs 17:17, and Isa 30:27–33 to argue that, despite Ahaz's being the first individual accused of offering a למלך sacrifice (2 Kgs 16:3), he was not the first Israelite actually to do so.[76] In particular, Mosca believes that the fact that neither Isaiah nor Micah, both contemporaries of Ahaz, condemn the practice proves that the rite had existed and was accepted in Jerusalem for some time.[77] However, despite acknowledging that the sacrifice was "officially sanctioned" and one that "Isaiah knew and, as a child of his century, accepted as orthodox," Mosca does not go so far as to claim that the rite was *originally* Yahwistic. Instead, it was "either of Canaanite or Phoenician origin," but was borrowed either during the "period of the Conquest" or perhaps as late as the tenth century. In Mosca's view, the rite was practiced, unchallenged, in both the North and the South until the fall of the former and until the reign of Josiah in the latter. Thus, Mosca argues that the rite was part of the Yahwistic cult in both Israel and Judah for the nearly the entirety of their existence as nations but nevertheless avoids concluding that it was a thoroughly Yahwistic practice. Instead, it was merely "adapted to the Yahwistic cult,"[78] albeit at a very early date.

Stavrakopoulou goes even further. In her view, the general sacrifice of firstborn children (see chapter 3 above), child sacrifices to the *šadday* gods,[79] and למלך offerings all were distinct in some respects but were probably interrelated. Together, these varied but related rites of child sacrifice are "likely to have existed in various forms, as a normative though infrequent element of indigenous, Judahite religious practice."[80] In Stavrakopoulou's opinion, the למלך sacrifices in particular represent "a royal specialization of the fertility rite of the firstborn sacrifice, in which a royal pregnancy was promised as a gift to *Yhwh*, the patron-deity of the Judahite royal family, and sacrificed in fire shortly after the birth as a means of encouraging the divine perpetuation

75. Eissfeldt, *Molk als Opferbegriff*, 56–59.

76. Mosca, "Child Sacrifice," 176–90.

77. Ibid., 219–20.

78. Ibid., 223, 239.

79. On Stavrakopoulou's argument that *šadday* gods were connected to child sacrifice, incorrect in my opinion, see the discussion of the Deir ʿAllā plaster inscriptions in chapter 2 above.

80. Stavrakopoulou, *King Manasseh and Child Sacrifice*, 299.

of the royal dynasty." Stavrakopoulou even finds an "echo" of the ancient connection between the royal dynasty at Jerusalem and the למלך sacrifices in the names of "David" and his son "Jedidiah" (2 Sam 12:24–25), both of which are lexically connected to √דוד and mean something like "Beloved (of Yah)." She posits that this term itself may have been in some way associated with child sacrifice.[81] Thus, Stavrakopoulou groups together the various child sacrifice rituals as essentially variations on a single theme, a thoroughly and unambiguously Yahwistic one.

More recently, in a similar vein, Tatlock has argued that the existence of Yahwistic למלך rites serves as evidence for his broader thesis that "child immolation was once widely accepted as a licit Yahwistic deed during the preexilic period, but was later viewed as inappropriate."[82] He, like Mosca before him, especially draws on Isa 30:33, which appears to link Yahweh to the sacrificial rites of the tophet. Since there is no evidence of disapproval on Isaiah's part, the rite presumably has old roots in the cult. Although Tatlock does not specify how early he believes such rites were accepted as legitimate, he makes no mention of the idea that these sacrifices offered למלך might have been some sort of foreign import or syncretism. Instead, in Tatlock's view, "*mōlek* and Yahweh were originally the same deity."[83] Thus, Tatlock also finds למלך sacrifices to be thoroughly Yahwistic and native to the cult of Yahweh in Jerusalem.

As argued in chapter 1 above, the weight of the evidence is that מלך is a sacrificial term, not the name of a foreign deity, and that the obvious recipient for the למלך sacrifices offered in the Jerusalem tophet was Yahweh. The corollary assumption, however, that if such sacrifices were offered to Yahweh, then they likely had a very old history in the Jerusalem cult, does not necessarily follow. In addition, just because one form of child sacrifice—for example, either type of firstborn sacrifice—may have had a long history among worshipers of Yahweh does not necessarily mean that the למלך offerings also had a similar history. There were several different child sacrifice rites in ancient Israel, and just as each variety of child sacrifice had a distinct function and purpose, each also had its own individual history. Thus, conclusions concerning the nature and history of the two types of firstborn sacrifice, both of which in my opinion do have old roots among at least some Yahwistic

81. Ibid., 296–97.

82. Tatlock, "How in Ancient Times," 213–16.

83. Ibid., 218. Contrary to the argument presented above in chapter 1, Tatlock argues that למלך refers to the recipient of the sacrifice, not to its victim.

groups, are ultimately of little relevance for tracing the antiquity of the למלך rite. Despite the tendency of many scholars to conflate the various forms of Israelite child sacrifice to one degree or another,[84] the למלך rite must be treated on its own terms.

This should be clear from the evidence that we can gather concerning the nature of the למלך rite itself. First, the victims of the למלך sacrifices are never referred to as "firstborn." In the instances in which the technical phrase למלך is explicitly used, the victims of the offerings are referred to as זרעך "your seed" (Lev 18:21; 20:2–4) or את בנו ואת בתו/את בניהם ואת בנתיהם "his son and his daughter/their sons and their daughters" (2 Kgs 23:10; Jer 32:35). Likewise, in the cases in which the phrase למלך is absent but the technical language √עבר (Hiphil) + באש "cause to pass over in fire" is used, the victims are referred to as בנו ובתו "his son and his daughter" (Deut 18:10), את בנו "his son/child" (2 Kgs 16:3; 21:6), את בניהם ואת בנתיהם "their sons and their daughters" (2 Kgs 17:7), את בניו "his sons/children" (2 Chr 33:6), or בניכם "your sons/children" (Ezek 20:31). In no case is a child that is offered למלך or "in fire" referred to as a "firstborn." So far as we can tell, birth order was of no importance for the למלך sacrifices.

In addition, the purpose of the למלך sacrifices appears to have been quite different from the purpose of either type of firstborn offering surveyed above. That is, there is no indication that למלך offerings were either made as part of a general sacrifice of firstborn children or that they were offered during periods of distress. Admittedly, it is difficult to determine the purpose of the למלך sacrifices solely on the basis of the biblical evidence; the biblical text is more interested in condemning the rite than expounding on the logic underlying it. The relevant Punic evidence, however, provides data for identically named rites involving child sacrifice and describes them in more detail. Although the biblical notices concerning למלך rites simply tell us that children were offered in fire, the Punic inscriptions provide ample testimony concerning their purpose. In their thorough examination of the standard formulae found on the Punic *mlk* stelae, Amadasi Guzzo and Zamora López identify three stages in the development of these inscriptions.[85]

84. See Eissfeldt, *Molk als Opferbegriff*, 46–61; Ackerman, *Under Every Green Tree*, 137–43. For his part, Mosca, while pointing to the evidence concerning Micah and Mesha ("Child Sacrifice," 162, 192, 223–25), dismisses the Jephthah narrative as not germane ("Child Sacrifice," 161). Stavrakopoulou also includes the general firstborn sacrifice and the alleged offerings to the *šadday*-god(s) as evidence for the indigenous character of למלך sacrifices (*King Manasseh and Child Sacrifice*, 283–99; eadem, "The Jerusalem Tophet," *SEL* 29–30 [2012–13], 147–49).

85. Amadasi Guzzo and Zamora López, "The Epigraphy of the Tophet," 159–92.

In the earliest phase (sixth century BCE), the standard formula on the relevant Punic stelae has the form:

> *nṣb mlk bʿl/ʾmr ʾš ytn + PN lbʿl ḥmn ʾdn*
>
> Stele of a *mlk* of *bʿl*/of a lamb that X gave to Baʿl Hammon, the Lord[86]

This provides little additional information about *mlk*-sacrifices, other than that a lamb could be offered instead of a child,[87] a practice unattested in the Hebrew Bible in relation to למלך sacrifices. It also seems likely that a stele was at least sometimes erected to commemorate these offerings, but this tells us little more than the existence of the stele itself reveals. A bit later (late sixth century BCE), a more detailed version of the formula appears:

> *lʾdn lbʿl ḥmn mlk bʿl/ʾdm/ʾmr (ʾz) ʾš ytn/ndr* + PN
>
> To the Lord Baʿl Hammon (this is) the *mlk* of *bʿl/ʾdm*/of a lamb that X gave/vowed[88]

In these instances, the variant √*ndr* "vowed" for √*ytn* "gave" is significant. This variant became dominant in later inscriptions (5th century BCE and later), where *ndr* "vow" even comes to replace the term *mlk* itself:

> *lʾdn lbʿl ḥmn ndr ʾš ndr* + PN
>
> To the Lord Baʿl Hammon a vow that X vowed[89]

Furthermore, in addition to the development toward explicit vow language, there are various other elements that might also appear attached to this basic formula, including the addition of a concluding formula *k šmʿ ql dbry* "for he [= Baʿl Hammon] heard the voice of his [= the offerer's] words," apparently indicating the deity's positive response to a request. In other cases, this concluding formula is presented in the imperfect/jussive *yšmʿ qlʾ* "may he hear his voice," apparently anticipating a positive divine response.[90]

86. Ibid., 169.

87. With *bʿl* referring either to a *baʿl*—that is, a "wealthy" child (so Mosca, "Child Sacrifice," 74–77)—or *b-ʿūl* "as an infant" (so Février, "Molchomor," 8–18; idem, "Le vocabulaire sacrificiel punique," 52–56). See also the discussion in *DNSWI*, 182–84. Whichever interpretation is correct, the term probably does refer to a human child.

88. Amadasi Guzzo and Zamora López, "The Epigraphy of the Tophet," 171.

89. Ibid., 172.

90. For a thorough survey of the various permutations, see ibid., 173–80. For a helpful collection of the texts themselves, along with a thorough discussion of the their contents, see Mosca, "Child Sacrifice," 61–97.

In sum, one can conclude on the basis of the Punic epigraphic evidence that *mlk*-sacrifices of both humans and sheep were associated with vows. More specifically, based on the appearance of *k šmʿ ql dbry* "for he heard the voice of his words" and/or *brkʾ* "he blessed him" in some inscriptions, it is possible to conclude that the sacrifice was offered after the deity had favorably responded to a petitioner's request. On the other hand, the clauses *yšmʿ qlʾ* "may he hear his voice" and/or *ybrkʾ* "may he bless him" might suggest that some of these sacrifices were offered prior to and in anticipation of receiving divine favor. In either case, however, the offerings appears to be of a *do ut des* nature and, so far as we can tell, organized at a family, not a national, level and offered for private rather than public ends.[91]

This general picture finds some external confirmation in Classical sources. Although both Philo and Porphyry situate Phoenician and Punic child sacrifice in the context of national emergencies,[92] the testimony of Kleitarchos (third century BCE) jibes remarkably well with the Punic epigraphic evidence:

> Κλείταρχος δέ φησι τοὺς Φοίνικας, καὶ μάλιστα Καρχηδονίους, τὸν Κρόνον τιμῶντας, ἐπάν τινος μεγάλου κατατυχεῖν σπεύδωσιν, εὔχεσθαι καθ' ἑνὸς τῶν παίδων, εἰ περιγένοιντο τῶν ἐπιθυμηθέντων, καθαγιεῖν αὐτὸν τῷ θεῷ. τοῦ δὲ Κρόνου χαλκοῦ παρ' αὐτοῖς ἑστῶτος τὰς χεῖρας ὑπτίας ἐκτετακότος ὑπὲρ κριβάνου χαλκοῦ, τοῦτον ἐκκαίειν τὸ παιδίον. τῆς δὲ φλογὸς τοῦ ἐκκαιομένου πρὸς τὸ σῶμα ἐμπιπτούσης, συνέλκεσθαί τε τὰ μέλη καὶ τὸ στόμα σεσηρὸς φαίνεσθαι τοῖς γελῶσι παραπλησίως, ἕως ἂν συσπασθὲν εἰς τὸν κρίβανον παρολίσθῃ. τὸν οὖν σεσηρότα γέλωτα σαρδάνιον ἐντεῦθεν λέγεσθαι, ἐπεὶ γελῶντες ἀποθνήσκουσι.
>
> And Kleitarchos says the Phoenicians, and above all the Carthaginians, venerating Kronos, whenever they were eager for a great thing to succeed, made a vow by one of their children. If they would receive the desired things, they would sacrifice it to the god. A bronze Kronos, having been erected by them, stretched out upturned hands over a bronze oven to burn the child. The flame of the burning child reached its body until, the limbs having shriveled up and the smiling mouth appearing to be almost laughing, it would slip into the

91. So also Amadasi Guzzo and Zamora López, "The Epigraphy of the Tophet," 179.
92. Both quoted by Eusebius (*Praep. ev.* 1.10.44 = 4.16.11 and 4.16.6).

> oven. Therefore the grin is called "sardonic laughter," since they die laughing.[93]

As one might expect, the section of this excerpt that often catches the reader's eye is the grisly description of the bronze statue of Kronos with its hands stretched out over a cauldron, holding an infant as it is slowly consumed and shriveled up into a "sardonically" grinning corpse. More pertinent for our purposes, however, is Kleitarchos's description of the motives of the Carthaginians who offered such sacrifices. He makes no mention of a national emergency but instead links the sacrifices with the fulfillment of vows. Even more specifically, the vows are said to have been made with the hope that the deity would bless a private undertaking. That the Carthaginian stelae themselves link these offerings to such vows indicates that Kleitarchos had at least roughly the correct idea about the rites he described. The testimony of Kleitarchos confirms the picture of the Punic epigraphic evidence: *mlk*-offerings were offered in fulfillment of vows, vows apparently made for the purpose of convincing the deity to grant success in one's private undertakings.[94]

The name given to the offering itself may support a connection with vows. There have been four major suggestions for the meaning of the Hebrew term מלך and the cognate Punic term *mlk* (transcribed in Latin as *molch*, *morch*, or *moch*[95]). The first is that *mōlek* represents a dysphemistic revocalization of *malk*/*melek* "king." This argument is that biblical "Molek" was originally a royal deity, but the biblical scribes have revocalized the consonants *mlk* with the vowels from *bōšet* "shame," similar to the way in which the divine epithet *baʿal* is occasionally replaced in its entirety with the word *bōšet* (see 2 Sam 2:8//1 Chr 8:33; Jer 3:24; 11:13). This suggestion was first

93. *FGrH* 137 F 9. For a convenient collection of Classical allegations of Punic child sacrifice, including that of Kleitarchos, Philo, Porphyry, and others, see Mosca, "Child Sacrifice," 2–23; and Day, *Molech*, 86–91. Mosca observes that "most of the epigraphic evidence, in fact, corresponds best to the witness of Kleitarchos" ("Child sacrifice," 102).

94. So also Mosca, "Child Sacrifice," 102–3. More recently, Mosca has suggested another possibility: that the rite involved an "act of divinization" rather than a "sacrifice" in the technical sense of the word. Mosca still holds, however, that the rites involved the killing of the child and that the children were given in fulfillment of vows. See P. G. Mosca, "The *Tofet*: A Place of Infant Sacrifice?" *SEL* 29–30 (2012–13): 119–36. Mosca's major objection to the term "sacrifice" is that the West Semitic term *dbḥ*/*zbḥ*, typically translated "sacrifice," denotes offerings intended to feed the god(s), and these *mlk*-offerings are not so intended (ibid., 127). Here I am content to use "sacrifice" in the broader, but admittedly less precise, sense of "ritual killing," which applies equally to these rites even if Mosca's "divinization" hypothesis is correct.

95. For the relevant Latin inscriptions, see Mosca, "Child Sacrifice," 57–58a.

made by Geiger,[96] and has more recently been followed by Day and Tatlock.[97] The vocalization *mulk/mōlek*, however, is confirmed both by the Greek rendering of the term by Μολοχ (OG 2 Kgs 23:10; Jer 29:35), as well as by the cognate Punic rite, which presents a *u*-class vowel in the first syllable when transcribed in Latin.[98]

The second suggestion is that *mōlek* derives from a Hiphil participle of √*ylk*. This was first suggested by von Soden[99] and has been more recently defended by Müller[100] and especially Reynolds.[101] In addition to a single attestation in the Phoenician portion of the Karatepe Bilingual A (*KAI* 26A:19), already noted by Müller,[102] Reynolds points to a Punic inscription from Carthage (*CIS* 1 5510:9–10) and a Neo-Punic inscription from Tripolitania (*Or* 33, 4:6)[103] to argue that √*ylk* (C-stem) is used in Phoenician and Punic as a verb meaning "to offer."[104] Reynolds also cites Num 17:11, where √*hlk* (Hiphil) is used in the context of Aaron's making atonement for the congregation, as evidence of a similar use of the word in Hebrew.[105] If √*ylk* (Hiphil) means "to offer," then *môlik/môlīk/môlēk* (< *mawlik*) could be a "causative nominal *maqtil*(*at*) form."[106] The difficulty with this suggestion, however, is twofold. First, there is no obvious way to derive Hebrew *mṓlek* from *môlīk/môlēk* from a historical-linguistic perspective. Müller suggests that the change is due to some sort of "linguistic degeneration";[107] Reynolds acknowledges the difficulty but observes that at least *mṓlek* contains an *i*-class vowel in its second syllable, albeit *e* rather than expected *i*, *ī*, or *ē*.[108] Even more problematic, however, is the Punic evidence, which points to a monosyllabic *quṭl*-type noun, *molk/mulk*.[109] Although a shift from one *i*-class

96. A. Geiger, *Urschrift und Übersetzungen der Bible in ihrer Abhängigkeit von der innern Entwicklung des Judentums* (Breslau: Hainauer, 1857), 299–308.

97. Day, *Molech*, 56–58, 84; Tatlock, "How in Ancient Times," 212–13.

98. See also Mosca's thorough refutation of this suggestion in "Child Sacrifice," 125–27.

99. W. von Soden, review of O. Eissfeldt, *Molk als Opferbegriff*, *TLZ* 61 (1936): 45–46.

100. Müller, "מֹלֶךְ *mōlek̠*," 376–77.

101. Reynolds, "Molek: Dead or Alive?" 138–46.

102. Müller, "מֹלֶךְ *mōlek̠*," 377.

103. G. Levi Della Vida, "Ostracon Neopunico dalla Tripolitania," *Or* 33 (1964): 1–14.

104. It should be noted that Reynolds is innovative in finding references to offerings in these two additional passages. In *CIS* 1 5510, especially, he finds a reference specifically to human sacrifice. His reading is possible but by no means certain in my opinion.

105. Reynolds, "Molek: Dead or Alive?" 142.

106. Müller, "מֹלֶךְ *mōlek̠*," 376.

107. Ibid.

108. Reynolds, "Molek: Dead or Alive?" 143.

109. The vocalized form can be reconstructed as *molk/mulk* on the basis of its appearance

vowel to another might not be entirely surprising, the complete disappearance of a vowel is more difficult to explain. Such phonological irregularities could be overlooked if not for the fact that a Hiphil participle form is lexically surprising. If *mlk* is a type of offering, then it would naturally refer to the victim—"that which is offered." Lexically speaking, however, a Hiphil participle of √*ylk/hlk* should indicate the agent of the action—"one who offers." If the word were to indicate the object offered, a passive form would be expected. Thus, in Phoenician and Punic, a C-passive participle, probably *mûlak/môlak*,[110] would be the expected form, but this is even farther from the attested forms of the term. For all of these reasons, the idea that *molk/mōlek* derives from a C-stem participle form of √*ylk/hlk* is unlikely.

No more satisfying is Heider's suggestion that biblical *mōlek* is to be derived from a Qal participle of √*mlk*, because this form should appear as *mōlēk* in Tiberian Hebrew, with the accent on the ultima rather than the penult. Heider explains the unexpected form by suggesting that it is a "frozen form" used as a proper name.[111] This seems unlikely, though, as there is again no obvious linguistic mechanism that would derive *mṓlek* from *mōlik/mōlēk* at any stage in the development of the language.[112] It is also worth noting that, since Heider takes *mōlek* as the name of a deity, not the name of a type of sacrifice, he is able to dismiss the Punic *molk* sacrifices as irrelevant for understanding the Hebrew term. If the argument presented here is followed, and if the Punic and Hebrew sacrifices are in fact cognate, then the Punic form *molk* must be accounted for, which is difficult to do if the form was orginally vocalized as a G participle, *mōlik*.

If, on the other hand, one begins with the vocalization of the term as we have it both in Hebrew and Punic, then Tiberian Hebrew *mōlek* and Punic *molk* can be derived from a **quṭl*-type nominal form of √*mlk*. Furthermore, the fact that these offerings appear to be be associated with vows in the Punic epigraphic corpus suggests that the root itself may have something to do with

in transliteration in Latin *mlk* inscriptions, where it appears as *morch*, *moch*, *molch*, or *morc*. For examples, see Mosca, "Child Sacrifice," 57–58a.

110. C-passive forms in Phoenician and Punic are difficult to identify, but their existence is likely. See J. Friedrich and W. Röllig, *Phönizisch-Punische Grammatik* (3rd ed.; Rome: Pontificio Istituto Biblico, 1999), §148; S. Segert, *A Grammar of Phoenician and Punic* (Munich: Beck, 1976), §54.38; C. R. Krahmalkov, *A Phoenician-Punic Grammar* (Leiden: Brill, 1999), 156.

111. Heider, *The Cult of Molek*, 226–27.

112. The difficulties with Heider's phonological reconstruction are well noted in Olyan and Smith, review of Heider, *The Cult of Molek*, 273–75.

vows. This line of argument long ago led Chabot,[113] followed by Eissfeldt,[114] to connect the term to Syriac √*mlk* II "to promise,"[115] a suggestion that remains impressive on both philological and contextual grounds, despite the fact that few today adopt it. The obvious difficulty with the suggestion is its reliance on a cognate attested only in a single Aramaic language, one that is somewhat distant both geographically and linguistically from Canaanite languages such as Hebrew and Phoenician/Punic. Nonetheless, this suggestion remains the least problematic solution, as it accounts both for the form of the term and for its apparent meaning.

If the above reconstruction of the function of *mlk* sacrifices in a Punic context is sound, then what conclusions can be drawn concerning the apparently cognate Hebrew למלך sacrifices? First, the למלך sacrifices are fundamentally different from either type of Israelite firstborn sacrifice. If the Punic *mlk* offerings are compared to the Yahwistic custom of offering children as part of a general sacrifice of firstborn children, the two rites are found to have little in common. In the latter, firstborn children were owed to Yahweh simply by virtue of their being firstborn children. Although those who acknowledged Yahweh's right to firstfruits and firstlings and offered them over to him did so in anticipation of a bountiful produce (see Prov 3:9–10), there is no question that no one could elect *not* to offer the firstfruits to Yahweh: firstborn and firstfruit offerings were compulsory, even in versions of the law in which the redemption of children was permitted or required (on which, see chapter 5 below). The laws concerning firstfruits and firstlings are thoroughly apodictic in nature, and failure to deliver the sacrifices constituted the sin of appearing before Yahweh "empty-handed" (Exod 22:28–29; 23:15; 34:19–20). Thus, firstborn children would have been unsuitable as objects of a special vow: one could hardly vow to Yahweh something that was already due him and expect some sort of additional favor in return.

Likewise, if *mlk*/למלך sacrifices were associated with vows to ensure success in private undertakings, then they are also quite different from Mesha's sacrifice. Mesha sacrificed his firstborn son during a time of distress. He did not vow his son, wait for divine favor, and only then offer him up. Mesha's sacrifice was in anticipation of divine aid, not in the wake of it. Likewise, the mention of firstborn sacrifice in Mic 6:7 makes no mention of vows, although in Micah the temporal relationship between the proposed offering and the presumed bestowal of divine favor is more ambiguous than in the case of Me-

113. Chabot, "Note complémentaire," 26–27.
114. Eissfeldt, *Molk als Opferbegriff*, 4–5.
115. Sokoloff, 771; Payne-Smith, 277; Brockelmann, 188.

sha's sacrifice. Thus, as in the case of the general offering of firstborn children, the offering of firstborn children during periods of distress is also distinct from *mlk*/למלך sacrifices.

The offering of Jephthah's daughter may be the closest parallel to the למלך offerings. In both cases, a vow is made with the purpose of obtaining divine aid, and in both cases is the vow fulfilled in response to receiving said aid. As observed above, however, the Jephthah story is problematic, both because Jephthah did not intend to sacrifice his daughter and because the story's genre (folktale) makes it problematic for historical reconstruction. Furthermore, Jephthah's daughter is sacrificed as an עולה, not as a מלך (Judg 11:31). Thus, although the tale of Jephthah's sacrifice appears to provide the clearest conceptual parallel to what we can reconstruct concerning the *mlk*/למלך sacrifices, the story remains too problematic to argue that Jephthah's vow is an early example of such a sacrifice.

In sum, so far as we can tell, both the victim and the function of the למלך rites were distinct from the other forms of child sacrifice attested in the Hebrew Bible. The למלך rites involved the sacrifice of children in general, not firstborn children in particular, and were associated with vows, at least in the Punic comparative material. Having established this, and treating these offerings in their own right, what can be said about their history in Jerusalem? Were they an old native rite, practiced in common with the Punic colonists due to a shared inheritance from their mutual Canaanite ancestors? This has been a common assumption since Eissfeldt's day, but it does not appear to have the weight of the evidence behind it. Indeed, if we confine our examination to the למלך rites themselves, leaving other Yahwistic child sacrifice rituals aside, there is good reason to believe that the למלך rites only appeared in Jerusalem at a relatively late period.

First, the absence of any mention of למלך sacrifices in the early parts of the Deuteronomistic History or Chronicles is notable. Only two individuals are singled out as having made such offerings, both kings of Judah during a relatively late period: Ahaz, who either "caused his son to pass through (העביר) by fire" (2 Kgs 16:3) or, more explicitly, "offered incense in the Valley of Ben-Hinnom and burned (יבער) his son in fire" (2 Chr 28:3); and Manasseh, who also "caused his son to pass through (העביר) by fire" (2 Kgs 21:6), more specifically "in the valley of Ben-Hinnom" (2 Chr 33:6). Despite the fact that he is the first king accused of making such offerings, few scholars have argued that Ahaz was in fact the first king to do so. Though Albright does allow for this possibility, arguing that it is "possible that Ahaz was one of the first to borrow the Syrian custom of sacrificing children to confirm a solemn vow or pledge,"[116] more recent scholars have tended to date the emergence of these sacrifices to a relatively early period. Indeed, one of the few issues of agreement among various scholars across the spectrum of opinions is that they can be traced back as least as early as the tenth century, if not earlier.[117] Despite this general consensus, however, there is very little evidence for למלך sacrifices prior to the reign of Ahaz, and there are several reasons to suspect that Ahaz himself may have been responsible for incorporating למלך sacrifices into the cult of Yahweh at Jerusalem.

First, it is significant that, despite its obviously polemical tone, the Deuteronomistic History is actually quite precise in leveling its accusations. A survey of the various "sins" of the kings of Israel and Judah reveals that the Deuteronomistic history is remarkably predictable and even formulaic in its lists of misdeeds. The people of Judah are accused of building and worshiping at במות, מצבות, and אשרים under Rehoboam (1 Kgs 14:22–24), the במות are said to have remained in operation during the reigns of his successors (1 Kgs 15:12–14; 22:43; 2 Kgs 12:3; 14:3; 15:4, 35), and these shrines are consistently traced to the "nations whom Yahweh drove out before the Israelites" (1 Kgs 14:24; 2 Kgs 17:11). That is, the religious practices are native to the land, even if the Deuteronomists would claim that they are foreign to Yahwism (usually; but cf. 1 Sam 9:12–13, 14, 19, 25; 10:5; 2 Kgs 3:3–4). The primary sin of the Southern kings involves the failure to eliminate the במות. On the other hand, the primary sin of the Northern kings is "the sin of Jeroboam"[118]—worship at the shrines at Dan and Bethel (1 Kgs 12:25–33; 2 Kgs 10:29). In addition, the Northern kings of the Omride dynasty in particular are accused of committing the additional the sin of importing the worship of the Phoenican god Baal upon Ahab's marriage to the Phoenician princess Jezebel (1 Kgs 16:32; 22:53). The Baal cult that is said to have been mitigated under the reign of Jehoram (2 Kgs 3:2) and eliminated altogether as part of Jehu's bloody purge (2 Kgs 10:18–28). Ahab is also accused of erecting an אשרה in Samaria (1 Kgs 16:33; 2 Kgs 13:6). The sin of the Omrides

116. W. F. Albright, *Archaeology and the Religion of Israel* (5th ed.; Baltimore: Johns Hopkins University Press, 1968), 163; idem, *Yahweh and the Gods of Canaan*, 242. Albright is followed by M. Cogan, *Imperialism and Religion: Assyria, Judah and Israel in the Eighth and Seventh Centuries BCE* (SBLMS; Missoula, MT: Society of Biblical Literature and Scholars Press, 1974), 81–83.

117. Eissfeldt, *Molk als Opferbegriff*, 46–61; Mosca, "Child Sacrifice," 223–25; Heider, *Cult of Molek*, 327; Day, *Molech*, 55, 82–85; Ackerman, *Under Every Green Tree*, 137–43; Stavrakopoulou, *King Manasseh and Child Sacrifice*, 299; eadem, "The Jerusalem Tophet," 147–49.

118. 1 Kgs 15:26, 30, 34; 16:2, 19, 26, 31; 21:22; 22:52; 2 Kgs 3:3; 10:29; 13:2, 6, 11; 14:24; 15:9, 18, 24, 28.

is not confined to the North, however. Two Judahite kings, Jehoram (2 Kgs 8:18) and Ahaziah (2 Kgs 8:27) are condemned for "walking in the way of the house of Ahab," in both cases due to their connection with Athaliah, the daughter of Ahab, and probably also due to the construction of a "house of Baal" in the South, a shrine whose altars and images were destroyed and whose priests were later killed, as reported in 2 Kgs 11:18.

After Hezekiah destroyed the במות, מצבת, and אשרה, along with Moses's bronze serpent (2 Kgs 18:4), Manasseh is said to have reestablished the במות and אשרה, the traditional sins of the kings of Judah; he also erected altars for Baal, the traditional sources of sin for the Omride kings of both Israel and Judah (2 Kgs 21:3, 7). In addition, he is said to have introduced new offenses: worshiping the "host of heaven" (צבא השמים) and consulting עונן, נחש, אוב, and ידענים, apparently various forms divination (2 Kgs 21:5–6).[119] The combined sum of Manasseh's offenses are gathered under the rubric גלולים, usually translated "idols"[120] (2 Kgs 21:11). His successor Amon is accused of having continued to serve the גלולים of his father (2 Kgs 21:21). Finally, all of the various offenses of all previous kings, the sins of both Judah and Israel, are said to have been eliminated during the reform of Josiah (2 Kgs 23). Despite the fact that his successors are said to have done "evil in the eyes of Yahweh" (2 Kgs 23:32, 37; 24:12, 19), none are explicitly accused of reversing Josiah's reforms. Thus, there are essentially three sorts of cultic violations recounted in the books of Kings: the sins of the kings of Judah (במות, מצבות, and אשרים), the sins of the kings of Israel (the "sin of Jeroboam"), and the

---

119. On necromancy and other forms of divination in ancient Israel, see R. Schmitt, "Divination, II. Hebrew Bible/Old Testament," *EBR* 6, 959–61; R. Albertz and R. Schmitt, *Family and Household Religion in Ancient Israel and the Levant* (Winona Lake, IN: Eisenbrauns, 2012), 467–69; C. B. Hays, *Death in the Iron Age II and in First Isaiah* (FAT 79; Tübingen: Mohr Siebeck, 2011), 168–75; A. Jeffers, *Magic and Divination in Ancient Palestine and Syria* (SHCANE 8; Leiden: Brill, 1996), 168–81; B. B. Schmidt, *Israel's Beneficent Dead*, esp. 150–54, 179–87; F. H. Cryer, *Divination in Ancient Israel and Its Near Eastern Environment: A Socio-Historical Investigation* (JSOTSup 142; Sheffield: JSOT Press, 1994), esp. 255–305. T. J. Lewis, *Cults of the Dead in Ancient Israel and Ugarit* (HSM 39; Atlanta: Scholars Press, 1989), esp. 99–181; E. Bloch-Smith, *Judahite Burial Practices and Beliefs about the Dead* (JSOTSup 123; Sheffield: JSOT Press, 1992), esp. 121–32; J. K. Kuemmerlin-McLean, "Magic, Old Testament," *ABD* 4, 468–71; J. Tropper, *Nekromantie: Totenbefragung im Alten Orient und im Alten Testament* (AOAT 223; Kevelaer: Butzon & Bercker/Neukirchen-Vluyn: Nerkirchener, 1989).

120. See M. I. Gruber, "Gillulim גלולים εἴδωλα," *DDD*², 346–47; H. D. Preuss, גִּלּוּלִים *gillûlîm*; גִּלֻּלִים *gillulîm*, *TDOT* 3, 1–5; *HALOT* 192; BDB 165. The term is especially common in Deuteronomic and Deuteronomically influenced literature. See M. Weinfeld, *Deuteronomy and the Deuteronomic School* (Oxford: Clarendon, 1972; repr., Winona Lake, IN: Eisenbrauns, 2014), 323.

Baal worship of the Omrides. Only the latter involves foreign syncretism, but even here the syncretism is the veneration of a foreign deity, not incorporating foreign elements into the cult of Yahweh.

For this reason, a distinctive notice concerning Ahaz's syncretistic renovations of the Jerusalem temple stands out as idiosyncratic. The Kings account of Ahaz's reign begins in the standard fashion: Ahaz's accession to the Judahite throne is dated to the current regnal year of the corresponding king of Israel; Ahaz's age at his accession and the length of his reign are indicated; and a notice that "he did not do right in the eyes of Yahweh" immediately follows the date formulae (2 Kgs 16:1–4). Next appears an account of the major interactions with foreign powers during Ahaz's reign, in this case the unsuccessful siege of Jerusalem waged by King Rezin of Aram and King Pekah of Israel and Ahaz's submission to the king of Assyria (2 Kgs 16:5–9). All this follows the standard formula for recounting the reigns of both Israelite and Judahite kings, with some minor variations.[121] Essentially this same pattern for every king from Rehoboam to Jotham, Ahaz's immediate predecessor, holds in Kings.[122]

Ahaz, however, is one of a handful of kings whose reign account is supplemented with a notice concerning alterations made to the temple. Similar reports include the temple restoration accounts of Joash (2 Kgs 12:5–17 [Eng. 12:4–16]) and Josiah (2 Kgs 22:3–7), along with details concerning the temple's role in the priestly coup initiated against Athaliah (2 Kgs 11). This material, along with the report concerning the temple's furnishings at the time of Solomon's dedication (1 Kgs 6–7; 8:1–13, 62–64), has sometimes been attributed to an independent source called a Temple Chronicle, although the unity of this source, its date of incorporation into the Deuteronomistic History, and its original nature have been disputed since Wellhausen first suggested its existence.[123] Taking a somewhat different ap-

121. For example, Israelite kings' accessions are dated to Judahite kings' regnal years, and as noted above, the prototypical sins of the two kingdoms are different; in the case of a few Judahite kings, there is a notice that they "did right in the eyes of Yahweh" in place of the claim that they "did not do right in the eyes of Yahweh"; and in some cases, a report of a coup stands in place of a king's interactions with foreign powers.

122. Minor exceptions to this pattern exist. For instance, there is no notice that Elah son of Baasha continued to commit the "sin of Jeroboam" between the report of his accession and the narrative concerning Zimri's coup (1 Kgs 16:8–11), and the notice concerning Zimri's sins is postponed until after that narrative is completed (1 Kgs 16:15–19). Similarly, no information is provided concerning Omri's foreign interactions, but a notice concerning his buying the hill of Samaria does immediately precede the notice concerning his sins (1 Kgs 16:23–27).

123. F. Bleek, A. Kamphausen, and J. Wellhausen, *Einleitung in das Alte Testament* (4th ed.; Berlin: Reimer, 1878), 257–59. Those following Wellhausen to one degree or another in-

proach, N. Na'aman traces these reports to various royal dedicatory inscriptions that recounted the building activities of Judahite kings in the temple precincts and that were still visible and available for use as sources by the Deuteronomistic historian(s), rather than representing a single, already unified source.[124]

Whatever the ultimate source of the report concerning Ahaz's temple renovations, it does on its face appear to be relatively historically reliable. The tone of the narrative is strikingly objective, even clinical, given the subject matter, without even a hint of the condemnation that one might expect in the Deuteronomistic History.[125] This stands in stark contrast to the account of the same event in 2 Chr 28:22–24, which unequivocally condemns Ahaz's activity vis-à-vis the temple. Although the Deuteronomistic writers clearly had a negative view of Ahaz (see 2 Kgs 16:2–4), there is no indication that his alterations to the temple were among the "abominations" (תעבות) that he committed (16:3). This surprising lack of polemic lends historical credibility to the report. That is, since the report is not put to a polemical use, its only function is to recount the occurrence of the event itself, and there is thus no obvious motivation for someone to manufacture it. Likewise, the fact that the activity recounted in the report does not represent any of the

clude I. Benzinger, *Die Bücher der Könige* (KHC 9; Freiburg: Mohr [Siebeck], 1899), 158–59, 170–71; A. Šanda, *Die Bücher der Könige* (vol. 2; EHAT 9; Münster: Aschendorffsch, 1912), 148–49; R. H. Pfeiffer, *Introduction to the Old Testament* (New York: Harper & Brothers, 1941), 401–2; Montgomery, *Kings*, 37–38; S. R. Driver, *An Introduction to the Literature of the Old Testament* (New York: Meridian, 1956), 189; J. Gray, *I & II Kings: A Commentary* (2nd ed.; OTL; Philadelphia: Westminster, 1970), 13–14; T. R. Hobbs, *2 Kings* (WBC 13; Waco, TX: Word, 1985), 148; K. A. D. Smelik, "The New Altar of King Ahaz (2 Kings 16): Deuteronomistic Re-Interpretation of a Cult Reform," in *Deuteronomy and Deuteronomic Literature: Festschrift C. H. W. Brekelmans* (ed. M. Vervenne and J. Lust; BETL 133; Leuven: Leuven University Press, 1997), 276; M. Cogan, *1 Kings: A New Translation with Introduction and Commentary* (AB 10; New York: Doubleday, 2000), 94–95.

124. N. Na'aman, "Royal Inscriptions and the Histories of Joash and Ahaz, Kings of Judah," *VT* 48 (1998): 333–49.

125. So Montgomery, *Kings*, 459–60; Smelik, "The New Altar of King Ahaz," 276–77; A. Lemaire, "The Evolution of the 8th-Century B.C.E. Jerusalem Temple," in *The Fire Signals of Lachish: Studies in the Archaeology and History of Israel in the Late Bronze Age, Iron Age, and Persian Period in Honor of David Ussishkin* (ed. I. Finkelstein and N. Na'aman; Winona Lake, IN: Eisenbrauns, 2011), 197; P. Dubovský, *The Building of the First Temple: A Study in Redactional, Text-Critical, and Historical Perspective* (FAT 103; Tübingen: Mohr Siebeck, 2015), 53–56. *Pace* Cohn who detects a critique conveyed "indirectly through the detailing of the despoliation and the remodeling of the access routes to the temple" (*2 Kings* [Berit Olam; Collegeville, MN: Liturgical, 2000], 115). So also Cogan and Tadmor (*II Kings*, 193), who claim that the innovations are "criticized." I find no critique in the account, either direct or indirect.

standard accusations leveled by the Deuteronomistic History likewise points to its having been primarily historical rather than polemical in nature.

The report itself runs as follows:

> King Ahaz went to meet Tiglath-pileser, king of Assyria, at Damascus, and he saw the altar that was in Damascus. King Ahaz sent the likeness of the altar, its construction, and all its details to Uriah the priest, and Uriah the priest built the altar. According to all that King Ahaz had sent him from Damascus, so Uriah the priest did prior to King Ahaz's coming from Damascus. The king came from Damascus, and the king saw the altar. The king approached the altar and ascended upon it. He offered its burnt offering and its offering, and he poured out its libation, and he sprinkled the blood of its peace offerings upon the altar. He removed the bronze altar that was before Yahweh from in front of the temple, between the altar and the temple of Yahweh, and he put it on the north side of the altar. King Ahaz commanded Uriah the priest, "Offer the morning burnt offering, the evening offering, the king's burnt offering, his offering, the burnt offering of all the people of the land, their offering, and their libations upon the great altar. All blood of a burnt offering and blood of a sacrifice you will sprinkle upon it. The bronze altar will be mine for inquiring. Uriah the priest did everything just as King Ahaz commanded. King Ahaz cut off the edges of the stands and removed the basin. He brought down the sea from upon the bronze oxen which were under it, and he set it upon a pavement of stones. He removed the covered way of the sabbath which they built in the temple and the outer entrance of the king from the temple of Yahweh, from before the king of Assyria. (2 Kgs 16:10–18)

There are several points worth noting concerning the altar report. First, it is likely that 16:10–16, the report about the construction, installation, and use of the altar, was originally independent from 16:17–18, which describe Ahaz's removal of various items from the temple, apparently for the purpose of paying tribute to the king of Assyria (2 Kgs 16:8). This latter section probably has no original connection with the altar report proper.[126] The report itself

126. So also Smelik, "The New Altar of King Ahaz," 275; Dubovský, *Building of the First Temple*, 60–61; Cogan and Tadmor, *II Kings*, 193; but cf. H.-D. Hoffmann, *Reform und Reformen: Untersuchungen zu einem Grundthema der deuteronomistischen Geschichtsschreibung* (AThANT 66; Zurich: Theologischer, 1980), 142–44, who takes 10–18 as a unit; and Na'aman, "Royal Inscriptions and the Histories of Joash and Ahaz," 345–47, who argues that 16:10–16, 18 are all drawn from the same inscription, while 16:17 comes from a separate source. A further subdivision—taking 16:12–14 as a secondary addition (or additions, taking 16:12–14 as a composite itself) to 16:10–11 and 16:15–16—has also been suggested (see R. Rendtorff, *Studien zur Geschichte des Opfers im alten Israel* [WMANT 24; Neukirchen-Vluyn: Neukirchener Verlag,

recounts how Ahaz saw an altar in Damascus, decided to have an identical one built in Jerusalem, and commissioned Uriah the priest to carry out the task. It was once common for scholars to assume that this action was motivated by Assyrian pressure on their Judahite vassal in the direction of religious and/or cultural assimilation.[127] Two almost contemporaneous examinations of the general Assyrian religious policy toward their vassal states in the mid-1970s—that of M. Cogan, whose starting point was the Assyrian evidence,[128] and that of J. W. McKay, who began with the biblical evidence[129]—convincingly demonstrated that there is no real evidence that the Neo-Assyrians ever attempted to control the worship of their vassals. It now appears more likely that Ahaz installed a new bronze altar in Jerusalem for the simple reason that he wanted to.[130] This altar was apparently of a Damascene style, but it is nonetheless likely that the offerings made on the altar were directed toward Yahweh, the national god of Judah; otherwise, we would expect the Deuteronomistic History to tell us so. Ahaz therefore appears to have imported foreign forms of worship into the cult of Yahweh at the Jerusalem temple. Of course, once such forms and rites were incorporated into the tradition, these practices would have been understood by the worshipers there as just as authentic expressions of the tradition as any others.[131] That is, there is no

1967], 46–50; E. Würthwein, *Die Bücher der Könige: 1. Kön. 17–2. Kön. 25* [ATD 11:2; Göttingen: Vandenhoeck & Ruprecht, 1984], 389–90; and S. A. Irvine, *Isaiah, Ahaz, and the Syro-Ephraimitic Crisis* [SBLDS 123; Atlanta: Scholars Press, 1990], 80–81). Whether 16:10–16 is a composite or an original unit, however, is ultimately unimportant for present purposes.

127. See especially T. Oestreicher, *Das deuteronomische Grundgesetz* (BFCT 27:4; Gütersloh: C. Bertelsmann, 1923), 38; and A. T. Olmstead, *History of Assyria* (New York: Charles Scribner's Sons, 1923), 198; idem, *History of Palestine and Syria to the Macedonian Conquest* (New York: Charles Scribner's Sons, 1931), 452. More recently, Schmidt has again argued in favor of the thesis that the altar can be traced to Assyrian "influence," although he hesitates to go so far as to suggest Assyrian "imposition" (*Israel's Beneficent Dead*, 222–36).

128. Cogan, *Imperialism and Religion*, esp. 72–77.

129. J. W. McKay, *Religion in Judah under the Assyrians 732–609 BC* (SBT 26; London: SCM, 1973), 5–12.

130. So also Smelik, "The New Altar of King Ahaz," 265–66; and Lemaire, "The Evolution of the 8th-Century B.C.E. Jerusalem Temple," 197–99.

131. The twin aspect—that is, the constantly changing yet conceptually continuous nature—of the historical development of the configurations of religious belief and practice has been dubbed "orthosyncretism" (a portmanteau constructed from "orthodoxy" and "syncretism") by T. Light, "Orthosyncretism: An Account of Melding in Religion," *Method & Theory in the Study of Religion* 12 (2000): 162–86. On the other hand, it is not uncommon for syncretism to generate an opposing "anti-syncretism" that attempts to preserve a more "authentic" religion, free of change—a descriptor that may aptly describe some of the traditions represented in the Hebrew Bible. In this regard, see especially the essays in C. Stewart and R. Shaw,

indication that Ahaz or Uriah would have understood their new altar as anything other than Yahwistic. Of course, the fact that the Chronicler viewed worship at this foreign altar as tantamount to worshiping foreign deities (2 Chr 28:23) indicates that other assessments of the legitimacy of Ahaz's syncretistic innovations were possible.

The most important detail for the present discussion, however, is that the report indicates that Ahaz was interested in incorporating foreign elements into the cult of Yahweh in Jerusalem. Notably, he is also the first king accused of "passing his son over by fire." That this latter claim also has some historical veracity is supported by the fact that there is no obvious motivation for attaching an accusation to Ahaz instead of one of the other "bad" kings of the Deuteronomistic History. Why not instead accuse Ahab, a much more "wicked" king, of the sin of child sacrifice? Or, on the other hand, why not save such an accusation for Manasseh, the "worst" of the Judahite kings? In short, there is no obvious reason for the Deuteronomistic writer(s) to manufacture this accusation against Ahaz in particular. It is possible then that he is the first king accused of making such sacrifices because he actually was the first to do so. If this logical thread is pursued, it follows that he introduced the rite into Jerusalem under foreign influence just as he rearranged the temple furnishings in imitation of the temple in Damascus. Contrary to the current scholarly consensus, למלך may actually be a late syncretistic import into Jerusalem under Ahaz, apparently a particularly syncretistic king.

None of this contradicts the arguments of chapter 1 that the למלך cult was Yahwistic in nature as practiced in Jerusalem. The sum of the evidence still points to למלך as meaning "as a *mōlek*-sacrifice" and to Yahweh as the

eds., *Syncretism/Anti-Syncretism: The Politics of Religious Synthesis* (New York: Routledge, 1994). The literature on the phenomenon and nature of religious and cultural syncretism—and even whether the use of the term "syncretism" is appropriate within academic discourse—is extensive. See especially, however, the seminal work by M. Pye, "Syncretism and Ambiguity," *Numen* 18 (1971): 83–93; idem, "Syncretism vs. Synthesis," *Method & Theory in the Study of Religion* 6 (1993): 217–29; as well as objections to some of Pye's allegedly essentialist assumptions by L. Martin, "Syncretism, Historicism, and Cognition: A Response to Michael Pye," *Method & Theory in the Study of Religion* 8 (1996): 215–24. Other important theoretical work on the topic includes A. Droogers, "Syncretism: The Problem of a Definition, the Definition of the Problem," in *Dialogue and Syncretism: An Interdisciplinary Approach* (ed. J. D. Gort et al.; Grand Rapids, MI: Eerdmans, 1989), 7–25; idem, "Syncretism, Power and Play," in *Syncretism and the Commerce of Symbols* (ed. G. Aijmer; Gothenburg: Institute for Advanced Studies in Social Anthropology, 1995), 38–59; D. N. Gellner, "For Syncretism: The Position of Buddhism in Nepal and Japan Compared," *Social Anthropology* 5 (1997): 275–89; C. Stewart, "Syncretism and Its Synonyms: Reflections on Cultural Mixture," *Diacritics* 29 (1999): 40–62; and M. Togawa, "Syncretism Revisited: Hindus and Muslims over a Saintly Cult in Bengal," *Numen* 55 (2008): 27–43.

divine recipient of these offerings. Thus, the reconstruction suggested here is that Ahaz adopted the למלך rite, previously unattested in Judah, from his (probably Phoenician) neighbors. If these sacrifices were associated with vows, as the relevant Punic evidence indicates, then they would not have been entirely innovative and out of place in Judah, which had a long history of rites involving vows and their fulfillment[132]—although Yahwistic vows are of course not otherwise connected to the practice of child sacrifice (Jephthah's unintended sacrifice excepted, of course). Just as the Damascus altar was a foreign import incorporated into the Yahwistic cult, so too would למלך rites be an originally foreign type of sacrifice that was nonetheless appropriated by the Jerusalem cult as fully Yahwistic.

This reconstruction of the history of the למלך sacrifices butts up against a few apparent difficulties. Those who trace the למלך rites to a much earlier period have typically brought forward two relevant pieces of evidence. The first is Isa 30:33, which many have argued is evidence of the antiquity of the tophet in the Ben-Hinnom Valley outside Jerusalem and of the למלך offerings that were offered there. The verse serves as the conclusion of an oracle against Aššur (33:27–33)—either the deity, the nation, or both. In this oracle, Yahweh declares that he (or, more properly, his Name [33:27]) will come crashing in like a torrent against Aššur, breaking the yoke of the Assyrian Empire. Yahweh's approach is marked by fire, storm, flood, and hail (33:30). The oracle works up to a climax, declaring that Aššur will be utterly destroyed, like the victim of a למלך sacrifice. The fact that the oracle is directed against Assyria has rightly led many to conclude that the most obvious date of composition for the oracle is during the time when Assyria actually was an imminent threat, probably during the campaign of Sennacherib.[133] The MT of 30:33 is unfortunately somewhat garbled, especially

132. See T. W. Cartledge, *Vows in the Hebrew Bible and the Ancient Near East* (JSOTSup 147; Sheffield: JSOT Press, 1992); J. Berlinerblau, *The Vow and the 'Popular Religious Groups' of Ancient Israel: A Philological and Sociological Inquiry* (JSOTSup 210; Sheffield: Sheffield Academic, 1996); Y. Ziegler, *Promises to Keep: The Oath in Biblical Narrative* (VTSup 120; Leiden: Brill, 2008).

133. So B. S. Childs, *Isaiah* (OTL; Louisville: Westminster John Knox, 2001), 227–28; H. Wildberger, *Isaiah 28–39* (trans. T. H. Trapp; CC; Minneapolis: Fortress, 2002), 189–94; J. J. M. Roberts, *First Isaiah* (ed. P. Machinist; Hermeneia; Minneapolis: Fortress, 2015), 396–400. Important dissenters, however, include R. E. Clements, *Isaiah 1–39* (NCB; Grand Rapids, MI: Eerdmans, 1980), 252–54; O. Kaiser, *Isaiah 13–39* (trans. R. A Wilson; OTL; Philadelphia: Westminster, 1974), 304–10; H. Barth, *Die Jesaja-Worte in der Josiazeit: Israel und Assur als Thema einer produktiven Neuinterpretation der Jesajaüberlierferung* (WMANT 48; Neukirchen-Vluyn: Neukirchener Verlag, 1977), 102–3; and J. Blenkinsopp, *Isaiah 1–39: A New Translation with Introduction and Commentary* (AB 19; New York: Doubleday, 2000), 423–24.

in the pointing. Nonetheless, Mosca has convincingly reconstructed it as follows:[134]

כי ערוך מאתמול תפתה	For his tophet[135] has been arranged from אתמול.[136]
גם הוא למלך הוכן	Even he[137] [= Aššur] is arranged as a *mōlek*-sacrifice.[138]
העמיק הרחב מדרתה	He [= Yahweh?] has widened and deepened its pyre.
אש ועצים הרבה	Fire and wood in abundance,
נשמת יהוה	the breath of Yahweh
כנחל גפרית	like a river of brimstone
בערה בה	is burning in it.

Thus, the oracle depicts Aššur as the victim of a למלך sacrifice, who will soon be consumed by a blazing fire, and on its basis Mosca draws five important conclusions concerning the למלך rite, which may be outlined as follows:[139]

1. "Passing children into the fire" involved their death, not merely their dedication (i.e., the passage obviously implies Aššur's destruction, not dedication).
2. The ritual accords well with what we can discern concerning the Carthaginian rites with the same name (see especially the description of Diodorus, who also has the rite take place in a pit filled with fire;[140] also compare the "timbrels and lyres" of Isa 30:32 with Plutarch's claim that the Carthaginian rite was accompanied by flutes and drums;[141] finally, Isa 30:27 sets the rite at night, as does a stele at Ngaous that refers to the sacrifice as a *sacrum magnum nocturnum*[142]).
3. Biblical מלך is a sacrificial term, not the name of a deity (i.e., in being "arranged as a מלך," Aššur is presented as the victim of a sacrifice, not its recipient).
4. The למלך rite is presented as a part of the official Yahwistic cultus (since it is unlikely that Yahweh would be presented as presiding over, and even initiating, a non-Yahwistic sacrifice).

---

134. The translation here broadly follows Mosca, "Child Sacrifice," 200–201, but diverges from it in a few important details, as discussed below.

135. MT vocalizes this word תָּפְתֶּה, an anomalous form. Mosca astutely suggests that the final ה is a mater for *-ô*, both here and elsewhere in the oracle, as in the orthography of contemporary inscriptions ("Child Sacrifice," 203).

136. On the significance of this word, see pp. 140–41 below.

137. Following K and Mosca, "Child Sacrifice," 206.

138. Reading *mulk/mōlek* for MT מֶּלֶךְ. So also Mosca, "Child Sacrifice," 202, 215–16.

139. Ibid., 212.

140. *Bibliotheca historica* 20.14.4–6.

141. *De superstitione* 171c–d.

142. Ngaous I; Mosca, "Child Sacrifice," 57.

5. Isaiah does not appear to have objected to the rite; there is no hint of condemnation of the rite by which Yahweh intends to destroy Aššur.

All five of Mosca's observations are sound, in my opinion. Mosca also suggests, correctly in my view, that the rite was practiced by Ahaz, as well as (at least) tolerated by Hezekiah and Isaiah, since there is no mention of a defilement of the tophet during the reform of the former nor any word of condemnation concerning it from the latter.[143] Mosca reaches the further conclusion that

> Isaiah's metaphorical use of Topheth and *mōlek* in a completely Yahwistic context is difficult to reconcile with a late eighth-century introduction or resurgence of child sacrifice under pagan Aramaic influence. If Ahaz, during his reign, had imported into Judah an essentially pagan or paganizing practice—especially one so awesome and, to an outsider, so loathsome—we would certainly expect the reform-minded Hezekiah and orthodox prophetic and priestly circles to react strongly against it. Yet on both fronts we are met only with silence.[144]

This final conclusion, however, is problematic: it makes several assumptions that are ultimately not warranted by the evidence. There is no reason to assume that the introduction of למלך rites into the Yahwistic cult would have aroused particular animosity by "orthodox" (whatever the term means in this context) individuals like Isaiah and Hezekiah. As I have argued above, there is evidence that at least two other forms of child sacrifice existed among Israelite Yahwists: the general sacrifice of firstborn children and the sacrifice of firstborn children during times of distress, both apparently with rather old Yahwistic roots. Likewise, offering sacrifices to Yahweh in fulfillment of vows is well attested in the Hebrew Bible.[145] Although the combination of sacrificing children with the fulfillment of vows may have been novel, neither element on its own would have necessarily been particularly "awesome" or "loathsome" in the context of eighth-century Judahite religious practice. There is thus no reason to assume that the "orthodox" biblical writers of the period would have necessarily objected to the late importation of such a rite into the Jerusalem cult.

143. Ibid., 219–20.

144. Ibid., 219.

145. See, e.g., Lev 22:21–25; Num 6:1–21; 30:2–17 [Eng. 30:1–16]; Deut 23:21–23 [Eng. 23:22–24]; Ps 22:26 [Eng. 22:25]; 50:14; 56:13 [Eng. 56:12]; 61:6, 9 [Eng. 61:5, 8]; 65:2 [Eng. 65:1]; 76:12 [Eng. 76:11]; 116:14, 18; 132:2.

In addition, the language of Isa 30:33 itself implies that the rite was new to Jerusalem. Its first line reads כי ערוך מאתמול תפתה, literally "for arranged from *yesterday* is his tophet." The phrase "from yesterday" has almost universally been understood and translated "from long ago,"[146] a translation that admittedly has good support from the versions: OG πρὸ ἡμερῶν "before days," Targum Jonathan מן עלמין "from eternity," Peshitta ܡܢ ܩܕܡ ܝܘܡܬܐ "from before days." Each appears to assume that מאתמול refers to a time in the distant past, just as modern translators do. Despite this consensus of both ancient and modern translators, however, this does not seem to be the most natural meaning of the phrase מאתמול.

It should first be noted that the term is vocalized אֶתְמוּל, rather than the more common אֶתְמוֹל,[147] although this difference in pronunciation is probably not significant. In addition, a more common form of the word lacks the initial *aleph*: תְּמֹל/תְּמוֹל.[148] The most basic meaning of the term is "yesterday"[149]—that is, "the day before today"—but it is attested in this literal sense only in 1 Sam 20:27. In the overwhelming majority of cases, the term is used in conjunction with שלשום "the day before yesterday." As a unit, the two terms form a merism simply meaning "formerly."[150] In all other cases, אתמול (and its related forms), when used in isolation, refers to the very *recent* past. For example, in Exod 5:14, the Egyptian taskmasters ask why the Israelite slaves have failed to complete their assigned quotas since the imposition of the new requirement that they gather straw in addition to making bricks. In this text, גם תמול גם היום "recently" (lit., "both yesterday and today") stands in contrast to תמול שלשם "formerly" (lit., "yesterday, the day before yesterday"). In 2 Sam 15:20, David exhorts Ittai the Gittite to return to his home in the wake of Absalom's coup. David asks, "Just recently (תמול) was your coming, and today (היום) will I make you wander with us?" The implication here is that, since Ittai had only joined David's band recently (lit., "yesterday"), he owed David no support during the present time of distress. In Job 8:9, the brevity of life is expressed: "For we are 'yesterday' (תמול) and we do not

---

146. So KJV, NRSV, JPS, Mosca, "Child Sacrifice," 200; Blenkinsopp, *Isaiah 1–39*, 422; Childs, *Isaiah*, 223; Wildberger, *Isaiah 28–39*, 186, 189; J. D. W. Watts, *Isaiah 1–33* (rev. ed.; WBC 24; Nashville: Nelson, 2005), 472–73; J. J. M. Roberts, *First Isaiah*, 397.

147. See 1 Sam 4:7; 14:21; 19:7; 2 Sam 5:2; Mic 2:8 (probably a scribal error there, however); Ps 90:4. In addition, in 1 Sam 10:11 the word is vocalized אִתְּמוֹל.

148. Gen 31:2, 5; Exod 4:10; 5:7, 8, 14 (2×); 21:29, 36; Deut 4:42; 19:4, 6; Josh 3:4; 4:18; 20:5; 1 Sam 20:27; 21:6; 2 Sam 3:17; 15:20; 2 Kgs 13:5; Job 8:9; Ruth 2:11; 1 Chr 11:2.

149. BDB 1069–70; *HALOT* 103, 1746.

150. Gen 31:2, 5; Exod 4:10; 5:7, 8, 14; 21:29, 36; Deut 4:42; 19:4, 6; Josh 3:4; 4:18; 20:5; 1 Sam 4:7; 10:11; 14:21; 19:7; 21:6; 2 Sam 3:17; 5:2; 2 Kgs 13:5; Ruth 2:11; 1 Chr 11:2.

know. For our days on earth are a shadow." Here the present generation is contrasted with former generations (דר רישון), mentioned in the previous verse; we are "recent" (תמול) but they are "bygone" (רישון). Finally, in Ps 90:4 the fleeting brevity of human life is compared to the everlasting nature of God: "For a thousand years in your eyes are like yesterday (יום אתמול) when it passes, or a watch in the night." Again, the אתמול/תמול expresses a short amount of time and is explicitly contrasted with a long duration of time. Indeed, if אתמול indicated "long ago" here, the entire rhetorical force of the comparison would be destroyed. "For a thousand years in your eyes are like the distant past" is the exact opposite of what the psalm seeks to convey. In sum, there is no instance in the Hebrew Bible in which the term /אתמול תמול is used to indicate the distant past, and it often refers specifically to the immediate or recent past.

This brings us back to Isa 30:33a: כי ערוך מאתמול תפתה, typically translated something like "For his burning place has *long been* prepared" (NRSV, emphasis mine). The consistent usage of the term elsewhere in the Hebrew Bible, however, points in precisely the opposite direction. Given the lexical analysis above, the phrase מאתמול—literally, "from yesterday"—should mean "just recently," and the line should instead be understood as something like "For his tophet has *just recently* been prepared." If the verse is referring to the tophet in Jerusalem, as Mosca and others have convincingly argued, then it also assumes that it had *not* been there for a particularly long time. This fits well with the circumstantial evidence that Ahaz is presented as the first king who "passed over a son by fire." Since Ahaz took the throne during Isaiah's own lifetime (Isa 6:1), if the tophet was established during Ahaz's reign, it certainly would qualify as "recently" (מאתמול) from Isaiah's perspective. Thus, Isa 30:33, like 2 Kgs 16, actually points to למלך as a syncretistic import during the late eighth century, not a rite with old roots in the Jerusalem cult, as most have assumed.

The other major evidence that seems to oppose a late eighth-century date for the first appearance of למלך offerings in Jerusalem is found in 2 Kgs 17:17a. Among the litany of sins that the Northern Kingdom is accused of having committed in the course of its existence as a nation we find, "And they caused their sons and their daughters to pass over in fire" (ויעבירו את בניהם ואת בנותים באש). As has already been observed several times, this language is closely associated with the למלך rite, and thus this verse implies that such sacrifices were practiced in the Northern Kingdom prior to its fall. Even though Ahaz's reign technically began prior to the fall of Samaria (2 Kgs 17:1) and it would therefore be possible to posit that these rites were introduced in

Israel at the same time as in Judah, there are a few reasons to be skeptical of the claim that למלך sacrifices were ever offered in the North.

First, no Northern king is singled out as having made such an offering. Almost all kings of Israel are accused of having continued in the "sin of Jeroboam"; and the Omrides, both in Israel and in Judah, are accused of worshiping the Phoenician god Baal. But there is no case in which Kings accuses a specific Northern king of "causing his sons and daughters to pass over by fire." Given its general antipathy toward the Northern Kingdom, it would be surprising if the Deuteronomistic History neglected to note the specific Northern kings who had offered such sacrifices if they in fact had done so.

The second reason to be suspicious is the rhetorical function of the litany in 2 Kgs 17 within the Deuteronomistic History itself. As Stavrakopoulou correctly observes, one of the overarching strategies employed in the books of Kings is to present the sins of King Manasseh as foreign, specifically Northern, in nature. The litany of sins in 2 Kgs 17:9–17 has a striking parallel in the list of Manasseh's sins in 2 Kgs 21:2–7. Both the Northern kings and Manasseh are accused of building "high places" (17:9, 11; 21:3) and asherim/an asherah (17:10; 21:3); serving גלולים (usually translated "idols"; 17:12; 21:11), the "host of heaven" (17:16; 21:5), and Baal (17:16; 21:3); practicing various forms of divination (קסם and נחש in 17:17; עונן and נחש in 21:6); and "causing their sons to pass over by fire" (17:17; 21:6). The fact that this particular cluster of accusations is only found in the report concerning Manasseh's sins and in the list of sins attributed to the fallen Northern monarchy signals that the Deuteronomistic History's twin sin litanies connect Manasseh to the Northern Kingdom. In particular, in Stavrakopoulou's view, the goal was to present Manasseh's sins as Northern sins, and thus "foreign."[151] Stavrakopoulou is no doubt correct, but the direction of dependence and the historical reality behind these charges is subject to debate.

One possibility is that the biblical text as we have it is essentially accurate: the Northern kings, Ahaz, and Manasseh all participated in the rite of "causing his son to pass over by fire." This is Mosca's view; he believes that the practice was more widespread than the evidence, strictly taken, indicates, with our sources only selectively applying the accusation in an effort to portray Ahaz, Manasseh, and the Northern Kingdom negatively.[152] Alterna-

151. Stavrakopoulou, *King Manasseh and Child Sacrifice*, 59–68. Similarly, see Smith, "Child Sacrifice as the Extreme Case," 9–12.

152. See Mosca, "Child Sacrifice," 189–92, 258–59 n. 157. Heider (*The Cult of Molek*, 403–5) and Stavrakopoulou (*King Manasseh and Child Sacrifice*, 87–88 and 299) agree that the למלך sacrifice was more widespread in Judah than the Kings narrative reports, but both are

tively, Smith suggests that all three accusations, given their obvious agenda of presenting Ahaz, Manasseh, and the kings of the North in a negative light, are tendentious—a "literary effort at heaping up the sins of the kings in question" and depicting Ahaz and Manasseh as partaking in an "extreme case of immoral non-Israelite behavior."[153] This analysis is possible, but it leaves no real basis for the accusation, which means that it would have to be essentially the product of imagination. I suggest a third option: the accusations against Ahaz and Manasseh are essentially accurate, but the similar accusations against the Northern Kingdom are the result of a tendentious attempt to link the fall of the North with the sins of the South. The Deuteronomists take the "sins" of Manasseh and retroactively apply them to the kings of Israel. As Stavrakopoulou rightly observes, presenting the sins of the North and the South as essentially identical serves to present Manasseh (as well as Ahaz) as behaving like a Northern (= foreign) king. It also has the effect of presenting the fall of Samaria as a precursor to the fall of Jerusalem; both kingdoms committed the same sins and suffered/will suffer the same fate. The fact that there is no other evidence for למלך sacrifices in the North, however, is probably a sign that the accusation as applied to Samaria reflects the rhetorical agenda of the Kings narrative and not the historical reality of Northern Israelite practice.[154]

Thus, the למלך offerings are an originally Phoenician/Punic rite that involved the sacrifice of children of both sexes in fulfillment of vows, probably made to ensure success in private undertakings. The earliest plausible evidence for the rite in Jerusalem is the notice that Ahaz "caused his son to pass over by fire," language elsewhere associated with the למלך rite, and the claim in Isa 30:33 that the tophet has "just recently" (מאתמול) been set up. These two pieces of evidence lead to the conclusion that the Phoenician/Punic למלך offerings were introduced into the Jerusalem cult by Ahaz. The tophet where these sacrifices were offered apparently continued in operation until the reform of Josiah, when it was defiled (2 Kgs 23:10). That Ahaz (2 Kgs 16:3) and Manasseh (2 Kgs 21:6) are accused of participating in the cult, but no mention is made of it during the accounts of the reigns of Hezekiah

more ambivalent about the veracity of the accusation that it also took place in the Northern Kingdom.

153. Smith, "Child Sacrifice as the Extreme Case," 11. Smith argues that the way in which both 2 Kgs 16:3 and 21:6 introduce the accusations with וגם may suggest that the accusations were textually secondary in nature ("Child Sacrifice as the Extreme Case," 9–10). Although the list of accusations may well be the result of a layered text, this does not necessarily mean that the accusation is tendentious, especially since Isa 30:33 (see above) presents the למלך rites as a recent import, thus supporting the accusation of 2 Kgs 16:3.

154. So also Day, *Molech*, 15 n. 1; *pace* Mosca, "Child Sacrifice," 258–59 n. 157.

and Amon, can probably be ascribed primarily to a Deuteronomistic agenda. The absence of an explicit notice concerning Amon's having supported the tophet and its rite can be explained by the apparent general lack of interest in his reign by the Kings writer(s). The notice concerning his sins is a cursory observation that he continued in the ways of his father Manasseh (2 Kgs 21:20–22), which of course includes the למלך sacrifices.

Only Hezekiah, who reigned between Ahaz and Manasseh, remains, but he is neither said to have participated in the למלך cult as they did, nor to have opposed it as Josiah did. It seems most likely that למלך rites continued to be offered during Hezekiah's reign[155] but that the Kings account omits any mention of them due to its generally pro-Hezekiah stance. If he had actively opposed it, on the other hand, it is unlikely that the Kings account would fail to mention that fact. Given the limited nature of our evidence, it is impossible to say whether Hezekiah merely tolerated or actively supported the למלך rites of the Jerusalem tophet, but despite the rite's foreign origin, it does not appear to have encountered any real or sustained opposition until the reform of Josiah.

Conclusions

This chapter has argued that there are several rites that involved the sacrifice of children in the Hebrew Bible. The first example is the application of the law of the firstborn to human children, a rite explored in detail in chapter 3. The version of the law in the Covenant Code (Exod 22:28b–29 [Eng. 29b–30]) shows that at least some Yahwists viewed the literal sacrifice of a firstborn child as the appropriate means of acknowledging Yahweh's claim to firstborn children. These sacrifices, like firstfruit offerings in general, served to ensure bounty and prosperity, and failing to give Yahweh his due would result in calamity and destruction. Applied to children, offering up a first child would be tantamount to giving up one's firstborn in exchange for divine protection of subsequent children, especially during the perils of birth and infancy, dangers that were particularly acute in the ancient world. As chapter 5 will demonstrate, however, sacrifice of firstborn children was not the only mechanism employed in ancient Israel for fulfilling this obligation, and there is no reason to suspect that this particular form of acknowledging Yahweh's rightful claim to firstborn children was ever universal, or even necessarily widespread, in ancient Israel.

155. So also Mosca, "Child Sacrifice," 218; and Heider, *The Cult of Molek*, 288–89.

The second form of child sacrifice attested in the Hebrew Bible is the offering of a firstborn child during times of distress. This form of child sacrifice is presented as a Moabite rite in 2 Kgs 3, where Mesha sacrifices his firstborn son, the heir to his throne, on the walls of Kir-hareseth. The sacrifice was only offered as a last resort, when all other hope was lost. There is good reason to suspect that this type of child sacrifice was not confined to Moab, however. The fact that the Kings account presents Mesha's sacrifice as effective—the Israelite-led coalition that threatened Mesha was driven off as a result of Mesha's sacrifice—as well as the reference to offering one's firstborn child to Yahweh at the end of the list of increasingly extravagant offerings in Mic 6:1–8, demonstrates that firstborn children were also perceived by at least some Israelites as appropriate sacrificial victims during times of distress. Unlike the case of firstborn children offered in compliance with Yahweh's claim to firstfruits and firstlings, these sacrifices would only have been offered in extraordinary circumstances and thus would have been quite rare, even among those who believed in their efficacy.

Unlike these two forms of child sacrifice, which appear to be "native" Israelite rituals, the למלך sacrifices seem to have been incorporated into the Yahwistic cult at a relatively late period. The earliest reliable evidence for the rite places it during the reign of Ahaz, and the fact that he is described as having introduced other syncretistic innovations in the Jerusalem cult—specifically, his incorporation of a new altar of Damascene design (2 Kgs 16:10–16)—supports the conclusion that he is the first Judahite king to offer למלך sacrifices. The tophet that he established for these offerings continued to operate for approximately a century before it was finally eliminated as part of Josiah's reform. The evidence for identically named *mlk* rites, which also involved the sacrifice of children, attested in the Punic central Mediterranean suggests that Ahaz borrowed the rite from Phoenicia, the original homeland of the Punic colonists. This conclusion is admittedly based on circumstantial evidence, because there is as yet no firm material evidence for the rite in the Phoenician homeland proper (see chapter 2 above). Because there is evidence for *mlk*/למלך sacrifices both in the Punic colonies and in Judah, however, Phoenicia is the most likely mediating link. If the למלך sacrifices served the same function in Judah that they did in the Punic colonies, then these sacrifices were associated with vows. Finally, despite the probable foreign origin of the rite, there is no reason to believe that these sacrifices were made to any deity other than Yahweh when they were offered in the Jerusalem tophet. As the discussion in the following chapter will reveal, even biblical writers who opposed these sacrifices tend to acknowledge that Yahweh was their intended recipient. Thus, למלך sacrifices were both syncretistic in origin and Yahwistic in nature; the two categories are not mutually exclusive.

Finally, in this chapter I have examined three other possible examples of child sacrifice in the Hebrew Bible: Jephthah's daughter, Hiel's alleged "foundation sacrifice," and the child sacrifices said to be offered by Sepharvites in Assyrian Samerina. In each case, the nature of the evidence is too problematic to allow us to draw confident historical conclusions concerning the reality of child sacrifice. Jephthah's sacrifice of his firstborn daughter appears as part of a literary trope common to folktales, and it would be imprudent to attempt to reconstruct historical practice on the basis of this type of evidence. In any case, even if the Jephthah story did contain a kernel of truth, it presents Jephthah's sacrifice of his firstborn daughter as unintended and surprising, not as a common or expected practice. In the case of Hiel, it is unlikely that a sacrifice is described at all; Hiel's son's are presented as having died as a consequence of his having rebuilt Jericho and thus as a divine punishment, not as any sort of "foundation sacrifice," a ritual for which little evidence exists in the first place. Finally, our current inability to identify either the Sepharvites or their deities, Adrammelech and Anammelech, makes it difficult to say much about the claim that they sacrificed their children to their gods. Even if we were willing to trust the claims of the writer(s) of Kings, however, this report would provide no real information about child sacrifice as practiced by Israelites and Judahites.

Thus, we are left with three distinct forms of child sacrifice attested in the Hebrew Bible. Two appear to have relatively old roots in the Israelite cult, while the third was likely the result of syncretistic borrowing. Each had a different function and purpose, and none of the various types of child sacrifice can be subsumed to another. Indeed, in the case of the two forms of firstborn sacrifice, the general and the extraordinary, the sacrifices stand in direct opposition, since a sacrifice of the firstborn child/son both on the eighth day (Exod 22:29 [Eng 22:30]) and during a time of crisis is impossible. There must have been some variety of practice among different Yahwistic groups, some of whom may have participated in one or more of these rites, while others may have participated in none. Unfortunately, given the nature of our evidence, it is difficult to say anything more than that a variety of belief and practice concerning child sacrifice existed concurrently.

Whatever the extent of child sacrifice, however, its historical reality came to present a problem for biblical writers of later periods. It is to these later texts that this study now turns its attention. As the next chapter demonstrates, the ways in which different biblical writers of the late monarchic, exilic, and postexilic periods dealt with the problem of the historical reality of Yahwistic child sacrifice varied considerably. Although some writers rejected all forms of child sacrifice as a foreign abomination, others sought instead to reinterpret or reappropriate some of these rites. Just as there was a variety of Israelite child sacrifice rites, there was also a variety of ways in which opponents of child sacrifices argued against their legitimacy.

CHAPTER 5

Biblical Reactions to Israelite Child Sacrifice

The previous four chapters have been devoted to exploring questions concerning the historical reality of child sacrifice in ancient Israel. This survey has concluded that there were at least three different forms of Israelite child sacrifice, all with different functions and purposes but all apparently offered by individuals who believed themselves to be "good Yahwists." In this final chapter, I will explore the views of biblical writers who rejected the idea that Yahweh ever condoned, much less commanded, the sacrifice of children. The idea that child sacrifice had no place in a "legitimate" cult of Yahweh is nearly unanimous among the various traditions preserved in the Hebrew Bible, but it will become clear in the analysis that follows that biblical rhetoric on the topic is actually quite varied in its details. The different streams of tradition in the Hebrew Bible employ divergent rhetorical strategies to oppose the legitimacy of child sacrifice, and these rhetorical differences sometimes reveal deeper differences regarding what constitute "authoritative" older traditions and their significance.

Deuteronomy

Deuteronomy had to deal with two separate and distinct forms of Israelite child sacrifice. The first were the למלך sacrifices. As argued above in chapter 4, three facts—(1) these offerings are not attested prior to the reign of Ahaz, (2) there is good reason to suspect that Ahaz himself had syncretistic tendencies, and (3) the most straightforward reading of Isa 30:33 is that the Jerusalem tophet where such sacrifices were offered was of relatively recent construction—point to the conclusion that the למלך offerings were of foreign origin and a relatively recent import. The most likely source for these sacrifices is Phoenicia, because our only other evidence for such sacrifices comes from the Punic central Mediterranean. Nonetheless, it is likely that, once these sacrifices were incorporated into the Jerusalem cult, their recipient was understood to be Yahweh. Given their foreign origin, however, it is unsurprising that the Deuteronomic writers choose to stress the foreign nature of the למלך sacrifices when they condemn them.

References to the למלך sacrifices occur in Deut 12:29–31 and 18:9–14, both using language of "sons and daughters," "in fire," and "causing to pass over"/"burning," which are characteristic of למלך sacrifices elsewhere. The former reads:

> For Yahweh your God will cut off the peoples whom you are going to dispossess before you there. You will dispossess them, and you will live in their land. Watch yourself lest you are ensnared by them after their being destroyed before you and lest you seek their gods and say, "How did these peoples serve their gods? I too will do likewise." Do not do so for Yahweh your God, for every abomination to Yahweh which he hates they do for their gods, for they even burn their sons and their daughters in fire to their gods (כי גם את בניהם ואת בנתיהם ישרפו באש לאלהיהם)."

The first thing to note is a point already mentioned in previous chapters: even in its denunciation of child sacrifice, the text acknowledges that Yahweh, not some foreign Molek deity, is the intended recipient of the sacrifices. The Israelites are warned not to imitate the cultic practices of the inhabitants of Canaan: "Do not do so *for Yahweh your God*."[1] Deuteronomy forbids worshiping Yahweh in the same way that the inhabitants of the land worship their gods. If Yahweh was not the perceived recipient of these offerings, it is difficult to imagine why Deuteronomy would concede so much rhetorical ground by introducing the notion.

Nonetheless, if the reconstruction above in chapter 4 is correct, then the rhetoric employed here contains a kernel of historical veracity. That is, when it paints the "burning of sons and daughters" as a foreign practice, it does so on an apparently solid historical basis. The most thorough treatment of the way in which the rhetoric of "foreignness" has been applied to the practice of child sacrifice is the work of Stavrakopoulou. She convincingly makes the case that child sacrifice was a practice at home in Yahwistic worship from an

1. Mosca suggests that the specific word choice is also intentional. In his view, the Canaanites are said to have "burned" (√שרף) their children because their veneration of idols made such rites entirely useless, while elsewhere the Israelites, who worshiped the true God, are said to have "caused to pass over" (√עבר; Hiphil) their children as part of an "effective" albeit "outlawed" rite (Mosca, "Child Sacrifice," 173–74).

early period and that the biblical authors only portray the rite as foreign in order to delegitimize it. Although the biblical rhetoric surrounding child sacrifice frequently distorts the data, I do not believe this to be entirely the case in Deuteronomy's condemnation of למלך rites. On a related note, it is also important to point out a major point of difference between Stavrakopoulou's approach, whose work I follow in many respects, and mine: I do not believe that it is helpful to discuss child sacrifice as a single type of ritual or even as a collection of rituals that can be subsumed under a common rubric.

Stavrakopoulou concludes her impressive survey of the evidence for the historical reality of child sacrifice in Judah: "Thus it would appear that three possible cults of child sacrifice may plausibly have existed within Judah: the firstborn sacrifice, the *mlk* sacrifice, and the sacrifice to the *šadday* gods." I largely agree with this statement, although, as discussed in chapter 4, I argue that there are actually two distinct forms of firstborn sacrifice that should not be conflated and, as discussed in chapter 2, I do not find the evidence for associating *šadday* gods with child sacrifice to be compelling. My major point of disagreement, however, is with her next sentence: "Though there are fundamental differences among these three cults which disallow their identification, they do exhibit striking parallels, which are suggestive of their possible interrelation at some point during the history of Judahite deity-worship or during the period of the formation of the biblical material."[2] She goes on to suggest that the rites may all share a common connection with fertility, a suggestion with which I agree with regard to a general sacrifice of firstborn children but not with regard to extraordinary firstborn sacrifices such as the one offered by King Mesha nor with regard to the למלך sacrifices. The former was offered in the context of distress, and the latter was associated with vows in the Punic central Mediterranean and probably in Judah as well. Neither had any direct connection to fertility. In short, although Stavrakopoulou is correct that "child sacrifice" played at least some role in the Yahwistic cult at a relatively early period, this does not necessarily mean that the Deuteronomic claims that the למלך rites were foreign in origin are entirely inaccurate and thus distortions of historical reality.

Further, Stavrakopoulou rightly notes regarding Deut 12:29–31: "The practice of child sacrifice is condemned not because it is ethically untenable, but because it is foreign. Consequently, because it is foreign, it is forbidden."[3] This statement is undoubtedly correct, but the question that naturally follows

2. Stavrakopoulou, *King Manasseh and Child Sacrifice*, 299.
3. Ibid., 149.

is *why* Deuteronomy would make this rhetorical move. Elsewhere, Stavrakopoulou suggests that "child sacrifice is intentionally presented as a foreign practice in order to distance the ancestors of the biblical writers and their god YHWH from this type of sacrifice." She suggests that this happened at a time when "YHWH's association with child sacrifice became theologically problematic for biblical writers of the post-monarchic era, who thus sought to distance their god from the practice and to preserve the sanctity of YHWH's name and reputation"; she concludes: "Child sacrifice is therefore deemed to be an abominable practice of the foreign nations, along with other religious rites with which it is associated."[4]

This is not entirely accurate, however. As will become clear below, it is not child sacrifice in general that is presented as foreign. It is the למלך rite in particular that attracts this rhetoric, and it is clear that Deuteronomy is specifically addressing the למלך rite. Despite its use of √שרף in place of the normal √עבר (Hiphil), Deuteronomy's identification of "sons and daughters" as the victims of the rite (see 2 Kgs 17:17; 23:10; Jer 32:35) along with the use of the phrase "in fire" (see 2 Kgs 16:3; 23:10; 2 Chr 33:6) both indicate that the למלך rite is in view. Both of these phrases are used specifically in reference to למלך sacrifices but not typically in the context of firstborn sacrifice. Furthermore, if the למלך sacrifice was a ritual incorporated into the Yahwistic cult during the reign of Ahaz, then the reason that Deut 12:29–31 presents it as "foreign" is because it indeed was of foreign origin. Of course, this does not mean that the rite was not also thoroughly Yahwistic when carried out in the Jerusalem tophet; it is unlikely that it could have been understood in any other way. Deuteronomy does appear to be less than precise in its presentation of historical reality, however, in tracing these sacrifices back to the pre-Israelite inhabitants of the land rather than to Phoenicians (and Punic colonists) of the first millennium—a depiction that in turn is predicated on a historically erroneous view that the Israelites came en masse from outside the land and dispossessed the Canaanites, bringing a pristine version of Yahweh veneration with them. Deuteronomy's picture of the formation of Israel stands in stark contrast to the current scholarly consensus that the Israelites developed a distinct ethnic identity in contrast to their Canaanite neighbors only gradually and do not represent a non-native group that invaded from outside, although some scholarly disagreement remains concerning which particular groups eventually came to be the people called Israel.[5]

4. Ibid., 310–11.

5. See, e.g., A. Faust, "The Emergence of Iron Age Israel: On Origins and Habitus," in *Israel's Exodus in Transdisciplinary Perspective: Text, Archaeology, Culture and Geoscience* (ed. T. E.

Nonetheless, details concerning the historical emergence of the Israelites aside, the Deuteronomic warning against incorporating a foreign child sacrifice rite into the cult of Yahweh does jibe well with what we can glean about the למלך sacrifice from other texts.

However, not all of Deuteronomy's rhetoric can be so easily reconciled with historical reality. Deut 18:9–14 begins similarly to 12:29–31, but then takes its rhetoric even further:

> When you come to the land which Yahweh your God is giving to you, you will not learn to act according to the abominations of those peoples. There will not be found among you one who causes his son or his daughter to pass over by fire (מעביר בנו ובתו באש) or who practices various sorts of divination and necromancy (קסם קסמים מעונן ומנחש ומכשף וחבר חבר ושאל אוב וידעני ודרש אל המתים). For anyone who does these things is an abomination to Yahweh, because these are the abominations that Yahweh your God is dispossessing from before you. You will be blameless with Yahweh your God. For these peoples whom you are dispossessing listen to diviners (אל מעננים ואל קסמים ישמעו). But Yahweh your God has not permitted such things for you.

This warning begins very much like the one in Deut 12:29–31, although here the act of sacrificing one's son or daughter is marked by the use of √עבר (Hiphil) "to cause to pass over," as is more common in the context of למלך sacrifices, rather than with √שרף "to burn," as in Deut 12:31. Also, notably absent here is any indication that the Israelites might offer these sacrifices to their own god, Yahweh, as was the case in 12:31. Finally, the warning here is considerably expanded, compared to the one in Deut 12:29–31; in addition

Levy, T. Schneider, and W. H. C. Propp; New York: Springer, 2015), 467–82; idem, *Israel's Ethnogenesis: Settlement, Interaction, Expansion, and Resistance* (Approaches to Anthropological Archaeology; London: Equinox, 2006); K. L. Sparks, "Religion, Identity, and Ancient Israel, *Religion Compass* 1 (2007): 587–614; idem, "Israel and the Nomads of Ancient Palestine," in *Community Identity in Judean Historiography: Biblical and Comparative Perspectives* (ed. G. N. Knoppers and K. A. Ristau; Winona Lake, IN: Eisenbrauns, 2009), 9–26; A. Killebrew, *Biblical Peoples and Ethnicity: An Archaeological Study of the Egyptians, Canaanites, Philistines, and Early Israel, 1300–1100* B.C.E. (ABS 9; Atlanta: Society of Biblical Literature, 2005); B. B. Schmidt, "Canaanites: I. Introduction, II. Archaeology, III. Ancient Near East and Hebrew Bible/Old Testament," *EBR* 4, 871–75; E. Bloch-Smith, "Israelite Ethnicity in Iron I: Archaeology Preserves What is Remembered and What is Forgotten in Israel's History," *JBL* 122 (2003): 401–25; and M. G. Brett, "Israel's Indigenous Origins: Cultural Hybridity and the Formation of Israelite Ethnicity," *BibInt* 11 (2003): 400–412.

to child sacrifice, this text includes references to all sorts of divination and necromancy. In this regard, it is significant that, unlike the case of למלך sacrifices, it is not clear that the other items in this list of illicit practices were syncretistic borrowings from Israel's neighbors. B. B. Schmidt, for example, points out that at least one of the various sorts of divination and necromancy enumerated here, קסם קסמים, is attested in relatively early biblical texts (Isa 3:2; Mic 3:6–7, 11), although he traces some of the other practices to foreign rites, which apparently originated in Mesopotamia.[6] He further argues that this section represents a relatively late, probably exilic "dtr 'Canaanizing' of the various rituals or performers listed" which "is clearly a rhetorical strategy designed to polemicize against formerly acceptable cults now competing with the contemporary dtr brand of Yahwism."[7] In ascribing a relatively late date to this text, Schmidt follows N. Lohfink and F. García López. Lohfink, beginning with the broader collection, dates the entire *Ämtergesetzen*—that is, the block of material contained in Deut 16:18–18:22 that deals with the distribution of power among various public offices (i.e., king, priest, and prophet)—to the early exilic period on the basis its treatment of Levites (who were not permitted to work in the temple in 2 Kgs 23:9, but who are in the Deut 18:6–8). A second factor supporting the early exilic date is its concern with false and true prophecy (Deut 18:15–22), a concern especially on display in the relatively late book of Jeremiah.[8] García López, who takes a different approach than Lohfink, traces several redactional layers in Deut 18:9–22 and points to lexical affinities between Deut 18:10–12 in particular and the list of sins committed by the kings of the North (2 Kgs 16:3), thus identifying the redactional activity as having a specifically Deuteronomistic bent.[9] Finally, E. Nicholson has argued that there is language in Deut 18:9–22 that appears

---

6. B. B. Schmidt, "Canaanite Magic vs. Israelite Religion: Deuteronomy 18 and the Taxonomy of Taboo," in *Magic and Ritual in the Ancient World* (ed. P. Mirecki and M. Meyer; RGRW 141; Leiden: Brill, 2002), 242–59.

7. Ibid., 256.

8. N. Lohfink, "Die Sicherung der Wirksamkeit des Gotteswortes durch das Prinzip der Schriftlichkeit der Tora und durch das Prinzip der Gewaltenteilung nach den Ämtergesetzen des Buches Deuteronomium (Dt 16,18–18,22)," in *Testimonium veritati: Philosophische und theologische Studien zu kirchlichen Fragen der Gegenwart* (ed. H. Wolter; Frankfurt: Knecht, 1971), 143–56. The essay appears in English translation: N. Lohfink, "Distribution of the Functions of Power: The Laws Concerning Public Offices in Deuteronomy 16:18–18:22," in *A Song of Power and the Power of Song: Essays on the Book of Deuteronomy* (ed. D. L. Christensen; trans. R. Walls; SBTS 3; Winona Lake, IN: Eisenbrauns, 1993), 336–52.

9. F. García López, "Un profeta como Moisés. Estudio crítico de Dt 18,9–22," in *Simposio Biblico Español (Salamanca, 1982)* (ed. N. Fernández Marcos, J. Trebolle Barrera, and J. Fernández Vallina; Madrid: Universidad Complutense, 1984), 289–308.

to have been influenced by the book of Jeremiah—the call narrative in Jer 1 in particular, itself some of the latest material in Jeremiah in Nicholson's view[10]—which would place Deut 18:9–22 later still.[11]

A late date, or at least a date later than Deut 12:29–31, can also be inferred for Deut 18:9–14 based on the fact that the latter seems to be a reworked version of the former or, more accurately, of the larger block of material in Deut 12:29–13:6.[12] Deut 12:29–13:6 consists of three discrete sections: a prohibition against adopting the cultic practices of the peoples whom the Israelites will dispossess, specifically the practice of child sacrifice (12:29–31);[13] a command not to add to or subtract from the laws (13:1 [Eng. 12:32]);[14] and warnings against listening to a "prophet' (נביא) or a "dreamer"

10. Here Nicholson follows W. McKane, *A Critical and Exegetical Commentary on Jeremiah I–XXV* (ICC; Edinburgh: T. & T. Clark, 1986), 25.

11. Compare, e.g., Deut 18:18 to Jer 1:9 or Deut 18:20 to Jer 28:15–16. E. Nicholson, "Deuteronomy 18:9–22, the Prophets and Scripture," in *Prophecy and Prophets in Ancient Israel: Proceedings of the Oxford Old Testament Seminar* (ed. J. Day; New York: T. & T. Clark, 2010), 151–71.

12. The connection between Deut 12:29–13:6 and Deut 18:9–22 has been noted by Lohfink, "Kerygmata," 96–97, and he has also suggested that the latter is dependent on the former (although he also admits that there may be other explanations). See also Lohfink, "Opferzentralisation, Säkularisierungsthese und mimetische Theorie," in *Studien zum Deuteronomium und zur deuteronomistischen Literatur* (vol. 3; SBAB 20; Stuttgart: Katholisches Bibelwerk, 1995), 256–57.

13. These verses have frequently been identified as making up a discrete unit, not tightly connected to the surrounding material. Although they do continue the theme of maintaining separation from the inhabitants of the land, which is stressed in Deut 12:2–7, the warning against sacrificing children in the manner of the land's inhabitants has no obvious connection with the regulations concerning cultic centralization immediately preceding 12:29–31 or with the material concerning heeding false prophets immediately following in Deut 13. Among those who detect a redactional hand at work in Deut 12:29–31 are T. Römer, "Cult Centralization in Deuteronomy 12: Between Deuteronomistic History and Pentateuch," in *Das Deuteronomium zwischen Pentateuch und Deuteronomistischem Geschichtswerk* (ed. E. Otto and R. Achenbach; FRLANT 206; Göttingen: Vandenhoeck & Ruprecht, 2004), 174; E. Otto, *Das Deuteronomium im Pentateuch und Hexateuch: Studien zur Literaturgeschichte von Pentateuch und Hexateuch im Lichte des Deuteronomiumrahmens* (FAT 30; Tübingen: Mohr Siebeck, 2000), 113; idem, *Das Deuteronomium: Politische Theologie und Rechtsreform in Juda und Assyrien* (BZAW 284; Berlin: de Gruyter, 1999), 235; B. M. Levinson, *Deuteronomy and the Hermeneutics of Legal Innovation* (New York: Oxford University Press, 1997), 24–25; and N. Lohfink, "Kerygmata des Deuteronomistischen Geschichtswerks," in *Die Botschaft und die Boten: Festschrift für Hans Walter Wolff zum 70. Geburtstag* (ed. J. Jeremias and L. Perlitt; Neukirchen-Vluyn: Neukirchener Verlag, 1981), 96–97.

14. Most regard this as a late intrusive element originally connected neither to what comes before nor after. So T. Veijola, *Das fünfte Buch Mose: Deuteronomium: Kapitel 1,1–16,17* (ATD 8:1; Vandenhoeck & Ruprecht, 2004), 284; J. Pakkala, *Intolerant Monolatry in the Deu-*

(חלם חלום) who would entice the people to serve other gods (13:2–6 [Eng. 13:1–5]).[15] Despite the broadly common theme of exhorting faithfulness to Yahweh and to Yahweh alone, the three units do not appear to be connected either logically or literarily. For instance, there is no indication that the prophet or diviner described in the final unit is following the practices of the peoples whom the Israelites will dispossess in the same way that those who burn their children in fire allegedly are; they are simply individuals who may "arise in your midst" (יקום בקרבך). Nor is there any obvious connection between the command not to add or take away laws and either the injunction against child sacrifice or that concerning prophets. Thus, in Deut 12:29–13:6, we appear to have three distinct exhortations concerning three

teronomistic History (Göttingen: Vandenhoeck & Ruprecht, 1999), 25; and A. D. H. Mayes, *Deuteronomy* (NCBC; Grand Rapids, MI: Eerdmans, 1979), 232. Though Levinson once argued that 13:1 formed a "colophon" to the altar law of Deut 12, added to mask the radical nature of its centralizing reform (*Deuteronomy and the Hermeneutics of Legal Innovation*, 48), more recently he has argued that it is integrally connected to chapter 13 and like the rest of that chapter can trace its origin to similar injunctions in Esarhaddon's Succession Treaty ("Esarhaddon's Succession Treaty as the Source for the Canon Formula in Deuteronomy 13:1," *JAOS* 130 (2010): 337–47; idem, "The Canon Formula in Deuteronomy 13:1," in *Scriptural Exegesis: The Shapes of Culture and the Religious Imagination: Essays in Honour of Michael Fishbane* [ed. D. A. Green and L. S. Lieber; Oxford: Oxford University Press, 2009], 25–45; see also B. M. Levinson and J. Stackert, "Between Covenant Code and Esarhaddon's Succession Treaty: Deuteronomy 13 and the Composition of Deuteronomy," *JAJ* 3 [2012]: 137–40.)

15. This section is generally seen as beginning a new unit, essentially independent from what precedes. See J. Pakkala, "Der literar- und religionsgeschichtliche Ort von Deuteronomium 13," in *Die deuteronomistischen Geschichtswerke: Redaktions- und religionsgeschichtliche Perspektiven zu "Deuteronomismus"-Diskussion in Tora und Vorderen Propheten* (ed. M. Witte et al.; BZAW 365; Berlin: de Gruyter, 2006), 126; Veijola, *Das fünfte Buch Mose*, 283; Levinson, *Deuteronomy and the Hermeneutics of Legal Innovation*, 48; P. E. Dion, "Deuteronomy 13: The Suppression of Alien Religious Propaganda in Israel during the Late Monarchical Era," in *Law and Ideology in Monarchic Israel* (ed. B. Halpern and D. W. Hobson; JSOTSup 124; Sheffield: JSOT Press, 1991), 147–216. Its content has also been traced by some to Esarhaddon's Succession Treaty; see Levinson and Stackert, "Between Covenant Code and Esarhaddon's Succession Treaty"; S. Parpola, "Assyria's Expansion in the 8th and 7th Centuries and Its Long-Term Repercussions in the West," in *Symbiosis, Symbolism, and the Power of the Past: Canaan, Ancient Israel, and Their Neighbors from the Late Bronze Age through Roman Palaestina* (ed. W. G. Dever and S. Gitin; Winona Lake, IN: Eisenbrauns, 2003), 104–5; B. M. Levinson, "'But You Shall Surely Kill Him!' The Text-Critical and Neo-Assyrian Evidence for MT Deuteronomy 13:10," in *Bundesdokument und Gesetz: Studien zum Deuteronomium* (ed. G. Braulik; HBS 4; Freiburg: Herder, 1995), 37–63; Otto, *Das Deuteronomium*, 34–90; Dion, "Deuteronomy 13," 205; and Weinfeld, *Deuteronomy and the Deuteronomic School*, 91–100. More skeptical about this connection are Pakkala, "Der literar- und religionsgeschichtliche Ort von Dtn 13," 129–34; and C. L. Crouch, *Israel and the Assyrians: Deuteronomy, the Succession Treaty of Esarhaddon, and the Nature of Subversion* (ANEM 8; Atlanta: SBL Press, 2014), esp. 78–92.

essentially unrelated topics, each laid one after the other with no attempt to link them.

In Deut 18:9–14, we find a similar series of commands, and although the order of injunctions is essentially the same, the two originally distinct commands against practicing child sacrifice like the peoples whom the Israelites will dispossess and against illicit prophecy have been intertwined. The text begins by forbidding imitating the inhabitants of the land, specifically in the areas of child sacrifice and divination: "There will not be found among you one who causes his son or his daughter to pass over by fire or who practices various sorts of divination and necromancy" (Deut 18:10–11). Thus, both practices are now linked to foreigners, unlike 12:31, where only child sacrifice appeared in this context. The addition of divination here likely has its basis in the fact that material concerning prophets and dreamers of dreams immediately follows the injunction against child sacrifice in 12:31–13:6, upon which Deut 18 is dependent, although the two blocks of material were not intertwined there in the same way as in 18:10–11. Next, in Deut 18:12–13, the command to avoid all sorts of divination is reiterated, and it is in this context that Yahweh presents the legitimate conduit for divine mediation: a prophet (נביא) whom he will raise up (יקים) in your midst (בקרבך) (Deut 18:15; note the lexical echoes of 13:2). Thus, what were two originally distinct commands—against child sacrifice and false prophecy—simply laid down next to one another without any obvious connection in 12:29–13:6 are now interwoven into a coherent unit in Deut 18:9–22. The direction of dependence is clear, since it would make sense for a scribe to smooth the sharp transitions in Deut 12:29–13:6, but there is no obvious reason why a scribe with Deut 18:9–22 before him would tease apart previously intertwined injunctions. Thus, yet another reason for suspecting that Deut 18:9–22 is relatively late is that it appears to be dependent upon Deut 12:29–13:6.

The upshot of all of this is that Deut 18:9–10 appears to misrepresent as foreign some practices, especially forms of divination, which had been well established among Israelite Yahwists for quite some time (e.g., קסם קסמים; see Isa 3:2; Mic 3:6–7, 11). This does not necessarily mean, however, that *all* of its accusations are distortions. If we trace the source material of Deut 18:9–10 to Deut 12:29–31, we find that only child sacrifice was *originally* associated with foreigners. None of the various forms of divination mentioned in Deut 18 are linked with child sacrifice or foreigners in Deut 12:29–13:6. It thus appears that Deut 18 has filled out its list of forbidden foreign practices with forms of illicit divination in order to provide a transition between following the practices of the peoples of the land and illicit prophecy, thereby both smoothing out the sharp shift in topics in Deut 12:29–13:6 and heightening its rhetoric against false prophecy by linking it to foreigners.

In contrast to the inconsistent and historically dubious association between illicit prophecy and foreignness in the rhetoric of Deuteronomy, Deuteronomy's consistent response to the form of child sacrifice elsewhere associated with the term למלך is to portray it as foreign and non-Israelite. This same claim that למלך offerings were foreign in origin is also found in the Deuteronomistic History. In each of the cases in which the "pass through fire" variety of child sacrifice is mentioned—the accusations against Ahaz (2 Kgs 16:3), the list of the Northern Kingdom's sins (17:15–17), and Manasseh (21:2–6)—the practice is identified as a foreign rite that was imitated by Israelites.[16] It is thus clear that this is a general Deuteronomic/Deuteronomistic rhetorical strategy to paint למלך sacrifices as foreign. It is worth reiterating that, given the rite's apparent late appearance on the scene in Jerusalem, only under foreign influence, this rhetoric is not entirely at odds with historical reality.

In contrast, Deuteronomy's rhetorical approach to opposing another form of Israelite child sacrifice, those offered in compliance with Yahweh's claim to firstborn children, is strikingly different. It is generally acknowledged that Deuteronomy was composed in response to the Covenant Code, and it has further been convincingly demonstrated that the legal material of Deuteronomy represents an intentional revision of the Covenant Code, either for the purpose of reinterpreting it or replacing it entirely.[17] Whether the inten-

16. In the cases of 2 Kgs 17:17 and 21:6, the association of these sacrifices with divination appears to follow in the tradition already established by Deut 18:9–10. See Cogan and Tadmor, *II Kings*, 205 and 266; Fritz, *1 & 2 Kings*, 390; and Hobbs, *2 Kings*, 306. Of course, one might also suggest that the relationship goes the other way and consider the possibility that Deut 18:9–10 has drawn upon and expanded the list of Manasseh's crimes in its reworking of Deut 12:29–13:6, and that 2 Kgs 21:6 is the source of Deut 18:9–10, rather than vice versa. On the suggestion that there may have been a "Deuteronomistic editing of Deuteronomy," see G. N. Knoppers, "Rethinking the Relationship between Deuteronomy and the Deuteronomistic History: The Case of Kings," CBQ 63 (2001): 393–415.

17. For an overview of the debate between those who believe that later law collections like Deuteronomy were intended to supersede earlier collections such as the Covenant Code and those who believe that these later collections were merely meant to be complementary, see J. Berman, "Supersessionist or Complementary? Reassessing the Nature of Legal Revision in the Pentateuchal Law Collections," *JBL* 135 (2016): 201–22. Berman himself argues in favor of a complementary model. For a defense of the complementary model as the appropriate way to understand Deuteronomy's relationship to the Covenant Code, see especially E. Otto, "Ersetzen oder Ergänzen von Gesetzen in der Rechtshermeneutik des Pentateuch: Zu einem Buch von Jeffrey Stackert," in *Die Tora. Studien zum Pentateuch: Gesammelte Schriften* (BZABR 9; Wiesbaden: Harrassowitz, 2009), 248–56; idem, "The Pre-exilic Deuteronomy as a Revision

tion was to replace or to supplement, we can say with some confidence that the scribes responsible for the Deuteronomic code knew the Covenant Code and drew upon it in composing their own work.[18] For this reason, it is worth comparing the law of the firstborn in Deuteronomy with its "source material" in the Covenant Code.

The Covenant Code's law of the firstborn (examined in detail above in chap. 3) is found in Exod 22:28b–29 [Eng 22:29b–30]:

> בכור בניך תתן לי כן תעשה לשרך לצאנך שבעת ימים יהיה עמו ביום השמיני תתנו לי
>
> The firstborn of your children/sons you shall give to me. Thus you shall do with your cattle and your sheep. Seven days he/it will be with his/its mother. On the eighth day you will give him/it to me.

Deuteronomy mentions firstlings (בכרת) of flocks and herds twice in passing in the context of its instructions concerning cult centralization (Deut 12:6–17). The only new information provided there, however, is that they are to be offered at "the place Yahweh your God will choose," as are all other sorts of offerings and sacrifices. It is in Deut 15:19–23, however, that Deuteronomy's detailed instructions concerning the sacrifice of firstlings is found:

> כל הבכור אשר יולד בבקרך ובצאנך הזכר תקדיש ליהוה אלהיך לא תעבד בבכר שורך ולא תגז בכור צאנך לפני יהוה אלהיך תאכלנו שנה בשנה במקום אשר יבחר יהוה אתה וביתך וכי יהיה בו מום פסח או עור כל מום רע לא תזבחנו ליהוה אלהיך בשעריך תאכלנו הטמא והטהור יחדו כצבי וכאיל רק את דמו לא תאכל על הארץ תשפכנו כמים
>
> Every male firstborn which is born in your herd and in your flock you will sanctify to Yahweh your God. You will not work with the firstborn of your oxen and you will not shear the firstborn of your flock. You, both you and your household, will eat it before Yahweh your

for the Covenant Code," in *Kontinuum und Proprium: Studien zu Sozial- und Rechtsgeschichte des Alten Orients und des Alten Testaments* (OBC 8; Wiesbaden: Harrassowitz, 1996), 112–22; and H. Najman, *Seconding Sinai: The Development of Mosaic Discourse in Second Temple Judaism* (JSJSup 77; Leiden: Brill, 2003), 20–29. For the supercessionist model, see especially B. Levinson, *Deuteronomy and the Hermeneutics of Legal Innovation*, and J. Stackert, *Rewriting the Torah: Literary Revision in Deuteronomy and the Holiness Legislation* (FAT 52; Tübingen: Mohr Siebeck, 2007).

18. The contrary view—that the Covenant Code is in some way dependent upon Deuteronomy—has been argued by Van Seters, *A Law Book for the Diaspora*. I continue to find the majority opinion to be more convincing. See p. 89 n. 46.

God year by year in the place which Yahweh will choose. But if there is in it a blemish, if it is lame or blind or has any bad blemish, you will not sacrifice it to Yahweh your God. Within your gates you will eat it, both clean and unclean together, like a gazelle or a deer. Only its blood you will not eat. You will pour it upon the ground like water.

Much could be said about Deuteronomy's version of the law of the firstborn in comparison to the Covenant Code's, including the incorporation of its demand for centralization (Deut 12:2–7) and its prohibition against eating blood (Deut 12:16). Also notable is the stipulation that the offering be carried out by being consumed by the offerer and his family (see also Deut 12:7) rather than "given," as in the Covenant Code. For our discussion, however, the interesting thing is the complete absence of any mention of firstborn children. Although the Covenant Code puts children first in its list of living beings subject to Yahweh's claim on firstlings, in Deuteronomy they are completely absent. Unlike the למלך sacrifices, Deuteronomy does not condemn these offerings; it simply ignores their existence altogether. If the Covenant Code and Deuteronomy were merely variant traditions, it could be that the group responsible for Deuteronomy was simply unaware of any custom making children subject to the law of the firstborn, even if the community responsible for the Covenant Code did know of such a tradition. As noted above, however, scholarly work on the relationships among the various biblical law codes has convincingly demonstrated that Deuteronomy's writers did know of and are in fact directly dependent on the Covenant Code. Thus, the only conclusion possible is that the scribes responsible for Deut 15:19–23 were well aware of the Covenant Code's application of the law of the firstborn to human beings but intentionally chose to omit this aspect of the law.[19] Although this was not the only possible rhetorical strategy to avoid the implication that the law of the firstborn demanded the sacrifice of children (see other possible responses below), omission and silence is perhaps the simplest, most direct solution. In any case, it is the approach adopted in Deuteronomy.[20]

19. For a discussion of the tendency for the Deuteronomic writers to omit and rewrite sections of their source text to suit their own purposes, albeit not in reference to the law of the firstborn in particular, see J. Pakkala, *God's Word Omitted: Omissions in the Transmission of the Hebrew Bible* (FRLANT 251; Göttingen: Vandenhoeck & Ruprecht, 2013), 118–34.

20. Finsterbusch thinks that the changes, especially limiting the application of the requirement to male cattle and the omission of human beings and unclean animals, represent a "farmer friendly" move ("The Firstborn between Sacrifice and Redemption, 98–99). *Pace* G. Brin, who argues that the reason why human firstborn and animals were not mentioned

There may be a faint hint of acknowledgment elsewhere in Deuteronomy that the Covenant Code in fact does apply the law of the firstborn to human children, specifically in Deuteronomy's "canon formula." One of the formula's two occurrences is in Deut 13:1 [Eng 12:32]:

> את כל הדבר אשר אנכי מצוה אתכם אתו תשמרו לעשות לא תסף עליו ולא תגרע ממנו
>
> Every word that I command you, you shall be careful to do. You will not add unto it and you will not take away from it.

This formula indicates that none of the material found in the Deuteronomic code should be omitted nor should it be supplemented with any other material—perhaps, for instance, a preexisting collection of laws such as those found in the Covenant Code? It may be significant that this canon formula immediately follows Deuteronomy's condemnation of the "cause to pass over by fire" variety of child sacrifice. Traditionally, scholars have viewed this verse as a late intrusive element, possibly cribbed from Deut 4:2, where an almost identical injunction appears, unrelated either to what comes before or after it.[21] If this is the case, then it may have been inserted here, immediately after Deuteronomy's injunction against child sacrifice, with the intention of subtly rejecting the Covenant Code's command to sacrifice children in fulfillment of the law of the firstborn. On the other hand, Levinson has suggested that the appearance of the canon formula in Deut 13:1 is original and that it, along with the material in Deut 13:2–12, ultimately derives from Esarhaddon's Succession Treaty.[22] If he is correct, then the prohibition against offering one's children by fire may have been placed just prior to this block of material in order to create essentially the same effect. Whatever the scribal mechanism, however, the fact that the command not to add or to take away from the Deuteronomic code appears in the immediate context of a mention of child sacrifice may be specifically aimed at the Covenant Code's law of the firstborn. Of course, this also assumes that whoever edited this material has subtly conflated the "cause to pass over by fire" variety of child sacrifice and the general sacrifice of firstborn children to some degree, but this would not

is because Deuteronomy only changed the law of the firstborn with regard to edible animals. Deuteronomy, in Brin's view, allowed the Covenant Code's stipulations concerning unclean animals and firstborn children to continue to apply (*Studies in Biblical Law*, 191 n. 35).

21. See pp. 154–55 nn. 13–15.

22. Levinson, "The Canon Formula in Deuteronomy 13:1."

be the only case of such a conflation in relatively late material in the Hebrew Bible, as we shall see below.

Whether or not a subtle critique of the Covenant Code's law of the firstborn is found in Deut 12:29–13:2, Deuteronomy clearly addresses two distinct forms of child sacrifice in two different ways: The "cause to pass over by fire"/ למלך sacrifice is rejected as the foreign practice of the Canaanites whom the Israelites would dispossess. On the other hand, the general sacrifice of firstborn children is passively rejected via omission. In this regard, Deuteronomy completely reframes the firstborn law, applying it only to the male offspring of clean animals, and firstborn offerings are now carried out during an annual pilgrimage to the central shrine; they are not offered on the eighth day. The firstborn is to be eaten by the offerer, not "given" as in the Covenant Code, which makes it nigh impossible to apply the regulation to human children.[23] Thus, Deuteronomy, while rejecting all forms of child sacrifice, does not entirely conflate various child sacrifice rites and employs different rhetorical strategies to reject each.

Later Legal Traditions

Although the Holiness material,[24] like Deuteronomy, rejects both the general sacrifice of firstborn children and the sacrifice of children offered למלך, its rhetoric is slightly different in the case of the latter and strikingly so in the case of the former. In examining these differences, it is important to keep in mind that there is little doubt that the Holiness material was composed by a person or persons who were aware of both the Covenant Code and Deuteronomy and who intentionally drew upon them, even while editing,

23. While there are a handful of references to cannibalism in the Hebrew Bible (Lev 26:29; Deut 28:53–57; 2 Kgs 6:28–29; Jer 19:9; Lam 2:20; 4:10; Ezek 5:10), all of these are in the context of extreme duress. There is no indication that cannibalism ever constituted any part of Israelite cultic practice.

24. Here I use the intentionally vague term "Holiness material" in reference to the "Holiness Code," which strictly speaking only refers to Lev 17–26, along with other material that I. Knohl has convincingly demonstrated derives from the same group, which he dubs the "Holiness School." This broader collection of material includes much material outside the "Holiness Code" proper (*The Sanctuary of Silence: The Priestly Torah and the Holiness School* [Minneapolis: Fortress, 1996], esp. 104–6; see also J. Milgrom, *Leviticus: A New Translation with Introduction and Commentary* [vol. 2; AB 3A; New York: Doubleday, 2000], 1319–67). Knohl refers both to the persons responsible for this material and to the text that they produced as the "Holiness School," a term that I find awkward when applied to a text rather than to a group of people.

revising, and perhaps even subverting its older source material.[25] Thus, differences between the treatment of either form of child sacrifice in the Holiness material and their treatment in other codes may represent intentional divergences in both its conception of and rhetoric concerning child sacrifice.

Beginning with the למלך sacrifices, unlike Deuteronomy, the Holiness material explicitly refers to such sacrifices by the term למלך. Indeed, five of the seven certain[26] references to מֹלֶךְ appear in the Holiness material of Leviticus. First, in Lev 18:21:

> ומזרעך לא תתן להעביר למלך ולא תחלל את שם אלהיך אני יהוה
>
> And from your seed you will not give, causing to pass over for a *mlk*-offering. You will not profane the name of your God. I am Yahweh.

The first part of the verse shows a connection to Deut 18:10a, although the paraphrase is rather loose. The latter reads:

> לא ימצא בך מעביר בנו ובתו באש
>
> There will not be found among you one who causes his son or daughter to pass over in fire.

The only lexeme that appears both in Deut 18:10a and in Lev 18:21 is √עבר, both governed by another verbal form (√מצא in Deut 18:10a and √נתן in Lev 18:21). In Lev 18:21, the victims of the rite are mentioned first and referred to as "your seed" (זרעך), while in Deut 18:10a the victims appear in the penultimate position and are referred to as "his son or his daughter" (בנו ובתו). The shift from third to first person is consistent with the Holiness material's general tendency to refer to the individual Israelite in the second-person singular.[27] The choice of "seed" rather than "son or daughter" may be influenced by the language of the previous verse (18:20), where sexual intercourse with

---

25. See J. Stackert, *Rewriting the Torah*; C. Nihan, *From Priestly Torah to Pentateuch* (FAT 25; Tübingen: Mohr Siebeck, 2007), esp. 401–545; K. Grünwaldt, *Das Heiligkeitsgesetz Leviticus 17–26: Ursprungliche Gestalte, Tradition und Theologie* (BZAW 271; Berlin: de Gruyter, 1999); esp. 139–379; A. Cholewiński, *Heiligkeitsgesetz und Deuteronomium: Eine vergleichende Studie* (AnBib 66; Rome: Biblical Institute Press, 1976).

26. 1 Kgs 11:5 should be emended to "Milcom"; see p. 6 n. 5 above. On Isa 57:9, see below.

27. See J. Joosten, *People and the Land in the Holiness Code: An Exegetical Study of the Ideational Framework of the Law in Leviticus 17–26* (VTSup 67; Leiden: Brill, 1966), 202; Milgrom, *Leviticus* 2, 1326; and Knohl, *Sanctuary of Silence*, 1 n. 3.

a compatriot's wife is forbidden employing the euphemism(?) "you will not give your laying down for seed" (לא תתן שכבך לזרע),[28] although in several other places offspring are referred to by the term זרע in the Holiness material (e.g., Lev 21:15, 17, 21; 22:3, 4; as well as Lev 20:2–4, which, however, may be dependent on 18:21). Additionally, in both cases, a prepositional phrase modifies the offering: "in fire" (באש) in Deut 18:10a and "as a *mlk*-offering" (למלך) in Lev 18:21. Thus, the first half of Lev 18:21 may be a rather loose reworking of Deut 18:10a.

Nonetheless, the rationale provided in the Leviticus version of the prohibition diverges from Deuteronomy's rationale even more than its language does. In both of Deuteronomy's commands not to "cause one's children to pass over in fire," the practice is traced to the inhabitants of the land whom the Israelites will dispossess (Deut 12:29–30; 18:9). In addition, this act is referred to as an "abomination" (תעבה; Deut 12:31; 18:9) that Yahweh "hates" (שנא; Deut 12:31). Lev 18:21, however, follows up its prohibition against למלך sacrifices with two Holiness material stock phrases: "you will not profane the name" of Yahweh (see also Lev 19:12; 21:6; 22:2, 32)[29] and "I am Yahweh" (see also Lev 18:2, 4, 5, 6, 30; 19:2, 3, 4, etc.).[30] In this way, the Holiness tradition has taken a Deuteronomic command and clothed it with distinctively Holiness language and rhetoric. The immediate issue at hand in Leviticus is the sanctity of Yahweh's name and the acknowledgment of Yahweh's authority. Israel must "be holy as Yahweh is holy" (Lev 19:2), and למלך sacrifices would not only compromise the people's holiness but would even defile Yahweh's name, a result otherwise brought about by making false oaths (Lev 19:12) or by the profanation of either the priests (Lev 21:6) or Yahweh's sacrifices (Lev 22:2, 32).

Interestingly, in its broader context, Lev 18:21 retains some of the flavor that it had in its Deuteronomic context. The entire corpus of injunctions contained in Lev 18 is framed by a warning against behaving like the inhabitants of the land (18:3, 24–27). This has its parallel, and probably ultimate source,[31] in Deut 12:29–31 and 18:9–14. This reappropriation of Deuteronomic rhetoric has the effect of applying Deuteronomy's claim that "causing to pass one's children over in fire" is a foreign Canaanite practice to

28. M. Noth, *Leviticus* (trans. J. E. Anderson; OTL; London: SCM, 1965), 136; B. Baentsch, *Exodus-Leviticus-Numeri* (HKAT 1:2; Göttingen: Vandenhoeck & Ruprecht, 1903), 394.

29. See Knohl, *Sanctuary of Silence*, 54; and Milgrom, *Leviticus* 2, 1552.

30. Milgrom refers to this phrase, extremely common in the Holiness material, as "H's signature seal" (*Leviticus* 2, 1517).

31. So Cholewiński, *Heiligkeitsgesetz*, 253–55.

all of the sins enumerated in Lev 18, not just to child sacrifice. Unlike Deut 18, however, rather than expanding the "abominations" of the Canaanites to include various forms of divination, in Lev 18 the ostensibly Canaanite practices are now sexual in nature.

Indeed, as others have already observed, the prohibition against למלך sacrifices fits rather uncomfortably among the litany of sexual violations listed in Lev 18. This has led scholars to posit quite an array of ingenious but ultimately unconvincing explanations for how למלך sacrifices were conceptually akin to illicit sexual acts.[32] But this is coming at the problem from the wrong angle. The Holiness material is conspicuous for its concern with sexual matters, much more so than other law codes. Admittedly, the Deuteronomic code contains a single prohibition against taking one's father's wife (Deut 23:1).[33] Furthermore, outside the Deuteronomic code proper, there is a cluster of prohibitions against incest and bestiality (Deut 27:20–23). Likewise, the Covenant Code contains a single sexual prohibition, one against bestiality (Exod 22:18). Neither Deuteronomy nor the Covenant Code, however, contains anything remotely resembling the litany of prohibited sexual acts contained in Lev 18 (and again in Lev 20, on which see below). Whatever the reason for this apparently novel concern with sexual matters, the Holiness material is genuinely innovative in its careful and tedious enumeration of illicit sexual acts.[34] In service of its argument in this regard, just as Deut 18:9–11 shoehorned various forms of divination into a reworked prohibition against "causing to pass over one's child in fire" (compare Deut 12:29–31) and thereby subsumed these forms of divination under the rubric of the "abomi-

32. J. E. Hartley and T. Dwyer, for example, propose four separate ways in which the two are connected: (1) both are kinship violations, (2) both disregard the personal integrity of the victim, (3) both involve the greatest pollution and stiffest penalties, and (4) there was a perceived connection between illicit sex and child sacrifice "deep in the tribal consciousness" ("An Investigation into the Location of the Laws on Offerings to Molek in the Book of Leviticus," in *Go to the Land I Will Show You: Studies in Honor of Dwight W. Young* [ed. J. Coleson and V. Matthews; Winona Lake, IN: Eisenbrauns, 1996], 90). Nihan suggests that "the sacrifice of one's child to Molech is contrary to the affirmation of Yahweh's control over man's reproductive activity and therefore represents another case of transgression against the boundaries set by society to sexual activity" (*From Priestly Torah to Pentateuch*, 438). For an overview of other previous suggestions, none of which are more persuasive than these two examples, see Nihan, *From Priestly Torah to Pentateuch*, 438 n. 159.

33. Nihan rightly observes that the primary concern in Deut 23:1 "is probably not a matter of incest properly speaking but rather of (mis)appropriating one's father's rights" (*From Priestly Torah to Pentateuch*, 480 n. 323).

34. See also Nihan, *From Priestly Torah to Pentateuch*, 480–81; and J. R. Ziskind, "Legal Rules on Incest in the Ancient Near East," *RIDA* 35 (1988): 97–99.

nations" of the peoples whom the Israelites would dispossess, Lev 18 has done the same with its litany of sexual prohibitions. It has bracketed the entire section with warnings against imitating the "abominations" of the people (Lev 18:3, 24–27), drawing on the rhetoric of Deuteronomy. As in Deut 12:29–31, the למלך rite appears as one item on its list of abominations. It fills out its list of offenses, however, with injunctions of a sexual nature. In this way, the Holiness material lumps together various forms of sexual depravity and presents them as the type of abominable behavior distinctive of Canaanites, behavior that the Israelites should not imitate.[35] Thus, Leviticus (re-)applies rhetoric originally associated with the למלך rite to all manner of sexual offenses.

The same strategy is used once again in Lev 20, which seems to be dependent on Lev 18.[36] In Lev 20, however, the rhetorical structure follows Deut 18:9–11 even more closely. The chapter opens with a long condemnation (the lengthiest in the Hebrew Bible) of למלך sacrifices. As in Lev 18, it connects the rite with "profaning" (√חלל Piel) Yahweh's name but adds a further notice that it has the effect of "defiling" (√טמא Piel) the sanctuary. Unlike elsewhere, Lev 20 specifically requires stoning as the penalty for offering these sacrifices (20:2–5). Next, like Deut 18:9–11 but unlike Lev 18, Lev 20 moves on to condemn various illicit forms of divination (20:6), followed by a handful of stock Holiness exhortations such as "be holy as I am holy" and "I am Yahweh your God" (Lev 20:7–8). Next, there is a command against disrespecting one's father or mother (20:9), another against illicit sex with one's neighbor's wife (20:10), and then a rather clever segue forbidding the combination of the two aforementioned practices—that is, of disrespecting family and illicit sexual acts—in the form of incest (20:11–12). This is followed in turn by a list of other illicit sexual acts, similar to the list in Lev 18 (20:13–21). Finally, there is a warning against behaving like the former inhabitants of the land (20:22–24), reminiscent of the frame of Lev 18, the opening section of Deut 18:9–11, and of course Deut 12:28–29. In Lev 20, the warning against behaving like Canaanites has been separated from the

35. Of course, this rhetorical strategy is almost certainly tendentious; there is no evidence that the Canaanites were generally perceived as sexual deviants. So also Milgrom, *Leviticus* 2, 1520.

36. So already L. B. Paton, "The Relationship of Lev. 20 to Lev. 17–19," *Hebraica* 10 (1894): 111–21; and more recently, Nihan, *From Priestly Torah to Pentateuch*, 446–54. I offer no opinion here on the debate about whether the author of Lev 20 is the same as that of Lev 18, what sort of traditional material lies behind one or both chapters, etc. For an overview of this discussion, see Nihan, *From Priestly Torah to Pentateuch*, especially the extensive notes on pp. 451–52. For the present, what is important is that the author of the present form of Lev 20 was aware of and in some way made use of the material in Lev 18.

למלך rite by so much intrusive material that the original link between this warning and "causing children to pass over by fire" has been almost entirely severed. The "anti-foreign" rhetoric originally connected with a particular form of child sacrifice, a practice that I have argued above did indeed have foreign roots, has snowballed to the point of subsuming divination, incest, and even bestiality. Nonetheless, despite this growth and development, the Holiness material continues to preserve Deuteronomy's connection between the למלך rite and the former inhabitants of Canaan, even if just barely. Despite all these innovations and rhetorical reworkings, the Holiness material and Deuteronomy are roughly compatible in their presentation of the למלך sacrifices, as well as in the basis for their condemnation. These sacrifices are wrong because they are foreign.

In the case of the general firstborn sacrifice, however, the Holiness material's rhetoric diverges sharply from that of Deuteronomy. As observed above, Deuteronomy's law of the firstborn (Deut 15:19–23) fails to mention children at all; they simply are not subject to its version of the command. The Holiness material, however, acknowledges Yahweh's claim to firstborn children but finds (or, probably more accurately, invents) an ingenious loophole that allows it to avoid requiring actual child sacrifice. Yahweh's claim to firstborn children is acknowledged three times in the Holiness material, first in Num 3:12–51, again in Num 8:14–19, and finally in Num 18:15–18.[37]

Num 3:12–13:

> I [= Yahweh] hereby take the Levites from the midst of the Israelites in place of every firstborn, a breach of a womb (כל בכור פטר רחם), from the Israelites. The Levites are mine (והיו לי הלוים). For every firstborn is mine (לי כל בכור). As on the day that I struck every firstborn in the land of Egypt, I sanctified (הקדשתי) for myself every firstborn in Israel from human to beast. They will be mine (לי יהיו). I am Yahweh.

Similarly, Num 8:14–19:

> You will separate the Levites from the midst of the Israelites. And the Levites will be mine (והיו לי הלוים). After this, the Levites will enter to serve the Tent of Meeting. I will cleanse them and you will

37. All of these are contained in the corpus of "Holiness material" that is found outside of the "Holiness Code" as traditionally defined (i.e., Lev 17–26). See Knohl, *Sanctuary of Silence*, 53–55, 83–85, 105.

> elevate them as an elevation offering. For given, indeed given, are they to me from the midst of the Israelites. In place of the breach of every womb, the firstborn (פטרת כל רחם בכור) of everyone from the Israelites, I have taken them for myself. For mine is every firstborn (לי כל בכור) among the Israelites, both human and animal, as of the day that I struck every firstborn in the land of Egypt. I sanctified (הקדשתי) them for myself. I accepted the Levites instead of every firstborn among the Israelites, and gave the Levites as gifts to Aaron and to his sons from the midst of the Israelites to carry out the service of the Israelites in the Tent of Meeting and to atone on behalf of the Israelites. There will not be among the Israelites a plague when the Israelites approach the holy place.

Here, as in the Covenant Code but unlike in Deuteronomy, the law of the firstborn applies both to human and animal firstborn. In the Holiness material, they are both called בכור, as in the earlier codes, as well as פטר(ת) רחם "breach of a womb." Further, as in the Covenant Code but unlike in Deuteronomy, there is no explicit distinction between the sexes. Additionally, here rather than "you will give" (√נתן) as in the Covenant Code, Yahweh speaking in the first person repeatedly declares that the firstborn "are mine" (לי). The agency of the claim is thus shifted from the individual Israelite onto Yahweh. This fact is further underlined by the connection of Yahweh's claim to Israelite firstborn with the original Passover event. By killing the Egyptian firstborn and sparing the Israelites, Yahweh has obtained a perpetual claim on Israelite firstborn, both children and cattle. Yahweh has decided, however, to accept the service of the Levites in lieu of Israelite firstborn.

The vicarious nature of the Levites' service is made even more explicit by the description of the exact manner by which this substitution was carried out. In Num 3:41, Yahweh tells Moses, "You will take the Levites for me—I am Yahweh—in place of the firstborn among the Israelites, and the cattle of the Levites in place of all the firstborn among the cattle of the Israelites." Thus, Yahweh's claim to Israelite firstborn children is set aside when he accepts the Levites in their place. It becomes clear that this substitution is meant quite literally in Num 3:42–43: Moses actually counts the Israelite firstborn and arrives at a sum of 22,273, which presents a problem, since there are only 22,000 Levites (Num 3:40). To solve this difficulty the Israelites are required to pay five shekels for each of the 273 extra Israelite firstborn—1,365 shekels—which is then handed over to Aaron and his sons (Num 3:46–51). Thus, contrary to Deuteronomy, the Holiness material acknowledges

Yahweh's claim to firstborn children but, like Deuteronomy, has no desire to see this requirement carried out via literal sacrifice. With some intellectual and rhetorical effort, the Holiness material manages both to affirm the statement of the Covenant Code concerning Yahweh's claim to firstborn children but also to avoid its implication that they actually be sacrificed to him. As a happy side effect, this rhetorical strategy also provides an etiology for the special devotion of the Levites to Yahweh's service.[38]

It would then seem that, with the payment of 1,365 shekels to make up the difference between the number of Israelite firstborn and the number of Levites, the Israelites and Yahweh should now be quits vis-à-vis firstborn children. Num 18:15–18, however, seems to assume that some obligation remains:

> Every breach of the womb (פטר רחם) of all flesh which is offered to Yahweh, both human and animal, shall be yours [= Aaron's]. But you will certainly redeem (פדה תפדה) the human firstborn (בכור), and the firstborn (בכור) of unclean animals you will redeem (תפדה). Its redemption, from one month of age, you will redeem (תפדה) according to its valuation: five shekels of silver, according to the sanctuary shekel (which is twenty gerahs). But the firstborn (בכור) of an ox, the firstborn (בכור) of a lamb, or the firstborn (בכור) of a goat you will not redeem; they are holy. You will sprinkle their blood on the altar, and you will turn their fat into smoke, a fire offering as a pleasant aroma to Yahweh. And their flesh will be yours [= Aaron's], just as the breast that is elevated and the right thigh will be yours.

This text presents another stark difference from Deuteronomy, where only clean animals are subject to the firstborn requirement and are consumed at the central shrine, and from the Covenant Code, where children are to be treated identically to clean animals ("*thus* you shall do" כן תעשה; Exod 22:29

38. See Levenson, *Death and Resurrection*, 43–52, for a nice discussion of the "transformation" of the law of the firstborn in various ways, including into Yahweh's claim on the Levites. W. Zimmerli traces the role of the Levites from their Deuteronomic elevation as the only legitimate priestly group to their degradation to menial temple servants in the later chapters of Ezekiel. He argues that Num 3 represents a sort of a "vollkommen geistliche Rehabilitierung" in which the Levites' service is once again elevated to a privilege, while at the same time solving the difficulty presented by a literal interpretation of the law of the firstborn as applied to humans ("Erstgeborene und Leviten: Ein Beitrag zur exilisch-nachexilischen Theologie," in *Near Eastern Studies in Honor of William Foxwell Albright* [ed. H. Goedicke; Baltimore: Johns Hopkins University Press, 1971], 459–69).

[Eng. 22:30]). In Num 18, there is an explicit contrast between humans and unclean animals on the one hand, who are both to be redeemed via the payment of five sanctuary shekels, and the firstborn of clean animals on the other, who are to be sacrificed. In addition, although the Covenant Code demands that all firstborn offerings be made on the eighth day, the Holiness material delays the offerings, both actual sacrifices and cash redemption, until one month after birth. These differences from the older codes have been observed before,[39] but what is less often observed is that the law of the firstborn in Num 18:15–18 also stands in tension with the claims of Num 3 and 8 that Yahweh has accepted the Levites in lieu of Israelite firstborn children and the Levite's cattle in lieu of the Israelites' firstborn cattle.[40] That is, if Yahweh had accepted the Levites in place of the Israelite firstborn and had even taken a cash payment of 1,365 shekels to compensate for the disparity between the number of Israelite firstborn and the number of Levites (Num 3:46–51), then why would the Israelites still need to offer the firstborn of clean animals as sacrifices and monetary payment in lieu of their firstborn children and unclean animals? Read together, these two forms of "redemption" appear to result in Yahweh's "double billing" the Israelites. There are clear similarities across the various Holiness claims. For instance, the price involved, either for the redemption of the "extra" firstborn children or for all of them, is five shekels in both cases. There is also similarity in language; both texts use פטר רחם and בכור to denote the firstborn. There are even similarities in how the offerings are conceived; in both cases, the offering of firstborn clean animals and the payment in lieu of human firstborn children serves to support the sanctuary. In all these ways, Num 18 on the one hand and Num 3 and 8 on the other stand together against the Deuteronomic and Covenant Code versions of the firstborn tradition. Nonetheless, even within the Holiness material itself, there remains some tension and even apparent contradiction concerning how Yahweh's claim to firstborn children should play out in actual practice.[41]

39. See, e.g., Finsterbusch, "The Firstborn between Sacrifice and Redemption," 100–102; Brin, *Studies in Biblical Law*, 170–235; J. Milgrom, *Numbers* (JPSTC; New York: Jewish Publication Society, 1990), 431–32; and M. Fishbane, *Biblical Interpretation*, 182.

40. A notable exception is Brin, who devotes some attention to the relationship between Num 18 and Num 3, concluding that the latter is dependent on the former and extrapolates its principle of Levite substitution from Num 18 (Brin, *Studies in Biblical Law*, 228–37).

41. A similar conception of the law of the firstborn, with sacrifice of clean animals and monetary redemption of unclean animals, appears in Lev 27:26–27, which is part of an apparent appendix or supplement to the Holiness Code proper (so Noth, *Leviticus*, 203; Tigay, *Leviticus*, 192; and Milgrom, *Leviticus* 2, 2407–9; although Milgrom argues that only the insertion of

In the Ritual Decalogue (Exod 34:11–26),[42] yet another means of dealing with the law of the firstborn as applied to human children appears. Traditionally, the Ritual Decalogue has been understood as the "J" counterpart to the Covenant Code, which may be linked to "E," although there has typically been more doubt about the relationship of the Covenant Code to E than that of the Ritual Decalogue to J.[43] Regardless of the relationship of these two codes to the narrative traditions of the Pentateuch, the traditional view presents them as two independent legal collections, both of which predate and serve as source material for D.[44] More recent work, however, has challenged this view and convincingly argued that the Ritual Decalogue is actually a post-Deuteronomic, perhaps even post-Priestly, reworking of Exod 23:14–

Lev 27 after the Holiness Code postdates the Code, not its actual *composition*, which he dates earlier). No mention of human beings appears in Lev 27:26–27, however, so it is not strictly germane to the present discussion.

42. I use the term "Ritual Decalogue" here only because it is the most common and widely recognized name for this block of material, one that ultimately traces its origins back to the suggestion of Goethe that these verses constitute the "original" Decalogue inscribed on Moses's tablets (J. W. von Goethe, "Zwo wichtige bisher unerörterte biblische Fragen, zum erstenmal gründlich beantwortet. Von einem Landgeistlichen in Schwaben. 1773" in *Göthe in Frankfurt am Main oder zerstreute Blätter aus der Zeit seines dortigen Aufenthalts in den Jahren 1757 bis 1775* [ed. H. Döring; Jena: Mauke, 1839], 24–39). Goethe's view was later supported and popularized by J. Wellhausen, *Die Composition des Hexateuchs und der historischen Bücher des Alten Testaments* (3rd ed.; Berlin: Reimer, 1899), 329–35. For a fascinating and informative overview of the early history of this idea, see B. M. Levinson, "Goethe's Analysis of Exodus 34 and Its Influence on Wellhausen: The *Pfropfung* of the Documentary Hypothesis," *ZAW* 114 (2002): 212–23. The use of the term "Ritual Decalogue" should not be understood as indicating that I believe that it is possible to tease out ten distinct commandments from the corpus; I readily admit that I cannot. For an overview of previous attempts to do so, see S. Gesundheit, *Three Times a Year: Studies on Festival Legislation in the Pentateuch* (FAT 82; Tübingen: Mohr Siebeck, 2012), 12–13 n. 3.

43. See, e.g., S. R. Driver, *The Book of Exodus in the Revised Version with Introduction and Notes* (CBSC; Cambridge: Cambridge University Press, 1911), 202–51, 363–74; R. Kittel, *Geschichte des Volkes Israel* (vol. 1; 5th ed.; HAG; Gotha: Klotz, 1923), 314–15, 327–28; D. J. McCarthy, *Treaty and Covenant: A Study in Form in the Ancient Oriental Documents and in the Old Testament* (2nd ed.; Rome: Biblical Institute Press, 1978), 256–76; R. E. Friedman, *Who Wrote the Bible?* (New York: Summit, 1987), 251, 259; E. Otto, "Deuteronomium und Pentateuch," in *Die Tora: Studien zum Pentateuch: Gesammelte Schriften* (BZABR 9; Wiesbaden: Harrassowitz, 2009), 196–201; and idem, *Das Deuteronomium*, 324–40.

44. Some scholars have even posited that the Ritual Decalogue predates the Covenant Code and that Exodus 23 in particular is dependent on it. See, e.g., Wellhausen, *Composition des Hexateuchs*, 90; G. R. Berry, "The Ritual Decalogue," *JBL* 44 (1925): 39–43; O. Eissfeldt, *The Old Testament: An Introduction* (trans. P. R. Ackroyd; New York: Harper and Row, 1965), 215–16; and J. Halbe, *Das Privilegrecht Jahwes: Ex 34,10–26: Gestalt und Wesen, Herkunft und Wirken in vordeuteronomischer Zeit* (FRLANT 114; Göttingen: Vandenhoeck & Ruprecht, 1975), esp. 391–505.

19.[45] Thus, when considering the Ritual Decalogue's law of the firstborn, we must allow for the possibility that it may be influenced not only by the Covenant Code but also by Deuteronomy and possibly even later material.

First, it is important to note that, unlike both Deuteronomy and the Holiness material, the Ritual Decalogue does not mention the offering of children למלך or by "causing them to pass over by fire" at all. The Ritual Decalogue is introduced by a preamble warning against worshiping the gods of the inhabitants of the land (Exod 34:11–17), similar to the warnings in both Deuteronomy and the Holiness material,[46] but no corresponding prohibition against making למלך offerings appears in conjunction with this warning, as was the case in those codes. The Ritual Decalogue does, however, contain a version of the law of the firstborn (Exod 34:19–20), which reads as follows:

> Every breach of the womb is mine (כל פטר רחם לי), and all of your male[47] cattle, the breach of your oxen and your sheep. A breach of a donkey you will redeem (תפדה) with a sheep. If you do not redeem it then you will break its neck. Every firstborn of your sons (בכור בניך) you will redeem. One will not appear before me empty-handed (ולא יראו פני ריקים).

---

45. See Gesundheit (Bar-On), *Three Times a Year*; idem, "The Festival Calendars in Exodus XXIII 14–19 and XXXIV 18–26," *VT* 48 (1998): 161–95; D. Carr, "Method in Determination of Direction of Dependence: An Empirical Test of Criteria Applied to Exodus 34,11–26 and Its Parallels," in *Gottes Volk am Sinai: Untersuchungen zu Ex 32–34 und Dtn 9–10* (ed. M. Köckert and E. Blum; VWGT 18; Gütersloh: Kaiser/Gütersloher, 2001), 107–40; E. Blum, "Das Sog. 'Privilegrecht' in Exodus 34,11–26: ein Fixpunkt der Komposition des Exodusbuches?" in *Studies in the Book of Exodus: Redaction – Reception – Interpretation* (ed. M. Vervenne; BETL 126; Leuven: Leuven University Press/Peeters, 1996), 347–66; and Fishbane, *Biblical Interpretation*, 194–97. This recent about-face is not entirely without precedent. Earlier research that argued that Exod 34 should be understood as later than and dependent on Exod 23 includes: J. F. L. George, *Die älteren Jüdischen Feste mit einer Kritik der Gesetzgebung des Pentateuch* (Berlin: Schroeder, 1835), 110–18; A. Dillmann and V. Ryssel, *Die Bücher Exodus und Leviticus* (KeHAT; 3rd ed.; Leipzig: Hirzel, 1897), 388–91; B. D. Eerdmans, *Das Buch Exodus* (vol. 3 of *Alttestamentliche Studien*; Giessen: Töpelmann, 1910), 85–92; Kittel, *Geschichte des Volkes Israel* 1, 314–15; R. H. Pfeiffer, "The Oldest Decalogue," *JBL* 43 (1924): 294–310; A. Šanda, *Moses und der Pentateuch* (ATA 9:4–5; Münster: Aschendorffsch, 1924), 185–86; A. Alt, *Die Ursprünge des israelitischen Rechts* (BVSAWLPHK 86; Leipzig: Hirzel, 1934), 52 n. 1; P. Heinisch, *Das Buch Exodus* (HSAT 1:2; Bonn: Hanstein, 1934), 241–44; and F. V. Winnett, *The Mosaic Tradition* (Toronto: University of Toronto Press, 1949), 30–37.

46. This has traditionally been understood as due to Deuteronomistic redactional activity. See Gesundheit, *Three Times a Year*, 37, especially the extensive literature cited in p. 37 n. 60.

47. Reading הזכר for MT תזכר with LXX.

In this text, various elements from previous versions of the law appear together. As in Deut 15:19, the law of the firstborn only applies to male offspring. As in the Holiness material, the firstborn are referred to both as בכור and as פטר רחם and the firstborn of clean animals, unclean animals, and humans are all subject to the law, not merely clean animals as in Deuteronomy. The Ritual Decalogue is innovative in demanding the vicarious sacrifice of a sheep in lieu of a donkey or, alternatively, the profane killing of the donkey, rather than redemption via a cash payment as in Num 18:15–16. As in Num 18:15–16, however, all human firstborn are to redeemed, but the mechanism for redemption is not specified. The context appears to imply, however, that a sacrifice of a sheep is what the Ritual Decalogue has in mind, as in the case of a donkey.[48] Although no explicit mention of the original Passover night is mentioned in the Ritual Decalogue's law of the firstborn, its version of the law appears immediately after its instructions concerning the Festival of Unleavened Bread, which is in turn explicitly linked to the Exodus event (Exod 34:18). This probably indicates that, as in the Holiness material, the Ritual Decalogue also assumes that the obligation to offer firstborn children and animals to Yahweh is connected with the original Passover night. Finally, the Ritual Decalogue's law of the firstborn ends with an injunction not to appear before Yahweh empty-handed, which otherwise appears only in the Covenant Code's instructions concerning the Festival of Unleavened Bread (Exod 23:15) and in the Deuteronomic festival calendar (Deut 16:16). Thus, this version of the law of the firstborn appears to be a conflation of all previous versions.[49] Its specific innovation is the redemption of an unclean donkey and apparently also human children, via vicarious sacrifice.

A similar tradition is also evident in Exod 13:2, 11–13:

48. Assuming that this is the case, there may be some connection between this version of the law of the firstborn and the redemption of Isaac via a ram in Gen 22. The latter, however, is far too overlaid with legend and etiology to provide reliable information about either the historical practice of child sacrifice or even biblical rhetoric surrounding the practice. As Levenson notes, "Genesis 22:1–19 is too much embedded in the specialness of Isaac for us to interpret it as addressing the general subject of human sacrifice," and, "The most that can be said on this topic is that the story reflects a situation in which the sacrifice of a sheep as a substitute for the favored son can meet with God's approval" (*Death and Resurrection*, 111–12, 119). Thus, although Gen 22, like the Ritual Decalogue, appears to be aware of the possibility of vicarious animal sacrifice in lieu of child sacrifice, any attempt to find an etiology for animal substitution in Gen 22 is fraught with difficulty. On this and related matters, see especially Levenson's thorough discussion of Gen 22 in *Death and Resurrection*, 111–24.

49. Gesundheit similarly argues that the Ritual Decalogue's law of the firstborn "is based on Exod 22:28b, but has been rewritten to accord with Priestly legislation" (*Three Times a Year*, 20).

> Sanctify to me every firstborn, the breach of every womb (קדש לי כל בכור פטר כל רחם), among the Israelites, both human and animal. It is mine.
>
> . . .
>
> It will happen when Yahweh brings you to the land of the Canaanites just as he swore to you and to your fathers and he will give it to you, you will cause to pass over every breach of a womb to Yahweh (והעברת כל פטר רחם ליהוה) and every breach of the offspring of an animal (וכל פטר שגר בהמה), the males (הזכרים) which you will have, to Yahweh. Every breach (פטר) of a donkey you will redeem (תפדה) with a sheep, and if you will not redeem you will break its neck. Every human firstborn among your sons (בכור אדם בבניך) you will redeem.

Although there has been much debate concerning the date of Exod 13:1–16,[50] Gertz, Zahn, and Gesundheit[51] have each convincingly demonstrated that this material is among the latest in the Pentateuch and draws upon language from earlier material in crafting its own version of both the Passover rite and the law of the firstborn.[52] This is especially evident in its version of the law of the firstborn, where בכור and פטר are both used in reference to firstborn creatures, as in the Holiness material and Exod 34. The specific mention of the donkey with a command either to redeem it with the vicarious sacrifice of a sheep or to break its neck and the command to redeem all human firstborn follow Exod 34:20 almost verbatim. Furthermore, as in the Holiness material and Exod 34, the law of the firstborn is presented in the context of the original Passover night. The only real innovation in Exod 13, albeit a fascinating one, is the use of the verb √עבר (Hiphil) in conjunction with firstborn offerings. This minor detail is surprising, since in all other cases examined thus far this verb has been specifically linked with the למלך rite. This is the

50. For an overview of the range of scholarly opinion concerning the passage, which includes ascribing the material to JE, to D, or to proto-D, see Gesundheit, *Three Times a Year*, 168–69; and M. M. Zahn, "Reexamining Empirical Models: The Case of Exodus 13," in *Das Deuteronomium zwischen Pentateuch und Deuteronomistischem Geschichtswerk* (ed. E. Otto and R. Achenbach; FRLANT 206; Göttingen: Vandenhoeck & Ruprecht, 2004), 42–43.

51. J. C. Gertz, *Tradition und Redaktion in der Exoduserzählung: Untersuchungen zur Endredaktion des Pentateuch* (FRLANT 186; Göttingen; Vandenhoeck & Ruprecht, 2000), 57–67; Zahn, "Reexamining Empirical Models," 36–55; and Gesundheit, *Three Times a Year*, 167–222.

52. *Pace* Carr, "Method in Determination," 127–30; and idem, *The Formation of the Hebrew Bible: A New Reconstruction* (Oxford: Oxford University Press, 2011), 267 n. 31, who argues that Exod 34 follows Exod 13, rather than vice versa.

first time the term has appeared in the context of the law of the firstborn. As we will see below, however, during later periods there appears to have been conflation in the terminology surrounding the two originally distinct rites: firstborn offerings and למלך sacrifices. Nonetheless, despite drawing its phrasing and terminology from a variety of traditions, the version of the law of the firstborn in Exod 13 is more or less of the same cloth as the version contained in the Ritual Decalogue.

Having surveyed the different legal traditions of the Hebrew Bible and their treatment of the various Israelite child sacrifice rites, we may note some general trajectories regarding both the למלך rite and the law of the firstborn. In the case of the למלך sacrifices, when it is addressed at all (i.e., in Deuteronomy and the Holiness material), the rite is unambiguously forbidden as an abominable practice of the inhabitants of the land whom the Israelites would dispossess. The Israelites are prohibited from worshiping Yahweh in a similar manner. This rhetoric may have its roots in historical reality, since there is reason to believe that this particular child sacrifice rite was foreign, probably Phoenician, in origin and was only incorporated into the Jerusalem cult, albeit almost certainly as a thoroughly Yahwistic rite, relatively late in Judah's history, during the reign of Ahaz. Although the Holiness material dresses this rhetoric in its own language—adding warnings against "defiling the name" of Yahweh and declarations that "I am Yahweh"—the rhetoric in both Deuteronomy and the Holiness material is more or less the same: למלך offerings are illicit in the context of a Yahwistic cult because they are foreign.

In the case of the law of the firstborn, several different means are employed to avoid the implication that firstborn children should be offered as sacrifices to Yahweh. In the case of Deuteronomy (15:19–23), the law of the firstborn is reimagined as a communal meal at the central shrine. Children are not even mentioned in its version of the law and thus are not subject to its stipulations; Deuteronomy thus avoids the implication that children ought to be sacrificed in compliance with the law of the firstborn by denying that they were ever subject to it. The Holiness material, on the other hand, acknowledges Yahweh's claim to firstborn children and further specifies that this claim is tied to Yahweh's having spared the Israelite firstborn on the original Passover night. However, the Holiness material avoids the conclusion that firstborn children actually need to be offered to Yahweh by introducing the idea of "redemption." This redemption plays out in two different ways, even within the Holiness material itself. Either the Levites are accepted as servants of Yahweh in place of offering Israelite firstborn (so Num 3:12–13; 8:14–19), or alternatively (or perhaps additionally?) a monetary payment by a child's parents in support of the priests serves to redeem Israelite firstborn children (so Num 18:15–18). Taking yet another approach, the Ritual Decalogue indicates that the firstborn of donkeys and (probably) human firstborn are redeemed by the vicarious sacrifice of a sheep (Exod 34:19–20), a tradition also taken up in Exod 13 and possibly also reflected in Gen 22. Furthermore, in the Ritual Decalogue as in the Holiness material, Yahweh's claim to firstborn children is connected to the original Passover night. Thus, while there is in the various legal collections a common desire to avoid the implication that children ought to be sacrificed in accordance with the law of the firstborn, there are a variety of mechanisms for reaching this conclusion.

Biblical rhetoric concerning child sacrifice is not confined to the legal material, however. In the prophetic corpus, both Ezekiel and Jeremiah address the topic of Israelite child sacrifice, sometimes participating in traditions that are aligned with the legal material but at other times diverging sharply from them and presenting different and in many ways quite radical claims concerning both the law of the firstborn and the למלך sacrifices.

Ezekiel

The book of Ezekiel refers to child sacrifice several times. First, in Ezek 16:20–21, in the context of one of the most graphic (and, for modern audiences, most disturbing) depictions of Israelite apostasy—a portrayal that includes Yahweh's jealous vengeance against his faithless bride played out via public stripping, humiliation, and execution—the following accusation against Yahweh's figurative bride, Jerusalem, occurs:

> You took your sons and your daughters (את בניך ואת בנותיך) whom you bore for me. You sacrificed them (תזבחים) to them [i.e., to "male images" צלמי זכר; see 16:17] to eat. Was your whoring ([53]תזנתך) not enough? You slaughtered (תשחטי) my children and you gave them (ותתנים), causing them to pass over (בהעביר) to them.

Similarly in Ezek 20:30–31:

> Therefore, say to the house of Israel: Thus says the Lord Yahweh, "Will you defile yourselves in the way of your fathers and are you whoring (זנים) after their detestable things? In offering your gifts [in

53. So K. Q תזנותיך.

> causing to pass your sons over in fire (בהעביר בניכם באש)][54] you defile yourselves with all your idols (גלולים) until this day. And I will be sought by you, house of Israel?! As I live," an utterance of the Lord Yahweh, "I will certainly not be sought by you."

Likewise, in Ezek 23:37–39, among the abominations committed by Samaria and Jerusalem (under the sobriquets "Oholah" and "Oholibah; see 23:4):

> For they have committed adultery, and blood is on their hands. They have committed adultery with their idols (גלוליהן). Even their sons (בניהן) which they bore to me they cause to pass over (העבירו) to them for food. Moreover, they did this to me: they defiled my sanctuary in that day and profaned my sabbaths. When they slaughtered their sons to idols (ובשחטם את בניהם לגלולים), they came to my sanctuary on that day to profane it. See, thus they do in the midst of my house.

There are several difficulties with these passages, not least of which is whether they refer to actual child sacrifice. On the one hand, the passages do contain terminology used elsewhere in reference to the למלך rite, especially "sons (and daughters)," "cause to pass over" (√עבר Hiphil), and in the case of MT 20:31 "in fire." In addition, the mention of "whoring" (√זנה) in Ezek 16:21 and 20:30 is a term also used in the context of condemning למלך sacrifices in Lev 20:5. Given Ezekiel's apparent infatuation with the root "to whore,"[55] however, it is entirely possible that the term's use here is coincidence. On the other hand, unlike in previously examined references to the למלך rite, Ezek 16:20 refers to the "sacrifice" (√זבח) of children, and Ezek 16:21 and 23:39 describes their "slaughter" (√שחט). Furthermore, these sacrifices are described as being offered for the purpose of feeding idols, despite the lack of evidence either in earlier biblical material or in the cognate Punic evidence that children offered למלך served as food for gods.

---

54. The bracketed phrase does not appear in the OG, probably an indication that it is a secondary gloss. So Stavrakopoulou, *King Manasseh and Child Sacrifice*, 162; W. Zimmerli, *Ezekiel 1: A Commentary on the Book of the Prophet Ezekiel, Chapters 1–24* (ed. F. M. Cross and K. Baltzer; trans. R. E. Clements; Hermeneia; Philadelphia: Fortress, 1979), 402; and W. Eichrodt, *Ezekiel: A Commentary* (trans. C. Quin; OTL; Philadelphia: Westminster, 1970), 260–61. Nonetheless, preferring to err on the side of comprehensiveness, I have included it among the relevant Ezekiel texts.

55. See Ezek 6:9 (2×); 16:15 (2×), 16, 17, 20, 22, 25, 26, 28 (2×), 29, 30, 31, 33 (2×), 34 (2×), 35, 36, 37, 41; 20:30; 23:3 (2×), 5, 8, 11 (2×), 14, 17, 18, 19 (2×), 27, 29 (2×), 30, 35, 43 (2×), 44.

Furthermore, Ezek 20:30–32 (if one assumes, against the evidence of the OG, that the mention of child sacrifice is original to the text) implies that Ezekiel's audience was *currently* making these offerings. Kings, however, testifies that למלך offerings ceased to be offered during Josiah's reform. Both the explicit statement that Josiah defiled the tophet (2 Kgs 23:10) and the notable absence of any accusation against the kings who came after Josiah (accusations that would have been particularly convenient for a historian interested in linking Jerusalem's fall to ritual apostasy) suggests that the למלך rites were a thing of the past by the time of Ezekiel's composition. Why then would the oracle refer to the Israelites' continuing to make such offerings "until this day" (Ezek 20:31)? The solution to this problem may be as simple as following the witness of the OG and excising the reference to child sacrifice in MT 20:31 as a secondary gloss.

This still leaves one question: why does Ezekiel's depiction of the "cause to pass over by fire" rites look so different from earlier descriptions of the למלך rite? One possibility is that Ezekiel's hyperbolic rhetoric is on full display in these passages. Mosca, for instance, suggests that Ezekiel uses terms like "slaughter" and "eating" tendentiously to connect child sacrifice with animal sacrifice.[56] Stavrakopoulou chalks up the over-the-top rhetoric to "the stereotypical usage of the biblical language of child sacrifice in these chapters, rather than, say, the reflections of an eye-witness to the practice."[57] In her extended treatment of child sacrifice language in Ezekiel, especially in Ezek 16, P. L. Day concludes that the text is not referring to child sacrifice but is instead figuratively using the trope of child sacrifice in a graphic depiction of the general destruction, and specifically the exile, of the inhabitants of Jerusalem by foreign nations. The "idols" are the nations and the "children" are the population of Jerusalem.[58] However one understands the unusually graphic imagery, there is good reason to suspect that the mentions of child sacrifice in Ezekiel represent rhetorical flamboyance more than historical veracity.

Nonetheless, if we are interested in tracing biblical rhetoric surrounding child sacrifice, then Ezekiel still has much to offer, despite dating to several decades after the practice of making למלך sacrifices had fallen into disuse. For Ezekiel, as in the Holiness material, למלך sacrifices constitute "whoring."

56. Mosca, "Child Sacrifice," 232.

57. Stavrakopoulou, *King Manasseh and Child Sacrifice*, 164.

58. P. L. Day, "Is the Language of Child Sacrifice Used Figuratively in Ezekiel 16?" in *Not Sparing the Child: Human Sacrifice in the Ancient World and Beyond: Studies in Honor of Professor Paul G. Mosca* (ed. V. D. Arbel et al.; New York: Bloomsbury, 2015), 91–113.

And, as in Deuteronomy, these sacrifices are presented as foreign. Ezekiel, however, takes Deuteronomy's "foreign" rhetoric to an entirely new level. Rather than simply accusing the inhabitants of Jerusalem of worshiping Yahweh in the same manner that the Canaanites' worshiped their gods (Deut 12:29–31), Ezekiel depicts the rite as involving the grotesque practice of feeding children to foreign idols, an accusation without precedent in previous biblical rhetoric surrounding למלך sacrifices. As argued above, there is likely a kernel of truth to the rhetoric of Deuteronomy, but Ezekiel's rhetoric appears to have no other source than the imagination of the scribe(s) responsible for the oracles. The fact that the oracles were composed at least a few decades after the last למלך sacrifice was offered in Jerusalem removed any restraint on this sort of rhetorical elaboration and intensification. Who would have had the means or motivation to correct Ezekiel's misrepresentation of the rite once no one in Jerusalem was participating in it? Thus, in Ezekiel's rhetoric, למלך sacrifices were presented not only as foreign in origin but also as offered to foreign, non-Yahwistic gods.

Significantly, however, Ezekiel takes an entirely different tack regarding the sacrifice of children in compliance with the law of the firstborn. Ezek 20:24–26, in the midst of a depiction of the exodus and wilderness wandering periods as a time of rebellion and disobedience on the part of the Israelites, states:

> Because they did not execute my judgments, rejected my statutes, profaned my sabbaths, and their eyes were after the idols of their fathers, I gave to them statutes that were not good and judgments by which they could not live. I defiled them in their gifts, in causing every breach of a womb to pass over (בהעביר כל פטר רחם). I desolated them so that they would know that I am Yahweh.

These two verses present a host of difficulties. Not only is there a theological problem—Yahweh's having intentionally misled the Israelites with "statutes that were not good"—but there is the question of the exact nature of these "statutes that were not good." C. Patton suggests that the phrase refers to the entire corpus of preexilic legal material, which included among its commands a requirement to sacrifice all firstborn children (Exod 22:28b–29 [Eng. 22:29b–30]). In Patton's view, Ezekiel rejects these older traditions in favor of its own corpus of legislation contained in Ezek 40–48.[59] S. W. Hahn and

59. C. Patton, "'I Myself Gave Them Laws That Were Not Good': Ezekiel 20 and the Exodus Traditions," *JSOT* 69 (1996): 73–90.

J. S. Bergsma, on the other hand, believe that it is only the corpus of Deuteronomic law that is rejected by (the generally Priestly-inclined) Ezekiel and that "every breach of a womb" refers not to the sacrifice of firstborn children but to Deuteronomy's allowance that non-firstlings may be slaughtered in a secular context (Deut 12:15–28), against Priestly traditions that require all animal slaughter to take place in a sacred context (see Lev 17:1–7). Thus, from a Holiness/Priestly perspective, the Deuteronomic Code represents "statutes that were not good" in that they required *only* firstborn (animals) to be sacrificed, but not others.[60] The most common suggestion, however, is that the "statutes that were not good" refers to some version of the law of the firstborn literally applied to humans without the application of a redemption clause, perhaps Exod 22:28b–29 (Eng. 22:29b–30), and thus, the "statutes that were not good" to which Ezekiel refers required the sacrifice of firstborn children.[61]

This final suggestion appears to be the most plausible for several reasons. First, the use of the verb √עבר (Hiphil) is commonly associated with the למלך rite, which also involved the sacrifice of children. Although Ezekiel appears to distinguish the למלך sacrifices and the firstborn offerings conceptually, in that the former are presented as sacrifices to feed foreign idols but the latter are given to Yahweh in compliance with "statutes that were not good," there appears to be some slippage in the language surrounding the two originally distinct varieties of child sacrifice. This conflation in language is especially characteristic of later periods. In only one other instance, Exod 13:12, does the verb √עבר (Hiphil) appear in conjunction with the law of the firstborn, and as noted above, this instance is in a passage that is probably among the

60. S. W. Hahn and J. S. Bergsma, "What Laws Were 'Not Good'? A Canonical Approach to the Theological Problem of Ezekiel 20:25–56," *JBL* 123 (2004): 201–18.

61. So D. E. Callender, "'I Gave Them Laws That Were Not Good' (Ezk 20:25): A Biblical Model of Complex Subjectivity and the Prospects of Multi-Ethnic Contextual Reading," *In die Skriflig* 48 (2014), Art. #1828, 8 pages. http://dx.doi. org/10.4102/ids.v48i1.1828; Smith, "Child Sacrifice as the Extreme Case," 8–9; idem, "Textual Interpretation in 7th–6th Century Israel: Between Competition, Textualisation and Tradition," in *Textual Criticism and Dead Sea Scrolls: Studies in Honour of Julio Trebolle Barrera: Florilegium Complutense* (ed. A. Piquer Otro and P. A. Torijano Morales; JSJSup 158; Leiden: Brill, 2012), 317–23; B. Halpern, "The False Torah of Jeremiah 8 in the Context of Seventh Century BCE Pseudepigraphy: The First Documented Rejection of Tradition," in *"Up to the Gates of Ekron": Essays on the Archaeology and History of the Eastern Mediterranean in Honor of Seymour Gitin* (ed. S. W. Crawford et al.; Jerusalem: The W. F. Albright Institute of Archaeological Research/The Israel Exploration Society, 2007), 339–40; Stavrakopoulou, *King Manasseh and Child Sacrifice*, 184–86; Levenson, *Death and Resurrection*, 4–8; M. Greenberg, *Ezekiel 1–20*: A New Translation with Introduction and Commentary (AB 22; Garden City, NY: Doubleday, 1983), 368–70; and Zimmerli, *Ezekiel* 1, 411–12.

the latest in the Pentateuch. Indeed, it is not impossible that the language of Exod 13:12 is influenced by Ezek 20:31 (or possibly vice versa). Despite this overlap in terminology, it does not appear that Ezekiel has entirely identified the למלך sacrifice with firstborn offerings, but the use of √עבר (Hiphil) probably does indicate that the "statutes that were not good" involved child sacrifice.

Another reason to suspect that the phrase "statutes that were not good" refers to child sacrifice is that, just a few verses later, in MT Ezek 20:31 an explicit reference to child sacrifice does appear, "in causing to pass your sons over in fire" (בנעביר בניהם באש). As observed above, the phrase does not appear in the OG and thus is likely a secondary gloss. Nonetheless, the gloss itself was probably occasioned by Ezek 20:25–26, suggesting that the glossator understood these verses as referring to child sacrifice. This late glossator apparently did not distinguish between the "causing to pass over by fire" sacrifices and the firstborn sacrifices; but, again, this type of confusion is common in later periods. Indeed, in the discussion below we will see that the late "C Material" of Jeremiah completely identifies the two rites. Although the original text of Ezek 20 kept the two rites conceptually separate, the glossator did not. In any case, the fact that our glossator finds child sacrifice in Ezek 20 supports the conclusion that the "statutes that were not good" probably involved child sacrifice.

Assuming that Ezek 20:25–26 refers to a version of the law of the firstborn that required child sacrifice, we are thus presented with yet another attempt both to affirm Yahweh's claim to firstborn children and to avoid arriving at the conclusion that Yahweh actually desired that firstborn children be sacrificed. Ezekiel's rhetorical strategy, however, is much more radical than any of the previously observed reactions to the law of the firstborn. Rather than indicating that firstborn children ought to be "redeemed," either by the vicarious sacrifice of a lamb as in Exod 34:20 and 13:13, via the service of the Levites as in Num 3:12 and 8:15–18, or by means of a monetary payment to the temple as in Num 18:15–16, Ezek 20:25–26 takes an entirely different rhetorical approach. Ezekiel claims that Yahweh actually did command that all firstborn children be sacrificed to him, but he only gave this command in response to the people's failure to follow the statutes that Yahweh had previously laid down, especially observance of the Sabbath (Ezek 20:12–13, 16, 20–21, 24). The obvious question, then, is why Ezekiel chose to make such a surprising, and theologically problematic, rhetorical move.

It seems unlikely that the book of Ezekiel, which clearly opposes child sacrifice in all its varieties, would have introduced an interpretation of the law of the firstborn that required the sacrifice of children. First, such a move would be rhetorically counterproductive; if one opposes child sacrifice, introducing the idea that Yahweh actually commanded it would run contrary to one's purposes. Second, Ezek 20:25–26 would have made little sense to a late sixth-century audience if they did not assume that the law of the firstborn did, or at the very least theoretically could, involve the sacrifice of children. The text assumes that there was at least one actual "statute" known to both the scribe and his audience that mandated that firstborn children be sacrificed. An obvious candidate for this statute is the Covenant Code's law of the firstborn (Exod 22:28b–29 [Eng. 22:29b–30]), which most naturally reads as requiring that firstborn children be "given" to Yahweh on the eighth day in the same manner that firstborn cattle and sheep were—that is, that they be sacrificed. Thus, both the scribe responsible for the oracle and his audience appear to have shared the assumption that the Covenant Code's law of the firstborn (or at least something similar to it) required the sacrifice of firstborn children. They also appear to have shared the belief that this tradition was authoritative. Smith observes that the scribe

> cannot change the older text due to the broadly recognized weight of tradition that has legitimized them—at least in some eyes. Instead, they refute its divine character—though not so much of the text itself, but of the way that it had been understood and interpreted. What people thought was commanded, it is now claimed, represents an incorrect understanding or interpretation of them.[62]

While I agree that the issue at stake concerns wrestling with a text that is broadly recognized as of divine origin in some sense, I partly demur: the issue is *not* whether the text has been properly interpreted; both parties agree about the interpretation of the law: it mandates the sacrifice of firstborn children. The issue at stake is the underlying motive for Yahweh's having given it in the first place. Ezek 20:25–26 concedes that Yahweh had given a command to sacrifice firstborn children but presents the giving of this command as a form of divine punishment. Thus, the authoritative status of the older text and even its interpretation is left undisputed, but its original purpose is radically reimagined.

A final issue to be addressed is the implied assumption that children were being sacrificed in compliance with Yahweh's claim to firstborn children during Ezekiel's day. If the Covenant Code's version of the law of the firstborn

62. Smith, "Textual Interpretation," 319.

is the text at issue, then it seems that both the oldest collection of legal material preserved in the Hebrew Bible and (at least some of) its interpreters in the late monarchic period believed that Yahweh's claim to firstborn children demanded their sacrifice. Is it possible that such a tradition lived on in actual practice throughout the generations between the formulation of the Covenant Code's law of the firstborn and the late monarchic period, even among a relatively small group of particularly "devout" Yahwists? Or could it be that over time the practice of child sacrifice in compliance with the law of the firstborn fell into disuse even among the group(s) that preserved the Covenant Code traditions, and then only at a relatively late period was there a resurgence of a literal interpretation of its law of the firstborn? Could it even be that the fairly recent importation of the למלך rite encouraged a renewed literal interpretation of the tradition? Or perhaps, on the other hand, the debate that underlies Ezek 20:25–26 was entirely "academic." Perhaps during the distress that accompanied the Babylonian conquest of Jerusalem, questions concerning what had angered Yahweh enough to allow such a calamity to befall the people of Judah were particularly pressing; perhaps some were arguing that the people had failed to apply Yahweh's commands rigorously and literally enough. Thus, it may be that Ezek 20 is engaged in an entirely theoretical debate and that at this late period no children were being sacrificed, although some may have been suggesting that they ought to be.

These questions are impossible to answer, given available evidence, and thus the historical reality of firstborn sacrifice in late monarchic Jerusalem or the lack thereof must remain a matter of uncertainty. Nonetheless, whatever the historical reality of child sacrifice during this period, Ezekiel's rhetoric concerning למלך sacrifices and the sacrifice of firstborn children diverges sharply from earlier biblical traditions. For Ezekiel, the למלך sacrifices involved feeding children to idols, a claim that goes beyond even the strong denunciations of Deuteronomy and the Holiness material. On the other hand, rather than claiming that the law of the firstborn did not apply to children at all, as in Deuteronomy, or that this requirement could be fulfilled by some sort of redemption, as in the Holiness material and Ritual Decalogue, Ezekiel acknowledged that Yahweh commanded that firstborn children be sacrificed as the Covenant Code literally says but avoided the conclusion that this was something that Yahweh actually wanted by transforming the command into a form of divine punishment. As the evidence from Jeremiah will reveal, however, this rather brilliant (but nonetheless troubling) rhetorical strategy would not be the last word on the matter, and some biblical writers found

Ezekiel's "solution" to the difficulty so problematic that they addressed it head on.

Jeremiah

In the book of Jeremiah, there are three particularly relevant, and nearly identical, oracles concerning the sacrifice of children. First, Jer 7:31:

> ובנו במות[63] התפת אשר בגיא בן הנם לשרף את בניהם ובנתיהם באש אשר לא צויתי ולא עלתה על לבי
>
> And they built the high places of the tophet which is in the Ben Hinnom Valley to burn their sons and their daughters in fire, which I did not command[64] and which did not enter my mind (lit., "arise upon my heart").

Next, Jer 19:5:

> ובנו במות הבעל לשרף את בניהם באש [עלות לבעל][65] אשר לא צויתי [ולא דברתי][66] ולא עלתה על לבי
>
> And they built the high places of the Baal to burn their sons/children in fire [as burnt offerings to the Baal], which I did not command [and which I did not speak] and which did not enter my mind (lit., "arise upon my heart").

Finally, Jer 32:35 [Greek 39:35]:

> ויבנו את במות הבעל אשר בגיא בן הנם להעביר את בניהם ובנתיהם למלך אשר לא צויתים ולא עלתה על לבי לעשות התועבה הזאת למען החטי[67] את יהודה
>
> And they built the high places of the Baal which is in the Ben Hinnom Valley to cause to pass over their sons and their daughters as a *mlk*-sacrifice, which I did not command them and which did not

63. OG reads a singular form τὸν βωμὸν.
64. OG adds "them" (αὐτοῖς)
65. Lacking in OG.
66. Lacking in OG.
67. So K. Q **החטיא**.

> enter my mind (lit., "arise upon my heart") to do this abomination in order to cause Judah to sin.

These three passages are obviously related to one another. Mowinckel assigns the first and last to the "C" material of Jeremiah,[68] while in his opinion 19:5 is part of a secondary reworking of Jer 19 ("B" material[69]) under the influence of Jer 7.[70] In viewing the three oracles as either coming from the same hand or in some way dependent on one another, Mowinckel has been followed by most scholars, despite some disagreement about specific details concerning the composition history of the three passages.[71] Whatever the precise relationship among them, however, it is clear that they all are essentially variations of the same oracle.

The most concise version is Jer 7:31, which has these essential elements: (1) a mention of the building of the high place(s) of the tophet in the Ben Hinnom Valley where (2) the burning of sons and daughters took place and (3) a denial that Yahweh ever commanded such a thing or even considered it. This outline is mostly followed in 19:5, aside from the expansions present in MT but absent from OG. The one major difference in the original text of 19:5 is that rather than building "the high place(s) of the tophet" the people are accused of building "the high places of the Baal." Finally, in 32:35 the language is a bit different from 7:31 and 19:5, but much more like the language found in Leviticus and Kings: instead of "being burned" (√שרף) the children are "caused to pass over" (√עבר Hiphil), here explicitly למלך. In addition, Yahweh's denial is even more emphatic in this final version, which adds the phrase "to do this abomination in order to cause Judah to sin." Nonetheless, despite these differences, the overarching message appears to be the same.

---

68. S. Mowinckel, *Zur Komposition des Buches Jeremia* (Kristiana: Dybwad, 1914), 31.
69. Ibid., 24.
70. Ibid., 8 n. 1.
71. See, e.g., W. Rudolph, *Jeremia* (HAT 12; Tübingen: Mohr [Siebeck], 1947), xv–xvii; J. Bright, *Jeremiah: A New Translation with Introduction and Commentary* (AB 21; Garden City, NY: Doubleday, 1965), 57–59, 131–33; E. Nicholson, *The Book of the Prophet Jeremiah, Chapters 1–25* (CBC; Cambridge: Cambridge University Press, 1973), 75–76, 162–63; W. Thiel, *Die deuteronomische Redaktion von Jeremia 1–25* (WMANT 41; Neukirchen-Vluyn: Neukirchener Verlag, 1973), 128–34; McKane, *Jeremiah I–XXV*, 455–56; G. H. Park-Taylor, *The Formation of the Book of Jeremiah: Doublets and Recurring Phrases* (SBLMS 51; Atlanta: Society of Biblical Literature, 2000), 192–95; C. Levine, "Das Kinderopfer im Jeremiabuch," in *Fortschreibungen: Gesammelte Studien zum Alten Testament* (BZAW 316; Berlin: de Gruyter, 2003), 227–41; G. Fischer, *Jeremiah 1–25* (HThKAT; Freiburg: Herder, 2005), 593–94; W. H. Schmidt, *Das Buch Jeremia: Kapitel 1–20* (ATD 20; Göttingen: Vandenhoeck & Ruprecht, 2008), 328.

Several features of this thrice-repeated oracle are worth noting. First, despite the fact that the term למלך only occurs in the third text, it is undoubtedly this rite—known from other passages as connected with the tophet in the Ben Hinnom Valley (2 Kgs 23:10) and with the fiery sacrifice of children (Deut 18:10; 2 Kgs 16:3; 17:17; 21:6 [//2 Chr 33:6]; 23:10; Ezek 20:31)—that is in view in all three cases. Unsurprisingly, as in nearly all earlier biblical texts that mention the rite (Isa 30:33 being the major exception), these למלך sacrifices are condemned in unambiguous terms. The rhetoric in Jeremiah, however, is a bit different. First, in Jer 19:5 and 32:35, the sacrifices are explicitly identified as having been offered at "the high place of the Baal." These two verses are the only instances in the Hebrew Bible in which the rite is in any way linked with Baal worship, and this connection is almost certainly the product of tendentious polemic rather than historical reality.[72] On the other hand, linking למלך offerings to the foreign god Baal is actually not *entirely* innovative but may be understood as a yet another step along one major rhetorical trajectory that has already been observed in earlier texts. As discussed above, the historical reality involved Ahaz incorporating למלך sacrifices into the Jerusalem cult, probably in imitation of his Phoenician neighbors. Deuteronomy, fairly accurately, describes these offerings as worshiping Yahweh in the same manner as foreigners (Deut 12:31). Next, the Holiness material and Ezekiel each link the rite with "whoring" (√זנה; Lev 20:25; Ezek 16:20–22), and Ezekiel in particular represents the recipients of these sacrifices as foreign idols.

In Jeremiah, several of these threads converge. First, the "foreign" nature of the למלך rite is even more pronounced. It is no longer merely a foreign rite or even a rite intended to feed foreign idols; in Jer 19:5 and 32:35, it is explicitly linked to Baal, Yahweh's chief rival in the Hebrew Bible, especially in the Deuteronomistic History and the book of Hosea. Thus, according to Jeremiah, not only are למלך rites foreign, they are rites associated with the foreign deity par excellence. Indeed, much of the groundwork for making this connection was laid by the "whoring" language used by the Holiness material and Ezekiel in conjunction with the rite because, other than Ezekiel, the book where such language most commonly occurs is Hosea,[73] which also happens to be the prophetic book most preoccupied with the worship of Baal.[74]

72. So also Mosca, "Child Sacrifice," 230–31; Heider, *The Cult of Molek*, 340; and Stavrakopoulou, *King Manasseh and Child Sacrifice*, 158–61.

73. Hos 1:2 [2×]; 2:7 [Eng. 2:5]; 3:3; 4:10, 12, 13, 14 [2×], 15, 18 [2×]; 5:3; 9:1.

74. Hos 2:10, 18 [Eng. 2:8, 16]; 13:1.

Already in Ezekiel, the למלך sacrifices were bound up in a rhetorical nexus of both "foreignness" and "whoring"; all the Jeremiah scribe(s) needed to do to attach these sacrifices to Baal was to incorporate Hosea's rhetoric connecting "whoring" with the worship of Baal. Thus, the relationship between למלך sacrifices and Baal in Jer 19:5 and 32:35 is certainly an innovation, but it is not one entirely without precedent.

Perhaps a more significant shift is the claim that Yahweh "did not command" such a thing. This passage is sometimes cited in conjunction with Ezekiel's "statutes that were not good" as another example of a prophet rejecting a law commanding child sacrifice. A common assumption is that Jeremiah and Ezekiel are essentially saying the same thing. For example, Halpern argues that "it would appear that Jeremiah and Ezekiel, in an era of the rejection of tradition, embrace the rejection of JE, probably already combined and promulgated in the early seventh century, in favor of the traditions represented by Deuteronomy, the Deuteronomistic History, and P."[75] Smith, on the other hand, argues that "these authors are arguing not only about the authority of an older text, but also about its interpretation, which had become part of their tradition surrounding such authoritative texts . . . they refute its divine character—though not so much of the text itself, but of the way that it had been understood and interpreted."[76] Thus, even while arguing against Halpern that the issue is the interpretation of divine law rather than its actual authority, Smith, too, treats the two texts as making the same basic argument. In the most literal sense, however, Jeremiah's argument is the exact *opposite* of Ezekiel's. Although Ezekiel says that Yahweh did give such a law (albeit a "not good" one), Jeremiah adamantly denies that he did. Levenson, however, does note this difference in rhetoric,[77] and Lundbom even goes so far as to assert regarding Ezekiel's claim: "Nothing remotely close to this comes out of the mouth of Jeremiah."[78] Carroll observes the "formal contradiction" and ascribes it to the "different traditions" of Ezekiel and Jeremiah.[79] Given this difference in rhetoric, one might ask why Jeremiah and Ezekiel, and their "different traditions," would take such diametrically opposed approaches toward reaching the common goal of denying that Yahweh ever actually desired

75. Halpern, "The False Torah of Jeremiah 8," 340.

76. Smith, "Textual Interpretation in 7th–6th Century Israel," 319.

77. Levenson, *Death and Resurrection*, 5.

78. J. R. Lundbom, *Jeremiah 1–20*: A New Translation with Introduction and Commentary (AB 21A; New York: Doubleday, 1999), 498.

79. R. P. Carroll, *Jeremiah*: *A Commentary* (OTL; Philadelphia: Westminster, 1986), 223.

child sacrifice. The solution may connected to the divergent attitudes toward the various legal corpora exhibited by different Yahwistic traditions.

It has long been observed that Jeremiah, and especially the so-called "C" material, has a strong affinity with the Deuteronomic literature of the Hebrew Bible.[80] Levinson, Stackert, and others have argued that Deuteronomy was intended to replace all earlier law collections, especially the Covenant Code.[81] Finally, it is important to recall that Deuteronomy's version of the law of the firstborn contains no mention whatsoever of firstborn children. Putting all this together, we can conclude that the scribes behind the Jeremiah C material could in good faith claim that Yahweh never gave any command requiring the sacrifice of children because they did not recognize as legitimate any body of legal material that made such a demand. That is, given the underlying assumptions of writers of a Deuteronomistic bent, the claim that Yahweh never gave such a law would be entirely accurate from their perspective. On the other hand, Ezek 20 seems to have recognized as authoritative the Covenant Code or some other collection with a similar law of the firstborn (i.e., one including children and lacking a redemption clause) and therefore had to take a more roundabout path to deny that Yahweh desired the sacrifice of children. Indeed, the strong rhetoric employed in Jer 7:31, 19:5, and 32:35 ("which I did not command and which did not enter my mind") leads us to suspect that these verses may in fact be directly responding to a claim that Yahweh *did* issue such a commandment. Jer 32:35 goes even further: "which I did not command them and which did not enter my mind to do this abomination in order to cause Judah to sin." Here the rhetoric sounds strikingly similar, although directly contrary, to that of Ezek 20:25–26, which claims that Yahweh *had* in fact given such a law in order to "defile" and "desolate" the people of Judah. This similarity seems too close to be mere coincidence, and it is possible that the Jeremiah passages are directly responding to the claims of Ezek 20. It may be that this is evidence of divergent beliefs about what constitutes the legitimate body of Yahwistic law spilling out into a debate about Yahweh's relationship to the practice of child sacrifice.

One final comment concerning the three Jeremiah passages: here, for the first time, the למלך rite and firstborn offerings are entirely conflated. Even as late as Ezekiel, the two forms of child sacrifice were treated as distinct, and

80. For a convenient collection of distinctly Deuteronomic phrases in the Jeremiah C material see, Weinfeld, *Deuteronomy and the Deuteronomic School*, 320–65.

81. See pp. 157–58 n. 17 above.

different rhetorical strategies were employed in addressing each. In Jeremiah, however, למלך language and firstborn sacrifice appear under a single blanket condemnation. The mention of "statutes that were not good" in Ezek 20 was specifically in reference to firstborn sacrifice, but the Jeremiah scribes respond to its arguments by employing למלך language. Further, in the case of Jer 19:5 and 32:35, both forms of child sacrifice are in turn identified with the worship of Baal. In this way, all forms of child sacrifice, despite their different purposes, functions, and histories, are rolled into a single undifferentiated mass, identified as anti-Yahwistic Baal worship and rejected as illegitimate.[82] Once this rhetorical strategy has been employed and all forms of child sacrifice are linked with foreign deities, the original connection between child sacrifice and Yahwism is completely severed. Thus, in Ps 106:37 the Israelites are said to have "sacrificed their sons and daughters to the *šēdîm*" (ויזבחו את בניהם ואת בנותיהם לשדים).[83] Likewise, if the mention of "slaughtering children in the wadis" in Isa 57:5 refers to child sacrifice in the context of an illicit (foreign?) cult (although I am not entirely certain that it does[84]), then it would be yet

82. This lack of concern for the finer points of (in its view) illicit worship is typical of Jeremiah's rhetoric. In this regard, the suggestion of W. R. Domeris is helpful: Jeremiah's rhetoric employs an "antilanguage" full of stock phrases like "a detestable thing that God hates," "Baal," "other gods," "false gods," etc., by means of which Jeremiah "intentionally lumps [particular forms of the religion of his society] together, so allowing the extremes to colour the more moderate shades of syncretism. In effect he tars all the religious expressions of his contemporaries with the same brush, creating both an artificial division (between his own extreme form of Yahwism, and all other expressions), and an artificial unity (within the other expressions, in spite of their obvious differences)" ("When Metaphor Becomes Myth: A Socio-Linguistic Reading of Jeremiah" in *Troubling Jeremiah* [ed. A. R. P. Diamond, K. M. O'Connor, and L. Stulman; JSOTSup 260; Sheffield: Sheffield Academic, 1999], 254).

83. *Pace* Stavrakopoulou (*King Manasseh and Child Sacrifice*, 274), this passage is not an indication of a historical connection between Yahweh's epithet "Shaddai" and the practice of child sacrifice. Instead, it represents yet another conflation of child sacrifice and the worship of foreign idols or deities, following in the steps of both Ezekiel and Jeremiah. Both here and in the other attestation of the term (Deut 32:17), the context makes clear that *šēdîm* do indeed refer to foreign deities or demons. For the possible connection to Akkadian *šēdu*(*m*), see *HALOT* 1417–18.

84. Isaiah 57:3–13 is notoriously difficult. The most convincing explanation of the oracle is that it represents an intertwining of sexual and death-cult imagery. See especially T. J. Lewis, "Death Cult Imagery in Isaiah 57," *HAR* 11 (1987): 267–84; idem, *Cults of the Dead*, 143–58. So also Ackerman, *Under Every Green Tree*, 143–52; J. Blenkinsopp, *Isaiah 56–66: A New Translation and Commentary* (AB 19B; New York: Doubleday, 2003), 152–66; and Stavrakopoulou, *King Manasseh and Child Sacrifice*, 170–79. The mention of "slaughtering children" in the context of cults of the dead is unprecedented in earlier literature, and if child sacrifice actually is in view here, Third Isaiah would be offering yet another twist on the rhetoric surrounding such offerings. The difficult nature of the text, however, allows only for tentative conclusions in this regard.

another variation on this theme. In later biblical texts, the historical variety of child sacrifice rites evident in earlier periods has been completely leveled. All forms of the practice are presented as examples of foreign idolatry and thus all stand in stark opposition to the worship of Yahweh.

Conclusions

Previous chapters explored the historical diversity of various Israelite child sacrifice rituals, but this chapter has attempted to trace the history of the biblical rhetoric surrounding the rites. We have seen that there is no unanimity on the issue, even among biblical writers who agree that Yahweh opposed all forms of child sacrifice. With regard to the למלך sacrifices, the general approach is to focus on the foreign origin of the practice. This rhetorical emphasis was likely encouraged by the fact that, so far as we can tell, the rite appeared relatively late on the scene in Jerusalem and probably was in reality an instance of foreign syncretism. Deuteronomy's rhetoric more or less reflects this historical reality, presenting it as a rite in which children are sacrificed to Yahweh in the same way that other peoples sacrifice their children to their gods. Later, however, this emphasis on the foreign origin of the rite morphed into Ezekiel's claim that these sacrifices also had foreign recipients, and eventually, in Jeremiah, to the claim that this foreign recipient was none other than Baal himself. Thus, the general trajectory was to paint the למלך rites as increasingly foreign to Israelite Yahwism as time went on.

On the other hand, although there is a general consensus among biblical writers that Yahweh did not desire the sacrifice of firstborn children, there are some significant disagreements concerning how to square this with Yahweh's legitimate claim to the firstborn of all humans and animals. Deuteronomy solves the problem by entirely omitting firstborn children from its version of the law of the firstborn, which later allowed Jeremiah's editors flatly to claim that no such law existed. Other biblical texts, however, take a less direct route. In the Ritual Decalogue, children are "redeemed" via the vicarious offering of a sheep. In Numbers, the Levites' service and/or financial support for the cult is accepted in lieu of firstborn children. Ezekiel takes the unique approach of acknowledging that Yahweh demanded the sacrifice of firstborn children, but claims that this command is one that is "not good," which was intended to punish the rebellious Israelites. In each case, we see different attempts to deal with earlier traditions, in some cases outright rejecting those traditions but in others trying to preserve and rework them in a more palatable direction.

It was only at the end of a long series of attempts to wrestle with the historical reality of Yahwistic child sacrifice that the solution of linking all such sacrifices to foreign deities emerged. This strategy was only possible at a relatively late period, when child sacrifice had fallen out of practice among Israelite Yahwists. Once the reality of child sacrifice had faded into the past, those denying that Yahweh ever desired such a thing were no longer constrained by the reality surrounding such rites and could take the simplest route—condemning all forms of child sacrifice by tying them all to the worship of foreign gods or idols. It was ultimately this final tactic that allowed and even encouraged the Greek translators of the Hebrew Bible to understand למלך as "to Molek," thereby enabling the creation of the grim and terrifying "Moloch" of Milton and Flaubert.

Summary and Conclusions

Israelite child sacrifice encompassed a range of rituals that do not appear to have had as much in common as we might assume. Insofar as we can tell, there were at least three different rites that involved the sacrifice of children to Yahweh in Iron Age Israel, each having its own distinct purpose and history. The general sacrifice of firstborn children served to acknowledge Yahweh's claim to all firstlings and firstfruits, applied specifically to children. Offering a firstborn child to Yahweh had the practical effect of ensuring that Yahweh would bless, multiply, and protect subsequent progeny—an entirely comprehensible concern in a society with infant mortality rates that may well have approached 50%. Although not all Israelites, and in my opinion probably far from most, actually sacrificed their firstborn children, there seems to be evidence that at least some took Yahweh's claim to firstborn children quite literally. Because such evidence is attested as early as the Covenant Code and as late as Ezekiel, the Yahwistic groups who engaged in actual firstborn sacrifice do not appear confined to a particular period of Israelite history. Instead, it appears that groups who literally offered their firstborn children existed simultaneously with those who did not, probably throughout a significant portion of Israel's history.

At the same time, there is also evidence for another form of firstborn sacrifice, apparently unrelated to the general sacrifice of firstborn children: the offering of a firstborn child during times of crisis. The primary evidence for this form of child sacrifice is the story of King Mesha of Moab in 2 Kgs 3 and the suggestion in Micah that Yahweh might be moved to act in response to a gift as extravagant as a firstborn child. This form of child sacrifice is conceptually distinct from a general sacrifice of firstborn children in that the concern is not with general blessing and fertility. Instead, this form of firstborn sacrifice was offered in the hope of obtaining direct divine intervention in the face of an extraordinary crisis. Indeed, practically speaking, the two forms of child sacrifice were incompatible, since a group that sacrificed all of their firstborn children on the child's eighth day could not have had any firstborn children left to offer during a time of crisis. We can thus assume that the two forms of firstborn sacrifice did not exist within a single group.

Third, we have the למלך sacrifices. Although the Hebrew Bible itself offers little information about the purpose of these sacrifices, Punic epigraphic evidence indicates that they were associated with personal vows made in order to obtain divine aid in private undertakings. Unlike either type of firstborn sacrifice, the victim of these offerings need not necessarily have been a firstborn child. The explicit mention of "daughters" in the context of למלך sacrifices shows that the sex of the child was not important in the way that it was in at least some versions of the law of the firstborn. Furthermore, while both forms of firstborn sacrifice appear to have had fairly old roots in the Yahwistic cult, the למלך offerings do not appear in Jerusalem until relatively late in Israel's history, under King Ahaz of Judah. Our evidence is far less complete that we would hope, but the most straightforward reading of the evidence that we do have suggests that Ahaz imported the rite, possibly from Phoenicia, and incorporated it into the Yahwistic cult in Jerusalem. Offered there, למלך sacrifices would most naturally have been understood as offered to Yahweh.

This historical sketch is of necessity tentative, which is unfortunately all that current evidence will allow. On some issues, information is completely lacking. For instance, we have almost no evidence whatsoever concerning the manner in which children were sacrificed, nor can we even assume that the means of sacrificing a child would have been consistent across the three different child sacrifice rites. The למלך offerings are said to have been made "by fire," but there is no evidence, for example, whether or not children sacrificed למלך were ritually killed before being burned or what sorts of other ritual acts accompanied these sacrifices. Mesha's sacrifice of his firstborn son is said to have taken place on a city wall and is referred to as an עלה, which may indicate burning in the case of the extraordinary firstborn offerings as well. Whether this would have been characteristic of all such sacrifices remains unclear. In the case of the general sacrifice of firstborn children, the one form of the law that appears to demand the sacrifice of firstborn children employs the vague verb "to give" (√נתן) and thus provides no details concerning how the rite was carried out. Finally, we have almost no information concerning how widespread any of these rites were. Although they appear to have been common enough to attract the notice of a variety of biblical writers, it is easy to imagine that it would not require many child sacrifices to arouse the attention of groups that did not endorse or practice such rites.

The groups that opposed child sacrifice also exhibit a diversity of approaches, even in their opposition to the various rites. A variety of rhetorical strategies are employed to avoid the conclusion that Yahweh's claim to first-born children entails their sacrifice. In some of the later legal material, a variety of means of "redemption" are offered. In some of these cases, the cultic service of the Levites is accepted in lieu of the sacrifice of Israelite firstborn children. In others, a sheep may be sacrificed as a substitute. In yet others, parents are required to make a cash payment to the temple in lieu of sacrificing their firstborn child.

The למלך sacrifices, on the other hand, are consistently rejected as foreign and non-Israelite. Relatively early texts such as Deuteronomy present these sacrifices as offered to Yahweh in imitation of the way the Canaanites worshiped their gods, but Ezekiel goes a step further and presents these sacrifices as feeding foreign idols. In Jeremiah, this rhetoric is again amplified, and the למלך sacrifices are depicted as offerings to Baal. In this way, biblical rhetoric surrounding למלך sacrifices can be observed on a trajectory of increasingly distancing Yahweh from the practice and tying it to foreigners and to foreign deities. There is a bit of historical truth in the original accusation, assuming that the rite in Israel originally derived from Ahaz's attempt to mimic the cults of his foreign neighbors; but over time, the rhetoric against למלך offerings became less and less anchored in historical reality, a shift that was probably facilitated by the fact that it no longer existed in Jerusalem when the oracles of Ezekiel and Jeremiah were being written. Thus, there would have been no contemporary cultic reality to serve as a check on their rhetoric.

So far as we can tell, all forms of child sacrifice disappeared some time during the exile. There is no evidence that any Yahwistic group continued to sacrifice their children according to any of the three known forms of child sacrifice after the fall of Jerusalem. Once all these forms of child sacrifice disappeared from practice, they could all be either explained away—for example, by assuming that redemption was intended even in forms of the law of the firstborn in which no redemption is actually mentioned—or reimagined as always having stood entirely in opposition to "legitimate" Yahwistic worship.

Bibliography

Aarne, A. *The Types of the Folktale: A Classification and Bibliography*. Translated by S. Thompson. 2nd ed. FFC 184. Helsinki: Suomalainen Tiedeakatemia, 1964.
Ackerman, S. *Under Every Green Tree: Popular Religion in Sixth-Century Judah*. HSM 46. Atlanta: Scholars Press, 1992.
Acquaro, E. "Il tofet di Tharros: note di lettura." Pp. 13–22 in *Riti funerari e di olocausto nella Sardegna fenicia e punica*. Quaderni della Soprintendza Archeologica per le Province di Cagliari e Oristano 6/1989, Supplemento. Cagliari: Edizioni della Torre, 1990.
Acquaro, E., F. Barreca, M. T. Francisi, S. Moscati, and M. L. Uberti. "Tharros – III." *RSF* 4 (1976): 197–228.
Acquaro, E., P. Bartoloni, S. Moscati, G. S. Petruccioli, V. Righini, A. Roderto Riaza, M. L. Uberti, and R. Zucca. "Tharros – VII." *RSF* 9 (1981): 29–119.
Acquaro, E., P. Bernardini, M. Blasco Arasanz, M. Madau, G. Manca Di Mores, L. I. Manfredi, and S. Moscati. "Tharros – XV–XVI." *RSF* 17 (1989): 249–306.
Acquaro, E., A. Caddeo, M. Madau, L.-I. Manfredi, and S. Moscati. "Tharros – XIII." *RSF* 15 (1987): 75–102.
Acquaro, E., A. Ciasca, S. Moscati, and M. L. Uberti. "Tharros – I." *RSF* 3 (1975): 89–119.
Acquaro, E., F. De Horatiis, F. Fedele, V. Righini, and M. L. Uberti. "Tharros – V." *RSF* 7 (1979): 49–124.
Acquaro, E., F. Fedele, S. Moscati, V. Santoni, and M. L. Uberti. "Tharros – IV." *RSF* 6 (1978): 63–99.
Acquaro, E., F. Fedele, L. Fozzati, R. Nisbet, V. Righini, and M. L. Uberti. "Tharros – VI." *RSF* 8 (1980): 79–142.
Acquaro, E., G. Garbini, and L.-I. Manfredi. "Tharros – XII." *RSF* 14 (1986): 95–107.
Acquaro, E., G. Garbini, S. Moscati, and V. Santoni. "Tharros – XI." *RSF* 13 (1985): 11–147.
Acquaro, E., C. Huertas Jiménez, F. Molina Fajardo, V. Righini Cantelli, A. Rodero Riaza, V. Santoni, and M. L. Ubert. "Tharros – VIII." *RSF* 10 (1982): 37–102.
Acquaro, E., M. Madau, and L.-I. Manfredi. "Tharros – XIV." *RSF* 16 (1988): 207–52.
Acquaro, E., L.-I. Manfredi, F. Molina Fajardo, and M. L. Uberti. "Tharros – X." *RSF* 12 (1984): 47–75.
Acquaro, E., V. Righini Cantelli, A. Simonetti, and M. L. Uberti. "Tharros – IX." *RSF* 11 (1983): 49–111.
Acquaro, E., and M. L. Uberti. "Tharros – II." *RSF* 3 (1975): 213–25.
Agelarakis, A. P., A. Kanta, and N. Stampolidis. "The Osseous Record in the Western Necropolis of Amathus: an Archaeo-Anthropological Investigation." Pp. 217–32 in *Eastern Mediterranean: Cyprus-Dodecanese-Crete 16th-6th Cent. B.C.* Edited by V. Karageorghis and N. Stampolidis. Athens: University of Crete, 1998.

Albertz, R., and R. Schmitt. *Family and Household Religion in Ancient Israel and the Levant*. Winona Lake, IN: Eisenbrauns, 2012.

Albright, W. F. *Archaeology and the Religion of Israel*. Baltimore: The Johns Hopkins University Press, 1942.

———. *Archaeology and the Religion of Israel*. 5th ed. Baltimore: The Johns Hopkins University Press, 1968.

———. Review of O. Eissfeldt, *Molk als Opferbegriff*. *JPOS* 15 (1935): 344.

———. *Yahweh and the Gods of Canaan: A Historical Analysis of Two Contrasting Faiths*. London: University College London, 1968.

Almagro-Gorbea, M. "Pozo Moro, el monumento orientalizante, su contexto socio-cultural y sus paralelos en la arquitectura funeraria ibérica." *Madrider Mitteilungen* 24 (1983): 177–293.

Alquier, A., and J. Alquier. "Stèles votives à Saturne découvertes près de N'Gaous (Algérie)." *CRAI* (1931): 21–26.

Alt, A. *Die Ursprünge des israelitischen Rechts*. BVSAWLPHK 86. Leipzig: Hirzel, 1934.

Amadasi, M. G., F. Barreca, P. Bartoloni, I. Brancoli, S. M. Cecchini, G. Garbini, S. Moscati, and G. Pesce. *Monte Sirai–II: Rapporto preliminare della Missione archeologica dell'Università di Roma e della Soprintendenza alle Antichità di Cagliari*. Studi semitici 14. Rome: Centro di studi semitici, Istituto de studi del vicino Oriente–Università, 1965.

Amadasi Guzzo, M. G., and J. Á. Zamora López. "The Epigraphy of the Tophet." *SEL* 29–30 (2012–2013): 159–192.

———. "Osservazioni sulle stele iscritte di Tiro." *RSF* 21 (1993): 157–63.

Andersen, F. I., and D. N. Freedman. *Micah: A New Translation with Introduction and Commentary*. AB 24 E. New York: Doubleday, 2000.

Andrado, P. N. de. "*Ḥesed* and Sacrifice: The Prophetic Critique in Hosea." *CBQ* 78 (2016): 47–67.

Ariès, P. *Centuries of Childhood: A Social History of Family Life*. Translated by R. Baldick. New York: Knopf, 1962.

Aro, J. Review of M. Birot, *Textes administratifs de la salle 5 du palais*. *OLZ* 56 (1961): 603–5.

Attridge, H. W., and R. A. Oden Jr. *Philo of Byblos, The Phoenician History: Introduction, Critical Text, Translation, Notes*. CBQMS 9. Washington, DC: Catholic Biblical Association of America, 1981.

Aubet, M. E. *The Phoenicians and the West: Politics, Colonies, and Trade*. 2nd edition. Translated by M. Turton. Cambridge: Cambridge University Press, 2001.

Avalos, H. "Sepharvaim." *ABD* 5, 1091.

Azize, J. J. "Was There Regular Child Sacrifice in Phoenicia and Carthage?" Pp. 185–206 in *Gilgameš and the World of Assyria: Proceedings of the Conference Held at Mandelbaum House, The University of Sydney, 21–23 July 2004*. Edited by J. J. Azize and N. Weeks. Ancient Near Eastern Studies Supplement 21. Leuven: Peeters, 2007.

Baentsch, B. *Exodus-Leviticus-Numeri*. HKAT 1:2. Göttingen: Vandenhoeck & Ruprecht, 1903.

Bar-On. *See* Gesundheit.

Barreca, F., G. Garbini, S. Moscati, and G. Pesce. *Monte Sirai–I: Rapporto preliminare della Missione archeologica dell'Università di Roma e della Soprintendenza alle Antichità di*

Cagliari. Studi semitici 11. Rome: Centro di studi semitici, Istituto de studi del vicino Oriente–Università, 1964.

Barth, H. *Die Jesaja-Worte in der Josiazeit: Israel und Assur als Thema einer produktiven Neuinterpretation der Jesajaüberlierferung*. WMANT 48. Neukirchen-Vluyn: Neukirchener Verlag, 1977.

Bartoloni, P. "Considerazioni sul 'tofet' di Tiro." *RSF* 21 (1993): 143–56.

———. "Monte Sirai 1981: La ceramica del *tofet*." *RSF* 10 (1982): 283–94.

———. *La necropoli di Monte Sirai – I*. Collezione di Studi Fenici 41. Rome: Consiglio Nazionale delle Ricerche, 2000.

———. "Urne cinerarie arcaiche a Sulcis." *RSF* 16 (1988): 165–79.

Barton, G. A. *Archaeology and the Bible*. Philadelphia: American Sunday-School Union, 1916.

Barton, J. "The Prophets and the Cult." Pp. 111–22 in *Temple and Worship in Biblical Israel*. Edited by J. Day. LHBOTS 422. New York: T. & T. Clark, 2005.

Bauks, M. "Kinderopfer als Weihe- oder Gabeopfer: Anmerkungen zum *mlk*-Opfer." Pp. 233–51 in *Israeliten und Phönizier: Ihre Beziehungen im Spiegel der Archäologie und der Literatur des Alten Testaments und seiner Umwelt*. Edited by M. Witte and J. F. Diehl. OBO 235. Fribourg: Academic Press, 2008.

Baumgartner, W. "Jephtas Gelübde: Jud. 11 30–40." *AR* (1915): 240–49.

Bea, A. "Kinderopfer für Moloch oder für Jahwe?" *Bib* 18 (1937): 95–107.

Beaumont, L. A. *Childhood in Ancient Athens: Iconography and Social History*. New York: Routledge, 2012.

Becking, B. *The Fall of Samaria: An Historical and Archaeological Study*. SHANE 2. Leiden: Brill, 1992.

Benichou-Safar, H. *Le tophet de Salammbô à Carthage: essai de reconstitution*. Rome: École française de Rome, 2004.

Benz, F. L. *Personal Names in the Phoenician and Punic Inscriptions: A Catalogue, Grammatical Study and Glossary of Elements*. Rome: Biblical Institute Press, 1972.

Benzinger, I. *Die Bücher der Könige*. KHC 9. Freiburg: Mohr (Siebeck), 1899.

Berger, P. "Les inscriptions de Constantine au Musée du Louvre." Pp. 273–94 in *Actes du 11e Congrès international des Orientalistes, 4e Section*. Paris: Imprimerie nationale, 1898.

Berlinerblau, J. *The Vow and the 'Popular Religious Groups' of Ancient Israel: A Philological and Sociological Inquiry*. JSOTSup 210. Sheffield: Sheffield Academic, 1996.

Berman, J. "Supersessionist or Complementary? Reassessing the Nature of Legal Revision in the Pentateuchal Law Collections." *JBL* 135 (2016): 201–222.

Bernardini, P. "Organized Settlements and Cult Places in the Phoenician Western Expansion between the 9th and 7th Centuries BCE: A Reflection on the Tophet." *SEL* 29–30 (2012–2013): 1–22.

———. "Per una rilettura del santuario tofet – I: il caso di Mozia." *Sardinia, Corsica et Baleares Antiquae* 3 (2005): 55–75.

———. "Recenti indagini nel santuario tofet di Sulci." Pp. 1059–69 in *Atti del V Congresso internazionale di studi fenici e punici: Marsala-Palermo, 2–8 ottobre 2000*. Palermo: Università degli Studi di Palermo. Facoltà di Lettere e Filosofia, 2005.

Berry, G. R. "The Ritual Decalogue." *JBL* 44 (1925): 39–43.

Berthier A., and R. Charlier. *Le sanctuaire punique d'El Hofra à Constantine*. 2 vols. Paris: Arts et métiers graphiques, 1952–1955.

Bevilacqua, F., A. Ciasca, G. Matthiae Scandone, S. Moscati, V. Tusa, and A. Tusa Cutroni. *Mozia – VII: Rapporto preliminare della Missione congiunta con la Soprintendenza alle Antichità della Sicilia Occidentale*. Studi semitici 40. Pubblicazioni del Centro di studio per la civiltà fenicia e punica 10. Rome: Consiglio nazionale delle ricerche, 1972.

Bhatnagar, R. D., R. Dube, and R. Dube. *Female Infanticide in India: A Feminist Cultural History*. New York: State University of New York Press, 2005.

Birot, M. *Textes administratifs de la salle 5 du palais*. ARMT 9. Paris: Imprimerie nationale, 1960.

———. *Textes administratifs de la salle 5 du palais*. 2e partie. ARMT 12. Paris: Imprimerie nationale, 1964.

Bisi, A. M. *Le stele puniche*. Studi semitici 27. Rome: Istituto di studi del vicino Oriente, Università di Roma, 1967.

Bleek, F., A. Kamphausen, and J. Wellhausen. *Einleitung in das Alte Testament*. 4th ed. Berlin: Reimer, 1878.

Blenkinsopp, J. *Isaiah 1–39: A New Translation with Introduction and Commentary*. AB 19. New York: Doubleday, 2000.

———. *Isaiah 56–66: A New Translation and Commentary*. AB 19B. New York: Doubleday, 2003.

Bloch-Smith, E."Israelite Ethnicity in Iron I: Archaeology Preserves What is Remembered and What is Forgotten in Israel's History." *JBL* 122 (2003): 401–25.

———. *Judahite Burial Practices and Beliefs about the Dead*. JSOTSup 123. Sheffield: JSOT Press, 1992.

Blum, E. "Die Kombination I der Wandinschrift vom Tell Deir ʿAlla: Vorschläge zur Rekonstruktion mit historisch-kritischen Anmerkungen." Pp. 594–98 in *Berührungspunkte: Studien zur Sozial- und Religionsgeschichte Israels und seiner Umwelt*. Edited by I. Kottsieper, R. Schmitt, and J. Wöhrle. AOAT 350. Münster: Ugarit-Verlag, 2008.

———. "Das Sog. 'Privilegrecht' in Exodus 34,11–26: ein Fixpunkt der Komposition des Exodusbuches?" Pp. 347–66 in *Studies in the Book of Exodus: Redaction – Reception – Interpretation*. Edited by M. Vervenne. BETL 126. Leuven: Leuven University Press/Peeters, 1996.

———. "'Verstehst du dich nicht auf die Schreibkunst...?' Ein weisheitlicher Dialog über Vergänglichkeit und Verantwortung: Kombination II der Wandinschrift vom Tell Deir ʿAlla." Pp. 33–53 in *Was ist Mensch, dass du seiner gedenkst? (Psalm 8,5)*. Edited by M. Bauks, K. Liess, and P. Riede. Neukirchen-Vluyn: Neukirchener Verlag, 2008.

Boer, A. M. den, and V. M. Hudson. "Sex-selective Infanticide and the 'Missing Females' in China and India." Pp. 337–71 in *Killing Infants: Studies in the Worldwide Practice of Infanticide*. Edited by B. H. Bechtold and D. C. Graves. Lewiston, NY: Mellen, 2006.

Boling, R. G. *Judges: Introduction, Translation, and Commentary*. AB 6. Garden City, NY: Doubleday, 1975.

Bonanno, A. and D. Cilia. *Malta: Phoenician Punic and Roman*. Malta: Midsea Books, 2005.

Bondì, S. F. "Monte Sirai 1985. Lo scavo del tofet." *RSF* 15 (1987): 179–90.

———. "Nuovi dati sul tofet di Monte Sirai." Pp. 23–43 in *Riti funerari e di olocausto nella Sardegna fenicia e punica*. Quaderni della Soprintendeza Archeologica per le province di Cagliari e Oristano 6/1989, Supplemento. Cagliari: Edizioni della Torre, 1990.

———. "Il tofet di Monte Sirai." Pp. 225–38 in *Carbonia e il Sulcis: Archeologia e territorio*. Edited by V. Santoni. Oristano: Editrice S'Alvure, 1995.

Boswell, J. *The Kindness of Strangers: The Abandonment of Children in Western Europe from Late Antiquity to the Renaissance*. New York: Pantheon, 1988.

Bottéro, J. *Textes économiques et administratifs*. ARMT 7. Paris: Imprimerie nationale, 1957.

Brancoli, I., A. Ciasca, G. Garbini, B. Pugliese, V. Tusa, and A. Tusa Cutroni. *Mozia – III: Rapporto preliminare della Missione archeologica della Soprintendenza alle Antichità della Sicilia occidentale e dell'Università di Roma*. Studi semitici 24. Rome: Istituto di studi del vicino Oriente, 1967.

Brett, M. G. "Israel's Indigenous Origins: Cultural Hybridity and the Formation of Israelite Ethnicity." *BibInt* 11 (2003): 400–412.

Bright, J. *Jeremiah: A New Translation with Introduction and Commentary*. AB 21. Garden City: Doubleday, 1965.

Brin, G. *Studies in Biblical Law: From the Hebrew Bible to the Dead Sea Scrolls*. Translated by J. Chipman. JSOTSup 176. Sheffield: JSOT Press, 1994.

Brockington, I. F. *Motherhood and Mental Health*. Oxford: Oxford University Press, 1996.

Brockington, I. F., J. Oates, S. George, D. Turner, P. Vostanis, M. Sullivan, C. Loh, and C. Murdoch. "A Screening Questionnaire for Mother-Infant Bonding Disorders." *Archives of Women's Mental Health* 3:4 (2001): 133–40.

Brown, S. *Late Carthaginian Child Sacrifice and Sacrificial Monuments in their Mediterranean Context*. JSOT/ASOR Monograph Series 3. Sheffield: Sheffield Academic, 1991.

Buber, M. *Königtum Gottes*. 2nd ed. Berlin: Schocken, 1936.

Burney, C. F. *The Book of Judges*. London: Rivingtons, 1918.

Butler, S. M. "A Case of Indifference? Child Murder in Later Medieval England." *Journal of Women's History* 19 (2007): 59–82.

Butler, T. C. *Judges*. WBC 8. Nashville: Nelson, 2008.

Callender, D. E. "'I Gave Them Laws That Were Not Good' (Ezk 20:25): A Biblical Model of Complex Subjectivity and the Prospects of Multi-Ethnic Contextual Reading." *In die Skriflig* 48 (2014), Art. #1828, 8 pages. http://dx.doi. org/10.4102/ids.v48i1.1828

Caquot, A., and A. Lemaire. "Les textes araméens de Deir ʿAlla." *Syria* 54 (1977): 189–208.

Caquot, A., and A.-S. Dalix, "Un texte mythico-magique." Pp. 393–405 in *Études ougaritiques I. Travaux 1985–1995*. Edited by M. Yon and D. Arnaud. RSOu 14. Paris: Éditions Recherche sur les Civilisations, 2001.

Carcopino, J. "Survivances par substitution des sacrifices d'enfants dans l'Afrique romaine." *RHR* 106 (1932): 592–99.

Carr, D. M. *The Formation of the Hebrew Bible: A New Reconstruction*. Oxford: Oxford University Press, 2011.

———. "Method in Determination of Direction of Dependence: An Empirical Test of Criteria Applied to Exodus 34,11–26 and Its Parallels." Pp. 107–40 in *Gottes Volk am Sinai: Untersuchungen zu Ex 32–34 und Dtn 9–10*. Edited by M. Köckert and E. Blum. VWGT 18. Gütersloh: Kaiser/Gütersloher, 2001.

Carroll, R. P. *Jeremiah: A Commentary*. OTL. Philadelphia: Westminster, 1986.

Cartledge, T. W. *Vows in the Hebrew Bible and the Ancient Near East*. JSOTSup 147. Sheffield: JSOT Press, 1992.

Carton, L. B. C. *Le sanctuaire de Baal-Saturne à Dougga: rapport sur les fouilles exécutées à Dougga en 1893*. Nouvelles archives des missions scientifiques 7. Paris: Imprimerie nationale, 1896.

Chabot, J.-B. "Mélanges épigraphiques et archéologiques." *Le Muséon* 37 (1924): 153–56.

———. "Note complémentaire." *CRAI* 75 (1931): 26–27.

———. "Punica XVIII. Stèles puniques de Constantine." *JA* 11:10 (1917): 38–79.

Charlier, R. "La nouvelle série de stèles puniques de Constantine et la question des sacrifices dits '*molchomor*,' en relation avec l'expression '*bsrm btm*.'" *Karthago* 4 (1953): 1–48.

Charpin, D., and J.-M. Durand. "Fils de Sim'al: les origines tribales des rois de Mari." *RA* 80 (1986): 141–83.

Chiera, G. *Testimonianze su Nora*. Collezione di studi fenici 11. Rome: Consiglio nazionale delle ricerche, 1978.

Childs, B. S. *Isaiah*. OTL. Louisville: Westminster John Knox, 2001.

Chisholm, R. B., Jr. "Israel's Retreat and the Failure of Prophecy in 2 Kings 3." *Bib* 92 (2011): 70–80.

Cholewiński, A. *Heiligkeitsgesetz und Deuteronomium: Eine vergleichende Studie*. AnBib 66 Rome: Biblical Institute Press, 1976.

Christou, D. "Cremations in the Western Necropolis of Amathus." Pp. 207–15 in *Eastern Mediterranean: Cyprus-Dodecanese-Crete 16th-6th Cent. B.C.* Edited by V. Karageorghis and N. Stampolidis. Athens: University of Crete, 1998.

Ciasca, A. "Mozia, sguardo d'insieme sul *tofet*." *Vicino Oriente* 8 (1992): 113–55.

Ciasca, A., G. Coacci Polselli, N. Cuomo di Caprio, M. G. Guzzo Amadasi, G. Matthiae Scandone, V. Tusa, A. Tusa Cutroni, and M. L. Uberti. *Mozia IX: Rapporto preliminare della Missione congiunta con la Soprintendenza alle Antichità della Sicilia Occidentale*. Studi semitici 50. Pubblicazioni del Centro di studio per la civiltà fenicia e punica 18. Rome: Consiglio nazionale delle ricerche, 1978.

Ciasca, A., R. Di Salvo, M. Castellino, and C. Di Patti. "Saggio preliminare sugli incinerati del 'tofet' di Mozia." *Vicino Oriente* 10 (1996): 317–46.

Ciasca, A., M. Forte, G. Garbini, S. Moscati, B. Pugliese, and V. Tusa. *Mozia – I: Rapporto preliminaire della Mission archeologica della Suprintendenza alle Antichità della Sicilia occidentale e dell'Università di Roma*. Studi semitici 12. Rome: Istituto di studi del vicino Oriente, 1964.

Ciasca, A., M. Forte, G. Garbini, V. Tusa, A. Tusa Cutroni, and A. Verger. *Mozia–II: Rapporto preliminaire della Mission archeologica della Suprintendenza alle Antichità della Sicilia occidentale e dell'Università di Roma*. Studi semitici 19. Rome: Istituto di studi del vicino Oriente, 1966.

Ciasca, A., G. Garbini, P. Mingazzini, B. Pugliese, and V. Tusa. *Mozia – IV: Rapporto preliminare della Missione archeologica della Soprintendenza alle Antichità della Sicilia oc-*

cidentale e dell'Università di Roma. Studi semitici 29. Rome: Istituto di studi del vicino Oriente, 1968.

Ciasca, A., M. G. Guzzo Amadasi, G. Matthiae Scandone, B. Olivieri Pugliese, A. Tusa Cutroni, and V. Tusa. *Mozia – V: Rapporto preliminare della Missione congiunta con la Soprintendenza alle Antichità della Sicilia Occidentale*. Studi semitici 31. Pubblicazioni del Centro di studio per la civiltà fenicia e punica 1. Rome: Consiglio nazionale delle ricerche, 1969.

Ciasca, A., M. G. Guzzo Amadasi, S. Moscati, and V. Tusa. *Mozia – VI: Rapporto preliminare della Missione congiunta con la Soprintendenza alle Antichità della Sicilia Occidentale*. Studi semitici 37. Pubblicazioni del Centro di studio per la civiltà fenicia e punica 7. Rome: Consiglio nazionale delle ricerche, 1970.

Ciasca, A., V. Tusa, and M. L. Uberti. *Mozia VIII: Rapporto preliminare della Missione congiunta con la Soprintendenza alle Antichità della Sicilia Occidentale*. Studi semitici 45. Pubblicazioni del Centro di studio per la civiltà fenicia e punica 14. Rome: Consiglio nazionale delle ricerche, 1973.

Cintas, P. "Le sanctuaire punique de Sousse." *Revue africaine* 91 (1947): 1–80.

Clements, R. E. *Isaiah 1–39*. NCB. Grand Rapids, MI: Eerdmans, 1980.

Cogan, M. *1 Kings: A New Translation with Introduction and Commentary*. AB 10. New York: Doubleday, 2000.

———. *Imperialism and Religion: Assyria, Judah and Israel in the Eighth and Seventh Centuries B.C.E.* SBLMS 19. Missoula, MT: Society of Biblical Literature and Scholars Press, 1974.

Cogan, M., and H. Tadmor. *II Kings: A New Translation with Introduction and Commentary*. AB 11. Garden City, NY: Doubleday, 1988.

Cohen, C. "Foam in Hosea 10:7." *JANES* 2 (1969): 25–29.

Cohn, R. L. *2 Kings*. *Berit Olam*. Collegeville, MN: Liturgical, 2000.

Cook, S. A. *The Religion of Ancient Palestine in the Second Millennium in the Light of Archæology and the Inscriptions*. London: Constable & Company, 1921.

Conder, C. R. "The Prayer of Ben Abdas on the Dedication of the Temple of Joppa." *PEFQS* (1892): 171–74.

Conheeny, J. and A. Pipe. "Note on Some Cremated Bones from Tyrian Cinerary Urns." *Berytus* 39 (1991): 83–87.

Cross, F. M. *Leaves from an Epigrapher's Notebook: Collected Papers in Hebrew and West Semitic Palaeography and Epigraphy*. Winona Lake, IN: Eisenbrauns, 2003.

Crouch, C. L. *Israel and the Assyrians: Deuteronomy, the Succesion Treaty of Esarhaddon, and the Nature of Subversion*. ANEM 8. Atlanta: SBL Press, 2014.

Cryer, F. H. *Divination in Ancient Israel and its Near Eastern Environment: A Socio-Historical Investigation*. JSOTSup 142. Sheffield: JSOT Press, 1994.

Daniels, D. R. "Is There a 'Prophetic Lawsuit' Genre?" *ZAW* 99 (1987): 339–60.

Day, J. *Molech: A God of Human Sacrifice in the Old Testament*. University of Cambridge Oriental Publications 41. Cambridge: Cambridge University Press, 1989.

———. *Yahweh and the Gods and Godesses of Canaan*. JSOTSup 265. Sheffield: Sheffield Academic, 2000.

Day, P. L. "From the Child is Born the Woman: The Story of Jephthah's Daughter." Pp. 58–74 in *Gender and Difference in Ancient Israel*. Edited by P. L. Day. Minneapolis: Fortress, 1989.

———. "Is the Language of Child Sacrifice Used Figuratively in Ezekiel 16?" Pp. 91–113 in *Not Sparing the Child: Human Sacrifice in the Ancient World and Beyond: Studies in Honor of Professor Paul G. Mosca.* Edited by V. D. Arbel, P. C. Burns, J. R. C. Cousland, R. Menkis, and D. Neufeld. New York: Bloomsbury, 2015.

Dearman, J. A. "The Tophet in Jerusalem: Archaeology and Cultural Profile." *JNSL* 22 (1996): 59–71.

Dever, W. G. "The Gezer Fortifications and the 'High Place': An Illustration of Stratigraphic Methods and Problems." *PEQ* 105 (1973): 61–70.

Delavault, B., and A. Lemaire. "Une stèle 'molk' de Palestine dédiée à Eshmoun? RES 367 Reconsidéré." *RB* 93 (1976): 569–89.

Delcor, M. "Reflexions sur la pâque du temps de Josias d'après 2 Rois 23, 21–23." *Henoch* 4 (1982): 207–19.

Derchain, P. "Les plus anciens témoignages de sacrifices d'enfants chez les sémites occidentaux." *VT* 20 (1970): 351–55.

Dewrell, H. D. "Child Sacrifice in Ancient Israel and Its Opponents." Ph.D. diss. The Johns Hopkins University, 2012.

———. "A 'Molek' Inscription from the Levant? Another Look at the Authenticity of RES 367." *RB* 123 (2016): 481–505.

———. "'Whoring after the mōlek' in Leviticus 20,5. A Text-Critical Examination." *ZAW* 127 (2016): 628–35.

Di Stefano, C. A. *Lilibeo Punica.* Rome: Libreria dello Stato: Istituto Poligrafico e Zecca dello Stato, 1993.

Dietrich, W. *Prophetie und Geschichte: Eine redaktionsgeschichtliche Untersuchung zum deuteronomistischen Geschichtswerk.* FRLANT 108. Göttingen: Vandenhoeck & Ruprecht, 1972.

Dijkstra, M. "Is Balaam Also Among the Prophets?" *JBL* 114 (1995): 43–64.

Dillmann, A., and V. Ryssel. *Die Bücher Exodus und Leviticus.* KeHAT. 3rd. ed. Leipzig: Hirzel, 1897.

Dion, P. E. "Deuteronomy 13: The Suppression of Alien Religious Propaganda in Israel during the Late Monarchical Era." Pp. 147–216 in *Law and Ideology in Monarchic Israel.* Edited by B. Halpern and D. W. Hobson. JSOTSup 124. Sheffield: JSOT Press, 1991.

Divale, W. T., and M. Harris, "Population, Warfare, and the Male Supremacist Complex." *American Anthropologist* 78 (1976): 521–38.

Dhorme, E. Review of O. Eissfeldt, *Molk als Opferbegriff. RHR* 113 (1936): 276–78.

Domeris, W. R. "When Metaphor Becomes Myth: A Socio-Linguistic Reading of Jeremiah." Pp. 244–62 in *Troubling Jeremiah.* Edited by A. R. P. Diamond, K. M. O'Connor, and L. Stulman. JSOTSup 260. Sheffield: Sheffield Academic, 1999.

Driver, S. R. *The Book of Exodus in the Revised Version with Introduction and Notes.* CBSC. Cambridge: Cambridge University Press, 1911.

———. *An Introduction to the Literature of the Old Testament.* New York: Meridian, 1956.

Dronkert, K. *De Molochdienst in het Oude Testament (With a Summary in English).* Leiden: Luctor et Emergo, 1953.

Droogers, A. "Syncretism, Power and Play." Pp. 38–59 in *Syncretism and the Commerce of Symbols*. Edited by G. Aijmer. Gothenburg: Institute for Advanced Studies in Social Anthropology, 1995.

———. "Syncretism: The Problem of a Definition, the Definition of the Problem." Pp. 7–25 in *Dialogue and Syncretism: An Interdisciplinary Approach*. Edited by J. D. Gort, H. Vroom, R. Fernhout, and A. Wessels. Grand Rapids, MI: Eerdmans, 1989.

Dubovský, P. *The Building of the First Temple: A Study in Redactional, Text-Critical, and Historical Perspective*. FAT 103. Tübingen: Mohr Siebeck, 2015.

Dussaud, R. *Les origines cananéennes du sacrifice israélite*. Paris: Leroux, 1921.

———. Review of O. Eissfeldt, *Molk als Opferbegriff*. *AfO* 11 (1936): 167–68.

———. Review of O. Eissfeldt, *Molk als Opferbegriff*. *Syria* 16 (1935): 407–09.

Eerdmans, B. D. *Das Buch Exodus*. Vol. 3 of *Alttestamentliche Studien*. Giessen: Töpelmann, 1910.

Eichrodt, W. *Ezekiel: A Commentary*. Translated by C. Quin. OTL. Philadelphia: Westminster, 1970.

Eissfeldt, O. *Molk as Opferbegriff im Punischen und Hebräischen und das Ende des Gottes Moloch*. Beiträge zur Religionsgeschichte des Altertums 3. Halle: Max Niemeyer, 1935.

———. *The Old Testament: An Introduction*. Translated by P. R. Ackroyd. New York: Harper and Row, 1965.

Ephʿal, I. *The City Besieged: Siege and Its Manifestations in the Ancient Near East*. CHANE 36. Leiden: Brill, 2009.

Ewald, H. *Die Propheten des Alten Bundes*. 2nd ed. Göttingen: Vandenhoeck & Ruprecht, 1867.

Ernst, A. B. *Weisheitliche Kultkritik: zu Theologie und Ethik des Sprüchbuchs und der Prophetie des 8. Jahrhunderts*. Biblisch-Theologische Studien 23. Neukirchen-Vluyn: Neukirchener Verlag, 1994.

Faerman, M., G. Kahila, P. Smith, C. Greenblatt, L. Stager, D. Filon, and A. Oppenheim, "DNA Analysis Reveals the Sex of Infanticide Victims." *Nature* 385 (1997): 212–13.

Faerman, M., G. Kahlila Bar-Gal, D. Filon, C. L. Greenblatt, L. Stager, A. Oppenheim, and P. Smith. "Determining the Sex of Infanticide Victims from the Late Roman Era through Ancient DNA Analysis." *Journal of Archaeological Science* 25 (1998): 861–65.

Faust, A. "The Emergence of Iron Age Israel: On Origins and Habitus." Pp. 467–82 in *Israel's Exodus in Transdisciplinary Perspective: Text, Archaeology, Culture and Geoscience*. Edited by T. E. Levy, T. Schneider, and W. H. C. Propp. New York: Springer, 2015.

———. *Israel's Ethnogenesis: Settlement, Interaction, Expansion, and Resistance*. Approaches to Anthropological Archaeology. London: Equinox, 2006.

Fedele, F., and G. V. Foster. "Tharros: ovicaprini sacrificali e rituale del *tofet*." *RSF* 16 (1988): 29–46.

Ferjaoui, A. *Le sanctuaire de Henchir el-Hami: de Ba'al Hammon au Saturne africain: Ier s. av. J.-C.-IVe s. ap. J.-C.* Tunis: Institut National du Patrimoine, 2007.

Février, J. G. "Essai de reconstitution du sacrifice Molek." *JA* 248 (1960): 167–87.
———. "Glanes néopuniques." *JA* 255 (1967): 61–64.
———. "Molchomor." *RHR* 143 (1953): 8–18.
———. "Le rite de substitution dans les textes de N'Gaous." *JA* 250 (1962): 1–10.
———. "Les rites sacrificiels chez les Hébreux et à Carthage." *REJ* 123 [1964]: 7–18
———. "Un sacrifice d'enfant chez les Numides." Pp. 161–71 in *Mélanges Isidore Lévy*. *AIPHOS* 13. Brussels: Secrétariat des Éditions de l'Institut, 1955.
———. "Le vocabulaire sacrificiel punique." *JA* 243 (1955): 49–63.
Finkelstein, I. "The Old Jephthah Tale in Judges: Geographical and Historical Considerations." *Bib* 97 (2016): 1–15.
Finlay, J. E., E. Özaltin, and D. Canning. "The Association of Maternal Age with Infant Mortality, Child Anthropometric Failure, Diarrhoea and Anaemia for First Births: Evidence from 55 Low- and Middle-Income Countries." *BMJ Open* 2011;1: e000226 doi:10.1136/bmjopen-2011–000226
Finsterbusch, K. "The First-Born between Sacrifice and Redemption in the Hebrew Bible." Pp. 87–108 in *Human Sacrifice in the Jewish and Christian Tradition*. Edited by K. Finsterbusch, A. Lange, and K. F. D. Römheld. SHR 112. Leiden: Brill, 2007.
Fishbane, M. *Biblical Interpretation in Ancient Israel*. Oxford: Oxford University Press, 1985.
Fischer, G. *Jeremiah 1–25*. HThKAT. Freiburg: Herder, 2005.
Flaubert, G. *Salammbô*. Translated by M. F. Sheldon. London: Saxon & Co, 1886.
Foster, B. R. "Humor and Cuneiform Literature." *JANES* 6 (1974): 69–85.
Foucher, L. *Hadrumetum*. Paris: Publications de l'Université de Tunis, 1964.
Franken, H. J. "Texts from the Persian Period from Deir 'Allā." *VT* 17 (1967): 480–81.
Friedman, R. E. *Who Wrote the Bible?* New York: Summit, 1987.
Friedrich, J., and W. Röllig. *Phönizisch-Punische Grammatik*. 3rd ed. Rome: Pontificio Istituto Biblico, 1999.
Fritz, V. *1 & 2 Kings*. Translated by A. Hagedorn. CC. Minneapolis: Fortress, 2003.
Fulco, W. J. "Anammelech." *ABD* 1, 223.
Galil, G. *The Lower Stratum Families in the Neo-Assyrian Period*. Leiden: Brill, 2007.
García López, F. "Un profeta como Moisés. Estudio crítico de Dt 18,9–22." Pp. 289–308 in *Simposio Biblico Español (Salamanca, 1982)*. Edited by N. Fernández Marcos, J. Trebolle Barrera, and J. Fernández Vallina. Madrid: Universidad Complutense, 1984.
Garnand, B. K., L. E. Stager, and J. A. Greene. "Infants as Offerings: Palaeodemographic Patterns and Tophet Burial." *SEL* 29–30 (2012–2013): 193–222.
Garroway, K. H. *Children in the Ancient Near Eastern Household*. EANEC 3. Winona Lake, IN: Eisenbrauns, 2014.
Geiger, A. *Urschrift und Übersetzungen der Bible in ihrer Abhängigkeit von der innern Entwicklung des Judentums*. Breslau: Hainauer, 1857.
Gelb, I. J. *Glossary of Old Akkadian*. MAD 3. Chicago: The University of Chicago Press, 1957.
Gelb, I., P. Purves, and A. MacRae. *Nuzi Personal Names*. Chicago: University of Chicago Press, 1943.
Gellner, D. N. "For Syncretism: The Position of Buddhism in Nepal and Japan Compared." *Social Anthropology* 5 (1997): 275–89.

George, J. F. L. *Die älteren Jüdischen Feste mit einer Kritik der Gesetzgebung des Pentateuch*. Berlin: Schroeder, 1835.
Gertz, J. C. *Tradition und Redaktion in der Exoduserzählung: Untersuchungen zur Engredaktion des Pentateuch*. FRLANT 186. Göttingen: Vandenhoeck & Ruprecht, 2000.
Gesundheit (Bar-On), S. *Three Times a Year: Studies on Festival Legislation in the Pentateuch*. FAT 82. Tübingen: Mohr Siebeck, 2012.
———. "The Festival Calendars in Exodus XXIII 14–19 and XXXIV 18–26." *VT* 48 (1998): 161–95
Gianto, A. "Some Notes on the Mulk Inscription from Nebi Yunis (*RES* 367)." *Bib* 68 (1987): 397–401.
Ginsberg, A. *Howl and Other Poems*. The Pocket Poets Series 4. New York: City Lights Books, 1956.
Goethe, J. W. von. "Zwo wichtige bisher unerörterte biblische Fragen, zum erstenmal gründlich beantwortet. Von einem Landgeistlichen in Schwaben. 1773." Pp. 24–29 in *Göthe in Frankfurt am Main oder zerstreute Blätter aus der Zeit seines dortigen Aufenthalts in den Jahren 1757 bis 1775*. Edited by H. Döring. Jena: Mauke, 1839.
Golden, M. *Children and Childhood in Classical Athens*. 2nd ed. Baltimore: Johns Hopkins University Press, 2015.
Graham, W. C., and H. G. May. *Culture and Conscience: An Archaeological Study of the New Religious Past in Ancient Palestine*. Chicago: University of Chicago Press, 1936.
Gray, J. *I & II Kings: A Commentary*. 2nd ed. OTL. Philadelphia: Westminster, 1970.
———. "The Desert God ʿAṯtr in the Literature and Religion of Canaan." *JNES* 8 (1949): 72–83.
———. *The Legacy of Canaan: The Ras Shamra Texts and Their Relevance to the Old Testament*. Leiden: Brill, 1957.
Grayson, A. K. "Adrammelech (Deity)." *ABD* 1, 79.
Green, A. R. W. *The Role of Human Sacrifice in the Ancient Near East*. ASOR Dissertation Series 1. Missoula, MT: Scholars Press, 1975.
Greenberg, M. *Ezekiel 1–20: A New Translation with Introduction and Commentary*. AB 22. Garden City: Doubleday, 1983.
Gressmann, H. *Die älteste Geschichtsschreibung und Prophetie Israels (von Samuel bis Amos und Hosea)*. Die Schriften des Alten Testaments 2:1. 2nd ed.. Göttingen: Vandenhoeck & Ruprecht, 1921.
Gruber, M. I. "Gillulim גלולים εἴδωλα." *DDD*², 346–47
Grünwaldt, K. *Das Heiligkeitsgesetz Leviticus 17–26: Ursprungliche Gestalt, Tradition und Theologie*. BZAW 271. Berlin: de Gruyter, 1999.
Gunkel, H. "Die israelitische Literatur." Pp. 51–102 in *Die orientalischen Literaturen*. Edited by P. Hinneberg. *Die Kultur der Gegenwart: ihre Entwicklung und ihre Ziele* 1:7. Berlin: Teubner, 1906.
Hackett, J. A. *The Balaam Text from Deir ʿAllā*. HSM 31. Chico, CA: Scholars Press, 1980.
———. "Religious Traditions in Israelite Transjordan." Pp. 125–36 in *Ancient Israelite Religion: Essays in Honor of Frank Moore Cross*. Edited by P. D. Miller, P. D. Hanson, and S. D. McBride. Philadelphia: Fortress, 1987.
Hahn, S. W., and J. S. Bergsma. "What Laws Were 'Not Good'? A Canonical Approach to the Theological Problem of Ezekiel 20:25–56." *JBL* 123 (2004): 201–18.

Halbe, J. *Das Privilegrecht Jahwes: Ex 34,10–26: Gestalt und Wesen, Herkunft und Wirken in vordeuteronomischer Zeit*. FRLANT 114. Göttingen: Vandenhoeck & Ruprecht, 1975.

Halpern, B. "The False Torah of Jeremiah 8 in the Context of Seventh Century BCE Pseudepigraphy: The First Documented Rejection of Tradition." Pp. 337–43 in *"Up to the Gates of Ekron": Essays on the Archaeology and History of the Eastern Mediterranean in Honor of Seymour Gitin*. Edited by S. W. Crawford, A. Ben-Tor, J. P. Dessel, W. G. Dever, A. Mazar, and J. Aviram. Jerusalem: The W. F. Albright Institute of Archaeological Research/The Israel Exploration Society, 2007.

Hanawalt, B. A. *Growing up in Medieval London*. Oxford: Oxford University Press, 1993.

———. "Medievalists and the Study of Childhood." *Speculum* 77 (2002): 440–60.

Harden, D. B. "The Pottery from the Precinct of Tanit at Salammbo, Carthage." *Iraq* 4 (1937): 59–89.

———. "Punic Urns from the Precinct of Tanit at Carthage." *AJA* 31 (1927): 297–310.

Hartley, J. E., and T. Dwyer, "An Investigation into the Location of the Laws on Offerings to Molek in the Book of Leviticus." Pp. 81–93 in *Go to the Land I Will Show You: Studies in Honor of Dwight W. Young*. Edited by J. Coleson and V. Matthews. Winona Lake, IN: Eisenbrauns, 1996.

Hays, C. B. *Death in the Iron Age II and in First Isaiah*. FAT 79. Tübingen: Mohr Siebeck, 2011.

Heider, G. C. *The Cult of Molek: A Reassessment*. JSOTSup 43. Sheffield: JSOT Press, 1985.

———. "Molech." *ABD* 4, 895–98.

Heinisch, P. *Das Buch Exodus*. HSAT 1:2. Bonn: Peter Hanstein, 1934.

Helmholz, R. H. "Infanticide in the Province of Canterbury During the Fifteenth Century." *History of Childhood Quarterly* 2 (1975): 379–90.

Hendel, R. S. "Away from Ritual: The Prophetic Critique." Pp. 59–70 in *Social Theory and the Study of Israelite Religion: Essays in Retrospect and Prospect*. Edited by S. Olyan. RBS 71. Atlanta: Society of Biblical Literature, 2012.

———. "Prophets, Priests, and the Efficacy of Ritual." Pp. 185–98 in *Pomegranates & Golden Bells: Studies in Biblical, Jewish, and Near Eastern Ritual, Law, and Literature in Honor of Jacob Milgrom*. Edited by D. P. Wright, D. N. Freedman, and A. Hurvitz. Winona Lake, IN: Eisenbrauns, 1995.

Hennessy, J. B. "Excavation of a Late Bronze Age Temple at Amman." *PEQ* 98 (1966): 155–62.

———. "Thirteenth Century B.C. Temple of Human Sacrifice at Amman." Pp. 85–104 in *Phoenicia and Its Neighbors*. Studia Phoenicia 3. Leuven: Peeters, 1985.

Herr, L. G. *The Amman Airport Excavations, 1976*. AASOR 48. Philadelphia: American Schools of Oriental Research, 1981.

———. "The Amman Airport Structure and the Geopolitics of Ancient Transjordan." *BA* 46 (1983): 223–29.

Hillers, D. R. *Micah: A Commentary on the Book of the Prophet Micah*. Edited by P. D. Hanson. Hermeneia. Philadelphia: Fortress Press, 1984.

Hobbs, T. R. *2 Kings*. WBC 13. Waco, TX: Word, 1985.

Hoffmann, H.-D. *Reform und Reformen: Untersuchungen zu einem Grundthema der deuteronomistischen Geschichtsschreibung*. AThANT 66. Zurich: Theologischer, 1980.
Hoftijzer, J. "Eine Notiz zum punischen Kinderopfer." *VT* 8 (1958): 288–92.
Hoftijzer, J., and G. van der Kooij. *Aramaic Texts from Deir ʿAlla*. Documenta et Monumenta Orientis Antiqui. Leiden: Brill, 1976.
———, eds. *The Balaam Text from Deir ʿAlla Re-Evaluated: Proceedings of the International Symposium Held at Leiden 21–24, 1989*. Leiden: Brill, 1991.
Hölscher, G. *Geschichte der israelitischen und jüdischen Religion*. Giessen: Töpelmann, 1922.
Hoop, R. de. *Genesis 49 in Its Literary and Historical Context*. OTS 29. Leiden: Brill, 1999.
Hughes, D. D. *Human Sacrifice in Ancient Greece*. New York: Routledge, 1991.
Hutton, J. "Southern, Northern, and Transjordanian Perspectives." Pp. 149–74 in *Religious Diversity in Ancient Israel and Judah*. Edited by F. Stavrakopoulou and J. Barton. New York: T. & T. Clark, 2010.
Irvine, S. A. *Isaiah, Ahaz, and the Syro-Ephraimite Crisis*. SBLDS 123. Atlanta: Scholars Press, 1990.
Jacobs, M. R. *The Conceptual Coherence of the Book of Micah*. JSOTSup 322. Sheffield: Sheffield Academic, 2001.
Jeffers, A. *Magic and Divination in Ancient Palestine and Syria*. SHCANE 8. Leiden: Brill, 1996.
Jongeling, K. *Handbook of Neo-Punic Inscriptions*. Tübingen: Mohr Siebeck, 2008.
Joosten, J. *People and Land in the Holiness Code: An Exegetical Study of the Ideational Framework of the Law in Leviticus 17–26*. VTSup 67. Leiden: Brill, 1996.
Judas, A.-C. *Étude démonstrative de la langue phénicienne et de la langue libyque*. Paris: Klincksieck, 1857.
Kaiser, O. *Isaiah 13–39*. Translated by R. A. Wilson. OTL. Philadelphia: Westminster, 1974.
Kaufman, S. A. "The Enigmatic Adad-Milki." *JNES* 37 (1978): 101–9.
———. "The Phoenician Inscription of the Incirli Trilingual: A Tentative Reconstruction and Translation." *Maarav* 14:2 (2007): 7–26.
Kaufmann, Y. *The Book of Judges*. Jerusalem: Kiryat Sepher, 1968. [Hebrew]
Keel, O. "Kanaanäische Sühneriten auf ägyptischen Tempelreliefs." *VT* 25 (1975): 413–69.
Kellum, B. A. "Infanticide in England in the Later Middle Ages." *History of Childhood Quarterly* 1 (1974): 367–88.
Kelsey, F. W. *Excavations at Carthage, 1925. A Preliminary Report*. New York: Macmillan, 1926.
Kempinski, A. "Death and Resurrection: The Early Evidence." *BAR* 21:5 (1995): 38–49.
Killebrew, A. E. *Biblical Peoples and Ethnicity: An Archaeological Study of the Egyptians, Canaanites, Philistines, and Early Israel, 1300–1100 B.C.E.* ABS 9. Atlanta: Society of Biblical Literature, 2005.
Kittel, R. *Geschichte des Volkes Israel*. 2 vols. 5th ed. HAG. Gotha: Klotz, 1923.
Klawans, J. *Purity, Sacrifice, and the Temple*. Oxford: Oxford University Press, 2006.
Knohl, I. *The Sanctuary of Silence: The Priestly Torah and the Holiness School*. Minneapolis: Fortress, 1996.
Knoppers, G. N. "Rethinking the Relationship between Deuteronomy and the Deuteronomistic History: The Case of Kings." *CBQ* 63 (2001): 393–415.

Koch, K. "Molek astral." Pp. 29–50 in *Mythos im Alten Testament und seiner Umwelt: Festschrift für Hans-Peter Müller zum 65. Geburtstag*. BZAW 278. Edited by A. Lange, H. Lichtenberger, and D. Römheld. Berlin: de Gruyter, 1999.

Koepf-Taylor, L. W. *Give Me Children or I Shall Die: Children and Communal Survival in Biblical Literature*. ES. Minneapolis: Fortress, 2013.

Kooij, G. van der. "Book and Script at Deir ʿAlla." Pp. in 239–62 *The Balaam Text from Deir ʿAlla Re-Evaluated: Proceedings of the International Symposium Held at Leiden, 21–24 August 1989*. Edited by H. Hoftijzer and G. van der Kooij. Leiden: Brill, 1991.

Kornfeld, W. "Der Moloch: eine Untersuchung zur Theorie O. Eissfeldts." *WZKM* 51 (1951): 287–313.

Krahmalkov, C. R. *A Phoenician-Punic Grammar*. Leiden: Brill, 1999.

Krandel-Ben Younès, A. *La présence punique en pays numide*. Tunis: République Tunisienne, Ministère de la culture, Institut national du patrimoine, 2002.

Kratz, R. G. "Chemosh's Wrath and Yahweh's No: Ideas of Divine Wrath in Moab and Israel." Pp. 92–121 in *Divine Wrath and Divine Mercy in the World of Antiquity*. Edited by R. G. Kratz and H. Spieckermann. FAT 2 33. Tübingen: Mohr Siebeck, 2008.

Krebernik, M. *Die Personennamen der Ebla-Texte: Eine Zwischenbilanz*. BBVO 7. Berlin: Reimer, 1988.

Krüger, T. "Erwägungen zur prophetischen Kultkritik." Pp. 37–55 in *Die unwiderstehliche Wahrheit: Studien zur alttestamentlichen Prophetie*. Edited by R. Lux and E.-J. Waschke. Arbeiten zur Bibel und ihrer Geschichte 23. Leipzig: Evangelische Verlagsanstalt, 2006.

Kumar, R. C. "'Anybody's Child': Severe Disorders of Mother Infant Bonding." *British Journal of Psychiatry* 171 (1997): 175–81.

Kuemmerlin-McLean, J. K. "Magic, Old Testament." *ABD* 4, 468–71.

Lafferty, T. V. *The Prophetic Critique of the Priority of the Cult: A Study of Amos 5:21–24 and Isaiah 1:10–17*. Eugene, OR: Pickwick, 2012.

Lagrange, M.-J. "Une inscription phénicienne." *RB* 1 (1892): 275–81.

Lange, A. "They Burn their Sons and Daughters—That Was No Command of Mine (Jer 7:31): Child Sacrifice in the Hebrew Bible and in the Deuteronomic Jeremiah Redaction." Pp. 109–32 in *Human Sacrifice in the Jewish and Christian Tradition*. Edited by K. Finsterbusch, A. Lange, and K. F. D. Römheld. BHR 112. Leiden: Brill, 2007.

Lantier, R and L. Poinssot. "Les stèles découvertes dans une favissa du temple de Saturne à Dougga." *Bulletin archéologique du Comité des travaux historiques et scientifiques* (1942): xii–xxviii.

Lemaire, A. "The Evolution of the 8th-Century B.C.E. Jerusalem Temple." Pp. 195–202 in *The Fire Signals of Lachish: Studies in the Archaeology and History of Israel in the Late Bronze Age, Iron Age, and Persian Period in Honor of David Ussishkin*. Edited by I. Finkelstein and N. Naʾaman. Winona Lake, IN: Eisenbrauns, 2011.

———. "The Mesha Stele and the Omri Dynasty." Pp. 135–44 in *Ahab Agonistes: The Rise and Fall of the Omri Dynasty*. Edited by L. L. Grabbe. LHBOTS 421 New York: T. & T. Clark, 2007.

Levenson, J. D. *The Death and Resurrection of the Beloved Son: The Transformation of Child Sacrifice in Judaism and Christianity*. New Haven: Yale University Press, 1995.

Levi Della Vida, G. "Iscrizioni neopuniche di Tripolitania." *Rendiconti delle sedute dell'Accademia Nazionale dei Lincei: Classe di Scienze morali, storiche e filologiche* 8 (1949): 399–412.

———. "Ostracon Neopunico dalla Tripolitania." *Or* 33 (1964): 1–14.

Levine, B. A. "The Deir ʿAlla Plaster Inscriptions." *JAOS* 101 (1981): 195–205.

———. *Numbers 21–36*. AB 4A. New York: Doubleday, 2000.

Levine, C. "Das Kinderopfer im Jeremiabuch." Pp. 227–41 in *Fortschreibungen: Gesammelte Studien zum Alten Testament*. BZAW 316. Berlin: de Gruyter, 2003.

Levinson, B. M. "'But You Shall Surely Kill Him!' The Text-Critical and Neo-Assyrian Evidence for MT Deuteronomy 13:10." Pp. 37–63 in *Bundesdokument und Gesetz: Studien zum Deuteronomium*. Edited by G. Braulik. HBS 4. Freiburg: Herder, 1995.

———. "The Canon Formula in Deuteronomy 13:1." Pp. 25–45 in *Scriptural Exegesis: The Shapes of Culture and the Religious Imagination: Essays in Honour of Michael Fishbane*. Edited by D. A. Green and L. S. Lieber. Oxford: Oxford University Press, 2009.

———. *Deuteronomy and the Hermeneutics of Legal Innovation*. Oxford: Oxford University Press, 1997.

———. "Esarhaddon's Succession Treaty as the Source for the Canon Formula in Deuteronomy 13:1." *JAOS* 130 (2010): 337–47.

———. "Goethe's Analysis of Exodus 34 and Its Influence on Wellhausen: The *Pfropfung* of the Documentary Hypothesis." *ZAW* 114 (2002): 212–23.

———. "Is the Covenant Code an Exilic Composition? A Response to John Van Seters." Pp. 272–325 in *In Search of Pre-Exilic Israel: Proceedings of the Oxford Old Testament Seminar*. Edited by J. Day. JSOTSup 406. New York: T. & T. Clark, 2004.

Levinson, B. M., and J. Stackert. "Between Covenant Code and Esarhaddon's Succession Treaty: Deuteronomy 13 and the Composition of Deuteronomy" *JAJ* 3 (2012): 123–40.

Lewis, T. J. *Cults of the Dead in Ancient Israel and Ugarit*. HSM 39. Atlanta: Scholars Press, 1989.

———. "Death Cult Imagery in Isaiah 57." *HAR* 11 (1987): 267–84.

Lidzbarski, M. *Ephemeris für semitische Epigraphik*. 3 Vols. Giessen: Ricker'sche (Töpelmann), 1902–15.

———. *Handbuch der nordsemitischen Epigraphik nebst ausgewählten Inschriften*. Weimar: Felber, 1898.

———. "Neue Götter." *Nachrichten von der königlichen Gesellschaft der Wissenschaften zu Göttingen, Phil.-hist. Klasse* (1916): 86–93.

———. *Phönizische und aramäische Krugaufschriften aus Elephantine*. Berlin: Königl. Akademie der Wissenschaften, in Kommission bei Georg Reimer, 1912.

Limburg, J. "The Root ריב and the Prophetic Lawsuit Speeches." *JBL* 88 (1969): 291–304.

Light, T. "Orthosyncretism: An Account of Melding in Religion." *Method & Theory in the Study of Religion* 12 (2000): 162–86.

Lightfoot, J. L. *Lucian: On the Syrian Goddess*. Oxford: Oxford University Press, 2003.

Lipiński, E. "The Plaster Inscription from Deir ʿAllā." Pp. 103–70 in *Studies in Aramaic Inscriptions and Onomastics*. Vol. 2. Leuven: Peeters, 1994.

Lohfink, N. "Kerygmata des Deuteronomistischen Geschichtswerks." Pp. in 87–100 *Die Botschaft und die Boten: Festschrift für Hans Walter Wolff zum 70. Geburtstag*. Edited by J. Jeremias and L. Perlitt. Neukirchen-Vluyn: Neukirchener Verlag, 1981.

———. "Opferzentralisation, Säkularisierungsthese und mimetische Theorie." Pp. 219–62 in *Studien zum Deuteronomium und zur deuteronomistischen Literatur*. Vol. 3. SBAB 20. Stuttgart: Katholisches Bibelwerk, 1995.

———. "Die Sicherung der Wirksamkeit des Gotteswortes durch das Prinzip der Schriftlichkeit der Tora und durch das Prinzip der Gewaltenteilung nach den Ämtergesetzen des Buches Deuteronomium (Dt 16,18–18,22)." Pp. 143–56 in *Testimonium veritati: Philosophische und theologische Studien zu kirchlichen Fragen der Gegenwart*. Edited by H. Wolter. Frankfurt: Knecht, 1971. [= "Distribution of the Functions of Power: The Laws Concerning Public Offices in Deuteronomy 16:18–18:22." Pp. 336–52 in *A Song of Power and the Power of Song: Essays on the Book of Deuteronomy*. Edited by D. L. Christensen. Translated by R. Walls. SBTS 3. Winona Lake, IN: Eisenbrauns, 1993.]

Lundbom, J. R. *Jeremiah 1–20: A New Translation with Introduction and Commentary*. AB 21A. New York: Doubleday, 1999.

Lust, J. "Molek and ΑΡΧΩΝ." Pp. 193–208 in *Phoenicia and the Bible*. Edited by E. Lipiński. Studia Phoenicia 11. Leuven: Peeters, 1991.

Macalister, R. *The Excavation of Gezer*. Vol. 2. London: John Murray, 1912.

Maltzan, H. von. *Reise in den Regentschaften Tunis und Tripolis*. Vol. 1. Leipzig: Dyk'sche Buchhandlung, 1870.

Marcus, D. *Jephthah and His Vow*. Lubbock, TX: Texas Tech Press, 1986.

Margalit, B. "Why King Mesha of Moab Sacrificed His Oldest Son." *BAR* 12:6 (1986): 62–63, 76.

Martin, L. "Syncretism, Historicism, and Cognition: A Response to Michael Pye." *Method & Theory in the Study of Religion* 8 (1996): 215–24.

Mayes, A. D. H. *Deuteronomy*. NCBC. Grand Rapids, MI: Eerdmans, 1979.

Mays, J. L. *Micah: A Commentary*. OTL. Philadelphia: Westminster, 1990.

Mays, S. "The Bioarchaeology of the Homicide of Infants and Children." Pp. 99–122 in *Tracing Childhood: Bioarchaeological Investigations of Early Lives in Antiquity*. Edited by J. L. Thompson, M. P. Alfonso-Durruty, and J. J. Crandall. Gainesville, FL: University Press of Florida.

———. "Infanticide in Roman Britain." *Antiquity* 67 (1993): 883–88.

Mays, S., and J. Eyers. "Perinatal Infant Death at the Roman Villa Site at Hambleden, Buckinghamshire, England." *Journal of Archaeological Science* 38 (2011): 1931–38.

Mazar, E. *The Northern Cemetery of Achziv (10th–6th Centuries BCE): The Tophet Site*. Cuadernos de Arqueología Mediterránnea 19–20. Barcelona: Publicaciones del Laboratorio de Arqueologia, Universidad Pompeu Fabra de Barcelona, 2009–2010.

McCarter Jr., P. K. "The Balaam Texts from Deir ʿAllā: The First Combination." *BASOR* 239 (1980): 49–60.

McCarthy, D. J. *Treaty and Covenant: A Study in Form in the Ancient Oriental Documents and in the Old Testament*. 2nd ed. AnBib 21. Rome: Biblical Institute Press, 1978.

McCarty, M. M. "Representation and the 'Meanings of Ritual Change: the Case of Hadrumetum." Pp. 197–228 in *Ritual Dynamics in the Ancient Mediterranean: Agency, Emotion, Gender, Representation*. Edited by A. Chaniotis. Heidelberger althistorische Beiträge und epigraphische Studien 49. Stuttgart: Steiner, 2011.

———. "Continuities and Contexts: The Tophets of Roman Imperial-Period Africa." *SEL* 29–30 (2012–2013): 93–118.

McKane, W. *The Book of Micah: Introduction and Commentary*. ICC. Edinburgh: T. & T. Clark, 1998.

———. *A Critical and Exegetical Commentary on Jeremiah I–XXV*. ICC. Edinburgh: T. & T. Clark, 1986.

McKay, J. W. *Religion in Judah under the Assyrians 732–609 BC*. SBT 26. London: SCM, 1973.

McKenzie, S. L. *The Trouble with Kings: The Composition of the Book of Kings in the Deuteronomistic History*. VTSup 42. Leiden: Brill, 1991.

Melchiorri, V. "Osteological Analysis in the Study of the Phoenician and Punic Tophet: A History of Research." *SEL* 29–30 (2012–2013): 223–58.

———. "Tophet: A Selected Bibliography." *SEL* 29–30 (2012–2013): 283–312.

———. "Le *tophet* de Sulci (S. Antioco, Sardaigne): État des études et perspectives de la recherche." *UF* 41 (2009): 509–24.

Meyers, C. "The Family in Early Israel." Pp. in 1–47 in *Families in Ancient Israel*. Edited by L. G. Perdue, J. Blenkinsopp, J. J. Collins, and C. Meyers. Louisville: Westminster John Knox, 1997.

Milgrom, J. *Leviticus: A New Translation with Introduction and Commentary*. 3 vols. AB 3–3B. New York: Doubleday, 1991–2001.

———. *Numbers*. JPSTC. New York: Jewish Publication Society, 1990.

Milinovich, T. M. "Form Criticism and the *rîb* in Isaiah 41,21–42,4." *BN* 136 (2008): 45–57.

Millard, A. R. "Adrammelech אדרמלך." *DDD*², 10–11.

———. "Anammelech ענמלך." *DDD*², 34–35.

Miller, J. M. "The Elisha Cycle and the Accounts of the Omride Wars." *JBL* 85 (1966): 441–54.

Miller, P. D. *The Religion of Ancient Israel*. Louisville, KY: Westminster John Knox, 2000.

Montgomery, J. A. *A Critical and Exegetical Commentary on the Books of Kings*. Edited by H. S. Gehman. ICC. New York: Charles Scribner's Sons, 1951.

Mosca, P. G. "Child Sacrifice in Canaanite and Israelite Religion: A Study in *Mulk* and מלך." Ph.D. diss. Harvard University, 1975.

———. "The *Tofet*: A Place of Infant Sacrifice?" *SEL* 29–30 (2012–2013): 119–36.

Moscati, S. *Italia archeologica: Centri greci, punici, etruschi, italici*. Vol. 1. Novara: Istituto geografico di Agostini, 1973.

———. "Non è un tofet a Tiro." *RSF* 21 (1993): 147–52.

———. *Il santuario dei bambini (tofet)*. Rome: Istituto Poligrafico e Zecca dello Stato, 1992.

Moscati, S., and M. L. Uberti. *Le stele puniche di Nora nel Museo nazionale die Cagliari*. Studi semitici 35. Rome: Consiglio nazionale delle ricerche, 1970.

Mowinckel, S. *Zur Komposition des Buches Jeremia*. Kristiana: Dybwad, 1914.

Mulder, M. J. "תֹּפֶת tōp̱eṯ." *TDOT 15*, 753–65.
Müller, H.-P. "Die aramäische Inschrift von Deir ʿAllā und die älteren Bileamsprüche." *ZAW* 94 (1982): 214–44.
———. "Hebraisch מֹלֶךְ und punisch *ml(')k(t)*." Pp. 243–53 in *Michael: Historical, Epigraphical and Biblical Studies in Honor of Prof. Michael Heltzer*. Edited by Y. Avishur and R. Deutsch. Tel Aviv: Archaeological Center, 1999.
———. "מֹלֶךְ *molæk*." *TDOT* 8, 375–88.
Mungello, D. E. *Drowning Girls in China: Female Infanticide since 1650*. New York: Rowman & Littlefield, 2008.
Naʾaman, N. "Royal Inscriptions and the Histories of Joash and Ahaz, Kings of Judah." *VT* 48 (1998): 333–49.
———. "Royal Inscriptions versus Prophetic Story: Mesha's Rebellion according to Biblical and Moabite Historiography." Pp. 145–83 in *Ahab Agonistes: The Rise and Fall of the Omri Dynasty*. Edited by L. L. Grabbe. LHBOTS 421. New York: T. & T. Clark, 2007.
Najman, H. *Seconding Sinai: The Development of Mosaic Discourse in Second Temple Judaism*. JSJSup 77. Leiden: Brill, 2003.
Nakhai, B. A. "Female Infanticide in Iron II Israel and Judah." Pp. 257–72 in *Sacred History, Sacred Literature: Essays on Ancient Israel, the Bible, and Religion in Honor of R. E. Friedman on His Sixtieth Birthday*. Edited by S. Dolansky. Winona Lake, IN: Eisenbrauns, 2008.
Nicholson, E. *The Book of the Prophet Jeremiah, Chapters 1–25*. CBC. Cambridge: Cambridge University Press, 1973.
———. "Deuteronomy 18:9–22, the Prophets and Scripture." Pp. 151–71 in *Prophecy and Prophets in Ancient Israel: Proceedings of the Oxford Old Testament Seminar*. Edited by J. Day. New York: T. & T. Clark, 2010.
Niditch, S. *Judges: A Commentary*. OTL. Louisville: Westminister John Knox, 2008.
Nielsen, K. *Yahweh as Prosecutor and Judge: An Investigation of the Prophetic Lawsuit (Rîb-Pattern)*. JSOTSup 9. Sheffield: JSOT Press, 1978.
Nihan, C. *From Priestly Torah to Pentateuch*. FAT 2 25. Tübingen: Mohr Siebeck, 2007.
Nissinen, M. "Adrammelech (Deity)." *EBR* 1, 442.
Noort, E. "Child Sacrifice in Ancient Israel: The *Status Quaestionis*." Pp. 103–25 in *The Strange World of Human Sacrifice*. Edited by J. N. Bremmer. Studies in the History of Anthropology of Religion 1. Leuven: Peeters, 2007.
Noth, M. *The Deuteronomistic History*. Translated by J. Doull, J. Barton, and M. D. Rutter. JSOTSup 15. Sheffield: JSOT Press, 1981.
———. *Leviticus*. Translated by J. E. Anderson. OTL. London: SCM, 1965.
Oestreicher, T. *Das deuteronomische Grundgesetz*. BFCT 27:4. Gütersloh: Bertelsmann, 1923.
Olmstead, A. T. *History of Assyria*. New York: Charles Scribner's Sons, 1923.
———. *History of Palestine and Syria to the Macedonian Conquest*. New York: Charles Scribner's Sons, 1931.
Olyan, S. M., and M. S. Smith. Review of G. C. Heider, *The Cult of Molek: A Reassessment*. *RB* 94 (1987): 273–75.
Orme, N. *Medieval Children*. New Haven: Yale University Press, 2001.

Otto, E. *Das Deuteronomium im Pentateuch und Hexateuch: Studien zur Literaturgeschichte von Pentateuch und Hexateuch im Lichte des Deuteronomiumrahmens*. FAT 30. Tübingen: Mohr Siebeck, 2000.

———. *Das Deuteronomium: Politische Theologie und Rechtsreform in Juda und Assyrien*. BZAW 284. Berlin: de Gruyter, 1999.

———. "Deuteronomium und Pentateuch." Pp. 168–228 in *Die Tora. Studien zum Pentateuch: Gesammelte Schriften*. BZABR 9. Wiesbaden: Harrassowitz, 2009.

———. "Ersetzen oder Ergänzen von Gesetzen in der Rechtshermeneutik des Pentateuch: Zu einem Buch von Jeffrey Stackert" Pp. 248–56 in *Die Tora. Studien zum Pentateuch: Gesammelte Schriften*. BZABR 9. Wiesbaden: Harrassowitz, 2009.

———. "The Pre-exilic Deuteronomy as a Revision for the Covenant Code." Pp. 112–22 in *Kontinuum und Proprium: Studien zu Sozial- und Rechtsgeschichte des Alten Orients und des Alten Testaments*. OBC 8. Wiesbaden: Harrassowitz, 1996.

———. Review of J. Van Seters, *A Law Book for the Diaspora: Revision in the Study of the Covenant Code*. *RBL* 7 (2004).

Otto, S. "The Composition of the Elijah-Elisha Stories and the Deuteronomistic History." *JSOT* 27 (2003): 487–508.

Pagan, J. M. *A Morphological and Lexical Study of Personal Names in the Ebla Texts*. ARES 3. Rome: Missione Archeologica Italiana in Siria, 1998.

Pakkala, J. *God's Word Omitted: Omissions in the Transmission of the Hebrew Bible*. FRLANT 251. Göttingen: Vandenhoeck & Ruprecht, 2013.

———. *Intolerant Monolatry in the Deuteronomistic History*. Göttingen: Vandenhoeck & Ruprecht, 1999.

———. "Der literar- und religionsgeschichtliche Ort von Deuteronomium 13." Pp. 125–37 in *Die deuteronomistischen Geschichtswerke: Redaktions- und religionsgeschichtliche Perspektiven zu "Deuteronomismus"-Diskussion in Tora und Vorderen Propheten*. Edited by M. Witte, K. Schmid, D. Prechel, and J. C. Gertz. BZAW 365. Berlin: de Gruyter, 2006.

Pallary, P. "Note sur les urnes funéraires trouvées à Salammbô près Carthage." *Revue Tunisienne* 152–54 (1922): 206–11.

Pardee, D. *Ritual and Cult at Ugarit*. WAW 10. Society of Biblical Literature: Atlanta, 2002.

———. "Ugaritic Prayer for a City Under Siege (1.88)." COS 1, 284–85.

Park-Taylor, G. H. *The Formation of the Book of Jeremiah: Doublets and Recurring Phrases*. SBLMS 51. Atlanta: Society of Biblical Literature, 2000.

Parker, J. F. *Valuable and Vulnerable: Children in the Hebrew Bible, Especially the Elisha Cycle*. BJS 355. Providence: Brown University, 2013.

Parpola, S. "Assyria's Expansion in the 8th and 7th Centuries and Its Long-Term Repercussions in the West." Pp. in 99–111 *Symbiosis, Symbolism, and the Power of the Past: Canaan, Ancient Israel, and Their Neighbors from the Late Bronze Age through Roman Palaestina*. Edited by W. G. Dever and S. Gitin. Winona Lake, IN: Eisenbrauns, 2003.

Paton, L. B. "The Relationship of Lev. 20 to Lev. 17–19." *Hebraica* 10 (1894): 111–21.

Patroni, G. "Nora, colonia fenicia in Sardegna." *Monumenti antichi* 14 (1904): 109–268.

Patton, C. "'I Myself Gave Them Laws That Were Not Good': Ezekiel 20 and the Exodus Traditions." *JSOT* 69 (1996): 73–90.

Pesce, G. *Tharros*. Cagliari: Editrice Sarda Fratelli Fossataro, 1966.
Pfeiffer, R. H. *Introduction to the Old Testament*. New York: Harper & Brothers, 1941.
———. "The Oldest Decalogue." *JBL* 43 (1924): 294–310.
Poinssot, C. *Les ruines de Dougga*. 2nd ed. Tunis: Ministère des affaires culturelles, Institut national d'archéologie et d'arts, 1983.
Poinssot, L., and R. Lantier. "Un sanctuaire de Tanit à Carthage." *RHR* 87 (1923): 32–68.
Pomponio, F., and P. Xella. *Les dieux d'Ebla: Étude analytique des divinités éblaïtes à l'époque des archives royales du IIIe millénaire*. AOAT 245. Münster: Ugarit-Verlag, 1997.
Preuss, H. D. גִּלּוּלִים *gillûlîm* גִּלֻּלִים *gillulîm*. *TDOT* 3, 1–5.
Procksch, D. O. *Die Genesis*. KAT 1. 2nd/3rd ed. Leipzig: Deichertsche, 1924.
Propp, W. H. C. *Exodus 19–40: A New Translation with Introduction and Commentary*. AB 2A. New York: Doubleday, 2006.
Provan, I. W. *1 and 2 Kings*. NIBCOT. Peabody, MA: Hendrickson, 1995.
Puech, E. "Le texte 'ammonite' de Deir ʿAlla: les admonitions de Balaam (première partie)." Pp. 13–30 in *La vie de la Parole: De l'Ancien au Nouveau Testament*. Paris: Desclée, 1987.
Puglisi, S. "Cagliari. Necropoli punica a incinerazione." *Notizie degli scavi antichità* (1942): 104–6.
Pye, M. "Syncretism and Ambiguity." *Numen* 18 (1971): 83–93.
———. "Syncretism vs. Synthesis." *Method & Theory in the Study of Religion* 6 (1993): 217–29.
Quinn, J. C. "The Cultures of the Tophet: Identification and Identity in the Phoenician Diaspora." Pp. 388–413 in *Cultural Identity in the Ancient Mediterranean*. Edited by E. S. Gruen. Los Angeles: Getty Research Institute, 2011.
———. "Tophets in the 'Punic World'." *SEL* 29–30 (2012–2013): 23–48.
Ramsey, G. W. "Speech-forms in Hebrew Law and Prophetic Oracles." *JBL* 96 (1977): 45–58.
Ransel, D. L. Review of J. Boswell, *The Kindness of Strangers*. *History of Education Quarterly* 30 (1990): 225–27.
Reis, P. T. *Reading the Lines: A Fresh Look at the Hebrew Bible*. Peabody, MA: Hendrickson, 2002.
Rendtorff, R. *Studien zur Geschichte des Opfers im alten Israel*. WMANT 24. Neukirchen-Vluyn: Neukirchener Verlag, 1967.
Reynolds, B. H. "Molek: Dead or Alive: The Meaning and Derivation of *mlk* and למלך." Pp. 133–50 in *Human Sacrifice in Jewish and Christian Tradition*. Edited by K. Finsterbusch, A. Lange, and K. F. D. Römheld. BHR 112. Leiden: Brill, 2007.
Roberts, J. J. M. *The Earliest Semitic Pantheon: A Study of the Semitic Deities Attested in Mesopotamia before Ur III*. Baltimore: The Johns Hopkins University Press, 1972.
———. *First Isaiah*. Edited by P. Machinist. Hermeneia. Minneapolis: Fortress, 2015.
Roche, M. de. "Yahweh's *Rîb* against Israel: A Reassessment of the So-Called 'Prophetic Lawsuit' in the Preexilic Prophets." *JBL* 102 (1983): 563–74.
Römer, T. C. "Cult Centralization in Deuteronomy 12: Between Deuteronomistic History and Pentateuch." Pp. 168–80 in *Das Deuteronomium zwischen Pentateuch und Deuteronomistischem Geschichtswerk*. Edited by E. Otto and R. Achenbach. FRLANT 206. Göttingen: Vandenhoeck & Ruprecht, 2004.

———. "Le sacrifice humain en Juda et Israël au premier millénaire avant notre ère." *Archiv für Religionsgeschichte* 1 (1999): 16–26.
———. "Why Would the Deuteronomists Tell about the Sacrifice of Jephthah's Daughter?" *JSOT* 77 (1998): 27–38.
Rudolph, W. *Jeremia*. HAT 12. Tübingen: Mohr (Siebeck), 1947.
Rundin, J. S. "Pozo Moro, Child Sacrifice, and the Greek Legendary Tradition." *JBL* 123 (2004): 425–47.
Russell, S. C. *Images of Egypt in Early Biblical Literature: Cisjordan-Israelite, Transjordan-Israelite, and Judahite Portrayals*. BZAW 403. Berlin: de Gruyter, 2009.
Sader, H. "Phoenician Stelae from Tyre." *Berytus* 39 (1991): 101–26.
———. "Phoenician Stelae from Tyre." *SEL* 9 (1992): 53–79.
Sagona, C. *The Archaeology of Punic Malta*. Ancient Near Eastern Studies 9. Leuven: Peeters, 2002.
Saint-Amans, S. *Topographie religieuse de Thugga (Dougga): ville romaine d'Afrique proconsulaire (Tunisie)*. Pessac: Ausonius, 2004.
Šanda, A. *Die Bücher der Könige*. 2 Vols. EHAT 9. Münster: Aschendorffsch, 1911–12.
———. *Moses und der Pentateuch*. ATA 9:4–5. Münster: Aschendorffsch, 1924.
Sasson, J. *Judges 1–12: A New Translation with Introduction and Commentary*. AYB 6D. New Haven: Yale University Press, 2014.
Scheper-Hughes, N. "Death Without Weeping: Has Poverty Ravaged Mother Love in the Shantytowns of Brazil?" *Natural History* 10 (1989): 8–16.
———. *Death Without Weeping: The Violence of Everyday Life in Brazil*. Berkeley: University of California Press, 1993.
———. "No More Angel Babies on the Alto." *Berkeley Review of Latin American Studies* (Spring 2013): 25–31.
———. "Social Indifference to Child Death." *The Lancet* 337:8750 (1991): 1144–47.
Schmidt, B. B."Canaanite Magic vs. Israelite Religion: Deuteronomy 18 and the Taxonomy of Taboo." Pp. 242–59 in *Magic and Ritual in the Ancient World*. Edited by P. Mirecki and M. Meyer. RGRW 141. Leiden: Brill, 2002.
———. "Canaanites: I. Introduction, II. Archaeology, III. Ancient Near East and Hebrew Bible/Old Testament." *EBR* 4, 871–75.
———. *Israel's Beneficent Dead: Ancestor Cult and Necromancy in Ancient Israelite Religion and Tradition*. FAT 11. Tübigen: Mohr Siebeck, 1994.
Schmidt, W. H. *Das Buch Jeremia: Kapitel 1–20*. ATD 20. Göttingen: Vandenhoeck & Ruprecht, 2008.
Schmitt, R. "Divination, II. Hebrew Bible/Old Testament." *EBR* 6, 959–61.
Schumacher, G. *Tell el-Mutesellim*. Vol. 1. Leipzig: Haupt, 1908.
Schwartz, G. M. "Archaeology and Sacrifice." Pp. 1–32 in *Sacred Killing: The Archaeology of Sacrifice in the Ancient Near East*. Edited by A. M. Porter and G. M. Schwartz. Winona Lake, IN: Eisenbrauns, 2012.
———. "Era of the Living Dead: Funerary Praxis and Symbol in Third Millennium BC Syria." Pp. in 59–77 in *(Re-)Constructing Funerary Rituals in the Ancient Near East*. Edited by P. Pfälzner, H. Niehr, E. Pernicka, and A. Wissing. Wiesbaden: Harrassowitz, 2012.
———. "Memory and its Demolition: Ancestors, Animals and Sacrifice at Umm el-Marra, Syria." *Cambridge Archaeological Journal* 23 (2013): 495–522.

———. "Status, Ideology, and Memory in Third-Millennium Syria: 'Royal' Tombs at Umm el-Marra." Pp. 39–68 in *Performing Death: Social Analyses of Funerary Traditions in the Ancient Near East and Mediterranean*. Edited by N. Laneri. Oriental Institute Seminars 3. Chicago: The Oriental Institute, 2007.

Schwartz, G. M., H. H. Curvers, S. S. Dunham, B. Stuart, and J. A. Weber. "A Third-Millennium Elite Mortuary Complex at Umm el-Marra, Syria: 2002 and 2004 Excavations." *AJA* 110 (2006): 603–41.

Schwartz, J. H. *What the Bones Tell Us*. New York: Holt, 1993.

Schwartz, J. H., F. D. Houghton, L. Bondioli, and R. Macchiarelli. "Bones, Teeth, and Estimating Age of Perinates: Carthaginian Infant Sacrifice Revisited." *Antiquity* 86 (2012): 738–45.

Schwartz, J. H., F. Houghton, R. Macchiarelli, and L. Bondioli. "Skeletal Remains from Punic Carthage Do Not Support Systematic Sacrifice of Infants." *PLoS ONE* 5 (2010): e9177.

Seeden, H. "A *Tophet* in Tyre?" *Berytus* 39 (1991): 39–82.

Segal, J. B. *The Hebrew Passover from the Earliest Times to A.D. 70*. London Oriental Series 12. London: Oxford University Press, 1963.

Segert, S. *A Grammar of Phoenician and Punic*. Munich: C. H. Beck, 1976.

Sellin, E. *Tell Ta'annek*. Denkschriften der Kaiserlichen Akademie der Wissenschaften in Wien, Philosophisch-Historische Klasse. Band 50:4. Vienna: Kaiserliche Akademie der Wissenschaften, 1904.

Smelik, K. A. D. "Moloch, Molekh, or Molk-Sacrifice? A Reassessment of the Evidence Concerning the Hebrew Term Molekh." *SJOT* 9 (1995): 133–42.

———. "The New Altar of King Ahaz (2 Kings 16): Deuteronomistic Re-Interpretation of a Cult Reform." Pp. 264–78 in *Deuteronomy and Deuteronomic Literature: Festchrift C.H.W. Brekelmans*. Edited by M Vervenne and J. Lust. BETL 133. Leuven: Leuven University Press, 1997.

Smith, M. "A Note on Burning Babies." *JAOS* 95 (1975): 477–79.

Smith, M. S. "Child Sacrifice as the Extreme Case and Calculation." Pp. 3–17 in *Not Sparing the Child: Human Sacrifice in the Ancient World and Beyond: Studies in Honor of Professor Paul G. Mosca*. Edited by V. D. Arbel, P. C. Burns, J. R. C. Cousland, R. Menkis, and D. Neufeld. New York: Bloomsbury, 2015.

———. *Early History of God: Yahweh and the Other Deities in Ancient Israel*. 2nd ed. Grand Rapids, MI: Eerdmans, 2002.

———. "Textual Interpretation in 7th–6th Century Israel: Between Competition, Textualisation, and Tradition." Pp. 317–23 in *Textual Criticism and Dead Sea Scrolls: Studies in Honour of Julio Trebolle Barrera: Florilegium Complutense*. Edited by A. Piquer Otro and P. A. Torijano Morales. JSJSup 158. Leiden: Brill, 2012.

Smith, P., G. Avishai, J. A. Greene, and L. E. Stager. "Age Estimations Attest to the Practice of Infant Sacrifice at the Carthage Tophet." *Antiquity* 87 (2013): 1191–99.

———. "Aging Cremated Infants: The Problem of Sacrifice at the Tophet at Carthage." *Antiquity* 85 (2011): 859–74.

Smith P., and G. Kahila. "Identification of Infanticide in Archaeological Sites: A Case Study from the Late Roman-Early Byzantine Periods at Ashkelon, Israel." *Journal of Archaeological Science* 19 (1992): 667–75.

Smith, W. R. *Lectures on the Religion of the Semites*. New York: D. Appleton & Company, 1889.
Soden, W. von. Review of E. Ebeling, *Tod und Leben nach den Vorstellungen der Babylonier*. *OLZ* 37 (1934): 411–19.
———. Review of O. Eissfeldt, *Molk als Opferbegriff*. *TLZ* 61 (1936): 45–46.
Soggin, J. A. *Judges: A Commentary*. OTL. Philadelphia: Westminster, 1981.
Sommer, B. J. "Dating Pentateuchal Texts and the Perils of Pseudo-Historicism." Pp. 85–108 in *The Pentateuch: International Perspectives on Current Research*. Edited by T. B. Dozeman, K. Schmid, and B. J. Schwartz. FAT 78. Tübingen: Mohr Siebeck, 2011.
Spalinger, A. J. "A Canaanite Ritual Found in Egyptian Reliefs." *JSSEA* 8 (1978): 47–60.
Sparks, K. L. "Israel and the Nomads of Ancient Palestine." Pp. 9–26 in *Community Identity in Judean Historiography: Biblical and Comparative Perspectives*. Edited by G. N. Knoppers and K. A. Ristau. Winona Lake, IN: Eisenbrauns, 2009.
———. "Religion, Identity, and Ancient Israel. *Religion Compass* 1 (2007): 587–614.
Spiegelberg, W. *Die demotischen Denkmäler: I. Die demotischen Inschriften*. Leipzig: Catalogue général des anitiquités égyptiennes du Musée du Caire, 1904.
Sprinkle, J. "Deuteronomic 'Just War' (Deut 20,10–20) and 1 Kings 2,27." *ZABR* 6 (2000): 285–301.
Stackert, J. *Rewriting the Torah: Literary Revision in Deuteronomy and the Holiness Legislation*. FAT 52. Tübingen: Mohr Siebeck, 2007.
Stager, L. E. "Carthage: A View from the Tophet." Pp. 155–66 in *Phönizier im Westen: die Beiträge des Internationalen Symposiums über "Die phönizische Expansion im Westlichen Mittelmeerraum" in Köln vom 24. bis 27. April, 1979*. Edited by H. G. Niemeyer. Mainz am Rhein: Zabern, 1982.
Stager, L. E., and A. Walker, eds., *American Expedition to Idalion, Cyprus 1973–1980*. OIC 24. Chicago: The Oriental Institute of the University of Chicago, 1989.
Stager, L. E., and S. R. Wolff. "Child Sacrifice at Carthage—Religious Rite or Population Control?" *BAR* 10:1 (1984): 31–51.
Stavrakopoulou, F. *King Manasseh and Child Sacrifice: Biblical Distortions of Historical Realities*. BZAW 338. Berlin: de Gruyter, 2004.
———. "The Jerusalem Tophet." *SEL* 29–30 (2012–2013), 147–49.
Steinberg, N. "The Problem of Human Sacrifice in War: An Analysis of Judges 11." Pp. 114–35 in *On the Way to Nineveh: Studies in Honor of George M. Landes*. Edited by S. L. Cook and S. C. Winter. ASOR Books 4. Atlanta: Scholars Press, 1999.
———. *The World of the Child in the Hebrew Bible*. HBM 51. Sheffield: Sheffield Phoenix, 2013.
Steuernagel, C. *Das Deuteronomium*. 2nd ed. HKAT 1:3,1. Göttingen: Vandenhoeck & Ruprecht, 1923.
Stewart, C. "Syncretism and Its Synonyms: Reflections on Cultural Mixture." *Diacritics* 29 (1999): 40–62.
Stewart, C., and R. Shaw, eds. *Syncretism/Anti-Syncretism: The Politics of Religious Synthesis*. New York: Routledge, 1994.
Stipp, H.-J. *Elischa–Propheten–Gottesmänner*. Arbeiten zu Text und Sprache im Alten Testament 24. St. Ottilien: EOS, 1987.

Sweeney, M. A. *I & II Kings: A Commentary*. OTL. Louisville: Westminster John Knox, 2007.

Tatlock, J. "How in Ancient Times They Sacrificed People: Human Immolation in the Eastern Mediterranean Basin with Special Emphasis on Ancient Israel and the Near East." Ph.D. Dissertation, the University of Michigan, 2006.

———. "The Place of Human Sacrifice in the Israelite Cult." Pp. 33–48 in *Ritual and Metaphor: Sacrifice in the Bible*. Edited by C. A. Eberhart. RBS 68. Atlanta: Society of Biblical Literature, 2011.

Teixidor, J. "Bulletin d'épigraphie sémitique 1978–1979." *Syria* 56 (1979): 353–405.

Tennyson, A. *The Death of Œnone, and Other Poems*. New York: Macmillan, 1892.

Thiel, W. *Die deuteronomische Redaktion von Jeremia 1–25*. WMANT 41. Neukirchen-Vluyn: Neukirchener Verlag, 1973.

Thompson, S. *Motif-Index of Folk-Literature*. 6 Vols. Revised edition. Bloomington, IN: Indiana University Press, 1955–58.

Tiemeyer, L.-S. "Prophecy as a Way of Cancelling Prophecy—The Strategic Uses of Foreknowledge." *ZAW* 117 (2005): 329–50.

Togawa, M. "Syncretism Revisited: Hindus and Muslims over a Saintly Cult in Bengal." *Numen* 55 (2008): 27–43.

Toti, M. P. "Gli scavi al Tofet di Giuseppe Whitaker." Pp. 499–509 in *Mozia X: Zona C. Il Kothon, Zona D. Le pendici occidentali dell'Acropoli, Zona F. La Porta Ovest*. Edited by L. Nigro. Studi semitici 50. Pubblicazioni del Centro di studio per la civiltà fenicia e punica 18. Rome: Consiglio nazionale delle ricerche, 1978.

Trexler, R. C. "Infanticide in Florence: New Sources and Results." *History of Childhood Quarterly* 1 (1973): 98–116.

Trible, P. *Texts of Terror: Literary-Feminist Readings of Biblical Narrative*. Philadelphia: Fortress, 1984.

Tronchetti, C. *Cagliari fenicia e punica*. Sardò 5. Sassari: Chiarella, 1990.

———. "Le *tophet* de Sulci (S. Antioco, Sardaigne): État des études et perspectives de la reserche." *UF* 49 (2009): 509–24.

Tropper, J. *Nekromantie: Totenbefragung im Alten Orient und im Alten Testament*. AOAT 223. Kevelaer: Butzon & Bercker/Neukirchen-Vluyn: Nerkirchener Verlag, 1989.

Trumbull, H. C. *The Threshold Covenant*. 2nd ed. New York: Charles Scribner's Sons, 1896.

Tsevat, M. בְּתוּלָה *bᵉthûlāh*; בְּתוּלִים *bᵉthûlîm*. *TDOT* 2, 338–43.

Tsukimoto, A. *Untersuchungen zur Totenpflege* (kispum) *im alten Mesopotamia*. AOAT 216. Kevelaer: Butzon und Bercker/Neukirchen-Vluyn: Neukirchener Verlag, 1985.

Uther, H.-J. *The Types of International Folktales: A Classification and Bibliography Based on the System of Antti Aarne and Stith Thompson*. 3 Vols. FFC 284–86. Helsinki: Suomalainen Tiedeakatemia, 2004.

Van Seters, J. *In Search of History: Historiography in the Ancient World and the Origins of Biblical History*. New Haven: Yale, 1983. Reprinted, Winona Lake, IN: Eisenbrauns.

———. *A Law Book for the Diaspora: Revision in the Study of the Covenant Code*. Oxford: Oxford University Press, 2003.

———. "Revision in the Study of the Covenant Code and a Response to My Critics." *SJOT* 21 (2007): 5–28.

Vaux, R. de. *Ancient Israel: Its Life and Institutions*. Translated by J. McHugh. New York: McGraw Hill, 1961.

———. Review of O. Eissfeldt, *Molk als Opferbegriff*. *RB* 45 (1924): 278–82.

———. *Les sacrifices de l'Ancien Testament*. CahRB 1. Paris: Galbalda, 1964.

———. *Studies in Old Testament Sacrifice*. Cardiff: University of Wales Press, 1964.

Veijola, T. *Das fünfte Buch Mose. Deuteronomium: Kapitel 1,1–16,17*. ATD 8:1. Vandenhoeck & Ruprecht, 2004.

Vella, N. C. "Vases, bones and Two Phoenician Inscriptions: An Assessment of a Discovery Made in Malta in 1816." Pp. 589–606 in *Ritual, Religion and Reason: Studies in the Ancient World in Honour of Paolo Xella*. Edited by O. Loretz, S. Ribichini, W. G. E. Watson and J. Á. Zamora. Münster: Ugarit-Verlag, 2013.

Volz, P. *Die biblischen Altertümer*. Calw & Stuttgart: Verlag der Vereinsbuchhandlung, 1914.

Ward, W. A. "The Scarabs, Scaraboid and Amulet-Plaque from Tyrian Cinerary Urns." *Berytus* 39 (1991): 89–99

Watts, J. D. W. *Isaiah 1–33*. Rev. ed. WBC 24. Nashville: Nelson, 2005.

Weber, J. A. "Elite Equids: Redefining Equid Burials of the Mid- to Late 3rd Millennium BC from Umm el-Marra, Syria." Pp. 499–519 in *Archaeozoology of the Near East*. Vol. 8. Edited by E. Vila, L. Gourichon, A. M. Choyke, and H. Buitenhuis. Lyon: Maison de l'Orient et de la Méditerranée, 2006.

Weinfeld, M. "Burning Babies in Ancient Israel: A Rejoinder to Morton Smith's Article in *JAOS* 95 (1975), pp. 477–479." *UF* 10 (1978): 411–13.

———. *Deuteronomy and the Deuteronomic School*. Oxford: Clarendon, 1972.

———. "The Worship of Molech and the Queen of Heaven and Its Background." *UF* 4 (1972): 133–54.

Weippert, H., and M. Weippert. "Die 'Bileam'-Inschrift von Tell Dēr 'Allā." *ZDPV* 98 (1982): 77–103.

Weiss, M. "Concerning Amos' Repudiation of the Cult." Pp. 199–214 in *Pomegranates & Golden Bells: Studies in Biblical, Jewish, and Near Eastern Ritual, Law, and Literature in Honor of Jacob Milgrom*. Edited by D. P. Wright, D. N. Freedman, and A. Hurvitz. Winona Lake, IN: Eisenbrauns, 1995.

Wellhausen, J. *Die Composition des Hexateuchs und der historischen Bücher des Alten Testaments*. 3rd ed. Berlin: Reimer, 1899.

Wendel, A. *Das Opfer in der altisraelitischen Religion*. Leipzig: Pfeiffer, 1927.

Wenham, G. J. "Betûlāh 'A Girl of Marriageable Age.'" *VT* 22 (1972): 326–48.

Westbrook, R. "Elisha's True Prophecy in 2 Kings 3." *JBL* 124 (2005): 530–32.

———. "Laws in Kings." Pp. 445–66 in *The Books of Kings: Sources, Composition, Historiography and Reception*. Edited by B. Halpern and A. Lemaire. Leiden: Brill, 2010.

Westermann, C. *Basic Forms of Prophetic Speech*. Translated by H. C. White. Philadelphia: Westminster, 1967.

Wevers, J. *Notes on the Greek Text of Leviticus*. SCS 44. Atlanta: Scholars Press, 1997.

Whitaker, J. I. S. *Motya: A Phœnician Colony in Sicily*. London: G. Bell and Sons, 1921.

Wildberger, H. *Isaiah 28–39*. Translated by T. H. Trapp. CC. Minneapolis: Fortress, 2002.

Williamson, L. "Infanticide: An Anthropological Analysis." Pp. 61–75 in *Infanticide and the Value of Life*. Edited by M. Kohl. Buffalo, NY: Prometheus, 1978.

Winnett, F. V. *The Mosaic Tradition*. Toronto: University of Toronto Press, 1949.

Wiseman, D. J. Review of M. L. Burke, *Texts administratifs de la salle III du palais*. *JSS* 10 (1965): 124–26.

Wolff, H. W. *Micah: A Commentary*. Translated by G. Stansell. CC. Minneapolis: Augsburg, 1990.

Würthwein, E. *Die Bücher der Könige*. ATD 11:1–2. Göttingen: Vandenhoeck & Ruprecht, 1977–84.

Xella, P. "'Tophet': An Overall Interpretation." *SEL* 29–30 (2012–2013): 259–81.

Xella, P., J. Quinn, V. Melchiorri, and P. van Dommelen. "Phoenician Bones of Contention." *Antiquity* 87 (2013): 1–9.

Zadok, R. "Geographical and Onomastic Notes." *JANES* 8 (1976): 113–26.

Zahn, M. M. "Reexamining Empirical Models: The Case of Exodus 13." Pp. 36–55 in *Das Deuteronomium zwischen Pentateuch und Deuteronomistischem Geschichtswerk*. Edited by E. Otto and R. Achenbach. FRLANT 206. Göttingen: Vandenhoeck & Ruprecht, 2004.

Zevit, Z. *The Religions of Ancient Israel: A Synthesis of Parallactic Approaches*. New York: Continuum, 2001.

Ziegler, Y. *Promises to Keep: The Oath in Biblical Narrative*. VTSup 120. Leiden: Brill, 2008.

Zimmerli, W. "Erstgeborene und Leviten: Ein Beitrag zur exilisch-nachexilischen Theologie." Pp. 459–69 in *Near Eastern Studies in Honor of William Foxwell Albright*. Edited by H. Goedicke. Baltimore: The Johns Hopkins Press, 1971.

———. *Ezekiel 1: A Commentary on the Book of the Prophet Ezekiel, Chapters 1–24*. Edited by F. M. Cross and K. Baltzer. Translated by R. E. Clements. Hermeneia. Philadelphia: Fortress, 1979.

Ziskind, J. R. "Legal Rules on Incest in the Ancient Near East." *RIDA* 35 (1988): 79–107.

Index of Authors

Index of Scripture

This index is ordered according to the traditional sequence of books in the Hebrew Bible. Chapter and verse are also cited according to the enumeration in the Hebrew Bible (not English translations thereof).

Index of Other Ancient Sources

www.ingramcontent.com/pod-product-compliance
Ingram Content Group UK Ltd.
Pitfield, Milton Keynes, MK11 3LW, UK
UKHW041058240926
475926UK00001B/66

9 781646 024186